The Subject's Matter

Representation and Mind

Hilary Putnam and Ned Block, Editors

Terence E. Horgan and Matjaž Potrč, *Austere Realism: Contextual Semantics Meets Minimal Ontology*

Michael Tye, *Consciousness Revisited: Materialism without Phenomenal Concepts*

Rocco J. Gennaro, *The Consciousness Paradox*

Frédérique de Vignemont and Adrian Alsmith (editors), *The Subject's Matter: Self-Consciousness and the Body*

The Subject's Matter

Self-Consciousness and the Body

edited by Frédérique de Vignemont and Adrian J. T. Alsmith

The MIT Press
Cambridge, Massachusetts
London, England

This book was set in Stone Serif by Westchester Publishing Services. Printed and bound in the United States of America.

Library of Congress Cataloging-in-Publication Data is available.

Names: Vignemont, Frédérique de, editor.
Title: The subject's matter : self-consciousness and the body / edited by Frédérique de Vignemont and Adrian J. T. Alsmith.
Description: Cambridge, MA : MIT Press, 2017. | Series: Representation and mind | Includes bibliographical references and index.
Identifiers: LCCN 2017010147 | ISBN 9780262036832 (hardcover : alk. paper)
Subjects: LCSH: Human body (Philosophy) | Self-consciousness (Awareness) | Self (Philosophy)
Classification: LCC B105.B64 S83 2017 | DDC 128/.6—dc23 LC record available at https://lccn.loc.gov/2017010147

10 9 8 7 6 5 4 3 2 1

Contents

Introduction: The Subject's Matter

Adrian J. T. Alsmith and Frédérique de Vignemont

We feel the wind pressing against us, as we in turn push against it. We feel the coldness of the snowball in our palm as we form it, and its lightness as we cast it forth. We feel the tickling sensation of the feather on our skin, and the convulsions of our chest as we recoil in laughter. In its continuous presence as that which "invariably accompanies the knowledge of whatever else we know" (James, 1890, p. 242) our body may be the object we know the best. It is the only object from which we constantly receive a flow of information through sight and touch. And it is the only object we can experience from the inside, through our proprioceptive, vestibular, and visceral senses.

Yet there have been very few books that have attempted to consolidate our understanding of the body as it figures in our experience and self-awareness. The only recent book that systematically addresses the topic is *The Body and the Self* (Bermúdez, Marcel, & Eilan, 1995), published by the MIT Press more than twenty years ago. It has become a landmark in the field and remains an almost unique reference. However, the study of the body in psychological disciplines such as cognitive psychology, cognitive neuroscience, psychiatry, and neuropsychology has boomed in the last twenty years. In this period, a range of new bodily illusions have emerged and pathologies of bodily experience have been studied in greater depth than ever before. Concomitantly, there has been a resurgence of philosophical attention paid to the significance of the body in our mental life, particularly in structuring the most basic aspects of perception and self-consciousness. The aim of this collected volume is to revisit conceptions of bodily self-awareness in the light of new empirical, technical, and theoretical advances. It comprises sixteen specially commissioned essays from philosophers and psychologists, which we hope collectively demonstrate the indispensability of each discipline in a complete understanding of the subject. The book is divided into three parts, each covering a topic central to an explanation of bodily self-awareness: representation of the body; the sense of bodily ownership; and representation of the self. What follows in the rest of the introduction is a summary of the background issues framing the discussion in each of these parts.

Part I: The Body Represented

The modern notion of a body representation can be traced back at least as far as Bonnier (1905), who used the term *body schema* to refer to the spatial organization of bodily sensations. Head and Holmes (1911–1912) posited the existence of *three* distinct body representations: a *body image*, which constitutes the conscious percept of the body, as well as two types of unconscious body representations, *body schemata*, one of which records every new posture or movement and the other maps the surface of the body on which bodily sensations are localized. Since then, a long tradition in psychology and in philosophy has defended the view that there are representations of the body, which structure and calibrate bodily experiences and bodily actions.

The notion of body representation is more general than that of the cortical maps of the body found in various parts of the central nervous system, the most famous of which was coined as the "homunculus" by Penfield and Rasmussen (1950). Such maps are highly distorted and thus cannot directly supply information about body size and shape required for action control and for bodily awareness (Medina & Coslett, 2016). For instance, although the homunculus in the primary somatosensory cortex generally follows the natural anatomical divisions of body parts, associating cortical areas to specific parts of the body, some body parts are overrepresented (e.g., hand), whereas others are underrepresented (e.g., torso). Furthermore, the homunculus does not represent the anatomical contiguity of body parts (e.g., the hand-specific area is next to the face-specific area) and does not obviously reflect the constitution and organization of the body (e.g., that the hand is next to the arm). To account for metric and structural properties of the body, one requires a more inclusive notion that can also encompass integrative representations of the body, which can serve to spatially organize sensory information concerning the body for a variety of purposes. Arguably, it is thanks to body representations that sensations are experienced as being at more than an isolated body point: if you are touched on the right index finger and on the right middle finger, you can feel these sensations to be both located *on your right hand* (O'Shaughnessy, 2008). It is also thanks to body representations that one can experience sensations in the complete absence of somatosensory input. For instance, when the sensory input from the lips and front teeth is fully blocked following anesthesia (e.g., for dental surgery) one feels one's lips and teeth increasing in size by as much as 100 percent (Gandevia & Phegan, 1999). Such an illusion cannot be explained by information coming from peripheral sensory receptors, since they are completely blocked; it seems best explained by the presence of a representation of the body functioning in independence of sensory input.

Perhaps the most commonly recognized form of body representation is that invoked by the experience of phantom body parts, especially phantom limbs, in amputees (Finger & Hustwit, 2003). Amputation is a clear case in which the body can be subject to radical change over time; the body can also gradually change size and shape from conception to mature adulthood. However, amputation and developmental changes are not the only kinds of change that body representations must track. There are also impermanent, short-term artificial changes to one's ability to affect the environment with one's body that are enabled by tool use. Representations of the body must accordingly adapt to these changes if they are to function adequately. It is unclear whether the nervous system treats having a body that grows in size over decades as a fundamentally different phenomenon to using a tool for a few minutes. But it is clear that as soon as we act without the tool, only representation of the body's original parameters (e.g., the actual size of our limbs) will be adequate.

Despite the intuitions prompted by phantom limbs, the fact that the nervous system must adapt, in many cases very quickly, to changes in the nature of the body and its ability to engage the environment might raise suspicion about whether the nervous system represents the body at all. Representations are computationally costly and arguably unnecessary if a system can retain perceptual contact with the objects of its cognition. As noted at the start of this introduction, the amount of information received from the body is quantitatively superior to that received from any environmental object. Modifying Brooks's (1991) expression, perhaps "the [body] is its own best model," given that the body presents a highly special feature compared to any other object in the world: it never leaves us; why do we then need an internal representation of the body?

Following Husserl (see Smith, 2007), Merleau-Ponty holds that there is a distinctive way in which the body manifests in experience as the subject of experience, such that it is "not one more [thing] among external objects" (2002, p. 105). Rather the body is our perceptual anchor, the singular structuring principle for every way in which we perceive the world as that which we can practically engage. Hence, according to Merleau-Ponty, it could not structure the presentation of a world of objects in this way if it were presented as just another object in the world. On this phenomenological understanding, the body schema ought to be understood as a set of relatively invariant functional relationships between sensing and acting, rather than a sensorimotor representation that might enable such a relationship (Gallagher, 2005). As for phantom limbs, Merleau-Ponty interprets them as resulting from the preserved readiness to move the amputated limbs, rather than a preserved representation of the limbs, as he puts it: "The phantom arm is not the representation of the arm, but the ambivalent presence of the arm" (2002, p. 94).

However, the virtue of a cognitive system's ability to "decouple" from the body itself by representing it ought not to be underestimated. In many biological systems (humans especially) peripheral signals specifying the dynamics of bodily movement are ambiguous and cannot travel fast enough to provide timely influence on central motor processes (Latash, 2008). Nevertheless, smooth sensorimotor control is achieved. According to a well-established—though still controversial—line of research in motor control, the reason for this is that the brain encodes a model of the musculoskeletal system. By feeding copies of the outflowing motor signals into this model, the system can then compute the likely sensory feedback that would be generated by the movements specified (see, e.g., Desmurget & Grafton, 2000). This enables the system to not only accommodate signal delay and unreliability, but also explore likely changes in the causal process without any obligation to implement such changes. If this is right, then skillful sensorimotor engagement is enabled precisely in virtue of driving a model (often known as a forward model) of the causal process, alongside or in absence of the actual control process. Representations, and in particular body representations, may thus be an efficient solution to the problems posed by our bodily interactions with the world.

All the contributions comprising part I of the volume concern the relationship between representations of the body and the body itself, including issues about the possibility of innate body representations (Bremner), the phenomenology and persistence of phantom limbs (Mezue & Makin), short-term changes in body representation after tool use (Martel, Cardinali, Roy, & Farnè), and spatial principles of body representations (Longo; Haggard, Cheng, Beck, & Fardo).

Part II: The Sense of Bodily Ownership

Each subject of experience has a "very special regard for just one body," such that each seems to "think of it as unique and perhaps more important than any other" (Strawson, 2003, p. 93). This selective concern for a particular body is an implicit but essential element of everyday thoughts about ourselves which involve the attribution of bodily properties. Perhaps you wish you were taller. Summer has passed and you had hoped to be more tanned. Do you ever think about losing a little weight? Entertaining such possibilities requires that these thoughts single out one's body as one's own. For one cannot think of one's body being some way by merely thinking about just any body.

One way of accounting for the ability to think about a particular body as one's own is to claim that experience of one's body is intimately bound to one's consciousness of oneself. Locke opened up this possibility in a suggestive passage:

> That this is so, we have some kind of evidence in our very bodies, all whose particles, whilst vitally united to this same thinking conscious self, so that we *feel* when they are touched, and are affected by, and are conscious of good or harm that happens to them, are a part of our *selves*, i.e., of our thinking conscious *self.* Thus the limbs of his body are to everyone a part of himself; he sympathizes and is concerned for them. Cut off an hand, and thereby separate it from that consciousness he had of its heat, cold, and other affections; and it is then no longer a part of that which is *himself*, any more than the remotest part of matter. (Locke, 1690/1997, bk. II, ch. 27, §11)

Locke seems to assert that experience of parts of the body is experience of parts of oneself, and even, that in order for a body *to be* a part of oneself, it must be connected to one's "consciousness" of its properties. But one might demur that a question about materialism concerning the self is obscuring the possibility of a weaker but highly significant psychological relation, namely that of *experiencing bodily ownership.* Just as one might admit that a dismembered limb remains one's limb—even perhaps if it is no longer a part of oneself—one can similarly admit that bodily experience can present one's body as one's own, whether or not it presents it as oneself.

A further issue that might obscure matters is that the notion of experiential ownership has been used to characterize what some argue to be an invariant feature of experience of all kinds (not just experience of one's body), namely "the quality of *mineness*, that is, the fact that the experiences are characterized by a first-personal givenness that immediately reveals them as one's own" (Zahavi, 2005, p. 124). Such a liberal application of the notion of experiencing something as one's own is clearly compatible with experiencing one's body as one's own. But one may wonder whether in order to experience one's body as one's own, one's experience itself must in general have the quality of presenting itself as owned by its subject. This would also be to obscure a particularly peculiar aspect of experiencing bodily ownership, which is that, in contrast to thoughts and experiences, there is a clear respect in which the body itself is an objective entity, as publicly accessible a material object as any other. Yet the body is presented as having a significance for the subject like no other such object.

The aim of these remarks has been to show the significance of the notion of experiencing ownership for self-conscious thought about one's bodily properties, while keeping the notion robustly distinct from that of bodily self-consciousness per se (in which the body is presented *as oneself*) and experiential ownership (in which all one's *experiences* are presented as one's own). These distinctions are important not only to make clear that typically the core notion of a sense of bodily ownership is that of an experience of bodily ownership, but also to make clear that drawing on the notion of bodily self-consciousness or experiential ownership in one's account of experiencing bodily ownership is a significant theoretical step.

Much of the present discussion of the sense of bodily ownership has been influenced by Mike Martin's (1995) discussion of the structure of bodily sensation. In brief, Martin seems to make the following claims:

• Modal contrast claim: There is a contrast present within the content of bodily sensation between regions where one could and regions where one could not experience bodily sensation.
• Bodily bounded sensation claim: Bodily sensations are necessarily experienced as falling within one's bodily boundaries.

On this basis, one might conclude that the sense of bodily ownership is no more than a consequence of the fact that one necessarily experiences bodily sensations to fall within one's bodily boundaries, which Bermúdez (2011) describes as a "deflationary conception." Martin also suggests that the correct understanding of the idea that we perceive our bodies in experiencing bodily sensation must hold what he calls a "sole-object view" of body awareness: in order for an instance of bodily experience to count as an instance of perception, it must be an experience of what is in fact the subject's actual body. This is, in effect, a metaphysical stipulation, contra a multiple-object view, in which a bodily experience may count as an instance of perception despite—perhaps through some strange circumstance—presenting the body of another. But in comparing the two views a little further, one can clarify certain motivations for studying the sense of ownership itself.

On Martin's sole-object view, the fact that the sense of ownership is veridical in the usual case is explained as a consequence of the nature of bodily sensation. When a subject perceives her body, her bodily sensations are necessarily presented as falling within the bounds of her body and this bodily experience is necessarily concerned with facts about her own actual body. On the multiple-object view, the fact that the sense of ownership is veridical in the usual case is a contingent fact. According to Martin, this sits uncomfortably with the fact that bodily sensations are necessarily bodily bounded and thus it makes mysterious the fact that we do experience ownership of our body parts.

But the mystery that Martin sees as trouble for the multiple-object view itself motivates positing a mechanism that generates the experience of bodily ownership. That is, the multiple-object view motivates the study of the sense of bodily ownership as an explanandum in its own right. This mechanism is given a particular explanatory role in instances of veridical perception, to explain why bodily sensations seem to present an experience of one's own body part as one's own. But it is also given a similar explanatory role in any potential instances of illusions of ownership, to explain why bodily sensations seem to present an experience of something that is not a part of one's body as one's own.

One of the major developments in the psychological literature since Martin's piece was written has been the intense study of just such an illusion of ownership, the rubber hand illusion (RHI), described by Botvinick and Cohen (1998). In the classic experimental set up, one sits with one's arm hidden behind a screen, while fixating on a rubber hand presented in one's bodily alignment; the rubber hand can then be touched either in synchrony or in asynchrony with one's hand. After a few minutes, one can find the following main effects after synchronous stroking.

At the phenomenological level (measured by questionnaires):

• Referred tactile sensations: Participants report that they feel tactile sensations as being located, not on their real hand that is stroked, but on the rubber hand.
• Sense of ownership: They report that it seems to them as if the rubber hand was their own hand.

At the behavioral level:

• Proprioceptive drift: They mislocalize the finger that was touched in the direction of the location of the finger of the rubber hand that was stroked in synchrony.

At the physiological level:

• Arousal: When they see the rubber hand threatened, they display an increased affective response (as measured by their skin conductance response).

Since 1998, several other bodily illusions manipulating the sense of ownership have been found, including out-of-body illusions (Ehrsson, 2007; Lenggenhager, Tadi, Metzinger, & Blanke, 2007) and the enfacement illusion (Sforza, Bufalari, Haggard, & Aglioti, 2010; Tsakiris, 2008), among others. Some of these bodily illusions use fake bodies while others appeal to virtual bodies or to another person's body. They can be local (restricted to the hand or to the face) or global (including the whole body). They can manipulate first-person or third-person perspective on the body. Despite these differences, in every variant participants have reported feeling as if a particular body (or body part) was their own, despite being aware that it does not belong to them.

Although many have become critical of the RHI paradigm, the fact that subjects report experiencing bodily ownership for another object than their own hand strongly suggests that the experience is contingently associated with the particular body that is one's own, which may seem incompatible with the sole-object view. The insistence that sensations are necessarily bodily bounded also seems potentially in conflict with certain pathological cases, in particular somatoparaphrenia, also known as asomatognosia or alien hand sign (de Vignemont, 2013). This pathology is caused by a lesion or an epileptic seizure in the right parietal lobe and it is often associated with somatosensory deficits and spatial neglect, but the main symptom is that patients deny that one of their limbs belongs to them (Vallar & Ronchi, 2009). Surprisingly, these patients can sometimes feel tactile and painful sensations to be located in their "alien" hand. It is not absolutely clear what to conclude from pathological cases such as these; as indeed, it is not absolutely clear what to conclude from studies of illusions of ownership. In part, this is because more work needs to be done in order to understand the precise nature of the experience in question.

The chapters in part II are concerned with the nature of bodily experience, the nature of the self-attributive quality involved in what is often referred to as the sense of bodily ownership, and the theoretical connection between the two. In particular, they cover questions about the deflationary conception (Gallagher), the spatial grounds of the sense of bodily ownership (Bermúdez), its agentive and affective grounds (de Vignemont), the relation between experiential ownership and bodily ownership (Billon), and pathological cases of bodily ownership (Garbarini, Pia, Fossataro, & Berti).

Part III: The Self Represented

A common theme in work on the nature of mental representation is that a subject's representation of herself is distinctive. Arguably this is so, even if subjects of experience are in a certain respect not distinctive. If subjects not only have bodies but are bodies, then they have a materiality in common with other entities of the world that they experience. Yet it cannot suffice for self-representation that one merely represents the world of which one is a part. For though there is a sense in which one then represents oneself, this situation is compatible with failing to represent oneself *as oneself*. To illustrate how a seemingly all-inclusive representation can fail in this way, consider David Lewis's (1979) story of the two gods. Imagine that there are two gods, living in different parts of the same world and each has a perfect and complete view of their world; for all the possible ways things could be, they know which of those ways holds true in their world. Yet, Lewis claims that we "can imagine [that] . . . neither one knows which of the two he is," noting that the trouble might be that "they have an equally perfect view of every part of their world, and hence cannot identify the perspectives from which they view it" (Lewis, 1979, pp. 520–521).

One way in which this is sometimes put is that although these (divine) subjects know their situation in logical space, they lack any knowledge of their situation in physical space. One of the most basic ways in which a subject can represent the world is spatially; and if at least one of the ways in which a subject can represent herself is to represent her body, it would seem sufficient to represent the spatial properties of the particular body that she is. The difficulty here is that it is conceivable that a subject could have a spatial representation, which includes the spatial properties of her body (e.g., its spatial situation) and fail to represent that object as itself. On the face of things, the natural solution is to appeal to a distinctive form of spatial representation, namely perspectival spatial representation, as representing the subject's body in the distinctive way required. Visual experiences, for instance, are perspectival, not only in that they present the world from somewhere, but also in that they present the world from the place at which one's body is. The spatial structure of visual experience would then seem to be sufficient to pick out the spatial properties of the subject of the experience. But even if the thing located at the place from which one perceives is identical with oneself, more needs to be said about how one comes to be aware of this fact. Indeed, a concern variously raised by philosophers since Schopenhauer is that the world-directedness of perceptual experience makes its content essentially inadequate to pick out the subject *as the subject*. If this is right, then one requires a further account of how it is that the subject is related to the world perceived, such that she can appropriately represent herself as being a part of it.

It should be noted that part of the worry here might be based on the assumption that genuine self-consciousness requires explicit representation of the subject. To this it might be replied that simply because the subject is not explicitly represented it does not follow that she is not represented at all. Indeed, it might be that as one's experience of the world accumulates, certain implicit assumptions about one's nature (as similar to certain objects that one perceives) and one's place in that world (as invariantly the same as the body from which one perceives) might form a conception of oneself as a body, as being the best explanation of the course of one's experience.

Moreover, it seems plausible that we can move from merely representing the world to representing ourselves, when our experience of the world interfaces with the unique way in which we experience a particular part of it. When one has a visual experience of a tree ahead, one is entitled to judge: "I am standing in front of a tree." One can be wrong about whether it is a tree (it can be a painting of a tree, for instance). But, as noted by Evans (1982, p. 222), one cannot have the following doubt: "someone is standing in front of a tree, but is it I?" Employing terminology Shoemaker (1968) introduced, Evans concludes that self-locating judgments are immune to error through misidentification relative to the first person. Similarly, one cannot be wrong about whose legs are crossed when one *feels* them that way (de Vignemont, 2012). Arguably, then, bodily judgments cannot fail to pick out the subject if they are appropriately grounded.

The immunity of bodily judgments to this kind of error is often explained by appeal to the fact that the body is the only object that we experience from the inside. The notion of experiencing something from the inside is somewhat vague, but may be taken to include the experience of our posture and the movement of our body parts, our translation, rotation and orientation, and the state of our internal milieu. Each of these ways of experiencing our body from the inside can variously inform a subject's representation of herself. Proprioception and kinesthesia present the posture and movement of the parts of the body with which one perceives the world. But they also provide a means by which perceptual experience can be connected to one's capacity for bodily action. The vestibular system—together with sight, touch, and perhaps even somatic graviceptive organs in the trunk (Mittelstaedt, 1996)—carries as much information about the external world as about one's body, by coding the relation between the two. Finally, interoception provides information about the physiological condition of the body, manifest in awareness as, for example, the thump of one's heart, and feelings of hunger, thirst, and bloatedness (Craig, 2002). Though often devoid of determinate spatial phenomenology, experiences such as these are perhaps the primary way in which one is presented with one's nature as a biological entity.

The final six chapters of the volume concern the relationship between the body and self-representation. Issues discussed include: whether visual experience ever represents its subject in a visual mode (Richardson); how bodily agency enables perceptual experience to represent its subject's location (Alsmith); how the metaphysics of subjects (as agents) affects the possibility of their representation (Peacocke); the significance of balance as a source of information about the subject (Wong); and how self-representation might emerge from the integration of internal and external bodily information channels (Tsakiris) and modeling the self as a deeply hidden cause of behavior (Hohwy & Michael).

A Note on the Structure of the Book

Each part and indeed each chapter can be read individually. Moreover, there are many chapters that could have easily appeared in other parts than those in which they appear. But there is a rationale to the organization that we have chosen: the complex relationship between the body and its mental representation (described in the first part) will in turn deepen one's understanding of the sense of bodily ownership (discussed in the second part) and bodily self-awareness more generally (in the third part). We hope, then, that this organization will benefit anyone with the luxury of enough time to read the volume from start to finish.

References

Bermúdez, J. L. (2011). Bodily awareness and self-consciousness. In S. Gallagher (Ed.), *The Oxford handbook of the self* (pp. 157–179). Oxford: Oxford University Press.

Bermúdez, J. L., Marcel, A. J., & Eilan, N. (Eds). (1995). *The body and the self.* Cambridge, MA: MIT Press.

Bonnier, P. (1905). L'aschématie. *Revue Neurologique, 13,* 605–609.

Botvinick, M., & Cohen, J. (1998). Rubber hands "feel" touch that eyes see. *Nature, 391*(6669), 756. doi:10.1038/35784.

Brooks, R. A. (1991). Intelligence without representation. *Artificial Intelligence, 47*(1–3), 139–159. doi:10.1016/0004-3702(91)90053-m

Craig, A. D. (2002). How do you feel? Interoception: The sense of the physiological condition of the body. *Nature Reviews: Neuroscience, 3*(8), 655–666. doi:10.1038/nrn894.

Desmurget, M., & Grafton, S. (2000). Forward modeling allows feedback control for fast reaching movements. *Trends in Cognitive Sciences, 4*(11): 423–431. doi:10.1016/S1364-6613(00)01537-0.

de Vignemont, F. (2012). Bodily immunity to error. In S. Prosser & F. Recanati (Eds.), *Immunity to error through misidentification: New essays* (pp. 224–246). Cambridge: Cambridge University Press.

de Vignemont, F. (2013). The mark of bodily ownership. *Analysis, 73*(4), 643–651. doi:10.1093/analys/ant080.

Ehrsson, H. H. (2007). The experimental induction of out-of-body experiences. *Science, 317*(5841), 1048. doi:10.1126/science.1142175.

Evans, G. (1982). *The varieties of reference*. Oxford: Oxford University Press.

Finger, S., & Hustwit, M. P. (2003). Five early accounts of phantom limb in context: Paré, Descartes, Lemos, Bell, and Mitchell. *Neurosurgery, 52*(3), 675–686.

Gallagher, S. (2005). *How the body shapes the mind*. Oxford: Oxford University Press.

Gandevia, S., & Phegan, C. (1999). Perceptual distortions of the human body image produced by local anaesthesia, pain and cutaneous stimulation. *Journal of Physiology, 514*(2), 609–616. doi:10.1111/j.1469-7793.1999.609ae.x.

Head, H., & Holmes, G. M. (1911–1912). Sensory disturbances from cerebral lesions. *Brain, 34*(2–3), 102–254. doi:10.1093/brain/34.2-3.102.

James, W. 1890. *Principles of psychology* (Vol. 1). New York: Dover.

Latash, M. L. (2008). *Neurophysiological basis of movement* (2nd ed.). Champaign, IL: Human Kinetics.

Lenggenhager, B., Tadi, T., Metzinger, T., & Blanke, O. (2007). Video ergo sum: Manipulating bodily self-consciousness. *Science, 317*(5841), 1096–1099. doi:10.1126/science.1143439.

Lewis, D. (1979). Attitudes de dicto and de se. *Philosophical Review, 88*(4), 513–543.

Locke, J. (1997). *An essay concerning human understanding*. London: Penguin Classics. (Originally published 1690.)

Martin, M. G. F. (1995). Bodily awareness: A sense of ownership. In J. L. Bermúdez, A. J. Marcel, & N. Eilan (Eds.), *The body and the self* (pp. 267–289). Cambridge, MA: MIT Press.

Medina, J., & Coslett, H. B. (2016). What can errors tell us about body representations? *Cognitive Neuropsychology, 33*(1–2), 5–25. doi:10.1080/02643294.2016.1188065.

Merleau-Ponty, M. (2002). *Phenomenology of perception*. New York: Routledge.

Mittelstaedt, H. (1996). Somatic graviception. *Biological Psychology, 42*(1–2), 53–74. doi:10.1016/0301-0511(95)05146-5.

O'Shaughnessy, B. (2008). *The will: A dual aspect theory* (2nd ed., Vol. 1). Cambridge: Cambridge University Press.

Penfield, W., & Rasmussen, T. (1950). *The cerebral cortex of man: A clinical study of localization of function.* New York: Macmillan.

Sforza, A., Bufalari, I., Haggard, P., & Aglioti, S. M. (2010). My face in yours: Visuo-tactile facial stimulation influences sense of identity. *Social Neuroscience, 5*(2), 148–162. doi:10.1080/17470910903205503.

Shoemaker, S. (1968). Self-reference and self-awareness. *Journal of Philosophy, 65*(19), 555–567.

Smith, A. D. (2007). The flesh of perception: Merleau-Ponty and Husserl. In T. Baldwin (Ed.), *Reading Merleau-Ponty: On the phenomenology of perception* (pp. 1–22). London: Routledge.

Strawson, P. F. (2003). *Individuals: An essay in descriptive metaphysics.* London: Routledge.

Tsakiris, M. (2008). Looking for myself: Current multisensory input alters self-face recognition. *PLoS One, 3*(12), e4040. doi:10.1371/journal.pone.0004040.

Vallar, G., & Ronchi, R. (2009). Somatoparaphrenia: A body delusion. A review of the neuropsychological literature. *Experimental Brain Research, 192*(3), 533–551. doi:10.1007/s00221-008-1562-y.

Wittgenstein, L. (1958). *The blue and brown books.* Oxford: Blackwell.

Zahavi, D. (2005). *Subjectivity and selfhood: Investigating the first-person perspective.* Cambridge, MA: MIT Press.

I   The Body Represented

1 The Origins of Body Representations in Early Life

Andrew J. Bremner

1 Introduction

There remains a striking disconnect in developmental psychology between studies addressing the development of our abilities to think and perceive (e.g., Arterberry & Kellman, 2016; Spelke & Kinzler, 2007), and those examining the development of action, how we learn to do things with our bodies (e.g., Adolph, 2015; Von Hofsten, 2007). Of course researchers have long acknowledged that perceptual development and the development of action are intertwined (e.g., Gibson & Pick, 2000); perceptual abilities are required when we act, and action changes the ways in which we perceive the world. Nonetheless, the body has fallen through the cracks. Those studying action development appear to treat perception and perceptual development as largely instrumental to that purpose. Those studying perceptual development often seem to ignore action and the body altogether, focusing on infants' perceptions of the external world (often the external world beyond reach). There are exceptions (e.g., Rochat, 2010), but it is as if we mostly forgot, or chose to ignore, that action and the body could *themselves* be objects of perception. Even Piaget (1952), for whom action and the body were so fundamental for cognitive and (arguably) perceptual development, has relatively little to say about how babies and children come to be able to perceive and represent themselves, their limbs, and their actions (Bremner & Cowie, 2013).

As discussed throughout this volume, the body is ubiquitous in, and inseparable from, our perceptual experiences and senses of self. And so, if we are to understand early experience, the possibility that at various stages in early life humans may have dramatically different representations of their own bodies is one to take particularly seriously. In this chapter I will show that, on the basis of recent and more established findings, there are good reasons to believe that the ways in which we perceive own bodies and limbs change substantially in infancy, and also likely in prenatal life.

I will first outline the relatively sparse theoretical accounts of the development of body representations.[1] I am unashamedly interested in how such representations develop in human infancy, so while I will give some consideration to the various different kinds of empirical research that speak to the ontogeny of body representations in infancy and childhood, I will focus particularly on investigations of the development of body representations in human infants, covering classic and more recent work on the development of imitation, sensorimotor abilities, and more particularly on recent work from my own lab and others' on body perception in infancy. In the later sections of the chapter I will discuss two particularly relevant (and interrelated) questions that bear on the early development of body representations: How and when do infants come to be able to sense their own bodies in the external spatial environment, and how does the development of multisensory processes underpin emerging body representations (see also Bremner, 2016)?

2   Innate Body Representations? (Problems with) Lessons from Neonatal Imitation and Congenital Phantom Limbs

Accounts concerning the ontogeny of representations of the body are relatively obscure, at least for the developmental psychologist. Although Piaget was certainly concerned with the development of representations of the self (and particularly how infants come to draw a distinction between the self and the external world; Russell, 1995), he gave little consideration to the structure of body representations. The most recognized contributions come from the phenomenological philosopher Merleau-Ponty, who articulated the view that perception of one's own body (underpinned by a postural schema—the internal model of the body and its layout which subserves action) develops postnatally, in response to physiological changes and as a result of experience (Merleau-Ponty, 1964, 2012).[2] He highlighted particularly the role of developing links between "exteroceptivity" (a sense of the external environment primarily from vision and audition), and "interoceptivity" (a sense of the body alone from touch and proprioception).

A role for experience in the development of body perception makes intuitive sense; there is clear scope for significant development in how we represent the body and limbs during childhood. For instance, any early ability to represent the whereabouts of one's hand would need to be continually retuned throughout development in order to cope with physical changes in the sizes, disposition, and movement capabilities of the hand and arms among the other parts of the body (Adolph & Avolio, 2000). As I shall discuss in section 5, a role for experience is also commensurate with the idea that multisensory processes are important in the development of body representations: As the body changes with development, the individual must reconfigure the ways in which the senses are combined (Bremner, Holmes, & Spence, 2008; Burr, Binda, & Gori, 2011).

Gallagher provides one prominent alternative to the idea that the development of body perception is driven by physiological changes and sensory experience. Drawing particularly on evidence and accounts of neonatal imitation (Meltzoff & Moore, 1997) and congenital phantom limbs (i.e., phantom limbs experienced by individuals who have never possessed the absent limb throughout development), Gallagher (2005; Gallagher & Meltzoff, 1996) argues that there are strong reasons to support the existence of innate components of our ability to perceive our body and limbs. A perhaps more extreme (nativist) position is adopted by Rochat (2010). Despite agreeing with many aspects of Merleau-Ponty's phenomenology of bodily perception, Rochat takes what seems to be an opposing view with regard to the development of body perception, arguing that a sense of the body is "innate" and that a postural schema is available from birth, providing "implicit awareness of relations between the body (the embodied self) and the environment in which it is embedded" (Rochat, 2010, p. 739).

Much of the evidence that Gallagher uses to support his argument for innate aspects of body perception comes from reports of congenital phantom limbs and neonatal imitation. It is somewhat frustrating (perhaps especially as a developmental psychologist) that the main evidence used to inform theoretical accounts of the development of body perception and representations is extracted either from a patient group who are relatively distant in age from the developmental events that seem likely to be involved (as is the case with work addressing congenital aplasia), or from behaviors that depend as much on a social motivation as they do on body representations (as is the case with work addressing imitation). Correspondingly, in this chapter I will focus particularly (as does Rochat, 1998, 2010) on what we know from empirical studies of infants' responses to, and actions with their own bodies. However, as imitation and congenital phantom limbs have set the scene for much of the theoretical speculation surrounding the development of body representations, it is important to first review what they can tell us.

Evidence gathered over a number of years by Meltzoff and Moore (see Meltzoff & Moore, 1997) indicates that newborn infants arrive in the outside world prepared to represent people and bodies via an ability to visually perceive and imitate representations of facial gestures. Given that newborns have very limited visual experience of either their own or others' faces, this ability must require some kind of prespecified crossmodal mapping between the seen gesture in the model and the motor responses made by the neonate. Neonatal imitation is thus a strong counter to Merleau-Ponty's argument that body representations which coordinate interoceptivity and exteroceptivity (multisensory body representations) are constructed through experience, or indeed through the postnatal maturation of neural pathways between sensory areas. However, in the ten or so years since Gallagher's (2005) account, a number of challenges to the evidential basis of neonatal imitation have accumulated (e.g., Jones, 2009; Ray & Heyes, 2011), leading to the most recent report which does not find evidence of true facial imitation until around six months of age (Oostenbroek et al., 2016). Six months is obviously plenty of time for imitation to be learned through postnatal sensorimotor experience (Heyes, 2016), and so the idea that imitation is an experience–independent ability is losing ground. No doubt debate and experimentation will continue following Oostenbroek and colleagues' recent paper, and so it will be interesting to follow this literature over the coming years. Crucially, however, because neonatal facial imitation requires a number of drivers in addition to a postural schema such as a certain social motivation, absence of imitation at birth does not rule out the possibility that newborns are able to form a postural schema.

Congenital phantom limbs are similarly controversial. Simmel (1966) showed that phantom limb experience in individuals who had lost a limb during development depends upon rather extensive prior experience of that limb in the first years of life. On this basis she argued that body representations are constructed gradually as a result of experience of the body. However, observations of a small number of individuals with limb aplasia who report congenital phantoms of those absent limbs (Brugger et al., 2000; Melzack, Israel, Lacroix, & Schultz, 1997) are used by Gallagher (2005; Gallagher, Butterworth, Lew, & Cole, 1998; Gallagher & Meltzoff, 1996) as an indication that there is an innate developmental driver of the body image, albeit one which is shaped and elaborated upon by experience (Simmel, 1966). Nonetheless, there are doubts as to whether or not phantom limbs in aplasia are genuinely comparable to those experienced by participants who have lost a limb during development. There are also alternative explanations of phantom sensations perceived in aplasia (Price, 2006). One such alternative is that the phantom sensations in a limb that someone has never had arise from a referral from experience of the available contralateral limb. Another is that observing touches in others could lead to a somatosensory empathy, like that seen in mirror-touch synesthesia (Banissy & Ward, 2007). In essence, the accumulation of significant pre and postnatal developmental experience prior to the report of phantom limbs in aplasia, leaves open a wide range of potential experiential explanations of this phenomenon.

As we have seen, there is currently considerable doubt concerning the status of both neonatal imitation and congenital phantom limbs, leaving Gallagher's (2005) account with less support. In the next sections I will discuss studies that trace body representations in early life, with a view to gaining more direct information about their developmental origins.

3 Body Representations in Human Fetuses and Neonates

The first clues to the emergence of body representations come from anatomical and motor development in utero. The human fetus's upper limbs develop earlier than the lower limbs; appearing first as "limb buds" around four weeks of gestation. The hands develop defined fingers, which remain joined at around six and a half weeks gestation, and are entirely distinct and separate from around eight weeks. It is at six and a half weeks that the hands start moving for the first time relative to the torso. The fingers begin practicing the movements involved in the "palmar grasp reflex" (in which the fingers clasp down on palm and alternately release) by the eleventh week of gestation. The lower limbs first appear as buds around one week after the upper limbs. Differentiation of fingers and the emergence of movement is similarly slower for the lower limbs.

Of course it is important not to overgeneralize what might be considered quite basic spontaneous or reflexive movements in order to imply the presence of representations (conscious or otherwise) of the limbs making such movements. Nonetheless, these early anatomical differentiations and movements seem likely to have a causal role in the early development of body representations. Milh et al. (2007) have reported "delta-brush" EEG oscillatory signals over central scalp sites of premature neonates (~30 weeks gestational age) which are apparent both when the hands and feet were stimulated by touch, and following spontaneous fetal movements which resulted in somatosensory feedback. The sites of these delta brush oscillations depended on the limb being stimulated, with feet movements and touches leading to signals at medial central sites, and hand movements and touches leading to signals at lateral central sites. On this basis, Milh and colleagues (2007) propose that spontaneous fetal motor activity may lead to the differentiation of somatosensory body maps in the infant brain (see also Marshall & Meltzoff, 2015; Nevalainen, Lauronen, & Pihko, 2014; Nevalainen et al., 2015), although we might also consider whether somatosensory differentiation of feet and hand areas in the brain might particularly encourage movements of these limbs due to somatosensory feedback.

Hand to mouth movements are an important feature of the early oral- manual behavior of the prenatal and newborn infant (Blass, Fillion, Rochat, Hoffmeyer, & Metzger, 1989; Butterworth & Hopkins, 1988; De Vries, Visser, & Prechtl, 1984). That a newborn's mouth will open in anticipation of the arrival of the hand at the mouth or the perioral region has been cited as evidence of intentionality of movement (Butterworth & Hopkins 1988), and an innate postural schema for this particular behavior (Gallagher, 2005). In fact, Gallagher et al. (1998) argue that an innate postural schema for moving the hand to the oral region would be sufficient to drive the development of the body image representation required for congenital phantom limb sensations in aplasia. Nonetheless, in the face of doubts about congenital phantom limbs (Price, 2006), the idea that early manual oral behaviors are underpinned by an innate postural schema deserves some reconsideration.

One immediate query concerning hand–mouth coordination in newborns is how we can characterize the representations underlying this behavior. Butterworth and Hopkins (1988) show that newborns anticipate the arrival of the hand at the mouth even before the hand has started moving. They also find that the open mouth posture is much more likely to be maintained throughout the arm movement when the arm movement results in contact with the mouth and face. This leads Rochat to conclude that: "What is instantiated in such systematic acts is . . . an *organized body schema*. These acts are not just random and cannot be reduced to reflex arcs. They need to be construed as functionally self-oriented acts proper" (2010, p. 740). Nonetheless, even if we accept that a representation of posture must be involved, we can still ask whether this is a case of a *single* (stand-alone) postural schema involving just hand–mouth coordination, or whether it is underpinned by a more general ability to represent the posture of the limbs across a wider range of contexts as Rochat seems to imply.

Gallagher et al. (1998) seem to promote the idea that hand–mouth coordination is a restricted (stand-alone) postural schema in newborns. They point out the existence of specialized neural networks underlying hand to mouth movements in mature primates (e.g., Graziano, 2016). It may be that hand–mouth coordination is a special case body schema, the early emergence of which might be explained by a particular ethological requirement in our evolutionary past (e.g., feeding). This interpretation is somewhat strengthened by the observation that administering sucrose under some circumstances leads to increased hand movements to the mouth (Blass et al., 1989). However, we should also remember that the newborn has already had significant experience of hand to mouth movements prenatally. De Vries, Visser, and Prechtl (1984) report that hand–face contact occurs in the fetus between fifty and one hundred times an hour from as early as twelve weeks gestation. In the restricted environment of the uterus, this may be due at least in part to the proximity of the hands to the face and may also be encouraged by the rich somatosensory innervation of the hands and face/mouth. Thus claims about innate postural schemas for hand–mouth coordination should be balanced against the possibility that such seemingly complex and functionally relevant behaviors may result from the complex interaction of a range of factors during the ample opportunities for learning in utero.

In sum, we should probably be reticent about drawing rich conclusions concerning body representations on the basis of hand–mouth coordination in newborns. There is no evidence that such behaviors are underpinned by more general competencies at representing the body and its postures across a wider range of sensorimotor scenarios. Furthermore, it is important to acknowledge that even a single stand-alone postural schema for hand–mouth coordination seems unlikely to have a straightforward origin in phylogenetic inheritance.

Moving away from the functional relevance of hand–mouth actions, let's consider the perceptual phenomenon. Rochat describes what he takes to be the newborn's perceptual experience during hand–mouth reaching: "Because they bring body parts in direct relation to one another . . . they provide neonates with invariant sensory information specifying the own body's quality as *bounded substance*, with an inside and an outside, specified by particular texture, solidity, temperature, elasticity, taste, and smell" (2010, p. 740). It is hard not to agree that self-touch provides us, as adults, with a particular kind of information which intuitively specifies aspects of the self including the current postural alignment of body parts. However, whether newborn infants perceive such sensorimotor events in the same way as adults is a question which we can at least start to ask empirically, as indeed Rochat has done. But before we get to the empirical data, let's look in more detail at the perceptual phenomenon of self-touch. Rochat refers to the perceptual phenomenon in which a double touch sensation occurs connecting *two different places on the body* (e.g., the hand and the mouth), in *the same place in external space*. I'll address these two spatial aspects in turn.

Can the newborn register that two places have been touched simultaneously on the body? To my knowledge, no work has assessed the ability to perceive tactile simultaneity as yet in newborns. On the face of it, such an ability, even at this early age, does not seem an entirely unlikely proposition given that the tactile perceptual system has been functional from the very early weeks of prenatal life (~4–7 weeks gestation; see Bremner, Lewkowicz, & Spence, 2012). However, in identifying tactile simultaneity, the central nervous system does have to overcome certain computational problems. Dr. Seuss's *Sleep Book* (1962), gives an illustration of one such problem concerning signal latency differences: the Chippendale Mupp has a very long tail which it bites just before going to sleep. Due to the length of its tail, it does not feel any pain until eight hours later, thus helping this excessively pragmatic creature to make the best of not having an alarm clock. As adult humans (in contrast to Mupps) we compensate for asynchronies in the arrival of somatosensory signals from different tactile sites on the body (e.g., Schicke & Röder, 2006). Nonetheless we know nothing of how this ability develops. This would be fascinating to investigate, and it is interesting to speculate how tactile simultaneity might be constructed while coping with the physical changes of the body through development. It may be that some kind of crossmodal calibration is required in order to tune tactile simultaneity (e.g., via reference to co-occurring visual or auditory stimuli; Harris, Harrar, Jaekl, & Kopinska, 2010; Burr et al., 2011).

As to whether newborn infants can determine that a simultaneous double touch event has happened in the same place in external space, I think we are on even less steady ground. One study has examined the question of whether newborn infants perceive the double touch sensation that occurs when they touch themselves. Rochat and Hespos (1997) compared newborns' and one-month-old infants' rooting responses to touches on their cheeks, specifically examining whether there was any difference in response when that touch was self-applied versus applied by the experimenter. This is certainly an ingenious test of an ability to differentiate self versus other touch. However, several problems mean that this study does not yield a clear test. Firstly, the experiment was particularly underpowered for the purpose of identifying statistically reliable effects, with eleven one-month-olds and only five newborns taking part. Rochat and Hespos do nonetheless find a significant interaction between age group and modality of touch (self vs. other), with greater rooting to self-touch in the one-month-olds, and greater rooting to other touch in the newborns. However, they also note that the newborns when inspected as a group on their own in fact showed *no* statistically reliable evidence of differentiating the self versus other touch in their rooting behaviors. The interaction thus only describes reliable trends in the one-month-old group that are not apparent in the newborns. Rochat and Hespos conclude that "newborns tended to display significantly more rooting responses . . . following external compared to self-stimulation," and cite this as "evidence of an innate ability to discriminate between self- vs. externally-caused stimulation" (1997, p. 105) but the absence of an effect in their newborn group contradicts these conclusions.

Irrespective of whether newborns are able to differentiate self versus other touch, I also want to question whether Rochat and Hespos's (1997) double touch study can tell us about perception of double touch *in a single place in external space*. Even with evidence of differential rooting in newborns, there would be no necessity that such a differential response to self versus other touch be based on a representation of the collocation of the two tactile sites in external space. In their study a proprioceptive difference (reaching to the face vs. not reaching to the face) is perfectly confounded with a tactile difference (double touch vs. single touch). The differential rooting response might therefore be due to either the proprioceptive difference (the infants might root more or less when the hand is near the face), the tactile difference (the infants might root more or less when they feel a single touch as opposed to a double touch), or to the combination of the two (the infants root more or less when they know that their hand is near their face and they feel a double touch). Rochat and Hespos (1997; also Rochat, 2010) seem to prefer this last explanation, inferring a spatial representation that encompasses a coordination of proprioception and touch. However, either of the other alternatives seem just as likely, and neither of these need to rest on a representation of external space in which touch and proprioception are coordinated. Even accepting Rochat and Hespos's (1997) claim of a differential rooting response, the simpler interpretations of this in newborns and one-month-olds outlined here are commensurate with recent work from my own lab, which indicates that external spatial coding of touch does not emerge until six months of age (Begum Ali, Spence, & Bremner, 2015; Bremner, Mareschal, Lloyd-Fox, & Spence, 2008; see section 4).

In sum, I think that it is safe to say that more empirical work remains to be done concerning fetal and newborn body representations. Despite a number of strident claims concerning innate body representations (e.g., Rochat, 2010), and innate postural schemas (e.g., Gallagher & Meltzoff, 1996), based on observations of newborn infants, the available data suggests that we are still (at best) a long way from unilateral support. Coordinated action between hand and mouth in newborns and fetuses certainly gives us a sign of the origins of the postural schemas that underlie a mature ability to perceive our bodies, and act with them. However, as explained in section 2, there is a danger of over interpreting such behaviors.

Irrespective of debate surrounding innate representations underlying hand–mouth coordination, it remains important to consider how early sensory and sensorimotor experience impacts on the development of body representations in utero. The fetus and newborn inhabit a very complex tactile milieu with constant and varying stimulation across the full body surface and internally. Given the difficulty of working with the crucial participant group (fetuses), we may learn more about how such information is decoded and capitalized upon from robotic simulations (e.g., see Kuniyoshi, 2016; Asada et al., 2009) than experimentation in the first instance (although see Milh et al., 2007 for a notable exception). However, we can at least draw some inferences about the developmental origins of body representations from studies of early postnatal development. I turn to those next.

4 Coming to Represent the Body in the Outside World

Arriving in the outside world, the newborn infant has to determine how the sensory stimulation experienced in utero relates to an entirely new external spatial environment. Proprioception and touch continue to provide the same kinds of information about the limbs and touches to the body, although being less enclosed will certainly enable the body to get into a new range of postures. But gone is the tightly enclosing tactile environment of the uterine walls. And rather than the low-pass filtered external sounds among the sloshes of the womb, the newborn now receives a much wider range of sound frequencies emanating from a much wider range of external places. Although recent modeling indicates that there is not an insignificant amount of visual stimulation that reaches the fetus (Del Giudice, 2011), at birth vision provides (for the first time) information about objects and events happening beyond immediate personal space. Sights, sounds, and even smells now offer up a much richer array of information about an external world than the newborn has been presented with before. He or she has to learn to make sense of this.

A casual observation of young infants' behavior with respect to their own hands suggests significant limitations in their appreciation of the relationship of their bodies to the externally sensed environment. The following anecdotal observation of a four-month-old infant suggests difficulties in appreciating the relationship between his or her own seen and felt hands: "Sometimes the hand would be stared at steadily, perhaps with growing intensity, until interest reached such a pitch that a grasping movement followed, as if the infant tried by an automatic action of the motor hand to grasp the visual hand, and it was switched out of the centre of vision and lost as if it had magically vanished" (Hall, 1898, p. 351). The picture given by this observation is reminiscent of Merleau-Ponty's (1964) proposal that the development of body perception is characterized by learning how sensations arising from their own body ("interoceptivity") relate in space and time to the new sensations regarding the external world ("exteroceptivity"). It is also supported by recent studies examining tactile spatial perception in infants, children, and blind people, which indicate that a sense of touch in external space takes some time to develop in early life. I cover these next.

Touch plays the dual roles of informing us about what is happening on the skin, and how the surface of our body interfaces with objects in the external spatial world (e.g., Martin, 1993). For the first of these roles we need only code the touch in somatotopic (or anatomical) spatial coordinates. But the second role requires an ability to code where the touch is externally. We can trace the emergence of external spatial coding of touch by examining effects of body posture on tactile localization. For instance, under certain circumstances, when adults are asked to localize touches on their hands they make more mistakes when their hands are crossed than when they are uncrossed (Schicke & Röder, 2006; Shore, Spry & Spence, 2002; Yamamoto & Kitazawa, 2001). This "crossed-hands deficit" (CHD) arises because adults are obliged to encode the location of tactile events in the external world (see fig. 1.1).

Work with blind adults demonstrates that external spatial coding of touch arises out of visual experience. Congenitally blind participants show no CHD even though blindfolded sighted and late blind adults (even those with only a few years of visual experience in early life) show the same CHD as sighted adults (Röder, Rossler, & Spence, 2004). More recently, no CHD was found in an individual who was born congenitally blind, but whose sight was restored at the age of two years through the removal of congenital cataracts (Ley, Bottari, Shenoy, Kekunnaya, & Röder, 2013). Thus, visual experience, seemingly at some point in the first two years of life, is important for the typical development of external spatial coding of touch.

When does external spatial coding of touch (as demonstrated through the CHD) develop? Two studies have found the CHD in early childhood (Begum Ali, Cowie, & Bremner, 2014; Pagel, Heed, & Röder, 2009) via verbal responses in which the participants had to identify which of two hands was touched (or which was touched first) during crossed and uncrossed postures. Studies with infants have tackled this question by examining the accuracy of infants' orienting responses to touches,

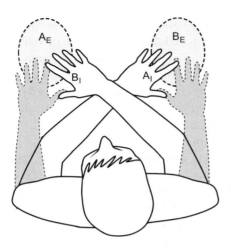

Figure 1.1
When the arms are crossed, intrinsic tactile locations on the skin (A_I and B_I) come to occupy less familiar places in the external environment (respectively B_E and A_E). Several studies now show that adults, children and even infants (Azañón & Soto-Faraco, 2008; Begum Ali et al., 2014, 2015; Bremner et al., 2008; Shore et al., 2002; Yamamoto & Kitazawa, 2001) are worse at localizing touches when the arms are crossed than when they are uncrossed. Some (Yamamoto & Kitazawa, 2001; Begum Ali et al., 2014; Bremner & Van Velzen, 2014), but not all (see Shore et al., 2002) have explained this as a bias to locate a touch (for example, to the left hand) in the external location where it would usually occur with the body in a canonical posture (A_E), and that this representation competes with representations of current location (on the body [A_I] or in external space [B_E]). The canonical posture is represented in this figure by the shaded arms with dashed outlines. (Figure reprinted with permission from Bremner & Van Velzen, 2015.)

particularly infants' orienting of their eyes, hands, and feet toward the tactile stimulation site. We (Bremner et al., 2008) found that 6.5-month-olds' first manual responses following a tactile stimulus were more likely to occur on the touched hand in the uncrossed-hands than the crossed-hands posture, indicating a CHD, and thus external coding of touch, in this age group.

Recently, my colleagues and I (Begum Ali et al., 2015) investigated whether external spatial coding of touch emerges in the first six months of post-natal life, comparing four- and six-month-old infants. Due to difficulties inherent in crossing four-month-old infants' arms, we examined the accuracy of their orienting responses to tactile stimuli on the feet across both crossed- and uncrossed-feet postures (fig. 1.2A). Crossed-feet effects have been observed in adults (Schicke & Röder, 2006). As you can see in figure 1.2B, the six-month-olds demonstrated the usual crossed-limb deficit with ~70 percent accuracy in the uncrossed posture, and chance (50 percent) performance in the crossed posture. In striking contrast, the four-month-olds showed no crossed-feet deficit, matching the performance of the six-month-olds in the uncrossed-feet posture and outperforming them in the crossed-feet posture.

So given that a crossed-feet deficit emerges between four and six months of age, we (Begum Ali et al., 2015) concluded that external spatial coding of touch develops between four and six months of age. This conclusion is commensurate with findings concerning tactile spatial coding in blind adults already mentioned (Ley et al., 2013; Röder et al., 2004), and in combination with this work indicates that visual experience somehow plays a role in bringing about the development external coding of touch between four and six months of age.

Our current explanation of the mediating effects of visual experience on the development of external coding of touch is that the onset of successful reaching at around four to five months of age brings about experiences of synchronous multisensory (visual-tactile) stimuli. Similar experiences are likely across hands and feet as infants' first reaches are made with both sets of limbs (Galloway & Thelen, 2004). Infants may well build up an expectation that tactile stimuli on the right hand (or foot) typically occur in right visual (or multisensory) space, and tactile stimuli on the left hand (or foot) typically occur in left visual (or multisensory) space (Bremner & Van Velzen, 2015; Yamamoto & Kitazawa, 2001; see fig. 1.1). Thus, multisensory interactions between vision and touch may be the developmental mechanism whereby infants come to represent the relation between their body and external space.

In the next section I will discuss what we know about the development of the multisensory underpinnings of body representations. However, it is first worth dwelling a little on what the findings described above mean with regard to the tactile experience of the human infant prior to four months of age. Given that location in external space does not appear to influence four-month-olds' responses to tactile stimuli we (Begum Ali et al., 2015) argue that up to and including this age infants, when they feel a unisensory tactile stimulus, experience that purely on the body and unrelated to the external environment, or the spatial sensations reaching their central nervous system via exteroceptors (e.g., vision, audition, and smell). This tactile solipsism seems profoundly different from the ways in which we as

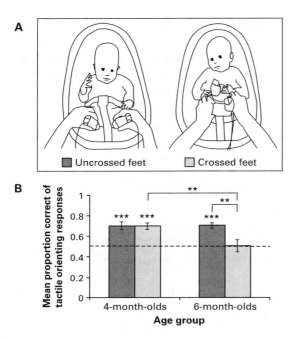

Figure 1.2
Probing infants' spatial representations of touch by crossing the legs (Begum Ali et al., 2015). (A) An infant participant in the uncrossed- and crossed-feet postures. The tactors, attached to the infants' feet using a cohesive bandage, were controlled remotely. The experimenter held the infant's feet in the assigned posture during tactile stimulation. (B) Mean proportion of correct first unilateral foot movements to vibrotactile stimuli (error bars indicate the standard error of the mean). The six-month-olds showed a crossed-feet effect whereas the four-month-olds performed equivalently across conditions, matching the best performance of the six-month-olds. Significant comparisons are indicated (*=$p<.05$, **=$p<.01$, ***=$p<.001$). (Figure reprinted with permission from Begum Ali et al., 2015.)

adults perceive and think about touch. If we're right, it must be strange to be a newborn infant.

5   The Early Development of the Multisensory Underpinnings of Body Representations

Perhaps the most direct sensory information concerning the body arises from cutaneous touch and proprioception, with signals from the vestibular system also providing direct information about the body's positioning with respect to the environment. Nonetheless, as adults our representations of limb and body position result from the combination and integration of information from these direct (and largely somatosensory) receptors with the visual and even auditory information which is more particularly suited to providing information about the external world (Holmes & Spence, 2004; cf. Merleau-Ponty, 1964). This multisensory nature of body representations gives rise to a number of computational challenges for the developing child. Not only do the senses convey information about the body and limbs in different neural codes and reference frames, but the spatial and temporal relationships between sensory modalities can vary dramatically from moment to moment. For instance, each time our arm changes posture the relations between tactile coordinates on the hands and locations in the external environment are realigned (see fig. 1.1).

While adults dynamically and automatically remap spatial correspondences among the senses across changes in the posture of the limbs (Holmes & Spence, 2004; although not perfectly: Yamamoto & Kitazawa, 2001), we cannot necessarily infer that the same is the case earlier in development. In fact the computational problems surrounding multisensory spatial perception are amplified during infancy and childhood. The number and variety of postural changes that a child makes in the service of purposeful skilled movement increases substantially in the first years of life. Furthermore, the spatial distribution of the limbs and the body also changes profoundly. Such physical and behavioral changes necessitate continuous adaptation of multisensory body representations in early life (Adolph & Avolio, 2000; Burr et al., 2011).

Some clear multisensory interactions concerning the body are known to be present at birth, including the vestibular–ocular reflex, in which vestibular signals concerning bodily movement are used to stabilize the visual image via eye movements (Rosander & Von Hofsten, 2000). Newborn head turning to tactile and auditory stimulation has also been observed (Moreau, Helfgott, Weinstein, & Milner, 1978; Butterworth & Castillo, 1976). Although there is relatively little information about the development of these cross-modal orienting responses, in some cases evidence indicates that they wane in the first months of postnatal life (e.g., Bremner et al., 2008; Clifton, Morrongiello, Kulig, & Dowd, 1981). Are these relatively isolated instances of neonatal multisensory reflexes, or indications of a broader multisensory competence enabling newborns and older infants to make sense of the multisensory milieu of their bodies? Although there is not the space to discuss this here, the latter account is very much implied by some current influential accounts of multisensory development (e.g., the intersensory redundancy hypothesis; Bahrick & Lickliter, 2012), although challenged elsewhere (Begum Ali et al., 2015).

Several studies using infants' looking preferences have investigated an early ability to make crossmodal links between cues about the body coming from somatosensation (proprioception, cutaneous touch) and vision. These studies typically examine infants' preferences for visual movements of limbs projected on a screen which are either congruent or incongruent with their own limb movements perceived proprioceptively (see fig. 1.3; Bahrick & Watson, 1985; Rochat, 1998). From as early as three months, infants' looking behavior demonstrates that they are able to differentiate multisensory bodily events on the basis of visual-proprioceptive (temporal and spatial) congruency. More recently researchers have examined whether infants can detect if a visually observed stroke to the skin occurs at the same time as a felt (tactile) stroke (Zmyj, Jank, Schütz-Bosbach, & Daum, 2011; Filippetti, Lloyd-Fox, Longo, Farroni, Johnson, 2015). Even newborn infants are able to do this (Filippetti, Johnson, Lloyd-Fox, Dragovic, & Farroni, 2013), and more recent data also indicates an ability to code spatial congruence between touches felt on the skin and seen on a video screen in newborns (Filippetti, Orioli, Johnson, & Farroni, 2015). Early crossmodal competencies of this kind provide fuel for speculation that an ability to perceive the bodily self is well specified from birth (e.g., Rochat, 2010).

One important limitation of the crossmodal matching studies just described (see fig. 1.3) is that they present visual bodily information on a screen well outside of personal space (sometimes as far as one meter distant). Thus, any crossmodal links that infants make in this context are necessarily abstracted from spatial frames of reference centered on the body and limbs. This prompts the question of whether an ability to link this screen-based visual information to somatosensory input is of relevance to spatial representations of the body and limbs that could provide the basis for sensorimotor coordination, and body representations more generally (Bremner & Cowie, 2013). While Rochat and Striano (2000) suggest

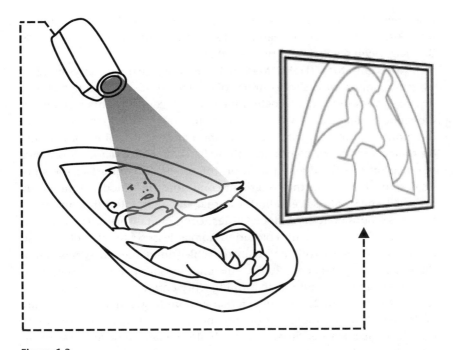

Figure 1.3
Crossmodal matching studies of multisensory body perception in infancy. Research-ers have measured infants' looking preferences for visual movements of limbs pro-jected on a screen which are either congruent or incongruent with their own limb movements perceived proprioceptively (Bahrick & Watson, 1985; Filippetti et al., 2013; Rochat, 1998). Differentiation of congruent and incongruent displays is typi-cally demonstrated by a looking preference for the incongruent presentation, but preferences for the congruent presentation are also observed under some circum-stances, and are equally as diagnostic of differentiation. (Figure reprinted with per-mission from Bremner, 2016.)

that infants' crossmodal matching of information concerning their bodies across spatial disparities points to an ability to "eject" representations of their own bodies to outside of personal space, I and my colleagues (e.g., Bremner & Cowie, 2013) have argued that such abilities might instead be underpinned by a quite different skill: recognizing specific associations between proprioceptive/somatosensory/kinesthetic cues to body movement and visual stimuli in the environment, *in the absence of a coherent multisen-sory representation of the body's posture and movements*. This interpretation is supported by well-established findings that there are significant devel-opmental changes in the ways multisensory information is used to guide reaching behaviors, with infants and even young children neglecting to make use of visual cues to hand position (e.g., Clifton, Rochat, Robin, & Bertheir, 1994; see Bremner, Holmes, et al., 2008).

In a recent study (Freier, Mason, & Bremner, 2016) we attempted to overcome some of the shortcomings of the crossmodal matching methods discussed above in order to determine whether young infants can register crossmodal collocation with respect to the body. We presented six- and ten-month-old infants with visual (flashes) and tactile (vibration) stimuli on their hands either colocated on one hand or spread across two hands (a touch on one hand and a light on the other). In contrast to the studies described above, in the congruent condition the bimodal stimuli only occupied one single place in both external and anatomical (bodily) space. Both age groups preferred to look at the incongruent displays. Thus, infants are sensitive to visual-tactile colocation from at least six months of age, and before they are able to orient visually to tactile stimuli presented in isolation (Bremner, Mareschal et al., 2008). This multisensory perceptual skill obviously plays an important role in forming representations of spatial relationships between the body and our external surroundings (Eilan, 1993). We are undertaking further studies to examine the origins of this ability prior to six months of age. Further questions which also remain to be addressed concern what kind of multisensory representation underlies this ability to perceive visual-tactile colocation. Do the infants perceive a unified (integrated) multisensory stimulus, or the colocation of two quite separate unisensory cues? The current work addressing the development of integration in multisensory perception more broadly (largely in the audiovisual domain) is quite limited, but points to an extended developmental trajectory later in infancy (Neil, Chee-Ruiter, Scheier, Lewkowicz, & Shimojo, 2006) and even into childhood (Burr et al., 2011).

Even once infants or children learn to colocate touches with visual stimuli in the external environment, a further hurdle involves developing an ability to update the location of a touch (and a limb) when the body moves into unfamiliar postures. The data from Freier et al. (2016) only pertain to a scenario in which the hands occupy fairly canonical places with respect to the body. We do not know what happens when the limbs are in unfamiliar places. Studies with adults demonstrate that when locating a touch in an unfamiliar posture we rapidly incorporate visual and proprioceptive information about limb position in order to remap the touch to its location in the external world (Azañón & Soto-Faraco, 2008). But how does the developing brain come to solve this task as the infant gradually builds up an increasingly complex repertoire of purposeful skilled movements across

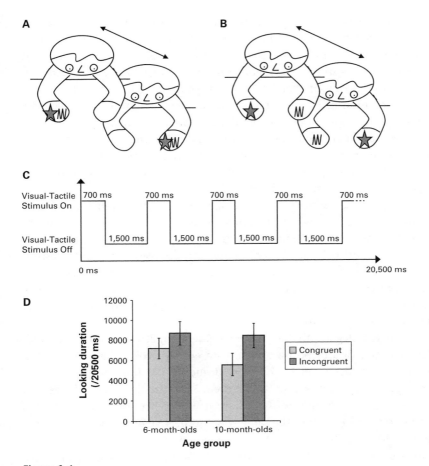

Figure 1.4
Determining whether six- and ten-month-old infants can perceive when tactile and visual stimuli are colocated on their hands (Freier et al., 2016). This figure provides a schematic illustration of the stimulus presentation protocols used in Freier et al.'s experiment, and the findings. (A) shows the spatially congruent visual-tactile event condition, and (B) shows the incongruent condition. In (A) colocated bimodal (visual-tactile) stimulation (700 ms) is presented synchronously on a single hand at a time, alternating between left and right hand. In (B) the visual and tactile stimuli alternate between the hands according to the same schedule, but although they are presented synchronously they never coincide on the same hand. (C) displays a schematic of the stimulus presentation schedule within a single trial. (D) shows the mean duration of infants' looking at their hands during congruent and incongruent test conditions (in seconds), plotted according to age group (error bars indicate the standard error of the mean). (Figure adapted from Freier et al., 2016.)

the first year of life? At six months of age we know that when infants are locating touches presented in isolation, they do not take account of current limb position and seemingly fall back on a reliance that the body is in a canonical posture (as evidenced by their crossed-hands and crossed-feet deficits; Begum Ali et al., 2015; Bremner, Mareschal et al., 2008). However, By ten months of age, infants maintain a consistent level of accuracy in their orienting responses across both familiar and unfamiliar postures. It seems that an ability to incorporate sensory information about current limb posture into representations of the external location of tactile events (referred to here as "postural remapping") develops significantly during the second half of the first year of life.

What processes underlie the development of postural remapping? One question here is whether development reflects a process of multisensory perceptual gains or whether we are seeing improvements in the infants' coordination of their crossmodal orienting responses. A second question concerns what sensory information infants are making use of to update their representations of limb position and remap their behavioral responses. A recent physiological study of tactile processing in infancy from our lab helps address both of these matters.

We (Rigato, Begum Ali, Van Velzen, & Bremner, 2014) investigated modulatory effects of arm posture on somatosensory evoked potentials (SEPs) recorded from the scalp in 6.5- and 10-month-old infants (see fig. 1.5). When presented with tactile stimuli, the 6.5-month-old infants showed no reliable effect of posture on their SEPs; it was as if these younger infants processed tactile events in the same way irrespective of the posture of their limbs, mirroring the findings from behavioral studies that this age group tended to respond to the same external location irrespective of limb posture (Bremner et al., 2008). However, the ten-month-old infants, like adults (Rigato et al., 2013; Soto-Faraco & Azañón, 2013) showed significant postural modulations of somatosensory processing. Thus, improvements in tactile localization across limb postures may well be underpinned by the increased role of postural information in somatosensory processing seen in the SEPs. Importantly, the modulatory effects of posture seen at ten months occur (as they do in adults) early in somatosensory processing (~60–120 ms). In answer to the first question raised above, this suggests that improvements in somatosensory processing and postural remapping at ten months of age occur largely at the early feed-forward (perceptual) end of neural processing in somatosensory cortex, rather than in terms of the responses to touches.

In addressing the second question raised earlier, we (Rigato et al., 2014) ran a further experiment investigating what sensory information

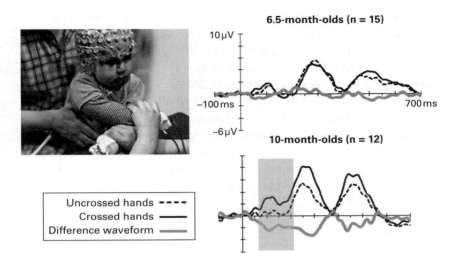

Figure 1.5
Researching the early development of body representations via somatosensory evoked potentials (SEPs). Rigato et al. (2014) examined the effect of arm posture on SEPs. The infants (as pictured on the left) received 200 ms vibrotactile stimuli to the hand in either an uncrossed- or a crossed-hands arm posture (the crossed-hands posture is shown). As in adults (Rigato et al., 2013) ten-month-olds' SEPs were modulated by posture from early in somatosensory processing, indicating a somatosensory postural remapping. Younger infants (6.5-month-olds) however, demonstrated SEPs which were unaffected by arm posture. (Figure reprinted with permission from Bremner, 2016.)

concerning limb position drives the postural modulation of somatosensory processing seen at ten months. We presented tactile stimuli again, but this time the infants' arms were obscured from their view by a cloak. In this case, the ten-month-old infants showed no effect of posture on their SEPs. Therefore, it seems that, at this point in development, visual cues to hand posture are required to remap tactile space.

Thus, by ten months of age, infants appear to be able not just to represent the location of touches in the external environment, but also to dynamically update tactile localization across changes in limb posture. Nonetheless, it is important to note that changes continue beyond the first year in the ways infants and even children combine multisensory cues to localize touches. For instance, in contrast to adults and older children, four-year-old children are actually worse at determining which hand felt a touch when they can see their hands (Begum Ali et al., 2014). It seems that visual cues to hand posture actually interfere with the process of localizing touches in early childhood. Indeed, an adult-like weighting of visual relative to proprioceptive hand position cues does not appear to mature until after nine years of age (Cowie, Sterling, & Bremner, 2016).

Given the variety of postures through which our limbs move from moment to moment, our ability to assemble coherent representations of the body and the world from the multisensory stream of information presented to the nervous system is fairly miraculous. While adults seemingly manage this with ease, the ways in which multisensory information concerning the body is combined change substantially in early life, as a result of sensory experience.

6 Summary

At the opening of this chapter I argued that there is a rich seam of enquiry into the developmental origins of our perception and understanding of our own bodies which has slipped through the cracks in developmental psychology. We ought to continue to try to paper over these cracks; investigating the development of the perceptual nature of body representations in early life of course has much broader implications beyond the development of body perception and extends to tracing the origins of our senses of self in the world, self concepts, and our understanding of others (Rochat, 2010).

Perhaps because of the relative neglect of the body in developmental psychology, theoretical accounts of the development of body representations have tended to be quite strident in flavor (and more recently nativist), frequently relying on evidence that is either controversial or not directly relevant to the matter, or both (e.g., research on congenital phantom limbs and neonatal imitation, see section 2). In sections 3 through 5 of this chapter I have examined what studies of early life (studies of fetuses and infants) can tell us about the developmental origins of body representations, examining relevant physiological and behavioral data, and referring to clinical conditions in adults (e.g., congenital blindness) where relevant. I have been quite critical of a number of "rich interpretations" of infant behavioral data, and the overall picture that I have extracted from the empirical literature is that pre and postnatal experience play important roles in the development of our abilities to sense the distributions of our limbs, and the relationship between our bodies and the external world. The evidence for well-specified experience independent components of body representations is not particularly strong at present. More empirical research and modeling, ideally focusing on very early development in utero as well as postnatal development, will be crucial for fully understanding how these abilities develop. I hope that I have also persuaded the reader that a full consideration of the development of the *multisensory nature* of body representations will be necessary to make significant progress in this area (see Bremner et al., 2012).

Acknowledgments

In preparing this chapter I was supported by an award from the ERC (241242). I would like to acknowledge helpful discussions with my colleagues; particularly JJ Begum Ali, Jo Johnston, Dorothy Cowie, Fran Le Cornu Knight, Silvia Rigato, Charles Spence, Rhiannon Thomas, and José van Velzen.

Notes

1. I am using the term "representation" in the fairly lazy way that I think psychologists usually use it—that is, to denote a particular pattern of neural firing corresponding to (an aspect of) a sensory stimulus. This is meant to encompass a wide range of possibilities, but I will try to be as precise as I can in distinguishing between different types of representation where appropriate.

2. It is worth noting here that interpretations of Merleau-Ponty's position with regard to the developmental origins of body perception are not always consistent. In contrast with Gallagher's (2005) interpretation (and my own), Rochat states that Merleau-Ponty "insists that what we perceive of the body, *presumably from birth on*, is primarily a 'postural schema'" (2010, p. 739; emphasis added).

References

Adolph, K. E. (2015). Motor development. In R. M. Lerner (Ed.), *Handbook of child psychology and developmental science* (7th ed., Vol. 2, pp. 114–157). New York: Wiley.

Adolph, K. E., & Avolio, A. M. (2000). Walking infants adapt locomotion to changing body dimensions. *Journal of Experimental Psychology: Human Perception and Performance, 26*(3), 1148–1166. doi:10.1037/0096-1523.26.3.1148.

Arterberry, M. E., & Kellman, P. J. (2016). *Development of perception in infancy: The cradle of knowledge revisited*. Oxford: Oxford University Press.

Asada, M., Hosoda, K., Kuniyoshi, Y., Ishiguro, H., Inui, T., Yoshikawa, Y., . . . Yoshida C. (2009). Cognitive developmental robotics: A survey. *IEEE Transactions on Autonomous Mental Development, 1*(1), 12–34. doi:10.1109/TAMD.2009.2021702.

Azañón, E., & Soto-Faraco, S. (2008). Changing reference frames during the encoding of tactile events. *Current Biology, 18*(14), 1044–1049. doi:10.1016/j.cub.2008.06.045.

Bahrick, L. E., & Lickliter, R. (2012). The role of intersensory redundancy in early perceptual, cognitive, and social development. In A. J. Bremner, D. J. Lewkowicz, & C. Spence (Eds.), *Multisensory development* (pp. 183–205). Oxford: Oxford University Press.

Bahrick, L. E., & Watson, J. S. (1985). Detection of intermodal proprioceptive-visual contingency as a potential basis of self-perception in infancy. *Developmental Psychology, 21*(6), 963–973. doi:10.1037/0012-1649.21.6.963.

Banissy, M. J., & Ward, J. (2007). Mirror-touch synesthesia is linked with empathy. *Nature Neuroscience, 10*(7), 815–816. doi:10.1038/nn1926.

Begum Ali, J., Cowie, D., & Bremner, A. J. (2014). Effects of posture on tactile localization by 4 years of age are modulated by sight of the hands: Evidence for an early acquired external spatial frame of reference for touch. *Developmental Science, 17*(6), 935–943. doi:10.1111/desc.12184.

Begum Ali, J., Spence, C., & Bremner, A. J. (2015). Human infants' ability to perceive touch in external space develops postnatally. *Current Biology, 25*(20), R978–R979. doi:10.1016/j.cub.2015.08.055.

Blass, E. M., Fillion, T. J., Rochat, P., Hoffmeyer, L. B., & Metzger, M. A. (1989). Sensorimotor and motivational determinants of hand–mouth coordination in 1–3-day-old human infants. *Developmental Psychology, 25*(6), 963–975. doi:10.1037/0012-1649.25.6.963.

Bremner, A. J. (2016). Developing body representations in early life: Combining somatosensation and vision to perceive the interface between the body and the world. *Developmental Medicine & Child Neurology, 58*(Suppl. 4), 12–16. doi:10.1111/dmcn.13041.

Bremner, A. J., & Cowie, D. (2013). Developmental origins of the hand in the mind and the role of the hands in the development of the mind. In Z. Radman (Ed.), *The hand, an organ of the mind: What the manual tells the mental* (pp. 27–55). Cambridge, MA: MIT Press.

Bremner, A. J., Holmes, N. P., & Spence, C. (2008). Infants lost in (peripersonal) space? *Trends in Cognitive Sciences, 12*(8), 298–305. doi:10.1016/j.tics.2008.05.003.

Bremner, A. J., Lewkowicz, D. J., & Spence, C. (2012). *Multisensory development.* Oxford: Oxford University Press.

Bremner, A. J., Mareschal, D., Lloyd-Fox, S., & Spence, C. (2008). Spatial localization of touch in the first year of life: Early influence of a visual code, and the development of remapping across changes in limb position. *Journal of Experimental Psychology: General, 137*(1), 149–162. doi:10.1037/0096-3445.137.1.149.

Bremner, A. J., & van Velzen, J. (2015). Sensorimotor control: Retuning the body–world interface. *Current Biology*, *25*(4), R159–R161. doi:10.1016/j.cub.2014.12.042.

Brugger, P., Kollias, S. S., Müri, R. M., Crelier, G., Hepp-Reymond, M. C., & Regard, M. (2000). Beyond re-membering: Phantom sensations of congenitally absent limbs. *Proceedings of the National Academy of Sciences of the United States of America*, *97*(11), 6167–6172. doi:10.1073/pnas.100510697.

Burr, D., Binda, P., & Gori, M. (2011). Multisensory integration and calibration in adults and in children. In J. Trommershauser, K. Kording, & M. S. Landy (Eds.), *Sensory cue integration* (pp. 173–194). Oxford: Oxford University Press.

Butterworth, G., & Castillo, M. (1976). Coordination of auditory and visual space in newborn human infants. *Perception*, *5*(2), 155–160.

Butterworth, G., & Hopkins, B. (1988). Hand–mouth coordination in the new-born baby. *British Journal of Developmental Psychology*, *6*(4), 303–314.

Clifton, R. K., Morrongiello, B. A., Kulig, J. W., & Dowd, J. M. (1981). Newborns' orientation toward sound: Possible implications for cortical development. *Child Development*, *52*(3), 833–838. doi:10.2307/1129084.

Clifton, R. K., Rochat, P., Robin, D. J., & Bertheir, N. E. (1994). Multimodal perception in the control of infant reaching. *Journal of Experimental Psychology: Human Perception and Performance*, *20*(4), 876–886. doi:10.1037/0096-1523.20.4.876.

Cowie, D., Sterling, S., & Bremner, A. J. (2016). The development of multisensory body representation and awareness continues to 10 years of age: Evidence from the rubber hand illusion. *Journal of Experimental Child Psychology*, *142*, 230–238. doi:10.1016/j.jecp.2015.10.003.

Del Giudice, M. (2011). Alone in the dark? Modeling the conditions for visual experience in human fetuses. *Developmental Psychobiology*, *53*(2), 214–219. doi:10.1002/dev.20506.

de Vries, J. I. P., Visser, G. H. A., & Prechtl, H. F. R. (1984). Fetal motility in the first half of pregnancy. *Clinics in Developmental Medicine*, *94*, 46–64.

Eilan, N. (1993). Molyneux's question and the idea of an external world. In N. Eilan, R. McCarthy, & B. Brewer (Eds.), *Spatial representation: Problems in philosophy and psychology* (pp. 236–255). Oxford: Oxford University Press.

Filippetti, M. L., Johnson, M. H., Lloyd-Fox, S., Dragovic, D., & Farroni, T. (2013). Body perception in newborns. *Current Biology*, *23*(23), 2413–2416. doi:10.1016/j.cub.2013.10.017.

Filippetti, M. L., Lloyd-Fox, S., Longo, M. R., Farroni, T., & Johnson, M. H. (2015). Neural mechanisms of body awareness in infants. *Cerebral Cortex*, *25*(10), 3779–3787. doi:10.1093/cercor/bhu261.

Filippetti, M. L., Orioli, G., Johnson, M. H., & Farroni, T. (2015). Newborn body perception: Sensitivity to spatial congruency. *Infancy, 20*(4), 455–465. doi:10.1111/infa.12083.

Freier, L., Mason, L., & Bremner, A. J. (2016). Perception of visual-tactile colocation in the first year of life. *Developmental Psychology, 52*(12), 2184–2190. doi:10.1037/dev0000160.

Gallagher, S. (2005). *How the body shapes the mind.* Oxford: Oxford University Press.

Gallagher, S., Butterworth, G. E., Lew, A., & Cole, J. (1998). Hand–mouth coordination, congenital absence of limb, and evidence for innate body schemas. *Brain and Cognition, 38*(1), 53–65. doi:10.1006/brcg.1998.1020.

Gallagher, S., & Meltzoff, A. N. (1996). The earliest sense of self and others: Merleau-Ponty and recent developmental studies. *Philosophical Psychology, 9*(2), 211–233. doi:10.1080/09515089608573181.

Galloway, J. C., & Thelen, E. (2004). Feet first: Object exploration in young infants. *Infant Behavior and Development, 27*(1), 107–112. doi:10.1016/j.infbeh.2003.06.001.

Gibson, E. J., & Pick, A. D. (2000). *An ecological approach to perceptual learning and development.* New York: Oxford University Press.

Graziano, M. S. (2016). Ethological action maps: A paradigm shift for the motor cortex. *Trends in Cognitive Sciences, 20*(2), 121–132. doi:10.1016/j.tics.2015.10.008.

Hall, G. S. (1898). Some aspects of the early sense of self. *American Journal of Psychology, 9*(3), 351–395. doi:10.2307/1411300.

Harris, L. R., Harrar, V., Jaekl, P., & Kopinska, A. (2010). Mechanisms of simultaneity constancy. In R. Nijhawan (Ed.), *Space and time in perception and action* (pp. 232–253). Cambridge: Cambridge University Press.

Heyes, C. (2016). Imitation: Not in our genes. *Current Biology, 26*(10), R412–R414. doi:10.1016/j.cub.2016.03.060.

Holmes, N. P., & Spence, C. (2004). The body schema and multisensory representation(s) of peripersonal space. *Cognitive Processing, 5*(2), 94–105. doi:10.1007/s10339-004-0013-3.

Jones, S. S. (2009). The development of imitation in infancy. *Philosophical Transactions of the Royal Society, Series B: Biological Sciences, 364*(1528), 2325–2335. doi:10.1098/rstb.2009.0045.

Kuniyoshi, Y. (2016). Constructive developmental science: A trans-disciplinary approach toward the fundamentals of human cognitive development and its disorders, centered around fetus simulation. In M. Inaba & P. Corke (Eds.), *Robotics research*

(pp. 291–303). Basel: Springer International Publishing. doi:10.1007/978-3-319
-28872-7_17.

Ley, P., Bottari, D., Shenoy, B. H., Kekunnaya, R., & Röder, B. (2013). Partial recovery of visual—spatial remapping of touch after restoring vision in a congenitally blind man. *Neuropsychologia, 51*(6), 1119–1123. doi:10.1016/j.neuropsychologia.2013.03.004.

Marshall, P. J., & Meltzoff, A. N. (2015). Body maps in the infant brain. *Trends in Cognitive Sciences, 19*(9), 499–505. doi:10.1016/j.tics.2015.06.012.

Martin, M. G. F. (1993). Sense modalities and spatial properties. In N. Eilan, R. McCarthy, & B. Brewer (Eds.), *Spatial Representation: Problems in Philosophy and Psychology* (pp. 206–218). Oxford: Oxford University Press.

Meltzoff, A. N., & Moore, M. K. (1997). Explaining facial imitation: A theoretical model. *Early Development & Parenting, 6*(3–4), 179–192. doi:10.1002/(SICI)1099-0917(199709/12)6:3/4<179::AID-EDP157>3.0.CO;2-R.

Melzack, R., Israel, R., Lacroix, R., & Schultz, G. (1997). Phantom limbs in people with congenital limb deficiency or amputation in early childhood. *Brain, 120*(9), 1603–1620. doi:10.1093/brain/120.9.1603.

Merleau-Ponty, M. (2012). *Phenomenology of perception.* London: Routledge.

Merleau-Ponty, M. (1964). *The primacy of perception: And other essays on phenomenological psychology, the philosophy of art, history, and politics.* J. M. Edie (Ed.). Evanston, IL: Northwestern University Press.

Milh, M., Kaminska, A., Huon, C., Lapillonne, A., Ben-Ari, Y., & Khazipov, R. (2007). Rapid cortical oscillations and early motor activity in premature human neonate. *Cerebral Cortex, 17*(7), 1582–1594. doi:10.1093/cercor/bhl069.

Moreau, T., Helfgott, E., Weinstein, P., & Milner, P. (1978). Lateral differences in habituation of ipsilateral head-turning to repeated tactile stimulation in the human newborn. *Perceptual and Motor Skills, 46*(2), 427–436. doi:10.2466/pms.1978.46.2.427.

Neil, P. A., Chee-Ruiter, C., Scheier, C., Lewkowicz, D. J., & Shimojo, S. (2006). Development of multisensory spatial integration and perception in humans. *Developmental Science, 9*(5), 454–464. doi:10.1111/j.1467-7687.2006.00512.x.

Nevalainen, P., Lauronen, L., & Pihko, E. (2014). Development of human somatosensory cortical functions – what have we learned from magnetoencephalography: A review. *Frontiers in Human Neuroscience, 8*, 158. doi:10.3389/fnhum.2014.00158.

Nevalainen, P., Rahkonen, P., Pihko, E., Lano, A., Vanhatalo, S., Andersson, S., . . . Lauronen, L. (2015). Evaluation of somatosensory cortical processing in extremely preterm infants at term with MEG and EEG. *Clinical Neurophysiology, 126*(2), 275–283. doi:10.1016/j.clinph.2014.05.036.

Oostenbroek, J., Suddendorf, T., Nielsen, M., Redshaw, J., Kennedy-Costantini, S., Davis, J., . . . Slaughter, V. (2016). Comprehensive longitudinal study challenges the existence of neonatal imitation in humans. *Current Biology, 26*(10), 1334–1338. doi:10.1016/j.cub.2016.03.047.

Pagel, B., Heed, T., & Röder, B. (2009). Change of reference frame for tactile localization during child development. *Developmental Science, 12*(6), 929–937. doi:10.1111 /j.1467-7687.2009.00845.x.

Piaget, J. (1952). *The origins of intelligence in the child.* London: Routledge and Kegan-Paul.

Price, E. H. (2006). A critical review of congenital phantom limb cases and a developmental theory for the basis of body image. *Consciousness and Cognition, 15*(2), 310–322. doi:10.1016/j.concog.2005.07.003.

Ray, E., & Heyes, C. (2011). Imitation in infancy: The wealth of the stimulus. *Developmental Science, 14*(1), 92–105. doi:10.1111/j.1467-7687.2010.00961.x.

Rigato, S., Begum Ali, J., van Velzen, J., & Bremner, A. J. (2014). The neural basis of somatosensory remapping develops in human infancy. *Current Biology, 24*(11), 1222–1226. doi:10.1016/j.cub.2014.04.004.

Rigato, S., Bremner, A. J., Mason, L., Pickering, A., Davis, R., & van Velzen, J. (2013). The electrophysiological time course of somatosensory spatial remapping: Vision of the hands modulates effects of posture on somatosensory evoked potentials. *European Journal of Neuroscience, 38*(6), 2884–2892. doi:10.1111/ejn.12292.

Rochat, P. (1998). Self-perception and action in infancy. *Experimental Brain Research, 123*(1), 102–109. doi:10.1007/s002210050550.

Rochat, P. (2010). The innate sense of the body develops to become a public affair by 2–3 years. *Neuropsychologia, 48*(3), 738–745. doi:10.1016/j.neuropsychologia .2009.11.021.

Rochat, P., & Hespos, S. J. (1997). Differential rooting response by neonates: Evidence for an early sense of self. *Early Development and Parenting, 6*(3–4), 105–112. doi:10.1002/(SICI)1099-0917(199709/12)6:3/4<105::AID-EDP150>3.0.CO;2-U.

Rochat, P., & Striano, T. (2000). Perceived self in infancy. *Infant Behavior and Development, 23*(3), 513–530. doi:10.1016/S0163-6383(01)00055-8.

Röder, B., Rösler, F., & Spence, C. (2004). Early vision impairs tactile perception in the blind. *Current Biology, 14*(2), 121–124. doi:10.1016/j.cub.2003.12.054.

Rosander, K., & von Hofsten, C. (2000). Visual-vestibular interaction in early infancy. *Experimental Brain Research, 133*(3), 321–333. doi:10.1007/s002210000413.

Russell, J. (1995). At two with nature: Agency and the development of self–world dualism. In J. L. Bermúdez, A. Marcel, & N. Eilan (Eds.), *The body and the self* (pp. 127–151). Cambridge, MA: MIT Press.

Schicke, T., & Röder, B. (2006). Spatial remapping of touch: Confusion of perceived stimulus order across hand and foot. *Proceedings of the National Academy of Sciences of the United States of America*, *103*(31), 11808–11813. doi:10.1073/pnas.0601486103.

Seuss, D. (1962). *Dr. Seuss's sleep book*. New York: Random House.

Shore, D. I., Spry, E., & Spence, C. (2002). Confusing the mind by crossing the hands. *Cognitive Brain Research*, *14*(1), 153–163. doi:10.1016/S0926-6410(02)00070-8.

Simmel, M. L. (1966). Developmental aspects of the body scheme. *Child Development*, *37*(1), 83–95. doi:10.2307/1126431.

Soto-Faraco, S., & Azañón, E. (2013). Electrophysiological correlates of tactile remapping. *Neuropsychologia*, *51*(8), 1584–1594. doi:10.1016/j.neuropsychologia.2013.04.012.

Spelke, E. S., & Kinzler, K. D. (2007). Core knowledge. *Developmental Science*, *10*(1), 89–96. doi:10.1111/j.1467-7687.2007.00569.x.

von Hofsten, C. (2007). Action in development. *Developmental Science*, *10*(1), 54–60. doi:10.1111/j.1467-7687.2007.00564.x.

Yamamoto, S., & Kitazawa, S. (2001). Reversal of subjective temporal order due to arm crossing. *Nature Neuroscience*, *4*(7), 759–765. doi:10.1038/89559.

Zmyj, N., Jank, J., Schütz-Bosbach, S., & Daum, M. M. (2011). Detection of visual-tactile contingency in the first year after birth. *Cognition*, *120*(1), 82–89. doi:10.1016/j.cognition.2011.03.001.

2 Immutable Body Representations: Lessons from Phantoms in Amputees

Melvin Mezue and Tamar R. Makin

Picture yourself waking up in the hospital. Your body is hurting, but you can't remember what happened. The doctor tells you that you had a severe accident causing you to lose your left arm. You think: "I definitely don't feel well, but surely the doctor must be mistaken; I can clearly feel the entirety of my hand and in fact it is hurting." You turn your gaze to the blanket covering your hand. You want to lift your hand to show it to the doctors, but when you do so nothing happens. On a second look you realize the doctor was correct; the hand you can feel and move is no longer there.

Phantom sensation is a curious phenomenon; we find it interesting because it raises challenging questions relevant to philosophy, psychology, and neuroscience. As such it has inspired a plethora of research and speculation in these fields, as well as clinical studies aimed at mitigating its most distressing manifestation—phantom pain. Also key among these is the question of how we construct an internal representation of our own bodies, and how this is affected by the disruption of amputation. However, the need for detailed consideration of this latter point precludes its discussion here.

In this chapter we will first describe how it feels to experience phantom sensations, then we will turn to the potential neural underpinnings of this intriguing phenomenon, which are still very much under debate. We will outline the case for the prevailing theory of disruptive nervous system changes as a cause for phantom pain, and will argue that past and recent evidence to the contrary should encourage us to look to a new model. Finally, we will discuss how such understanding has guided clinical attempts at relieving phantom pain.

How Does It Feel to Have a Phantom Limb?

It is well recognized that even decades following amputation, people report a continuous sensation of the limb that is no longer there. Phantom sensations are almost ubiquitous, often beginning immediately following amputation; at least nine out of ten people who have undergone an amputation of their arm report experiencing the lingering sensation of their missing hand (Weeks, Anderson-Barnes, & Tsao, 2010). The term "phantom limb" was coined by American surgeon Silas Weir Mitchell in the mid-nineteenth century, in a report of clinical studies in amputees. However, various authors had described the condition long before this, dating as far back as the sixteenth century (Finger & Hustwit, 2003; Schott, 2014). The "ghost" of the hand can be perceived as vividly as you might feel your own hand. The sensations that people report can differ, ranging between pressure, warmth, cold, tingling, itch, and pain (Melzack, 1992). One amputee, who lost her hand and arm to cancer, describes her sensations as follows: "To anyone looking at me, I have no arm. But I can feel the entirety of my phantom hand and arm. Imagine you are wearing an elbow length evening glove . . . everywhere the glove touches your skin it's crushing your arm constantly. . . . On top of it you get pains like burning pains. It's like when you burn yourself on the grill. Your instinct is to pull your hand away, but with this pain you can't. It's a nerve sensation and it stays there, until 'it' decides to pull away" (*Labyrint*, 2013).

Many amputees report that they are able to perform voluntary movements of their phantom, which generally increase the vividness of the sensations (Raffin, Giraux, & Reilly, 2012; Reilly, Mercier, Schieber, & Sirigu, 2006); immobility and involuntary movements are also common. Broadly, phantom sensations can be categorized into kinetic, kinesthetic, and exteroceptive components (Weinstein, 1998). Kinetic sensations include voluntary or involuntary perceptions of movement, kinesthetic sensations include the position and shape of the missing body part, while exteroceptive perceptions include sensory aspects such as touch, temperature, and vibration. The phantom limb typically mimics the sensory experience of the missing limb with amputees even reporting feeling that the limb is wet, sweaty, or tickly. The posture of the phantom is also variable, with phantom arms commonly partially flexed at the elbow, and the phantom fingers curled (either partially or completely clenched into a fist). Sometimes the position of the limb preamputation is assumed by the phantom following amputation, suggesting a role for sensory memories in creating the phantom (Katz & Melzack, 1990). Further, this can change into awkward and painful positions (either transiently, or chronically), without necessarily having any relationship to the position of the residual arm (i.e., the arm to which the missing hand was attached). Importantly, amputees perceive the phantom as an integral part of their body, and often adjust their movements and habits to accommodate the position of the phantom (Ramachandran & Hirstein, 1998).

As mentioned above, phantom sensations are very common even in long-term amputees. However, it is interesting to note that the experience of the phantom sensations can change over time. A striking example is the phenomenon of "telescoping," a common distortion of perception (in approximately 30 percent of amputees; see Katz, 1992), where over the years, the phantom arm or leg is perceived as shortened, with the hand or foot felt closer to the residual limb (Nikolajsen, 2013). While for most amputees, the telescoped hand or leg position is stable, some amputees are able to extend their telescoped hands (e.g., when reaching out for items, or when wearing their prosthesis), implying that body representation remains dynamic even years after limb loss. Since the hand benefits from a larger representation in the brain (compared with the arm), it has been speculated that telescoping is related to slower fading of the hand representation in the central nervous system (Ramachandran & Hirstein, 1998). However, this theory hasn't been formally tested. Occasionally, painful and nonpainful phantom sensations can be elicited by tactile nonpainful stimulation of the residual limb and to a lesser extent also in other body regions such as the ipsilateral face or chin (Grüsser et al., 2004; Ramachandran, Stewart, & Rogers-Ramachandran, 1992). Suggested neural mechanisms for this will be discussed later.

The phenomenon of phantoms is not restricted to limbs following amputation. Supernumerary phantom limbs and even whole body phantoms have been reported in patients with central nervous system injuries (Cipriani, Picchi, Vedovello, Nuti, & Di Fiorino, 2011). Some have reported phantom sensations in individuals who were born with a missing limb (Brugger et al., 2000), however evidence here is mostly anecdotal and this phenomenon remains controversial (Price, 2006). Further, beyond amputation of limbs, phantom sensations have also been reported secondary to loss of internal organs, teeth, breasts, and genitalia, as well as deafferentation from nerve damage in the absence of limb loss (Flor, 2002; Foell, Bekrater-Bodmann, Flor, & Cole, 2011). Limb phantoms, and hand phantom sensations in particular, are more vivid and common than other types of phantoms (Ephraim, Wegener, MacKenzie, Dillingham, & Pezzin, 2005; Weeks et al., 2010). As such, upper limb amputation (hereafter arm amputation) provides a good model for understanding the mechanisms of phantom sensations, and will provide the focus of this chapter. There is not enough research to determine whether phantoms of the limb are similar in etiology to other bodily distortions described above, however lessons on the mechanisms underlying the genesis of hand and arm phantom sensations may be translatable to the study of other types of phantoms.

Phantom limb sensations are commonly painful, as reported by up to 80 percent of arm amputees (phantom limb pain [PLP]; Weeks et al., 2010; Nikolajsen, 2013). Pain onset typically occurs immediately following amputation, but can also be delayed for several months or years (Schley et al., 2008). The pain is often intermittent with episodes occurring daily or weekly and lasting seconds to hours at a time (Desmond & Maclachlan, 2010). Constant pain is however not uncommon. PLP is variably characterized as shooting, burning, pricking, tingling, cramping, and crushing, and can be localized or diffused; these sensations are most common in the phantom hand (Nikolajsen, 2013). Although most arm amputees experience phantom pain, its frequency and severity may decrease with time following amputation (Bosmans, Geertzen, Post, & Schans, 2010). PLP is distinct from pain arising from the remaining part of the arm (residual limb pain) and is possibly mediated by a separate neural mechanism (Flor, Nikolajsen, & Jensen, 2006).

Despite being very common, PLP is notorious for being very difficult to treat with conventional medicine (Knotkova, Cruciani, Tronnier, & Rasche, 2012). As such, PLP presents a serious medical problem. The unusual challenge that clinicians face is that the body part to be treated is not physically present. To aid the treatment of PLP, both clinicians and researchers are searching for the neural correlates of this unique phenomenon. The hope is that a mechanistic understanding of the neural basis of PLP will promote successful treatment. This clinically driven research presents opportunities to further our understanding of the neural underpinning of phantom sensations. For our purposes in this chapter, we consider phantom pain and phantom sensations together and assume similar causative mechanisms. This is consistent with the observation that treatments targeting phantom limb pain typically decrease the vividness of nonpainful phantom sensations, suggesting that both are on the same clinical spectrum (Nikolajsen, 2013). However we note that the relationship between phantom sensation and pain is not yet fully established (as demonstrated by Bolognini, Olgiatia, Maravitaa, Ferraroc, & Fregnid, 2013). For example, voluntary phantom movements that increase vividness of phantom sensations have been associated with decreased phantom pain (Gagné, Reilly, Hétu, & Mercier, 2009) and with analgesia (Foell, Bekrater-Bodmann, Diers, & Flor, 2014). Next we consider which parts of the nervous system may contribute to the development of the conspicuous and disabling phenomenon of phantom pain.

Where in the Nervous System Is the Phantom?

The neural basis of phantom pain is still under debate. Early theories of PLP proposed it to be a consequence of injury caused to the peripheral nerves transmitting information into the spinal cord. This was due to early observations showing that PLP can be evoked by pressing the end of the residual arm (the stump; Mitchell, 1872). Nyström and Hagsbarth (1981) elegantly demonstrated, using intraneural microelectrode recordings of peripheral nerves in a human amputee, that even when the receptors of the peripheral nerve are amputated, the residual axons still remain active (i.e., transmitting action potentials). Importantly, both spontaneous and evoked PLP were reflected in the activity of the residual nerve. Based on this line of findings, a simple explanation for the mechanism of phantom sensations and pain has been established: As these peripheral nerves normally provide information about touch and pain originating from the hand, inputs provided by these nerves would be interpreted by the central nervous system as arising from the missing hand. Such misinterpretation of information will result in the persistent experience of touch, proprioception, and pain as arising from the missing hand (Wall & Gutnick, 1974; Fried Govrin-Lippmann, Rosenthal, Ellisman, & Devor, 1991). Unfortunately, clinical treatment inspired by this theory has been unsuccessful. Specifically, anesthetic blockade of the peripheral nerve ending (as well as surgical interventions designed to reduce the malleability of the peripheral nerve to transmit action potentials) has been shown to be only partly effective at eliminating spontaneous PLP (Nikolajsen, Black, Kroner, Jensen, & Waxman, 2010). Since clinical translation of the peripheral theory did not produce a cure for PLP, the scientific community has turned to study the involvement of more central mechanisms. Nevertheless, recent findings showing dramatic relief from painful and nonpainful phantom sensations following blockade of the cell bodies of the peripheral nerve (Vaso et al., 2014; see also Borghi, et al. 2010.) suggest that the marginalization of the peripheral theory might have been premature. This new evidence demonstrates that phantom pain can be caused by aberrant inputs that originated in the peripheral nervous system. However, to conclusively show that pain relief depends solely on peripheral nerve blockade, more research is necessary.

Inspired by contemporary theories about the significance of the central nervous system in the experience of pain (Melzack, 1989), researchers in the 1990s began to focus on the role of the spinal cord and higher structures. Inputs from the hand normally transfer from the peripheral nervous system into the spinal cord, which is also the first terminal of the central nervous system for processing touch and pain. Research in animals suggests that input changes into the spinal cord due to nerve injury will affect the processing of pain (Wall, 1977; Woolf, 2011). While this modification of input may have a role in PLP in humans, direct evidence is lacking. Despite poor mechanistic understanding, invasive treatments using spinal cord stimulation have been trialed in the management of postamputation pain, with mixed results (Deer et al., 2014).

Currently, the prevailing theory for the development of PLP is that of *maladaptive brain plasticity*. In various parts of the sensorimotor system, different regions of the brain are responsible for representing and controlling specific body parts. In nonhuman primates (monkeys), loss of input to the brain's hand area (e.g., following amputation) leads to redistribution of brain resources—termed brain plasticity, or reorganization (Merzenich et al., 1983; Pons et al., 1991). In other words, a body part that was previously not represented by the (now deprived) hand area, such as the face, begins to activate the area. This phenomenon is most commonly demonstrated in the first terminal for touch processing (and potentially pain) in the cortex, the primary somatosensory cortex. The contribution of subcortical structures has been debated, with recent work suggesting a critical role for the brainstem (Jain, Florence, Qi, & Kaas, 2000; Kambi et al., 2014). Intuitively, you might expect that the brain's ability to reassign resources across body parts based on altered demand should be helpful, and perhaps even allow amputees to better adapt to their disability. An example of this would be early-blind individuals, in whom studies show adaptive crossmodal plasticity of the occipital cortex, such that the visual cortex becomes involved in nonvisual processing for language and Braille reading (Sadato et al., 1996; Cohen et al., 1997; Amedi, Raz, Pianka, Malach, & Zohary, 2003; Amedi, Floel, Knecht, Zohary, & Cohen, 2004). But according to the theory of maladaptive brain plasticity, reorganization in the adult brain at this scale is harmful. This view purports that the deprivation of sensory input following amputation results in striking brain plasticity, where primary sensory representations of cortically neighboring body parts (i.e., lower face) take over the area previously devoted to the missing limb (Pons et al., 1991; Jain, Qi, Collins, & Kaas, 2008). This is reflected in inter-hemispheric asymmetry of the cortical representation of the face measured in amputees using electrical source imaging (Elbert et al., 1994). Importantly this cortical asymmetry following limb loss, which is thought to reflect reorganization, has been shown to be correlated (Flor et al., 1995; Flor et al., 1998) or associated with PLP (Birbaumer et al., 1997; Lotze, Flor, Grodd, Larbig, & Birbaumer, 2001; Flor, Denke, Schaefer, & Grüsser, 2001).

Consequently, cortical reorganization was proposed to trigger pain representations in the missing hand by responding to inputs intended for the neighboring cortical regions (Ramachandran et al., 1992). The mismatch between body representations (new facial inputs vs. other signals relating to the original affiliation of the area) is thought to result in an "error" signal that is interpreted by the brain as pain arising from the missing hand. This theory attempts to explain various sensory phenomena associated with phantom sensations, such as referred sensations (although see Knecht et al., 1996) and the proclivity for phantom sensations and pain in the upper limb extremities, which have a greater cortical representation (Nikolajsen, 2013; Ramachandran, Brang, & McGeoch, 2010).

The theory for maladaptive brain plasticity has been extremely influential, not only in the neuroscience community (Flor et al., 2006), but also for clinicians (Subedi & Grossberg, 2011). Over the years it has been expanded upon in an attempt to explain other neuropathic pain conditions, such as complex regional pain syndrome (Maihofner et al., 2003; Gustin et al., 2012). Beyond insights into the soft wiring of the brain, this theory provides clear predictions on how best to treat phantom pain: if pain is caused by maladaptive reorganization, then to alleviate phantom pain we need to reverse it. One popular approach known as mirror box therapy attempts to do this by reinstating the representation of the missing hand to its original territory, using illusory visual information about the missing hand (Ramachandran & Rogers-Ramachandran, 1996; for more, see below).

Challenging the Maladaptive Theory of Phantom Pain

As mentioned above, the relatively simple early theory that phantom limb pain is driven by false input from the injured limb nerve has gained new support (Vaso et al., 2014). Recently, the main assumption underlying the maladaptive plasticity theory—that input loss from the hand triggers a maladaptive domino effect of changed body representation in the brain—has also been challenged.

In order to demonstrate maladaptive plasticity, one must determine whether this new representation (e.g., lips) actually invades the cortical territory of the missing hand. We recently showed that this is not the case (Makin, Scholz et al., 2015). Here, we used measurements that take into consideration the unique architecture of each participant's brain, in order to provide an accurate measurement of lip shifts. As previously reported by other groups, we found that, on the side of the brain directly affected by the amputation, the representation of the lips was shifted. The direction of this shift was toward the hand area. However, although statistically robust, the magnitude of the shift was much smaller than previously reported, and did not result in invasion into the hand area. Other measurements of activity levels in the missing hand's territory during lip movement (activating the primary somatosensory and primary motor cortex), also showed no increased lip representation in amputees (both compared with the intact hand hemisphere and compared with controls). It appears that, while local shifts in lip representation occur in the brain following amputation, they do not necessarily involve the missing hand's territory (see Raffin, Richard, Giraux, & Reilly, 2016, for similar results).

Another key assumption of the maladaptive theory is that plasticity is triggered by a lack of inputs, which unmasks displaced inputs, and further leads to a mismatch between body part inputs. It is interesting to note, however, that displaced signals in the somatosensory cortex (experimentally induced activity via direct or indirect brain stimulation to the somatosensory cortex, e.g., via electrical stimulation or transcranial direct current stimulation), do not induce pain in the underlying body part (Mazzola, Isnard, & Mauguiere, 2006; Flesher et al., 2016). This suggests that displaced signals are not a sufficient trigger for pain sensations, as suggested by the model. Furthermore, we (Makin, Scholz et al., 2013; Kikkert et al., 2016) and others (Mercier, Reilly, Vargas, Aballea, & Sirigu, 2006; Raffin, Mattout, Reilly, & Giraux, 2012; Raffin et al., 2016), found that despite hand amputation, representations relating to the phantom hand persist in the brain (see Makin & Bensmaia, 2017 for extended discussion). Specific to the current discussion, we showed that amputees suffering from worse phantom pain tended to have more preserved structure and function in their missing hand's brain area (Makin, Scholz et al., 2013b). These findings are consistent with previous theories about the role of residual peripheral inputs in generating PLP and contradict the maladaptive brain plasticity theory. If input is not lost to the hand's brain area, how is maladaptive plasticity triggered? One recent study has attempted to unify these different theories by proposing a dissociation between postamputation representation of the hand, and plasticity of the upper limb and lips representation, with the latter driving phantom limb pain (Raffin et al., 2016). However, since the majority of the participants in this study (eight out of eleven) had amputation above the elbow, and as upper limb representation and plasticity was probed using phantom elbow movements, the suggested dissociation remains unreconciled.

Using functional connectivity analyses of resting state we also studied spontaneous fluctuations in the functional MRI brain signal. We observed that functional coupling was reduced in amputees as compared to controls, between the phantom and intact hand areas (Makin, Scholz et al., 2013), as well as within the sensorimotor system (Makin, Filippini et al., 2015). This means that regions of the brain that are normally functionally coupled (presumably due to coactivation) become less associated with each other. This might be due to the lack of reinforcement from synchronized inputs between the intact and deprived cortices following amputation. Indeed, phantom sensations, and phantom pain in particular are best characterized as internal states of sensation, as they are mostly dissociated from events in the external world to which the sensorimotor system is normally tuned. This decreased connectivity was further shown to be associated with higher PLP scores and thus implies that the integrity of the deprived region cannot be fully preserved by the residual inputs. We propose this *persistent represen-tation* model to suggest that both sensory deprivation and phantom pain experience have modulatory effects—sensory deprivation is associated with decreased local functional and structural representations, while coexisting phantom pain experience is associated with maintained local cortical rep-resentations and functional inter-hemispheric decoupling.

We also challenge the notion that reorganization involving the terri-tory of the missing hand is necessarily harmful. Instead, recent work sug-gests that the brain territory of the missing hand might be utilized in order to support compensatory behavior that amputees adopt in order to cope with their disability (Makin, Cramer et al., 2013; Philip & Frey, 2014; see also Hahamy et al., 2015, 2017 for related research). As such, the brain region that normally represents sensorimotor activity of the amputated hand may be recruited to represent body parts which are now used in its place (e.g., the intact hand). According to this line of research, brain plasticity following amputation is supportive, rather than maladaptive.

Finally, criticism has been raised regarding the level of evidence support-ing the maladaptive theory (Jutzeler, Curt, & Kramer, 2015). More experi-mental evidence is needed concerning the central mechanism of phantom sensations. Next we will consider lessons learned from neuromodulatory interventions targeted at phantom pain.

What Do Neuromodulatory Therapies Tell Us about PLP Mechanisms?

A further limitation of the maladaptive theory is the paucity of clinical results from therapies designed based on its predictions (Knotkova et al., 2012). For example, to support this theory, one should demonstrate that phantom pain is alleviated by therapies that either increase the representation of the missing hand, or decrease representation of the displaced body part in the missing hand area, or both. Visual feedback (or mirror box therapy) is an intervention designed to reverse maladaptive cortical reorganization of the sensorimotor cortices, by reinstating the representation of the missing hand. When a mirror is placed in the observer's midline with the intact hand in front of the mirror and the phantom hand behind the mirror, on looking at the reflection of their intact hand moving, some amputees report that they can start to feel movement sensations in their phantom hand (Ramachandran & Rogers-Ramachandran, 1995). This sensation has been suggested to reflect the brain's prioritization of visual sensory information over proprioceptive feedback, although it is questionable whether visual representation is sufficient to activate the primary somatosensory cortex (Chan & Baker, 2015). Evidence supporting the integration of mirror therapy or virtual mirror therapy into the management of PLP is based on a collection of anecdotal data, case reports, uncontrolled studies and a few controlled trials (Chan et al., 2007; Brodie, Whyte, & Niven, 2007; Moseley, Gallace, & Spence, 2008; Foell et al., 2014; Ortiz-Catalan et al., 2016). The notable lack of high quality evidence and double-blind, sham-controlled studies in particular, results in continued skepticism over the clinical efficacy of this approach (Rothgangel, Braun, Beurskens, Seitz, & Wade, 2011; Thieme et al., 2016). Other neuromodulatory approaches such as sensory discrimination feedback-guided training (asking patients to distinguish intensity/location of stimulation on the residual arm using electrodes), and intensive use of myoelectric prostheses to provide sensory feedback through the residual arm have been designed to target putative mechanisms of maladaptive plasticity but have shown very limited evidence of long-term efficacy (Lotze et al., 1999; Dietrich et al., 2012; Flor et al., 2001). Conversely, motor imagery—another such behavioral therapy (Moseley, 2006)—appears to have a distinct neural signature to motor execution of the phantom (Raffin, Mattout et al., 2012), which may suggest that the mechanism of relief is not as simple as rekindling the limb's sensorimotor representation.

Summary and Concluding Remarks

Phantom sensations and pain are extremely common following upper limb amputation. Beyond the interest in understanding this curious phenomenon, PLP is a debilitating pain syndrome, which is notorious for being difficult to treat. After decades of PLP research, the origin of this mysterious syndrome remains unclear. Clinicians struggle to treat pain in a body part that no longer exists and it is therefore the joint responsibility of clinical and scientific researchers to provide an understanding of the neural basis of this condition. Recent evidence challenges the prevalent theory for maladaptive cortical reorganization, by questioning the extent of spontaneous reorganization, as well as its causal role in generating PLP. Moreover, current treatments designed based on the maladaptive theory are often ineffective. It therefore remains unclear whether brain reorganization following amputation is indeed maladaptive.

Based on recent and classical evidence, we propose that despite reorganization, cortical representations of the lost limb are largely immutable. Evidence is accumulating to suggest that the persistence of cortical representations of the missing hand, likely reflecting ongoing contributions from the peripheral nervous system despite amputation, may associate with PLP. Nevertheless, the dissociation between phantom sensations and the physical world may result in a functional detachment between the phantom cortex and the rest of the sensorimotor cortex. We suggest that this loss of connectivity may contribute to the manifestation of phantom pain. Simultaneously, processing of pain signals by the central nervous system may further contribute to altered connectivity with the missing hand territory, thus amplifying this chronic state. According to our suggested account, changes in the representation of adjacent cortical areas may reflect central influences on the processing of pain, rather than be the causative process itself. New therapies aimed at integrating peripheral and central nervous system modulation may therefore prove more effective at alleviating phantom limb pain.

The discovery of the immutability of amputees' missing hand representations, despite the absence of the physical limb, opens a host of questions with immediate implications for philosophy, psychology, neuroscience, and medicine. Why do these body representations remain immutable? How does the preserved representation interact with (or facilitate) adaptive reorganization of other body parts into the missing hand territory? And how can we utilize the persistence of the body representation to provide clinical interventions? We believe it is necessary to integrate the immutability of body representation into contemporary theories of body representation and related disorders in order to better understand its role.

References

Amedi, A., Floel, A., Knecht, S., Zohary, E., & Cohen, L. G. (2004). Transcranial magnetic stimulation of the occipital pole interferes with verbal processing in blind subjects. *Nature Neuroscience, 7*(11), 1266–1270. doi:10.1038/nn1328.

Amedi, A., Raz, N., Pianka, P., Malach, R., & Zohary, E. (2003). Early "visual" cortex activation correlates with superior verbal memory performance in the blind. *Nature Neuroscience, 6*(7), 758–766. doi:10.1038/nn1072.

Birbaumer, N., Lutzenberger, W., Montoya, P., Larbig, W., Unertl, K., Töpfner, S., et al. (1997). Effects of regional anesthesia on phantom limb pain are mirrored in changes in cortical reorganization. *Journal of Neuroscience, 17*(14), 5503–5508.

Bolognini, N., Olgiatia, E., Maravitaa, A., Ferraroc, F., & Fregnid, F. (2013). Motor and parietal cortex stimulation for phantom limb pain and sensations. *Pain, 154*(8), 1274–1280. doi:10.1016/j.pain.2013.03.040.

Borghi, B., D'Addabbo, M., White, P. F., Gallerani, P., Toccaceli, L., Raffaeli, W., et al. (2010). The use of prolonged peripheral neural blockade after lower extremity amputation: The effect on symptoms associated with phantom limb syndrome. *Anesthesia and Analgesia, 111*, 1308–1315. doi:10.1213/ANE.0b013e3181f4e848.

Bosmans, J. C., Geertzen, J., Post, W. J., & Schans, C. P. (2010). Factors associated with phantom limb pain: A 31/2-year prospective study. *Clinical Rehabilitation, 24*(5), 444–453. doi:10.1177/0269215509360645.

Brodie, E., Whyte, A., & Niven, C. A. (2007). Analgesia through the looking-glass? A randomized controlled trial investigating the effect of viewing a "virtual" limb upon phantom limb pain, sensation and movement. *European Journal of Pain, 11*(4), 428–436. doi:10.1016/j.ejpain.2006.06.002.

Brugger, P., Kollias, S. S., Müri, R. M., Crelier, G., Hepp-Reymond, M.-C., & Regard, M. (2000). Beyond re-membering: Phantom sensations of congenitally absent limbs. *Proceedings of the National Academy of Sciences of the United States of America, 97*(11), 6167–6172. doi:10.1073/pnas.100510697.

Chan, A., & Baker, C. (2015). Seeing is not feeling: Posterior parietal but not somatosensory cortex engagement during touch observation. *Journal of Neuroscience, 35*(4), 1468–1480. doi:10.1523/JNEUROSCI.3621-14.2015.

Chan, B., Witt, R., Charrow, A. P., Magee, A., Howard, R., Heilman, K. M., et al. (2007). Mirror therapy for phantom limb pain. *New England Journal of Medicine, 357*(21), 2206–2207. doi:10.1056/NEJMc071927.

Cipriani, G., Picchi, L., Vedovello, M., Nuti, A., & Di Fiorino, M. (2011). The phantom and the supernumerary phantom limb: Historical review and new case. *Neuroscience Bulletin, 27*(6), 359–365. doi:10.1007/s12264-011-1737-6.

Cohen, L., Celnik, P., Pascual-Leone, A., Corwell, B., Faiz, L., Dambrosia, J., et al. (1997). Functional relevance of cross-modal plasticity in blind humans. *Nature, 389*(6647), 180–183. doi:10.1038/38278.

Deer, T., Nagy, M., Provenzano, D., Pope, J., Krames, E., Leong, M., et al. (2014). The appropriate use of neurostimulation of the spinal cord and peripheral nervous system for the treatment of chronic pain and ischemic diseases: The Neuromodulation Appropriateness Consensus Committee. *Neuromodulation, 17*(6), 515–550. doi:10.1111/ner.12208.

Desmond, D., & Maclachlan, M. (2010). Prevalence and characteristics of phantom limb pain and residual limb pain in the long term after upper limb amputation. *Journal of Rehabilitation Research, 33*(3), 279–282. doi:10.1097/MRR.0b013e 328336388d.

Dietrich, C., Walter-Walsh, K., Preißler, S., Hofmann, G. O., Witte, O. W., Miltner, W. H. R., et al. (2012). Sensory feedback prosthesis reduces phantom limb pain: Proof of a principle. *Neuroscience Letters, 507*(2), 97–100. doi:10.1016/j.neulet.2011.10.068.

Elbert, T., Flor, H., Birbaumer, N., Knecht, S., Hampson, S., Larbig, W., et al. (1994). Extensive reorganization of the somatosensory cortex in adult humans after nervous system injury. *Neuroreport, 5*(18), 2593–2597.

Ephraim, P. L., Wegener, S. T., MacKenzie, E. J., Dillingham, T. R., & Pezzin, L. E. (2005). Phantom pain, residual limb pain, and back pain in amputees: Results from a national survey. *Archives of Physical Medicine and Rehabilitation, 86*(10), 1910–1919. doi:10.1016/j.apmr.2005.03.031.

Finger, S., & Hustwit, M. P. (2003). Five early accounts of phantom limb in context: Paré, Descartes, Lemos, Bell, and Mitchell. *Neurosurgery, 52*(3), 675–686.

Flesher, S. N., Collinger, J. L., Foldes, S. T., Weiss, J. M., Downey, J. E., Tyler-Kabara, E. C., et al. (2016). Intracortical microstimulation of human somatosensory cortex. *Science Translational Medicine, 8.* doi:10.1126/scitranslmed.aaf8083.

Flor, H. (2002). Phantom-limb pain: Characteristics, causes, and treatment. *Lancet Neurology, 1*(3), 182–189. doi:10.1016/S1474-4422(02)00074-1.

Flor, H., Denke, C., Schaefer, M., & Grüsser, S. M. (2001). Effect of sensory discrimination training on cortical reorganisation and phantom limb pain. *Lancet, 357,* 1763–1764. 9270. doi:10.1016/S0140-6736(00)04890-X.

Flor, H., Elbert, T., Knecht, S., Wienbruch, C., Pantev, C., Birbaumer, N., . . . Taub, E. (1995). Phantom-limb pain as a perceptual correlate of cortical reorganization following arm amputation. *Nature, 375,* 482–484. doi:10.1038/375482a0.

Flor, H., Elbert, T., Mühlnickel, W., Pantev, C., Wienbruch, C., & Taub, E. (1998). Cortical reorganization and phantom phenomena in congenital and traumatic upper-extremity amputees. *Experimental Brain Research, 119*(2), 205–212. doi:10.1007/ s002210050334.

Flor, H., Nikolajsen, L., & Jensen, T. S. (2006). Phantom limb pain: A case of maladaptive CNS plasticity? *Nature Reviews: Neuroscience, 7*(11), 873–881. doi:10.1038/nrn1991.

Foell, J., Bekrater-Bodmann, R., Diers, M., & Flor, H. (2014). Mirror therapy for phantom limb pain: Brain changes and the role of body representation. *European Journal of Pain, 18*(5), 729–739. doi:10.1002/j.1532-2149.2013.00433.x.

Foell, J., Bekrater-Bodmann, R., Flor, H., & Cole, J. (2011). Phantom limb pain after lower limb trauma: Origins and treatments. *International Journal of Lower Extremity Wounds*, *10*(4), 224–235. doi:10.1177/1534734611428730.

Fried, K., Govrin-Lippmann, R., Rosenthal, F., Ellisman, M., & Devor, M. (1991). Ultrastructure of afferent axon endings in a neuroma. *Journal of Neurocytology*, *20*(8), 682–701. doi:10.1007/BF01187069.

Gagné, M., Reilly, K. T., Hétu, S., & Mercier, C. (2009). Motor control over the phantom limb in above-elbow amputees and its relationship with phantom limb pain. *Neuroscience*, *162*(1), 78–86. doi:10.1016/j.neuroscience.2009.04.061.

Grüsser, S. M., Mühlnickel, W., Schaefer, M., Villringer, K., Christmann, C., Koeppe, C., et al. (2004). Remote activation of referred phantom sensation and cortical reorganization in human upper extremity amputees. *Experimental Brain Research*, *154*(1), 97–102. doi:10.1007/s00221-003-1649-4.

Gustin, S. M., Peck, C. C., Cheney, L. B., Macey, P. M., Murray, G. M., & Henderson, L. A. (2012). Pain and plasticity: Is chronic pain always associated with somatosensory cortex activity and reorganization? *Journal of Neuroscience*, *32*(43), 14874–14884. doi:10.1523/JNEUROSCI.1733-12.2012.

Hahamy, A., Macdonald, S. N., van den Heiligenberg, F., Kieliba, P., Emir, U., Malach, R., Johansen-Berg, H., Brugger, P., Culham, J., C., & Makin, T. R. (2017). Representation of multiple body parts in the missing hand territory of congenital one-handers. *Current Biology*, *27*, 1350–1355.

Hahamy, A., Sotiropoulos, S. N., Slater, D. H., Malach, R., Johansen-Berg, H., & Makin, T. R. (2015). Normalisation of brain connectivity through compensatory behaviour, despite congenital hand absence. *eLife*, *4*, e04605. doi:10.7554/eLife.04605.

Jain, N., Florence, S., Qi, H.-X., & Kaas, J. H. (2000). Growth of new brainstem connections in adult monkeys with massive sensory loss. *Proceedings of the National Academy of Sciences of the United States of America*, *97*(10), 5546–5550. doi:10.1073/pnas.090572597.

Jain, N., Qi, H.-X., Collins, C., & Kaas, J. H. (2008). Large-scale reorganization in the somatosensory cortex and thalamus after sensory loss in macaque monkeys. *Journal of Neuroscience*, *28*(43), 11042–11060. doi:10.1523/JNEUROSCI.2334-08.2008.

Jutzeler, C. R., Curt, A., & Kramer, J. L. K. (2015). Relationship between chronic pain and brain reorganization after deafferentation: A systematic review of functional MRI findings. *NeuroImage: Clinical*, *9*, 599–606. doi:10.1016/j.nicl.2015.09.018.

Kambi, N., Halder, P., Rajan, R., Arora, V., Chand, P., Arora, M., et al. (2014). Large-scale reorganization of the somatosensory cortex following spinal cord injuries is due to brainstem plasticity. *Nature Communications*, *5*, 3602. doi:10.1038/ncomms4602.

Katz, J. (1992). Psychophysiological contributions to phantom limbs. *Canadian Journal of Psychiatry, 37*(5), 282–298.

Katz, J., & Melzack, R. (1990). Pain "memories" in phantom limbs: Review and clinical observations. *Pain, 43*(3), 319–336. doi:10.1016/0304-3959(90)90029-D.

Kikkert, S., Kolasinski, J., Jbabdi, S., Tracey, I., Beckmann, C. F. Johansen-Berg, H., & Makin, T. R. (2016). Revealing the neural fingerprints of a missing hand. *elife, 5*, e15292. doi:10.7554/eLife.15292.

Knecht, S., Henningsen, H., Elbert, T., Flor, H., Höhling, C., Pantev, C., et al. (1996). Reorganizational and perceptional changes after amputation. *Brain, 119*(4), 1213–1219. doi:10.1093/brain/119.4.1213.

Knotkova, H., Cruciani, R., Tronnier, V., & Rasche, D. (2012). Current and future options for the management of phantom-limb pain. *Journal of Pain Research, 5*, 39–49. doi:10.2147/JPR.S16733.

Labyrint. (2013, September 29). Het zelfreparerende lichaam. https://www.vpro.nl/speel~VPWON_1181871~het-zelfreparerende-lichaam-labyrint~.html.

Lotze, M., Flor, H., Grodd, W., Larbig, W., & Birbaumer, N. (2001). Phantom movements and pain. An fMRI study in upper limb amputees. *Brain, 124*(11), 2268–2277. doi:10.1093/brain/124.11.2268.

Lotze, M., Grodd, W., Birbaumer, N., Erb, M., Huse, E., & Flor, H. (1999). Does use of a myoelectric prosthesis prevent cortical reorganization and phantom limb pain? *Nature Neuroscience, 2*(6), 501–502. doi:10.1038/9145.

Maihofner, C., Handwerker, H. O., Neundorfer, B., & Birklein, F. (2003). Patterns of cortical reorganization in complex regional pain syndrome. *Neurology, 61*, 1707–1715.

Makin, T. R., & Bensmaia, S. J. (2017). Stability of sensory topographies in adult cortex. *Trends in Cognitive Sciences, 21*(3), 195–204. doi:10.1016/j.tics.2017.01.002.

Makin, T. R., Cramer, A. O., Scholz, J., Hahamy, A., Slater, D. H., Tracey, I., et al. (2013). Deprivation-related and use-dependent plasticity go hand in hand. *eLife, 2*, e01273. doi:10.7554/eLife.01273.

Makin, T. R., Filippini, N., Duff, E. P., Slater, D. H., Tracey, I., & Johansen-Berg, H. (2015). Network-level reorganisation of functional connectivity following arm amputation. *NeuroImage, 114*, 217–225. doi:10.1016/j.neuroimage.2015.02.067.

Makin, T. R., Scholz, J., Filippini, N., Slater, D. H., Tracey, I., & Johansen-Berg, H. (2013). Phantom pain is associated with preserved structure and function in the former hand area. *Nature Communications, 4*, 1570. doi:10.1038/ncomms2571.

Makin, T. R., Scholz, J., Slater, D. H., Johansen-Berg, H., & Tracey, I. (2015). Reassessing cortical reorganization in the primary sensorimotor cortex following arm amputation. *Brain, 138*(8), 2140–2146. doi:10.1093/brain/awv161.

Mazzola, L., Isnard, J., & Mauguiere, F. (2006). Somatosensory and pain responses to stimulation of the second somatosensory area (SII) in humans. A comparison with SI and insular responses. *Cerebral Cortex, 16*(7), 960–968. doi:10.1093/cercor/bhj038.

Melzack, R. (1989). Phantom limbs, the self and the brain (The D. O. Hebb Memorial Lecture). *Canadian Psychology, 30*(1), 1–16. doi:10.1037/h0079793.

Melzack, R. (1992). Phantom limbs. *Scientific American, 266*(4), 120–126. doi:10.1038/scientificamerican0492-120.

Mercier, C., Reilly, K. T., Vargas, C. D., Aballea, A., & Sirigu, A. (2006). Mapping phantom movement representations in the motor cortex of amputees. *Brain, 129*(8), 2202–2210. doi:10.1093/brain/awl180.

Merzenich, M. M., Kaas, J. H., Wall, J., Nelson, R. J., Sur, M., & Felleman, D. (1983). Topographic reorganization of somatosensory cortical areas 3b and 1 in adult monkeys following restricted deafferentation. *Neuroscience, 8*(1), 33–55. doi:10.1016/0306-4522(83)90024-6.

Mitchell, S. W. (1872). *Injuries of nerves, and their consequences.* Philadelphia: J.B. Lippincott.

Moseley, G. L. (2006). Graded motor imagery for pathologic pain: A randomized controlled trial. *Neurology, 67*(12), 2129–2134. doi:10.1212/01.wnl.0000249112.56935.32.

Moseley, G. L., Gallace, A., & Spence, C. (2008). Is mirror therapy all it is cracked up to be? Current evidence and future directions. *Pain, 138*(1), 7–10. doi:10.1016/j.pain.2008.06.026.

Nikolajsen, L. (2013). Phantom Limb. In S. McMahon, M. Koltzenburg, I. Tracey, & D. Turk (Eds.), *Wall and Melzack's textbook of pain* (6th ed., pp. 915–925). Philadelphia: Elsevier Saunders.

Nikolajsen, L., Black, J. A., Kroner, K., Jensen, T. S., & Waxman, S. G. (2010). Neuroma removal for neuropathic pain: Efficacy and predictive value of lidocaine infusion. *Clinical Journal of Pain, 26*(9), 788–793.

Nyström, B., & Hagsbarth, K.-E. (1981). Microelectrode recordings from transected nerves in amputees with phantom limb pain. *Neuroscience Letters, 27*(2), 211–216. doi:10.1016/0304-3940(81)90270-6.

Ortiz-Catalan, M., Guðmundsdóttir, R. A., Kristoffersen, M. B., Zepeda-Echavarria, A., Caine-Winterberger, K., Kulbacka-Ortiz, K., et al. (2016). Phantom motor execution facilitated by machine learning and augmented reality as treatment for phantom limb pain: A single group, clinical trial in patients with chronic intractable phantom limb pain. *Lancet, 388*(10062), 2885–2894. doi:10.1016/S0140-6736(16)31598-7.

Philip, B., & Frey, S. (2014). Compensatory changes accompanying chronic forced use of the nondominant hand by unilateral amputees. *Journal of Neuroscience, 34*(10), 3622–3631. doi:10.1523/JNEUROSCI.3770-13.2014.

Pons, T., Garraghty, P. E., Ommaya, A. K., Kaas, J. H., Taub, E., & Mishkin, M. (1991). Massive cortical reorganization after sensory deafferentation in adult macaques. *Science*, *252*(5014), 1857–1860.

Price, E. H. (2006). A critical review of congenital phantom limb cases and a developmental theory for the basis of body image. *Consciousness and Cognition*, *15*(2), 310–322. doi:10.1016/j.concog.2005.07.003.

Raffin, E., Giraux, P., & Reilly, K. (2012). The moving phantom: Motor execution or motor imagery. *Cortex*, *48*(6), 746–757. doi:10.1016/j.cortex.2011.02.003.

Raffin, E., Mattout, J., Reilly, J., & Giraux, P. (2012). Disentangling motor execution from motor imagery with the phantom limb. *Brain*, *135*(2), 582–595. doi:10.1093/brain/awr337.

Raffin, E., Richard, N., Giraux, P., & Reilly, K. (2016). Primary motor cortex changes after amputation correlate with phantom limb pain and the ability to move the phantom limb. *NeuroImage*, *130*, 134–144. doi:10.1016/j.neuroimage.2016.01.063.

Ramachandran, C., Brang, D., & McGeoch, P. (2010). Dynamic reorganization of referred sensations by movements of phantom limbs. *Neuroreport*, *21*(10), 727–730. doi:10.1097/WNR.0b013e32833be9ab.

Ramachandran, V. S., & Hirstein, W. (1998). The perception of phantom limbs. The D. O. Hebb lecture. *Brain*, *121*(9), 1603–1630. doi:10.1093/brain/121.9.1603.

Ramachandran, V. S., & Rogers-Ramachandran, D. (1996). Synaesthesia in phantom limbs induced with mirrors. *Proceedings of the Royal Society, Series B: Biological Sciences*, *263*(1369), 377–386.

Ramachandran, V. S., Rogers-Ramachandran, D., & Cobb, S. (1995). Touching the phantom limb. *Nature*, *377*(6549), 489–490. doi:10.1038/377489a0.

Ramachandran, V. S., Stewart, M., & Rogers-Ramachandran, D. (1992). Perceptual correlates of massive cortical reorganization. *Neuroreport*, *3*, 583–586.

Reilly, K. T., Mercier, C., Schieber, M. H., & Sirigu, A. (2006). Persistent hand motor commands in the amputees' brain. *Brain*, *129*(8), 2211–2223. doi:10.1093/brain/awl154.

Rothgangel, A., Braun, S. M., Beurskens, A. J., Seitz, R. J., & Wade, D. T. (2011). The clinical aspects of mirror therapy in rehabilitation: A systematic review of the literature. *International Journal of Rehabilitation Research. Internationale Zeitschrift für Rehabilitationsforschung. Revue Internationale de Recherches de Readaptation*, *34*(1), 1–13.

Sadato, N., Pascual-Leone, A., Grafmani, J., Ibañez, V., Deiber, M.-P., Dold, G., et al. (1996). Activation of the primary visual cortex by Braille reading in blind subjects. *Nature*, *380*(6574), 526–528. doi:10.1038/380526a0.

Schley, M. T., Petra, W., Stephanie, T., Hanns-Peter, S., Martin, S., Konrad, C. J., et al. (2008). Painful and nonpainful phantom and stump sensations in acute traumatic amputees. *Journal of Trauma, 65*(4), 858–864. doi:10.1097/TA.0b013e31812eed9e.

Schott, G. (2014). Revealing the invisible: The paradox of picturing a phantom limb. *Brain, 137*(30, 960–969. doi:10.1093/brain/awt244.

Subedi, B., & Grossberg, G. T. (2011). Phantom limb pain: Mechanisms and treatment approaches. *Pain Research and Treatment, 864605.* doi:10.1155/2011/864605.

Thieme, H., Morkisch, N., Rietz, C., Dohle, C., & Borgetto, B. (2016). The efficacy of movement representation techniques for treatment of limb pain—a systematic review and meta-analysis. *Journal of Pain, 17*(2), 167–180. doi:10.1016/j.jpain.2015.10.015.

Vaso, A., Adahan, H.-M., Gjika, A., Zahaj, S., Zhurda, T., Vyshka, G., et al. (2014). Peripheral nervous system origin of phantom limb pain. *Pain, 155*(7), 1384–1391. doi:10.1016/j.pain.2014.04.018.

Wall, P. D. (1977). The presence of ineffective synapses and the circumstances which unmask them. *Philosophical Transactions of the Royal Society of London, Series B: Biological Sciences, 278*(961), 361–372. doi:10.1098/rstb.1977.0048.

Wall, P. D., & Gutnick, M. (1974). Ongoing activity in peripheral nerves: The physiology and pharmacology of impulses originating from a neuroma. *Experimental Neurology, 43*(3), 580–593. doi:10.1016/0014-4886(74)90197-6.

Weeks, S., Anderson-Barnes, V., & Tsao, J. (2010). Phantom limb pain: Theories and therapies. *Neurologist, 16*(5), 277–286. doi:10.1097/NRL.0b013e3181edf128.

Weinstein, S. M. (1998). Phantom limb pain and related disorders. *Neurologic Clinics, 16*(4), 919–935.

Woolf, C. J. (2011). Central sensitization: Implications for the diagnosis and treatment of pain. *Pain, 152*(3 Suppl.), S2–S15. doi:10.1016/j.pain.2010.09.030.

3 Tool Use Unravels Body Morphology Representation in the Brain

Marie Martel, Lucilla Cardinali, Alice C. Roy, and Alessandro Farnè

Introduction

Performing accurate and efficient movements implies the brain can access and integrate neural representations of both the body and the space around it. This integrated processing is even more challenging in the case of actions performed with tools, as one needs to transfer the control of its body to that of a mechanical effector. Humans have come to an exquisite level of mastery in tool use, as dramatically witnessed when brain damage brakes this capability down leading to apraxic deficits. The cognitive motor and neural processes that allow for accurate tool use have been extensively studied (Osiurak & Massen, 2014; Tarhan, Watson, & Buxbaum, 2015). In the present chapter, we focus on the possibility that part of tool mastery may emerge from the capability of incorporating tools into body representations (BR), as postulated by several theories (Arbib, Bonaiuto, Jacobs, & Frey, 2009; Cardinali et al., 2012). Many different approaches have been used to address the issue of how tools get incorporated into neural representations. Since the seminal monkey electrophysiology work by Iriki and colleagues (Iriki, Tanaka, & Iwamura, 1996), tool use has been repeatedly reported to cause transient changes in a spatial representation termed peripersonal space (PPS). As it has recently become clear that tool use may also affect bodily representations (Cardinali, Frassinetti et al., 2009), a certain degree of confusion remains on how tool incorporation can and should be investigated as a function of the nature of the target brain representation. Here, we chose to detach ourselves from the seminal work on space remapping, and instead focus on some of the body representations and try to identify the conditions under which their plasticity becomes apparent following tool-use tasks.

1   Tool Use Modifies the Represented Body Morphology

Besides changing the space around us by extending our peripersonal space (see, for review, Brozzoli, Ehrsson, & Farnè, 2014; Dijkerman & Farnè, 2015), tool use has been shown to modify the representation of our own body. In this section, we will pursue two main objectives. The first one is to testify about the benefits of tool use as a paradigm to assess body representation plasticity. The second aim is to suggest some points one should take into consideration when using such a tool-use based approach to tackle body representations. In the present chapter we will focus on two of the body representations described in the literature, namely the body schema (BS) and the body image (BI; see Martel, Cardinali, Roy, & Farnè, 2016, for a thorough taxonomy of body representations).

Body Schema
The body schema is a highly plastic representation of the body parts' posture, shape, and size, used to execute or imagine executing movements (Medina & Coslett, 2010). It allows for execution and constant monitoring of our actions and appears to be fed mainly by proprioceptive, but also tactile and kinesthetic information (Head & Holmes, 1911; Shenton, Schwoebel, & Coslett, 2004). Our group has contributed converging evidence for body schema plasticity after tool use (Cardinali, Frassinetti et al., 2009; Cardinali et al., 2011, 2012; Cardinali, Brozzoli, Finos, Roy, & Farnè, 2016; Cardinali, Brozzoli, Luauté, Roy, & Farnè, 2016). Indeed, Cardinali and colleagues (2009) reported for the first time that the BS, specifically the arm representation, was modified after using a mechanical grabber for ten minutes. We recorded neurotypical participants' free hand movement kinematics before and after using this tool. Tool reach and grasp actions modified the subsequent free hand movement kinematic profile. As compared to the same bare hand movements performed before tool use, after tool use the velocity and deceleration peaks occurred later and were of smaller amplitude resulting in a longer movement duration. In addition, the amplitude of both velocity and deceleration peaks was smaller, as compared to that observed during the bare hand movements performed before tool use. Such changes did not occur for the grasping component of the movement (e.g., finger opening), but were limited to the transport one, suggesting a selective modification of the forearm representation. This result points to the fact that BS update is very specific and involves only the body parts which morphology is affected by the tool. Subjects literally acted as if they had a longer arm after tool use. Indeed, when compared to people with short(er)

arms, participants with long(er) arms naturally displayed bare hand reach-to-grasp movements characterized by velocity and deceleration peaks of longer latencies and smaller amplitude, with overall longer movement times. The kinematic pattern of long-armed people is thus similar to that observed after tool use, irrespective of the real arm length (see Cardinali, Frassinetti et al., 2009, supplementary material). These findings were taken as evidence for tool incorporation into the arm representation and hence, plasticity of the BS.

Similar effects of "represented arm lengthening" were obtained when subjects were required to quickly point with their left index fingertip at anatomical landmarks of their right arm (elbow, wrist, middle finger) where an unseen tactile stimulus was delivered. After tool use, subjects pointed to the wrist and elbow as if they were farther apart, hence they clearly relied on an extended arm length representation. Interestingly, their hand length representation, as indexed by the distance between the wrist and the middle fingertip end-pointing locations, remained unchanged, supporting the body part specificity showed by the kinematic results (Cardinali, Frassinetti et al., 2009). Accordingly, using a tool that modifies the fingers, but not the arm length, selectively affects finger representation (Cardinali, Brozzoli, Finos et al., 2016).

Recently, we investigated the hypothesis according to which mental imagery of tool use could be sufficient to modify one's arm's length representation. Given that both actual and mental imagery of tool use are known to alter space perception (Davoli, Brockmole, & Witt, 2012; Witt & Proffitt, 2008), we reasoned that tool-use imagery should trigger, on subsequent hand movement kinematics, similar effects to those induced by actual tool use (Baccarini et al., 2014). In this study, we asked healthy participants to perform free hand reach-to-grasp movements, before and after merely imagining performing this movement either with their hand (day one), or with a mechanical grabber passively held in their hand (day two). We ensured that motor imagery was accurately performed by introducing changes in the orientation of the thumb–finger opposition axis needed to grasp the target object (after Frak, Paulignan, & Jeannerod, 2001), thus making the task more difficult for some orientations. The results showed that movement time was similarly affected by this manipulation of task difficulty in both actual and imagined reach-to-grasp movements. Crucially, after tool-use imagery participants displayed reduced amplitude peaks for the transport component (velocity and deceleration peaks), while there was no kinematic change after imagining to use the hand to execute the same movements (Baccarini et al., 2014). These results are similar to those observed after actual tool use. Taken together, these findings converge to indicate that imagining reaching out an object with a tool may be sufficient to trigger its plastic incorporation in the BS.

Noteworthy, participants were familiarized with the tool in the preceding day, and could see it while holding it, so both vision and proprioception were possibly at stake in producing the effects following mental tool-use imagery (Baccarini et al., 2014). The longitudinal study of a deafferented patient enabled us to show that tool incorporation requires intact proprioceptive feedback (Cardinali, Brozzoli, Luauté et al., 2016). By using the same paradigm as in Cardinali, Frassinetti et al. (2009), we found that without proprioception, the tool-use effects on BS—which are typically observed in healthy subjects—were no longer present. Instead, tool use required a period of learning and only subsequently it affected movements in a way that was unspecific (as it involved both arm and finger behavior) and restricted to the specific movement performed with the tool (in our case grasping, but not pointing movements). We are currently gathering further empirical evidence that the plasticity of BS could occur without recurring to any visual inputs, proprioception being in principle sufficient to trigger body representation changes (Martel et al., 2014). This line of study is in keeping with the old tenet that proprioception and more generally somatosensation should allow for a privileged access to the BS (Cardinali, Brozzoli, & Farnè, 2009; Dijkerman & de Haan, 2007). In a related study, Cardinali and colleagues (Cardinali et al., 2011) asked healthy blindfolded participants to point quickly and accurately with their left index fingertip, to a specific location on their right arm that had previously been touched by the experimenter (finger, wrist, or elbow). In another condition, subjects had to verbally report where (on their right arm) they had been touched, by reading aloud the number on a ruler kept parallel to their (unseen) right arm. The distance between the different landing and read-out points was then calculated to assess the represented length of the hand (fingertip to wrist distance) and the forearm (wrist to elbow distance), both before and after using the same mechanical grabber to perform reach-to-grasp movements. Participants' performance revealed a significant effect of tool use on both tasks, but only for the representation of forearm length, the hand length remaining unchanged. When making either conscious verbal judgments about, or unconscious movements toward the tactile stimulation, the represented distance between the elbow and the wrist was extended after tool use (Cardinali et al., 2011).

In the same way as peripersonal space remapping, BS plasticity following tool use relies on the functional importance of the tool (Sposito, Bolognini,

Vallar, & Maravita, 2012). In their study, Sposito and colleagues tackled this question by designing a forearm bisection task, consisting in estimating the midpoint of one's own forearm before and after diversified tool-use training. After using a sixty-centimeter-long tool, subjects indicated a more distal midpoint, according to the hypothesis of an increased arm length representation. Interestingly, no midpoint shift was observed after using a twenty-centimeter-long tool, which did not alter the reaching space, thus highlighting the importance of the reachability gain to the BS update. Similarly, we found that when a same tool is used in a way that is not functionally meaningful, the effects on the arm representation are only partial (Cardinali et al., 2012).

In some particular cases, the role played by the conscious feeling of ownership toward the arm using the tool has been reported to be critical. It is the case of brain-damaged patients suffering from a pathological embodiment of other people's arm, at the place of their own hemiplegic arm. Garbarini and colleagues (Garbarini et al., 2015) asked four of these patients to estimate the midpoint of their contralesional forearm before and after fifteen minutes of tool-use training (similar to Sposito et al., 2012). When the patients were convinced to use the tool with their own paralyzed arm (though they were merely looking at the experimenter arm + tool usage) they misjudged their forearm midpoint more distally (i.e., toward the hand), just as neurotypical participants did with respect to their real own arm. This finding points to the existence of intimate relationships between the body representations and the sense of ownership, as the possibility that tool use affects the BS seems clearly conditional to the (possibly implicit) self-attribution of the effector acting with a tool. These authors, considering tool use in terms of tool embodiment, opened the field to studies about prosthetic arms, and the way they are integrated into the body representations, for an optimal sensorimotor control (Romano, Caffa, Hernandez-Arieta, Brugger, & Maravita, 2015). Prosthesis can indeed be considered as tools in the sense that they allow the user to perform movements and actions otherwise not possible. Prosthesis use, as tool use, changes the shape and size of the user's body in an attempt to restore it to its original state by replacing a missing limb. If the concept of a tool becoming a body part as been around since the beginning of the nineteenth century, the idea that a prosthesis can become a body part has been accepted as true and obvious even more easily. The main issue with the research about embodiment is the quite vague definition of embodiment. Murray defines embodiment as "the way in which people experience their own body" (2008, p. 127). This definition, while correct, includes many different phenomena and processes.

More recently, de Vignemont (2011) proposed a systematic definition of embodiment that postulates the existence of three layers: motor embodiment (an object is embodied if it moves as a body part and is perceived as under one's control); spatial (an object is embodied if the space it is located in is processed as body space); and affective (an object is embodied if the individual shows the same affective reactions as for his or her own body). When all the three aspects are present, one can talk about full embodiment.

A seminal work by Fraser (1984) used a kinematic approach to assess whether prosthesis can become a body part. The rationale behind the study was that if the prosthesis is embodied it should be moved as a body part. Indeed, she found that the participant had a similar kinematic profile when performing movements with her intact arm as well as with her prosthesis. A few years later, McDonnell and colleagues (McDonnell, Scott, Dickison, Theriault, & Wood, 1989) investigated prosthesis embodiment in a group of congenital and acquired amputees by using a pointing task. They found that, when asked to point to the (unseen) position in space of their stump, amputees consistently overestimated the length of their arm but only while wearing a prosthesis. These two studies support the idea that prostheses can be embodied into the body schema, that is they show motoric embodiment. However they do not per se justify the claim that prostheses are fully embodied.

Interviews have been used to test affective embodiment (Murray, 2004, 2008). These studies reported that amputees can experience and describe various degrees of embodiment, which seems to be related to the amount of use of the prosthesis. Such relation between use and embodiment doesn't seem to be linear or unidirectional. Embodiment seems to arise after protracted use, necessary to reach a level of comfort with the prosthesis. On the other hand, embodiment is suggested to play a role in supporting amputees in continuing using the prostheses. Pazzaglia and colleagues (Pazzaglia, Galli, Scivoletto, & Molinari, 2013; see also Galli, Noel, Canzoneri, Blanke, & Serino, 2015) developed a new comprehensive questionnaire to investigate wheelchair embodiment in patients with spinal cord injury. A principal component analysis on eleven questions addressing various aspects of patients' personal experience revealed that the majority of patients experienced the wheelchair as being part of their body. Interestingly, they also perceived it a functional substitute of their legs but not as an external tool. That is, the wheelchair *is* the legs rather than a tool supporting or extending them.

Finally, a growing number of studies used a modified rubber hand illusion (RHI) protocol where the participant stump and the prosthesis were synchronously or asynchronously stimulated (D'Alonzo, Clemente, & Cipriani, 2015; Ehrsson et al., 2008; Giummarra, Georgiou-Karistianis, Nicholls, Gibson, & Bradshaw, 2010; Rosén et al., 2009; Schmalzl, Kalckert, Ragnö, & Ehrsson, 2014). They reported that amputees can experience a rubber hand or a prosthesis as their own hand as shown by the fact that they feel the tactile stimulation on the stump as coming from the rubber hand or prosthesis and show physiological responses, as assessed with skin conductance response measures, at a threat to the prosthesis. These data show spatial and affective embodiment of prosthesis in amputees. However, the RHI-like paradigm might not be representative of real life experience with prosthesis. In such quite artificial situations, amputees are not asked to control or act with the prosthesis (hence not addressing motoric embodiment), as they would in real life, but rather passively observed it. As such, they speak more of whether a RH-like illusion can be induced using a prosthetic hand then of prosthesis embodiment on amputees, providing weak insight on whether and how embodiment can support prosthesis use and reduce rejection.

In addition, tool-use dependent plasticity of the BS seems to be limb specific, as recently suggested by Jovanov and colleagues (Jovanov, Clifton, Mazalek, Nitsche, & Welsh, 2015). In this study, participants were asked to look at a screen with a picture of a woman holding a rake, with the arm outstretched perpendicular to her body. Then they had to respond as fast as possible to targets appearing on the hand, the tip of the rake, or the woman's foot, either with their own hand or foot. This task was performed before and after using a rake to grasp and move a tennis ball. The authors found a body-part compatibility effect for which RT were faster when the responding limb matched the one the target appeared on (i.e., hand response to a target appearing on the woman's hand). Crucially, after using the rake, the compatibility effect was present also for hand (but not foot) responses to target appearing on the rake image.

Regarding limb specificity, one crucial aspect has been neglected for a long time: the tool morphology, as studied recently by Miller and colleagues (Miller, Longo, & Saygin, 2014). These authors referred to an implicit body representation, and even if they prefer the term "body model" (Longo & Haggard, 2010), a supposedly distinct representation from both the BS and the BI, we will discuss its findings in terms of their relevance to the BS. In their study, Miller et al. (2014) asked subjects to perform a tactile distance judgment task (TDJ): they stimulated them in two distinct points, at two different locations (hand/arm and forehead), and asked participants to judge where the distance was bigger. Although clearly conscious and perceptive, we previously suggested (Cardinali et al., 2012) that tactile inputs may allow access to the body metrics, assessing (at least partly) the BS. The TDJ task was performed before and after using a tool to grasp a balloon, either a mechanical arm-shaped grabber, or a hand-shaped tool. Crucially, after using the mechanical arm-shaped grabber, tactile distance perception on the hand was not modified, while that on the arm was. Conversely, after using the hand-shaped tool, only tactile perception on the hand was modified. Those changes were opposite in direction: increased width and decreased length of the hand or the arm. These findings highlight that tool morphology itself, linked with the functional role of the tool, is crucial in the updating of the BS.

Several studies (Baccarini et al., 2014; Cardinali, Frassinetti et al., 2009; Martel et al., 2014) employing tools whose basic property was to lengthen the participants' arm, have found kinematic changes following tool use that were limited to the reaching component of the movement. This consistently replicated finding reinforces the idea that with an arm-lengthening tool, the representation of the arm is selectively modified. The changes in the hand perceptual representation reported by Miller et al. (2014) after using a hand-widening tool could thus be concomitant with kinematic changes that could be selective of the grasping part of the movement. Results from our group confirm this prediction: when the distal length of the thumb and index fingers is lengthened, subsequent free hand prehensile movements are altered selectively with respect to the grasping component of the movement, leaving the transport component unchanged (Cardinali, Brozzoli, Finos et al., 2016). One finding that deserves discussion is that the reduced length in the arm perceptual representation reported by Miller and colleagues after the use of the long grabber does not readily fit the increased arm length representation described by the post-tool kinematics (Baccarini et al., 2014; Cardinali, Frassinetti et al., 2009; Martel et al., 2014) or the post-tool somatosensory driven pointing (Cardinali et al., 2011; Cardinali, Frassinetti et al., 2009). Miller and collaborators have suggested that this discrepancy could be the result of the difference between the tasks across studies. Critically, to our best knowledge, the only other study that observed a shortening of perceived arm length after tool use (Ganesh, Yoshioka, Osu, & Ikegami, 2014) required, once again, the conscious participants' estimation of their effectors size. They proposed that the earliest stage of tool incorporation goes with a shortening of the perceived arm length, which then turns in the previously reported lengthening of perceived arm length with further tool use. Finally, tool use can shape both PPS and BS when both were tested at perceptual level (Canzoneri et al., 2013), although the similar outcome does not necessarily call for an identity between these representations and cognitive processes (see, for a dissociation, Bassolino, Finisguerra, Canzoneri, Serino, & Pozzo, 2015). One further possibility is that once directly modified by tool use, the change induced within the BS can spill over the BI, the PPS, or both (Cardinali et al., 2011; Cardinali, Brozzoli et al., 2009).

Here we have tried to gather the available pieces of evidence suggesting that tool use allows for the access to body representations and their plasticity. Several studies converge in indicating that, when used in real life, or even merely by mental imagery, tools can be incorporated in what we have identified as the body schema (Baccarini et al., 2014; Cardinali et al., 2011, 2012; Cardinali, Frassinetti et al., 2009; Cardinali, Brozzoli, Finos et al., 2016; Cardinali, Brozzoli, Luauté et al., 2016; Martel et al., 2014). In this respect it is important to notice that in all these studies, the object to be grasped with either the tool or the hand was always located inside the reaching space of the arm. Far from being a methodological detail, the fact of acting in the same space with the tool and the hand allows to isolate tool use specific effects, ruling out possible confounds due to the fact of acting with either effector in different sectors for space. Tool-use remapping also appears to be limb specific (Cardinali, Brozzoli, Finos et al., 2016; Jovanov et al., 2015), and dependent upon the function and morphology of the tool (Miller et al., 2014; Cardinali, Brozzoli, Finos et al., 2016) to perform a specific action (Sposito et al., 2012).

Body Image

In our view, the rubber hand illusion is to the body image, what tool use is to the peripersonal space: for decades researchers have used tool-use paradigms to testify of the plasticity of the PPS, to the point that one might think that PPS exists only to subserve tool use. Similarly, the RHI has been used to study BI plasticity and until recently, the BI has mainly been referred to the concept of body ownership in RHI studies.

The RHI consists in inducing the illusion of owning a fake rubber hand, by brushing the participants' unseen hand synchronously with a fake hand (see, for review Kilteni, Maselli, Kording, & Slater, 2015; Tsakiris, 2010). Again, BI and PPS are the models of body and space representations commonly used, so far, to explain how the body is owned and represented in the brain (Blanke, Slater, & Serino, 2015; Makin, Holmes, & Ehrsson, 2008). However, as tool use started to "dig its way" as a paradigm to interrogate other body representations such as the body schema, the interest started to grow regarding the relationships between tools, their use, and the

BI, particularly since it seemed difficult to feel ownership over non-hand-shaped tools (de Vignemont & Farnè, 2010; Tsakiris, Carpenter, James, & Fotopoulou, 2010), a limit that could possibly extend to enacted, but not necessarily self-sensed robotic hands (Romano et al., 2015). In this rich but complex theoretical framework, the BI initially appeared to be immune to tool use. For example, in the work by Cardinali and colleagues alluded to above (Cardinali et al., 2011) there were two additional conditions that, by manipulating the type of the input and output task modalities, were designed to tackle more specifically the BI. In one condition, blindfolded subjects had to point quickly and accurately with their left index finger to a specific location on their right arm that, instead of being signaled by tactile stimulation, was named by the experimenter ("finger," "wrist," or "elbow"). In another condition, subjects had to verbally report the position of the named anatomical landmark by reading aloud the number corresponding to these landmarks from a ruler that was visible in front of them. The distance between the landing and read aloud locations was then calculated to assess the represented length of arm and hand, before and after using the same long mechanical grabber. Results showed no change in the arm (or hand) representation after tool use in either condition. Noteworthy, the same subjects actually showed significant changes of arm (but not hand) length estimation in the two conditions where touch was used as input modality to indicate the anatomical landmarks, thus designed to mainly tackle the BS (Cardinali et al., 2011). Overall, this pattern of results suggests that tool use had no consequences on the conscious representation of the body (e.g., the BI).

Among the main features of the BI, besides that of being typically accessed via conscious explicit tasks, there is its heavy dependence upon vision. Miller and colleagues (Miller, Longo, & Saygin, 2013) addressed this issue by asking participants to judge whether a depicted hand was wider than their own before and after practicing with a hand-shaped tool that was much bigger than average human hands. When tool use was performed with visual feedback, most of the subjects judged to have a wider and shorter hand. In contrast, when blindfolded participants used the mechanical hand, no modification of the conscious hand representation occurred. Hence visual feedback could be necessary to update the BI. However, we anticipate this debate is far from being over, as for example, the RHI has been observed even without visual input, when blindfolded subjects reported the impression of stroking their own hand while the experimenter was stroking it and at the same time using their other hand to touch a rubber hand (Ehrsson, Holmes, & Passingham, 2005).

2 Tool Use: An Open Window into Body Representations

Although tool-use paradigms have allowed researchers to gain considerable knowledge about body representations and their plasticity, several interesting questions remain to be addressed. A major question is related to the dynamics of the BS updating. Ganesh and colleagues (Ganesh et al., 2014) testified of a fast initial reduction of the arm representation, which is then followed by the repeatedly reported extension of BS. Whether this apparent discrepancy is entirely attributable to the differences in the tasks used remains unclear, and future investigations are awaited to elucidate the temporal and spatial dynamics of the processes bringing to tool embodiment (see, for review, de Vignemont, in press). In addition, all the effects that have been reported so far following tool use are (supposedly) temporary. This assumed transient character can actually be contrasted by what seem to be a rather permanent change in blind, expert cane users (Serino, Bassolino, Farnè, & Làdavas, 2007), and prolonged tool use may actually translate in more permanent neural changes of BRs. Yet, if we readily accept the term "plasticity" to deal with such tool-use dependent effects, we should probably think in terms of plasticity also when those effects disappear. This spatiotemporal plasticity remains so far unexplored: is the shrinking back gradual, or immediate like an elastic band going back to its default size (de Vignemont & Farnè, 2010), as it has been observed for the peripersonal space retraction in adults and children (Caçola & Gabbard, 2012)?

A closely related question is whether BS plasticity always goes in the direction of and expansion/elongation, or can also account for shortening/shrinkage. By using an arm-immobilization paradigm, Bassolino and others (Bassolino et al., 2015) found that the arm representation did not shrink. This favors the hypothesis that, as the body cannot biologically shrink, BRs could only extend, without changing in the opposite direction (Bassolino et al., 2015; Cardinali, Brozzoli et al., 2009; de Vignemont et al., 2005; but see Ganesh et al., 2014; Miller et al., 2014). Several studies have established that after surgical extension of limbs in achondroplastic patients, body representations namely the BS and the explicit BI, were modified toward a "normalization" when compared to body-typical subjects (Cimmino et al., 2013; Di Russo et al., 2006).

Another so far unanswered question is how to test the BI to definitely ascertain whether it is immune to tool use or not. Cardinali and colleagues (Cardinali et al., 2011) tried identifying which combination of inputs and outputs was needed to exclusively or preferentially assessing body representations: a pure motor task will allow access to the BS, and be sensitive to tool use, while a pure perceptual and verbal task will trigger the BI, with no mark of tool use. Strikingly, with a verbal input and a motor output, no effect of tool use was observed, suggesting that this combination provides marginal or no access to BS, being possibly more related to BI. Conversely, a tactile input with a perceptual output was sufficient to make the key signature of tool incorporation visible. This finding may suggest that such a combination is sufficient to reveal that BI is also sensitive to tool use. An alternative interpretation is however possible, namely that the BS, once affected by tool use, may have mediated this plastic change into the BI. This consideration also raises the point of the possible functional interactions between BRs, that remain however outside the scope of the present chapter (see Kammers et al., 2010).

Before concluding we wish to consider some potential advantages that may emerge from conducting a systematic approach of tool use as a model paradigm for the study of body representations. Such an approach may hold the potential to elucidate whether and to what extent different body representations are generally or rather specifically tackled by tool- and task-related manipulations. Moreover, the critical conditions to be met for a given BR to become, if possible, sensitive to the representational plasticity induced by tool use may be unraveled. Tool use could thus keep the promise of opening a window into the study of body representations and their plasticity. Last but not least, the systematic questioning of BR via tool-use paradigms can help refine the current models we use to frame these BR, by clarifying in more mechanistic terms their operational definitions.

3   Tool Use, Body Schema, and Internal Models

One final aspect that we would like to start considering here is the relationship between two research domains that, despite being both related to motor action performance, have often times in the past walked parallel paths: the body representations literature and the motor control literature. While interested in similar topics, especially when it comes to the BS and tool use, these research fields have developed influential models that, in our opinion, are highly complementary and would benefit from a deeper collaboration. In particular, we suggest that the body schema can find its place inside the current internal model theories, a place that may functionally correspond to the internal representations of the motor apparatus (called "the plant"; Gaveau et al., 2014; Kawato, 1999; Miall, 2002; see also Desmurget & Grafton, 2000).

In the attempt to test this computational hypothesis of the body schema, we will recall here the main components and functioning of the computational framework within which motor control has been mostly developed (for reviews, see Grush, 2004; Shadmehr & Krakauer, 2008). In brief, the first model, the inverse model, uses an internal representation of all the available perceived information to define a motor command as accurate as possible to reach a desired change in the state of the effector and world; that is, it calculates the necessary feedforward control (Miall & Wolpert, 1996). Classically, internal models consider mostly the positional information about the hand, whereas they take into account several features about objects (size, weight, orientation, etc.). For instance, in a reach-to-grasp movement, the inputs of the inverse model would be the actual state of the limb (e.g., hand position close to the body), as well as the desired state of the limb (e.g., specific object in hand, arm away from the body, at a specific distance). The output would be the required motor command to reach this desired state. As this command is sent to the effector, an efference copy of the arm motor command is also created to feed the forward model. In this respect, as a first step toward mutual enrichment between domains, we suggest that not only the position, but also other features of the effector should feed the forward model, such as the weight, shape, and size of the arm or hand, that is to say, the features typically attributed to the body schema.

In a complementary way, the forward model predicts the sensory consequences of the movement from the efference copy of the motor command (Wolpert, Ghahramani, & Jordan, 1995; Wolpert & Kawato, 1998; Miall & Wolpert, 1996). Hence, the efference copy itself becomes the forward model's input to estimate the arm's predicted trajectory. Comparison between the predicted feedbacks and the actual ones is considered as the basis of motor learning, as any difference (e.g., missing the target object) would trigger an error signal and initiate updating the inverse model (Imamizu et al., 2000; Ioffe, Chernikova, & Ustinova, 2007; Tseng, Diedrichsen, Krakauer, Shadmehr, & Bastian, 2007). Many studies have indicated that a critical role in acquiring and maintaining new internal models through motor learning is played by the cerebellum (Imamizu et al., 2000; Ioffe et al., 2007; Ishikawa, Tomatsu, Izawa, & Kakei, 2015; Tseng et al., 2007; Wolpert, Miall, & Kawato, 1998). In an elegant study, Imamizu and colleagues (2000) taught healthy participants inside an MRI scanner to use a computer mouse with a novel rotational transformation. As the dynamics of this action was totally new and unusual, it required motor learning based upon the initial error signals, and the inverse and forward model progressively

tuned to perform an adequate movement with the mouse. After participants learned to follow a random target on the screen with the mouse, a
specific activity in the cerebellum remained, reflecting the acquisition of an
internal model of the new dynamics of the mouse. Hence, acquisition of a
new object dynamics appears really close to acquisition of a new movement
(Rieger, 2012).

A point we wish emphasizing within this computational framework is
that, when reaching for an object with the hand, a state estimation is made
depending upon both the object to grasp (i.e., the state of the world), and
the effector to use (i.e., most typically, the state of the body). Different
dynamics and kinematic characteristics of objects will then lead to different
internal models, readily accessible, as our central nervous system can use
predictive coding and anticipation to reduce the unnecessary high costs of
online control (Davidson & Wolpert, 2004; Flanagan et al., 1999). Davidson
and Wolpert (2004), for example, revealed that when reaching for objects
of different weights with their hand, subjects could easily swap between
internal models for a light or a heavy object alternatively, and could also
quite appropriately combine them based on their previous experience of
each weight. Thus, we can both learn new internal models and flexibly swap
among already learned ones.

If we now turn considering our tool-use paradigms (Cardinali et al., 2011,
2012; Cardinali, Frassinetti et al., 2009; Cardinali, Brozzoli, Finos et al.,
2016), we are brought to suggest that they did not require the acquisition of
a new internal model for estimating the state of the world. The object weight,
size, and position were indeed the same, as well as the distance from the
hand starting position, throughout the experiments. In short, we kept the
"state of the world" constant to isolate the "state of the body." We should
rather consider the possibility that a new internal model would have been
necessary for the effector model (i.e., the arm). In this view, the BS and its
plasticity would consist of an update of the inverse model of the state of
the body. Although it may be difficult to determine whether we learn an
internal model of the tool, or adapt the model of our arm (Kluzik, Diedrichsen, Shadmehr, & Bastian, 2008; Malfait & Ostry, 2004), one important
aspect to notice is that we found no evidence of major learning processes
in the kinematics of the tool-use sessions: when comparing the kinematics
of the initial tool-use actions with those of the terminal ones (i.e., block
one vs. block four, twelve trials per block), the kinematics did not differ
(Cardinali et al., 2012; Cardinali, Frassinetti et al., 2009). The lack of statistically observable differences in tool-use kinematics across blocks may
suggest that the participants' sensorimotor system was immediately apt to

transfer the control from the arm to the arm + tool configuration (Arbib et al., 2009). This apparent lack of motor learning could thus indicate that there was no need to learn an entirely new internal model when using the tool. Rather, it seems reasonable to suggest that participants could keep using their own arm model, with the simple trick of updating its length parameter. For this alternative to be viable within the internal models framework, one should admit that, during tool use, a set of small error signals, produced by tool-use actions, may be available to update the length parameter in the body-state estimation. Such signals would consist in much finger-grained error feedbacks than missing the target (which never happened in our tool-use studies) and may actually reflect a way to optimize motor control within a given inverse model.

Additionally, broad generalization of tool effects on free-hand movement appears to suggest an update of the arm model when using the tool, rather than a new model for the world (Heuer & Hegele, 2015; Kluzik et al., 2008); in other words, the inverse and forward models optimize themselves when the arm suddenly appears to display new dynamics and kinematic movement characteristics. Although we had no evidence of major learning processes (nor aftereffects), we have indeed observed that grasping with a tool (in a sagittal direction) affected both subsequent free hand grasping and pointing movements (Cardinali, Frassinetti et al., 2009), and affected free-hand grasping both in the frontal and sagittal directions (Martel et al., 2014). We therefore suggest that tool incorporation into the body schema may require minimal motor learning based on fine-grained error signals to update the body-effector parameter that has been affected by the use of a given tool, for example, the arm length (Cardinali et al., 2011, 2012; Cardinali, Frassinetti et al., 2009). As such, tool incorporation may impose minimal requirements to motor learning processes in healthy participants, at least for such simple tools that do not alter the regular dynamics of natural reach and grasp movements. Accordingly, motor learning does become necessary when proprioceptive information is not available to support BS plasticity and tools can not readily be incorporated (Cardinali, Brozzoli, Luauté et al., 2016).

If tools are incorporated in the BS by updating the body-state estimates, then one should also explain how the kinematic "traces" of this incorporation can still be observable afterwards, when people are using their free hand to reach and grasp the objects. Our suggestion that the BS update takes place via subtle changes in the motor learning process, might accommodate this finding. In motor control terms, the presence of very small "error signals" during tool use would indeed imply using a control policy with small weights (or gains) assigned to the actual feedback. This, in turn, would leave tool-use-induced plasticity effects visible across the subsequent free-hand trials. To date, these effects were still observed after about twenty trials of reaching with the hand alone (up to ten to fifteen minutes, following about fifty trials with the tool), and we might expect that after some more trials, the update would occur reversely.

As internal models include a representation of the body—as an effector—on which the motor command is implemented, it is thus reasonable to consider that the internal model can adapt to a change in the effector representation (Kluzik et al., 2008). Shadmehr and Krakauer indeed suggested that a fundamental step in motor control is "to form a belief about the state of our body and the world (called state estimation)" (Shadmehr & Krakauer, 2008, p. 359). While using the tool employed in our studies (Cardinali et al., 2011, 2012; Cardinali, Frassinetti et al., 2009; Cardinali, Brozzoli, Finos et al., 2016), subjects may update an already available internal model of the arm effector, which "becomes" longer (e.g., represented by body state estimations as being a longer forearm).

Another possibility that should be considered is that the body schema and its plasticity would be mainly embedded in the forward model. Indeed, one important result from our studies on tool use that we need to take into account when referring to internal models is the qualitatively similar, albeit less important, effect that we found on free-hand kinematics after subjects were asked to merely imagine to use the tool (as compared to the control condition of imagining to use their hand). As it is the case for some very fast movements (e.g., saccades), motor imagery would—by definition—impede any major integration of sensory feedbacks with the sensory consequences predicted of the basis of the forward model. Thus, the beliefs about the state of the body (and environment) would not be modified and, in this case, no (major) change in the internal model would be possible (as no error signal can be fed back to trigger learning processes). As limpidly set out by Shadmehr and Krakauer: "to imagine a movement we need to change the weight associated with measured sensory feedback to zero, making our control process rely entirely on our predictions" (Shadmehr & Krakauer, 2008, p. 375). Although tentatively, we therefore try to interpret the body schema plasticity in the computational framework of motor control in such a way that it is embedded in the forward model (at least when vision, proprioception, and kinesthetic motor imagery are available). The above recalled lack of major signs of learning processes, as well of opposite aftereffects, could indeed support the hypothesis that people can access previously built models of functionally elongated arms. However, there is quite ample evidence that swapping from one internal model to another one would have no consequences in terms of updating of the internal model as, again, swapping would bypass any learning processes. The hypothesis that people can swap from an "arm" to an "arm + tool" model would thus be incompatible with the finding that tool-use dependent effects on kinematics were visible, subsequently, when people reached objects with their hand alone. Then, to explain the minor, but significant presence of imagined tool-use effects on subsequent free-hand kinematics, one should consider the possibility that body-state estimates may not only be updated based upon the observed error (i.e., the integration of predicted and actual sensory consequences, but also based upon the predicted error (i.e., the integration of predicted consequences and results). Although relatively rare, there have been previous reports that exposure to visuo-proprioceptive discrepancy without any observation of reaching errors (subjects did not receive visual feedback of their pointing movement) was sufficient to develop aftereffects (see, for example, Block & Bastian, 2012; Michel, Gaveau, Pozzo, & Papaxanthis, 2013).

To date, we believe that the available findings do not allow us to disentangle between these alternatives based mainly on the inverse or the forward models, which could also be non-mutually exclusive. It could also be possible that their relative contribution in determining the degree of tool incorporation into the BS would vary, according to the current availability of sensory information and the particular constraints of the task at hand. The purpose of this last paragraph, far from being to solve a debate, it is rather to instantiate the debate and to propose that it may be very valuable to merge research on tool use pursued under the perspective of its effects on body representations with that pursued under the perspective offered by current computational models of motor control.

Conclusion

To conclude, we believe that tool-use paradigms hold the potential to reveal many valuable aspects to deepening our understanding of body representations and their plasticity. Its specificity and selectivity to affect different BR may empower our capability to disentangle the still unsolved questions about body representations and their plastic modification. While it remains an open question whether and under which conditions tool use modifies the existing action models, or instead creates new tool-specific internal models, we believe that merging the still relatively separate domains of neuropsychological conceptions about the body representations and computational theories of motor control may open promising and exciting new questions and hypotheses to be tested through tool-use paradigms.

Acknowledgments

A.F. and A.C.R. were supported by grants from the Fédération pour la Recherche sur le Cerveau, Neurodon. A.C.R. was also supported by ANR SAMENTA. A.F. was also supported by ANR-CeSaMe, LABEX CORTEX (ANR-11-LABX-0042), and the J. S. McDonnell Foundation Scholar Award. L.C. was supported by NSERC-CREATE IRTG program (449313-2014). M.M. was supported by a grant from the French Ministry of Higher Education and Research.

References

Arbib, M. A., Bonaiuto, J. B., Jacobs, S., & Frey, S. H. (2009). Tool use and the distalization of the end-effector. *Psychological Research, 73*(4), 441–462. doi:10.1007/s00426-009-0242-2.

Baccarini, M., Martel, M., Cardinali, L., Sillan, O., Farnè, A., & Roy, A. C. (2014). Tool use imagery triggers tool incorporation in the body schema. *Frontiers in Psychology, 5*, 492. doi:10.3389/fpsyg.2014.00492.

Bassolino, M., Finisguerra, A., Canzoneri, E., Serino, A., & Pozzo, T. (2015). Dissociating effect of upper limb non-use and overuse on space and body representations. *Neuropsychologia, 70*, 385–392. doi:10.1016/j.neuropsychologia.2014.11.028.

Blanke, O., Slater, M., & Serino, A. (2015). Behavioral, neural, and computational principles of bodily self-consciousness. *Neuron, 88*(1), 145–166. doi:10.1016/j.neuron.2015.09.029.

Block, H. J., & Bastian, A. J. (2012). Cerebellar involvement in motor but not sensory adaptation. *Neuropsychologia, 50*(8), 1766–1775. doi:10.1016/j.neuropsychologia.2012.03.034.

Brozzoli, C., Ehrsson, H. H., & Farnè, A. (2014). Multisensory representation of the space near the hand: From perception to action and interindividual interactions. *Neuroscientist, 20*(2), 122–135. doi:10.1177/1073858413511153.

Caçola, P., & Gabbard, C. (2012). Modulating peripersonal and extrapersonal reach space via tool use: A comparison between 6- to 12-year-olds and young adults. *Experimental Brain Research, 218*(2), 321–330. doi:10.1007/s00221-012-3017-8.

Canzoneri, E., Ubaldi, S., Rastelli, V., Finisguerra, A., Bassolino, M., & Serino, A. (2013). Tool-use reshapes the boundaries of body and peripersonal space representations. *Experimental Brain Research, 228*(1), 25–42. doi:10.1007/s00221-013-3532-2.

Cardinali, L., Brozzoli, C., & Farnè, A. (2009). Peripersonal space and body schema: Two labels for the same concept? *Brain Topography, 21*(3), 252–260. doi:10.1007/s10548-009-0092-7.

Cardinali, L., Brozzoli, C., Finos, L., Roy, A. C., & Farnè, A. (2016). The rules of tool incorporation: Tool morpho-functional and sensori-motor constraints. *Cognition, 149*, 1–5. doi:10.1016/j.cognition.2016.01.001.

Cardinali, L., Brozzoli, C., Luauté, J., Roy, A. C., & Farnè, A. (2016). Proprioception is necessary for body schema plasticity: Evidence from a deafferented patient. *Frontiers in Human Neuroscience, 10*, 272. doi:10.3389/fnhum.2016.00272.

Cardinali, L., Brozzoli, C., Urquizar, C., Salemme, R., Roy, A. C., & Farnè, A. (2011). When action is not enough: Tool-use reveals tactile-dependent access to body schema. *Neuropsychologia, 49*(13), 3750–3757. doi:10.1016/j.neuropsychologia.2011.09.033.

Cardinali, L., Frassinetti, F., Brozzoli, C., Urquizar, C., Roy, A. C., & Farnè, A. (2009). Tool-use induces morphological updating of the body schema. *Current Biology, 19*(12), R478–R479. doi:10.1016/j.cub.2009.05.009.

Cardinali, L., Jacobs, S., Brozzoli, C., Frassinetti, F., Roy, A. C., & Farnè, A. (2012). Grab an object with a tool and change your body: Tool-use-dependent changes of body representation for action. *Experimental Brain Research, 218*(2), 259–271. doi:10.1007/s00221-012-3028-5.

Cimmino, R. L., Spitoni, G., Serino, A., Antonucci, G., Catagni, M., Camagni, M., et al. (2013). Plasticity of body representations after surgical arm elongation in an achondroplasic patient. *Restorative Neurology and Neuroscience, 31*(3), 287–298. doi:10.3233/RNN-120286.

D'Alonzo, M., Clemente, F., & Cipriani, C. (2015). Vibrotactile stimulation promotes embodiment of an alien hand in amputees with phantom sensations. *IEEE Transactions on Neural Systems and Rehabilitation Engineering, 23*(3), 450–457. doi:10.1109/TNSRE.2014.2337952.

Davidson, P. R., & Wolpert, D. M. (2004). Internal models underlying grasp can be additively combined. *Experimental Brain Research, 155*(3), 334–340. doi:10.1007/s00221-003-1730-z.

Davoli, C. C., Brockmole, J. R., & Witt, J. K. (2012). Compressing perceived distance with remote tool-use: Real, imagined, and remembered. *Journal of Experimental Psychology, 38*(1), 80–89. doi:10.1037/a0024981.

Desmurget, M., & Grafton, S. (2000). Forward modeling allows feedback control for fast reaching movements. *Trends in Cognitive Sciences*, *4*(11), 423–431. doi:10.1016/S1364-6613(00)01537-0.

de Vignemont, F. (2011). Embodiment, ownership and disownership. *Consciousness and Cognition*, *20*(1), 82–93. doi:10.1016/j.concog.2010.09.004.

de Vignemont, F. (in press). The extended body hypothesis. In A. Newen, L. de Bruin, & S. Gallagher (Eds.), *Oxford handbook of 4E cognition*. Oxford: Oxford University Press.

de Vignemont, F., Ehrsson, H. H., & Haggard, P. (2005). Bodily illusions modulate tactile perception. *Current Biology*, *15*(14), 1286–1290. doi:10.1016/j.cub.2005.06.067.

de Vignemont, F., & Farnè, A. (2010). Widening the body to rubber hands and tools: What's the difference? *Revue de Neuropsychologie*, *2*(3), 203–211.

Di Russo, F., Committeri, G., Pitzalis, S., Spitoni, G., Piccardi, L., Galati, G., et al. (2006). Cortical plasticity following surgical extension of lower limbs. *NeuroImage*, *30*(1), 172–183. doi:10.1016/j.neuroimage.2005.09.051.

Dijkerman, H. C., & de Haan, E. H. F. (2007). Somatosensory processes subserving perception and action. *Behavioral and Brain Sciences*, *30*(2), 189–239. doi:10.1017/S0140525X07001392.

Dijkerman, H. C., & Farnè, A. (2015). Sensorimotor and social aspects of peripersonal space. *Neuropsychologia*, *70*, 309–312. doi:10.1016/j.neuropsychologia.2015.03.005.

Ehrsson, H. H., Holmes, N. P., & Passingham, R. E. (2005). Touching a rubber hand: Feeling of body ownership is associated with activity in multisensory brain areas. *Journal of Neuroscience*, *25*(45), 10564–10573. doi:10.1523/JNEUROSCI.0800-05.2005.

Ehrsson, H. H., Rosén, B., Stockselius, A., Ragnö, C., Köhler, P., & Lundborg, G. (2008). Upper limb amputees can be induced to experience a rubber hand as their own. *Brain*, *131*(12), 3443–3452. doi:10.1093/brain/awn297.

Flanagan, J. R., Nakano, E., Imamizu, H., Osu, R., Yoshioka, T., & Kawato, M. (1999). Composition and decomposition of internal models in motor learning under altered kinematic and dynamic environments. *Journal of Neuroscience*, *19*(20), RC34.

Frak, V., Paulignan, Y., & Jeannerod, M. (2001). Orientation of the opposition axis in mentally simulated grasping. *Experimental Brain Research*, *136*(1), 120–127. doi:10.1007/s002210000583.

Fraser, C. (1984). Does an artificial limb become part of the user? *British Journal of Occupational Therapy*, *47*(2), 43–45.

Galli, G., Noel, J. P., Canzoneri, E., Blanke, O., & Serino, A. (2015). The wheelchair as a full-body tool extending the peripersonal space. *Frontiers in Psychology*, *6*, 639. doi:10.3389/fpsyg.2015.00639.

Ganesh, G., Yoshioka, T., Osu, R., & Ikegami, T. (2014). Immediate tool incorporation processes determine human motor planning with tools. *Nature Communications*, 5, 4524. doi:10.1038/ncomms5524.

Garbarini, F., Fossataro, C., Berti, A., Gindri, P., Romano, D., Pia, L., et al. (2015). When your arm becomes mine: Pathological embodiment of alien limbs using tools modulates own body representation. *Neuropsychologia*, 70, 402–413. doi:10.1016/j.neuropsychologia.2014.11.008.

Gaveau, V., Pisella, L., Priot, A.-E., Fukui, T., Rossetti, Y., Pélisson, D., et al. (2014). Automatic online control of motor adjustments in reaching and grasping. *Neuropsychologia*, 55, 25–40. doi:10.1016/j.neuropsychologia.2013.12.005.

Giummarra, M. J., Georgiou-Karistianis, N., Nicholls, M. E. R., Gibson, S. J., & Bradshaw, J. L. (2010). The phantom in the mirror: A modified rubber-hand illusion in amputees and normals. *Perception*, 39(1), 103–118. doi:10.1068/p6519.

Grush, R. (2004). The emulation theory of representation: Motor control, imagery, and perception. *Behavioral and Brain Sciences*, 27(3), 377–396. doi:10.1017/S0140525X04000093.

Head, H., & Holmes, G. (1911). Sensory disturbances from cerebral lesions. *Brain*, 34(2–3), 102–254. doi:10.1093/brain/34.2-3.102.

Heuer, H., & Hegele, M. (2015). Explicit and implicit components of visuo-motor adaptation: An analysis of individual differences. *Consciousness and Cognition*, 33, 156–169. doi:10.1016/j.concog.2014.12.013.

Imamizu, H., Miyauchi, S., Tamada, T., Sasaki, Y., Takino, R., Pütz, B., et al. (2000). Human cerebellar activity reflecting an acquired internal model of a new tool. *Nature*, 403(6766), 192–195. doi:10.1038/35003194.

Ioffe, M., Chernikova, L. A., & Ustinova, K. I. (2007). Role of cerebellum in learning postural tasks. *Cerebellum (London, England)*, 6(1), 87–94. doi:10.1080/14734220701216440.

Iriki, A., Tanaka, M., & Iwamura, Y. (1996). Coding of modified body schema during tool use by macaque postcentral neurones. *Neuroreport*, 7(14), 2325–2330.

Ishikawa, T., Tomatsu, S., Izawa, J., & Kakei, S. (2015). The cerebro-cerebellum: Could it be loci of forward models? *Neuroscience Research*, 104, 72–79. doi:10.1016/j.neures.2015.12.003.

Jovanov, K., Clifton, P., Mazalek, A., Nitsche, M., & Welsh, T. N. (2015). The limb-specific embodiment of a tool following experience. *Experimental Brain Research*, 233(9), 2685–2694. doi:10.1007/s00221-015-4342-5.

Kammers, M. P. M., Kootker, J. A., Hogendoorn, H., & Dijkerman, H. C. (2010). How many motoric body representations can we grasp? *Experimental Brain Research*, 202(1), 203–212. doi:10.1007/s00221-009-2124-7.

Kawato, M. (1999). Internal models for motor control and trajectory planning. *Current Opinion in Neurobiology*, *9*(6), 718–727. doi:10.1016/S0959-4388(99)00028-8.

Kilteni, K., Maselli, A., Kording, K. P., & Slater, M. (2015). Over my fake body: Body ownership illusions for studying the multisensory basis of own-body perception. *Frontiers in Human Neuroscience*, *9*, 141. doi:10.3389/fnhum.2015.00141.

Kluzik, J., Diedrichsen, J., Shadmehr, R., & Bastian, A. J. (2008). Reach adaptation: What determines whether we learn an internal model of the tool or adapt the model of our arm? *Journal of Neurophysiology*, *100*(3), 1455–1464. doi:10.1152/jn.90334 .2008.

Longo, M. R., & Haggard, P. (2010). An implicit body representation underlying human position sense. *Proceedings of the National Academy of Sciences of the United States of America*, *107*(26), 11727–11732. doi:10.1073/pnas.1003483107.

Makin, T. R., Holmes, N. P., & Ehrsson, H. H. (2008). On the other hand: Dummy hands and peripersonal space. *Behavioural Brain Research*, *191*(1), 1–10. doi:10.1016/j .bbr.2008.02.041.

Malfait, N., & Ostry, D. J. (2004). Is interlimb transfer of force-field adaptation a cognitive response to the sudden introduction of load? *Journal of Neuroscience*, *24*(37), 8084–8089. doi:10.1523/JNEUROSCI.1742-04.2004.

Martel, M., Cardinali, L., Jouffrais, C., Finos, L., Farnè, A., & Roy, A. C. (2014, April). *Proprioception alone drives body schema plasticity*. Presented at the Twenty-First Cognitive Neuroscience Society Annual Meeting, Boston, MA.

Martel, M., Cardinali, L., Roy, A. C., & Farnè, A. (2016). Tool-use: An open window into body representation and its plasticity. *Cognitive Neuropsychology*, *33*(1–2), 82–101. doi:10.1080/02643294.2016.1167678.

McDonnell, P. M., Scott, R. N., Dickison, J., Theriault, R. A., & Wood, B. (1989). Do artificial limbs become part of the user? New evidence. *Journal of Rehabilitation Research and Development*, *26*(2), 17–24.

Medina, J., & Coslett, H. B. (2010). From maps to form to space: Touch and the body schema. *Neuropsychologia*, *48*(3), 645–654. doi:10.1016/j.neuropsychologia.2009 .08.017.

Miall, R. C. (2002). Motor control, biological and theoretical. In M. A. Arbib (Ed.), *The handbook of brain theory and neural networks* (2nd ed., pp. 686–689). Cambridge, MA: MIT Press.

Miall, R. C., & Wolpert, D. M. (1996). Forward models for physiological motor control. *Neural Networks*, *9*(8), 1265–1279. doi:10.1016/S0893-6080(96)00035-4.

Michel, C., Gaveau, J., Pozzo, T., & Papaxanthis, C. (2013). Prism adaptation by mental practice. *Cortex*, *49*(8), 2249–2259. doi:10.1016/j.cortex.2012.11.008.

Miller, L. E., Longo, M. R., & Saygin, A. P. (2013). Tool use modulates both conscious and unconscious representations of body shape. Paper presented at ASSC17 in San Diego, CA.

Miller, L. E., Longo, M. R., & Saygin, A. P. (2014). Tool morphology constrains the effects of tool use on body representations. *Journal of Experimental Psychology: Human Perception and Performance, 40*(6), 2143–2153. doi:10.1037/a0037777.

Murray, C. D. (2004). An interpretative phenomenological analysis of the embodiment of artificial limbs. *Disability and Rehabilitation, 26*(16), 963–973. doi:10.1080/0 9638280410001696764.

Murray, C. D. (2008). Embodiment and prosthetics. In P. Gallagher, D. Desmond, & M. MacLachlan (Eds.), *Psychoprosthetics* (pp. 119–129). London: Springer.

Osiurak, F., & Massen, C. (2014). The cognitive and neural bases of human tool use. *Cognition, 5*, 1107. doi:10.3389/fpsyg.2014.01107.

Pazzaglia, M., Galli, G., Scivoletto, G., & Molinari, M. (2013). A functionally relevant tool for the body following spinal cord injury. *PLoS One, 8*(3), e58312. doi:10.1371/journal.pone.0058312.

Rieger, M. (2012). Internal models and body schema in tool use. *Zeitschrift fur Psychologie mit Zeitschrift fur Angewandte Psychologie, 220*(1), 50–52. doi:10.1027/2151 -2604/a000091.

Romano, D., Caffa, E., Hernandez-Arieta, A., Brugger, P., & Maravita, A. (2015). The robot hand illusion: Inducing proprioceptive drift through visuo-motor congruency. *Neuropsychologia, 70*, 414–420. doi:10.1016/j.neuropsychologia.2014.10.033.

Rosén, B., Ehrsson, H. H., Antfolk, C., Cipriani, C., Sebelius, F., & Lundborg, G. (2009). Referral of sensation to an advanced humanoid robotic hand prosthesis. *Scandinavian Journal of Plastic and Reconstructive Surgery and Hand Surgery, 43*(5), 260–266. doi:10.3109/02844310903113107.

Schmalzl, L., Kalckert, A., Ragnö, C., & Ehrsson, H. H. (2014). Neural correlates of the rubber hand illusion in amputees: A report of two cases. *Neurocase, 20*(4), 407–420. doi:10.1080/13554794.2013.791861.

Serino, A., Bassolino, M., Farnè, A., & Làdavas, E. (2007). Extended multisensory space in blind cane users. *Psychological Science, 18*(7), 642–648. doi:10.1111/j.1467 -9280.2007.01952.x.

Shadmehr, R., & Krakauer, J. W. (2008). A computational neuroanatomy for motor control. *Experimental Brain Research, 185*(3), 359–381. doi:10.1007/s00221-008-1280-5.

Shenton, J. T., Schwoebel, J., & Coslett, H. B. (2004). Mental motor imagery and the body schema: Evidence for proprioceptive dominance. *Neuroscience Letters, 370*(1), 19–24. doi:10.1016/j.neulet.2004.07.053.

Sposito, A., Bolognini, N., Vallar, G., & Maravita, A. (2012). Extension of perceived arm length following tool-use: Clues to plasticity of body metrics. *Neuropsychologia*, *50*(9), 2187–2194. doi:10.1016/j.neuropsychologia.2012.05.022.

Tarhan, L. Y., Watson, C. E., & Buxbaum, L. J. (2015). Shared and distinct neuroanatomic regions critical for tool-related action production and recognition: Evidence from 131 left-hemisphere stroke patients. *Journal of Cognitive Neuroscience*, *27*(12), 2491–2511. doi:10.1162/jocn_a_00876.

Tsakiris, M. (2010). My body in the brain: A neurocognitive model of body-ownership. *Neuropsychologia*, *48*(3), 703–712. doi:10.1016/j.neuropsychologia.2009.09.034.

Tsakiris, M., Carpenter, L., James, D., & Fotopoulou, A. (2010). Hands only illusion: Multisensory integration elicits sense of ownership for body parts but not for non-corporeal objects. *Experimental Brain Research*, *204*(3), 343–352. doi:10.1007/s00221-009-2039-3.

Tseng, Y.-W., Diedrichsen, J., Krakauer, J. W., Shadmehr, R., & Bastian, A. J. (2007). Sensory prediction errors drive cerebellum-dependent adaptation of reaching. *Journal of Neurophysiology*, *98*(1), 54–62. doi:10.1152/jn.00266.2007.

Witt, J. K., & Proffitt, D. R. (2008). Action-specific influences on distance perception: A role for motor simulation. *Journal of Experimental Psychology: Human Perception and Performance*, *34*(6), 1479–1492. doi:10.1037/a0010781.

Wolpert, D. M., Ghahramani, Z., & Jordan, M. I. (1995). An internal model for sensorimotor integration. *Science*, *269*(5232), 1880–1882.

Wolpert, D. M., & Kawato, M. (1998). Multiple paired forward and inverse models for motor control. *Neural Networks*, *11*(7–8), 1317–1329. doi:10.1016/S0893-6080(98)00066-5.

Wolpert, D. M., Miall, R. C., & Kawato, M. (1998). Internal models in the cerebellum. *Trends in Cognitive Sciences*, *2*(9), 338–347. doi:10.1016/S1364-6613(98)01221-2.

4 Body Representations and the Sense of Self

Matthew R. Longo

It has been widely observed that we perceive our bodies in two fundamentally different ways. First, we perceive our body from inside, as the seat of our sensations and the reference of the first-person perspective. Sensations experienced in this way, for example coming from the body surface or viscera, cannot be experienced by others in the same way one experiences them oneself, different from publically available sensations, such as visual and auditory impressions of external objects, which may be experienced in much the same way by several observers. Second, we also perceive our body as a physical object in the world, just like any other. This duality indicates two modes under which we can experience our body: (1) prereflectively, from the inside, as an object of immediate experience, or (2) from the outside, as a physical and biological stimulus and object of cognitive reflection.

The first of these modes describes a way in which our own body is unique, in which it is experienced in a way qualitatively different from all other forms of experience. The second mode, in contrast, describes a way in which our body is an unremarkable physical and biological object, perceived and experienced in much the same way as any other object in the world. This distinction has some similarities with that made by philosophers such as Cassam (1997), who emphasize the role of awareness of oneself as a *physical* object in shaping self-consciousness. It is certainly true that awareness of our body inherits many properties from the category PHYSICAL OBJECT, such as solidity or being affected by gravity. I wish to emphasize, however, the body's status as a *biological* object, and the more specific categories which this provides, such as of BODIES, which produce many more properties, such as engaging in digestion or having a pancreas.

Perhaps unsurprisingly, discussions of this duality have generally focused on the first mode of perceiving the body, showing a natural interest in the way in which our experience of our body is special and unlike other forms of perception and experience, rather than the way in which it is a mundane instance of more general processes. This has resulted, for instance, in a remarkable dissociation between research on the representation of one's own body (for reviews see, e.g., Longo, Azañón, & Haggard, 2010; Medina & Coslett, 2010) and research on the visual perception of other people's bodies (for review see, e.g., Peelen & Downing, 2007).

In this chapter, I wish to consider the second mode of experiencing the body, the ways in which the body is *not* special, but merely one body among an entire population of other bodies. I will consider this issue from three different perspectives. First, I will discuss research on different types of body representation, asking which represent *my* body and which bodies in general, and how these might interact. Second, I will discuss some evidence for shared representations of one's own body and of others' bodies, focusing on ways in which the categorization of my body as an instance of the wider categories of BODIES influences its representation. Finally, I will end with a speculative discussion of two ways in which bodily structure might be represented, either *absolutely* as a fully specified form, or *relatively* as a vector deviation from an average or typical body.

Which Body Representation Represents Me?

We appear to have a single, unified sense of self. While the experience of embodiment can be decomposed into distinct elements (Longo, Schüür, Kammers, Tsakiris, & Haggard, 2008), outside of unusual situations such as the split-brain (Sperry, 1968) our self seems to be highly integrated into a single, unified entity. We seem to have just a single self. Research on body representations, however, has revealed a striking diversity of distinct representations of the body (for reviews, see Schwoebel & Coslett, 2005; Longo, 2016). The most discussed distinction among body representations is that between the *body image* and *body schema* (Gallagher & Cole, 1995; Paillard, 1999; de Vignemont, 2010), but several other representations have also been identified, including the *superficial schema* (Coslett & Lie, 2004; Mancini, Longo, Iannetti, & Haggard, 2011) mediating localization of stimuli onto the body surface; the *body structural description* (Buxbaum & Coslett, 2001; Corradi-Dell'Acqua, Hesse, Rumiati, & Fink, 2008), underlying representation of the spatial layout of body parts; the *body model* (Longo & Haggard, 2010; Longo et al., 2010), specifying the metric properties of the body; and *body semantics* (Coslett, Saffran, & Schwoebel, 2002; Kemmerer & Tranel, 2008), underlying general knowledge about the body and words for body parts. The contrast between the unity of the self and the diversity of body representations raises a basic question: Which of these representations corresponds to my bodily self, which body representation represents *me*?

One approach to this question would be to deny that any single body representation ought to correspond to our bodily self. By analogy, we might observe that though a cake appears to have a unified existence as an integrated object, it is nevertheless comprised of distinct ingredients (flour, eggs, sugar, etc.). The question which of these ingredients corresponds to the "cakeness" of the final product is, of course, entirely spurious. Perhaps the bodily self, similarly, arises from the contributions of the various individual body representations (body image, body schema, etc.) and, like the cake, has a distinct existence over and above the sum of its ingredients. Thus, the bodily self might be a type of gestalt, being more than—and different in kind from—the sum of its component parts (Koffka, 1935).

While this interpretation is difficult to exclude entirely, it does seem that certain body representations are at least closer to our subjective bodily self than others. For example, whereas the body image is thought of as an intrinsically subjective representation of our bodily properties, the body schema is thought of as inaccessible to conscious awareness and used to guide motor behavior. The question of whether the body schema makes any contribution to the self notwithstanding, it is impossible to imagine a situation in which the body image makes no such contribution. Perhaps we might say that even if the six cups of flour do not correspond directly to the cakeness of the finished pastry, they nevertheless fill this role much better than does the pinch of cinnamon added at the end. So too, the body image, even if not in a one-to-one relation with the bodily self, seems almost certain to be more central to it than the body schema.

Another way of approaching this problem is to think about the seeming unity of visual experience, alongside the diversity of visual representations, from neurons with center-surround receptive fields in the lateral geniculate nucleus, to simple, complex, and hypercomplex neurons in the visual cortex (Hubel & Wiesel, 1998). In this case, the different types of representations appear to be arranged hierarchically, with each stage reflecting a computational generalization upon the previous stage. Thus simple cells (preferring oriented edges at specific locations) can be constructed from a population of center-surround cells (preferring points of light in specific locations), complex cells (preferring oriented edges at *any* location) from a population of simple cells, and so forth (Hubel & Wiesel, 1998). Progressive stages of visual processing, then, move closer and closer to our subjective experience of the world, though each stage in this sequence is causally necessary to the final percept. Might body representations be similarly organized hierarchically, with the top level of the hierarchy corresponding to the bodily self?

I recently suggested that at least some body representations are organized hierarchically, specifically in terms of the spatial scale at which they represent the body (Longo, 2015a). At the lowest level, the somatosensory system represents the body as a pixelated map of individual receptive fields on the skin, while at the highest level, the body is represented visually as an integrated whole. And, indeed, our subjective bodily self certainly corresponds more closely to a visual depiction of the entire body than to the receptive fields of individual somatosensory neurons. Nevertheless, it does not seem that a hierarchy of this kind can fully capture the diversity of body representations. There is no single dimension along which body representations differ. The body schema, mediating control of skilled action, seems to differ qualitatively from, for example, the superficial schema mediating localization of stimuli on the skin surface.

Higher levels of the visual system offer another way of thinking about this problem. Here, the hierarchical processing seen at lower levels breaks down and brain areas appear specialized for processing specific aspects of stimuli. For example, area V4 appears specialized for color processing (Lueck et al., 1989), area MT for motion processing (Zeki et al., 1991), and the fusiform face area (FFA) for face processing (Kanwisher, McDermott, & Chun, 1997). When we see someone we know, we may simultaneously recognize their identity, notice the color of their cheeks, and process the motion of their mouth. All these features, moreover, may be aspects of a single, unified experience of seeing that person. Here, we would not want to ask which brain area (V4, MT, or FFA) represents this experience. Rather, we would say that each area processes a different aspect of the stimulus and these are then merged into a unified percept through a process of "binding" (Treisman & Gelade, 1980).

Perhaps, analogously, the various body representations might process distinct aspects of our experience of the body, with the seemingly unified bodily self resulting from a process of binding of these several features. For example, the body schema might contribute information about body posture, the body image about the body's visual appearance, the body structural description about the spatial layout of body parts, and the body model about the metric scale of the body. Here, again, we would not say that any single body representation corresponds directly to the bodily self. Rather, our bodily self would have several qualitatively distinct characteristics (e.g., posture, size, appearance), each of which would be processed by a different body representation. Against this interpretation, however, the current descriptions of body representations does not seem conducive to thinking about each as processing a single dimension of bodily properties or state. For example, the body schema is usually discussed not as a simple representation of posture, but as a more general representation of the disposition and state of the body underlying skilled action (e.g., Paillard, 1999; Gallagher & Cole, 1995). It is linked to a cognitive function (motor control) rather than a specific aspect of the body. In other cases, different body representations appear to represent the same dimensions, such as descriptions of the body image and body model both including information about body size and shape, though with different distortions (Longo & Haggard, 2010).

Thus far, I have discussed three types of potential relation between the bodily self and the various body representations. First, body representations might be like the ingredients in a cake, which lose their independent identity to form a whole fundamentally different from any of the constituent ingredients. Second, body representations might be like the hierarchically-structured levels of processing at early stages of the visual system, with each representation being a generalization upon the preceding one, and with the final stage corresponding to the bodily self. Third, body representations might be like the specialized modules at higher levels of the visual system, each dedicated to processing one aspect of the body, which are bound into an integrated percept with each nevertheless preserving its distinct character.

Finally, I wish to suggest that a better way to think about this relation from a distinction raised by Longo and colleagues (2010). We distinguished between two main classes of higher-order body representation. In analogy to somato*sensation*, we referred to these classes as somato*perception* and somato*representation*. Somatoperception refers to the construction of higher-level percepts of the body and objects in contact with the body, involving representations such as the body schema, body image, and body model. Somatorepresentation, in contrast, refers to abstract beliefs, knowledge, and attitudes about bodies generally and one's own body in particular, related to the body as an object of third-person perception and cognitive reflection, relating to body representations such as the body structural description and body semantics. Returning to the discussion above about the two modes by which the body can be experienced, somatoperception corresponds to the first mode, building on the body's unique status as a private source of first-person information. Somatorepresentation, in contrast, corresponds to the second mode, relating to the body's existence as a physical object in the world just like any other and its membership in categories such as that of human bodies or mammalian bodies.

Given the distinction between somatoperception and somatorepresentation, it is very natural to relate the bodily self to the former, rather than the latter. Our sense of self seems much more intimately connected to our immediate perceptual experience of embodiment than to our cognitive reflection on our body or our categorization of our body as an instance of more general types. For instance, we take for granted that our body has a spleen, based on our knowledge of bodies generally. Most of us have no experience perceiving or interacting with our spleen, nor any sensations or other experiences which we link to it. Our belief in our spleen seems entirely inherited from abstract knowledge we have about superordinate categories to which our body belongs. In this sense, it seems to remain entirely intellectual and have little or no impact on our bodily self.

Evidence for Shared Body Representations

Is all somatorepresentation like our knowledge of our spleen in this respect, completely intellectual and removed from our sense of self? In the remainder of this chapter I will discuss some ways in which it may not be and our categorization of our body may influence our bodily self. In particular, I will focus on the relation between the way we represent our body in particular and our more general representation of human bodies.

A first place one might start to think about shared body representations is in terms of mirror neurons, which appear to show some level of mapping between actions of one's own body and those of other's bodies (Rizzolatti & Craighero, 2004). Jeannerod and Pacherie (2004) develop the idea that the human mirror system implies the existence of shared action representations between self and other, *naked intentions* which specify the content of an action but leave ambiguous whether the actor is oneself or someone else. More directly relevant to the present discussion, de Vignemont (2014) extends this idea to bodies, asking whether there are similar shared representations of bodies, which may specify the form or characteristics of a body but leave open whose body it is, one's own or someone else's.

My concern here, however, is somewhat different from de Vignemont's, who focuses on the feeling of body ownership, whether a body is "mine" or someone else's. My focus in asking whether there are shared body representations is on how the categorization of one's own body as a member of the larger category BODIES is affected by the properties we consider prototypical of that category. I will discuss four lines of evidence which might be taken as suggesting the operation of shared body representations in this sense.

Perceptual and conceptual distortions. One line of evidence for shared body representations comes from distortions common to one's own body and other bodies. For example, recent results have shown overestimations of the location of the knuckles in the hand (Longo, 2015b; Margolis & Longo, 2015). Asked to point to the location on the palm directly opposite to the knuckle of each finger, participants judged the knuckles of the nonthumb fingers as dramatically farther forward in the hand than their actual location (Longo, 2015b). Importantly, very similar results were found when participants judged the locations of the knuckles of the experimenter's hand. This suggests that the biases in judging knuckle location do not reflect a perceptual distortion of the participant's hand in particular, but rather their more abstract understanding of the configuration of hands in general. More critically in the present context, they also show that a common representation of hand configuration underlies both the representation of one's own and of others' hands.

Other recent results have shown that not all distortions of body representation have this characteristic. Longo and Haggard (2010) developed a paradigm for measuring implicit representations of the size and shape of the hand underlying position sense, the perception of the location of the body in external space. The participant's hand is covered by an occluding board and they use a long baton to judge the location of different landmarks on the hand (i.e., the knuckles and fingertips) underneath the board. By comparing the judged locations of each landmark, perceptual maps of hand size and shape can be constructed and compared to actual hand form. Longo and Haggard (2010) found that these maps showed highly stereotyped patterns of distortion. Specifically, the length of the fingers (i.e., the distance between the knuckle and fingertip) is substantially underestimated, whereas overall hand width (i.e., the distance between the knuckles of the index and little fingers) is substantially overestimated. Thus, overall, these maps reveal a squat, fat hand representation, as shown in figure 4.1.

Do these distortions represent a perceptual distortion of the participant's own hand specifically, or a conceptual distortion of hands in general? The distal mislocalization of the knuckles, described above, provides a natural interpretation of the underestimation of finger length. Indeed, the magnitude of knuckle mislocalization is correlated across participants with the

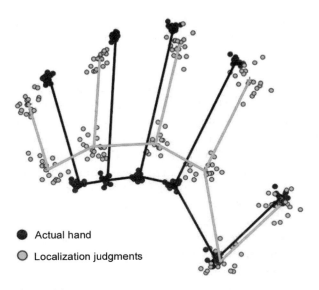

● Actual hand
○ Localization judgments

Figure 4.1
Perceptual maps underlying human position sense from experiment 1 of Longo and Haggard (2010). The black points show the actual locations of the knuckles and fingertips from each participant, put into Procrustes alignment to show average hand shape across individuals (black lines). The gray points and lines show the judged locations of these landmarks, again in Procrustes alignment to show the average perceptual map (gray lines).

magnitude of underestimation of finger length (Longo, Mattioni, & Ganea, 2015). As the mislocalization of the knuckles is not specific to one's own hand, this suggests that the underestimation of finger length may not be either. Critically, however, the mislocalization of the knuckles cannot account for the overestimation of hand width. To investigate the extent to which the distorted hand maps reflect perceptual versus conceptual distortions, Longo and colleagues (2015) asked participants to localize either the knuckles and fingertips of their own hand under the occluding board, or those of a prosthetic rubber hand which they viewed for ten seconds before it was covered. Underestimation of finger length was present for both the participants' own hands and the rubber hand, and was of similar magnitude. Conversely, overestimation of hand width was apparent only for the participants' own hands and not the rubber hand. Similar results were found by Saulton and colleagues (Saulton, Longo, Wong, Bülthoff, & de la Rosa, 2016). This dissociation suggests the existence of both perceptual and conceptual distortions of body representations underlying position sense.

Phantom limbs in congenital limb absence. A second potential line of evidence for shared body representations comes from the existence of phantom limbs in congenital limb absence. Phantom experiences are nearly universal in the case of amputated limbs (Melzack, 1990; Ramachandran & Hirstein, 1998), which may result from a lifetime's experience with the limb. Phantom limbs have also been reported in cases of congenital limb absence (e.g., Brugger et al., 2000; Saadah & Melzack, 1994; Vetter & Weinstein, 1967; Weinstein & Sersen, 1961; Weinstein, Sersen, & Vetter, 1964), though such reports have also been challenged (e.g., Simmel, 1966).

What factors might cause phantom limbs in cases of congenital limb absence? One possibility is an innately specific body image (Melzack, 1990; Gallagher, Butterworth, Lew, & Cole, 1998). If a central representation of bodily structure were genetically specified, independent from the actual development of the physical body itself, this innate representation might produce phantom experiences when, for whatever reason, the actual development of the body diverges from this innate plan, as in congenital limb absence. Brugger and colleagues (2000), however, offer another possibility, that phantoms might arise from generalization from the visual experience of other people. A person born without a limb will nevertheless interact with and perceive innumerable other people throughout their lives, most of whom will have all four limbs. This will presumably result in the formation of a category of HUMAN BODIES, including two arms and two legs. Given that their own body is clearly also a member of this category, the representation of all four limbs may thus be inherited from this superordinate category, even if the individual themselves has only three limbs. Conceivably, this could result in the experience of phantom experiences of a limb that has never actually existed.

To my knowledge, no existing research strongly differentiates between these different interpretations of the origins of phantom limbs in cases of congenital limb absence. In one study, Longo, Long, and Haggard (2012) investigated implicit hand maps of a congenitally absent limb in an individual, C.L., born without a left arm, using the paradigm described above (Longo & Haggard, 2010). Because this paradigm does not involve any stimulation delivered to the occluded hand, it is uniquely suitable to measurement of the representation of a nonexistent body part. Perceptual maps could thus be obtained for C.L.'s left hand, which she felt as being located underneath the occluding board. Assuming that C.L.'s left hand would have had the same size and shape as her intact right hand, she showed very similar distortions for the representation of both hands, with large over-estimation of hand width and underestimation of finger length. Because these distorted hand maps are unlikely to be similar to hands that C.L. has visually experienced in other people, Longo and colleagues (Longo et al., 2012) suggested that these results argue against her phantom experiences reflecting visual generalization. Nonetheless, the possible role of visual generalization in the experience of phantom sensations in cases of congenital limb absence is another potential source of evidence for shared body representations.

The media and body image distortion. Another possible piece of evidence for shared body representations comes from the putative role of exposure to extreme body types in the mass media in causing distortions of body image (Becker & Hamburg, 1996; Derenne & Beresin, 2006), such as those seen in eating disorders (Treasure, Claudino, & Zucker, 2010) and body dysmorphic disorder (Phillips, 2005). Epidemiological studies have provided clear evidence for a causal influence of exposure to Western media depictions of bodies on bodily dissatisfaction and development of disordered eating (e.g., Field et al., 1999; Becker, Burwell, Gilman, Herzog, & Hamburg, 2002). Unfortunately, however, little experimental research has investigated the direct effects of seeing other peoples' bodies on one's own body image. One experimental study (Hamilton & Waller, 1993), however, did find that exposure to images of models from fashion magazines produced rapid increases in perceived body size, though the stimuli used were largely uncontrolled. Overall, research on media effects does suggest important connections between the representation of one's own body and that of others, though further experimental research is needed to understand this connection.

Prototypical bodies. Finally, I wish to discuss the possibility that the membership of our own body in the wider category BODIES may bias the perception of our own body toward the characteristics that we consider typical for bodies more generally. What is the relation between our representation of the characteristics of a specific object and our representation of the typical characteristics of objects of that type? In an elegant series of studies over the past three decades, Janellen Huttenlocher and her colleagues have addressed this question, showing that categorical information systematically biases estimation across a range of domains.

Consider, for example, the study of Huttenlocher, Hedges, and Duncan (1991). Participants were shown a sheet of paper with a large circle containing a small black dot for one second, then given a new sheet with an empty circle and asked to mark the location they judged the dot as having been located. The results showed that judgments were systematically biased. Participants appear to have implicitly subdivided the circle into quadrants by imposing boundaries along the vertical and horizontal meridians. Responses were biased in the direction of the center of mass of each quadrant. Huttenlocher and colleagues (1991) interpret these results as reflecting the existence of "spatial prototypes" at the center of each quadrant. The final location estimate will thus reflect a Bayesian-weighted integration of fine-grain information about the specific stimulus seen and categorical information. Indeed, when a visual interference task was administered between stimulus presentation and response, which should reduce the weight given to fine-grained information, the magnitude of the bias toward the quadrant centers was increased. Thus, participants' memory of stimulus location was systematically distorted by the presence of categorical information.

Similarly, Huttenlocher, Newcombe, and Sandberg (1994) showed children a toy being hidden in a long, thin sandbox. After a delay, the child was allowed to search for the toy. Ten-year-olds, like adults, appeared to implicitly subdivide the sandbox at the center into two categories. Searches were biased toward the center of each half (i.e., 25 percent of the way from each edge). In contrast, four- and six-year-olds appeared not to subdivide the sandbox into two halves. Their searches were biased toward the center of the sandbox. In both cases, memory for the location of the toy was systematically biased by categorical information, with developmental change in how the sandbox was segmented into regions.

While the two examples given so far both concern judgments of spatial location, analogous biases can also be found in very different domains. For example, Huttenlocher, Hedges, and Vevea (2000) showed participants images of schematic fish that varied in fatness. When asked to reproduce the fatness of a previously seen fish, participants judged the fish as closer in fatness to the average of all fish seen than it actually was. This suggests that the memory trace of the specific stimulus being judged is integrated with categorical information about the distribution of stimuli in general.

Huttenlocher and colleagues (1991, 2000) argue that where memory is noisy, accuracy can be maximized by integrating both fine-grained information about a specific stimulus with category-level information. Though this results in some level of systematic bias, overall performance will nevertheless be higher.

What are the implications of such category effects for the body image? Is our experience of our own body similarly biased by category-level information about the distribution of bodies in general? A handful of studies have provided some evidence that this may indeed be the case (Cornelissen, Johns, & Tovée, 2013; Cornelissen, Bester, Cairns, Tovée, & Cornelissen, 2015; Kuskowska-Wolk, & Rössner, 1989). For example, Cornelissen and colleagues (2015) measured body image by having participants judge whether images of bodies were fatter or thinner than they were, estimating the body mass index (BMI) that they perceive themselves as being and comparing it to their actual BMI. Interestingly, there was a systematic relation between actual and judged BMI, with thin participants overestimating their body weight and heavy participants underestimating. Thus, in both cases, there was a perceptual bias in the direction of an average body. This effect is highly similar to the effects described by Huttenlocher and colleagues (1991, 1994, 2000) in very different domains. These results suggest that our subjective experience of our body itself may also be shaped by a combination of both immediate sensory information about our body and categorical information about bodies in general.

Absolute and Relative Body Representations

In the final section of this chapter, I will discuss two ways in which body representations might be specified. On the one hand, representations such as the body image could be specified absolutely, in a self-contained manner that requires no additional information or linkage to any other representation. On the other hand, such representations could be specified in terms of the ways in which they differ from other bodies, such as from an average or prototypical body. As an example of this distinction, consider two ways in which the height of a person might be reported, either as "João is 180 centimeters tall" or as "João is 1.5 standard deviations taller than an average Portuguese man." The former description is absolute, requiring no further information; the latter is relative, requiring information about the distribution of heights of Portuguese men to determine João's height in centimeters.

Quetelet and l'homme moyen. Before further discussing the concept of a relative body representation, I wish first to introduce some nineteenth century conceptions of statistical variation which, though of purely historical interest statistically, have interesting conceptual analogues in the present context. The Belgian scientist Adolphe Quetelet (1796–1874) was among the first to apply methods of statistics and probability to social issues. My description follows the excellent discussions of Quetelet, his antecedents, and his influence on subsequent developments in the social sciences in Porter (1986) and Stigler (1986). Previous work had demonstrated highly lawful regularities in the distributions of observations in cases such as errors of astronomical observation of star transit times and gambling contexts, such as coin flips. Examining rates of events such as births, deaths, murders, and suicides, Quetelet was struck by their year-on-year regularity, which suggested to him the operation of laws of society, analogous to physical laws, which he believed could be developed into a rigorous "social physics" (*physique sociale*).

The predictable rate at which, for example, people in France were convicted of crimes suggested that the French had a measureable proclivity, or penchant, for criminality, independent of the characteristics of any individual French person. Moreover, that such rates seemed to differ from place to place, for example between the Low Countries and France, suggested the existence of different national types. This led Quetelet in 1835 to the introduction of his famous construct *l'homme moyen*, or the average man, a hypothetical being who represented a particular social type, for example the average Frenchman. The average man (or woman) embodied all the physical characteristics and moral and behavioral penchants seen in a given type, which could be estimated by calculating the average value or rate across a large number of examples. Porter describes the concept thus:

> Quetelet's most celebrated construct, *l'homme moyen*, or the average man, was similarly dependent on his belief in the regularity of statistical events. Quetelet maintained that this abstract being, defined in terms of the average of all human attributes in a given country, could be treated as the "type" of the nation, the representative of a society in social science comparable to the center of gravity in physics. After all, deviations from the average must necessarily cancel themselves out whenever a great number of instances is considered. Hence for the average man, "all things will occur in conformity with the mean results obtained for a society. If one seeks to establish, in some way, the basis of a social physics, it is he whom one should consider, without disturbing oneself with particular cases or anomalies, and without studying whether some given individual can undergo a greater or lesser development in one of his faculties." Quetelet allowed his average man a temporal dimension as well as physical and moral ones, thus giving him a mean rate of growth and moral development over his average life. (Porter, 1986, pp. 52–53)

The most interesting aspect of Quetelet's reasoning in the present context concerns his conception of individual differences between people. Not every Frenchman will have the same characteristics or penchants as the average Frenchman (in the same way that while the average American may have 2.3 children, no individual American does). What then is the relationship between any specific Frenchman and *l'homme moyen francais*? Quetelet was struck by the fact that the distribution of individual differences in a population mirrored the Gaussian distribution known to characterize errors in several domains. For example, Friedrich Wilhelm Bessel had shown in 1818 that the distribution of disagreements between astronomers' estimates of ascensions and declinations of celestial bodies was well described by a Gaussian, normal distribution (Stigler, 1986). Similarly, the binomial distribution shows that errors in estimating the true probability of a flipped coin coming up heads also have a Gaussian distribution. For example, Quetelet calculated that a fair coin flipped 999 times would come up heads exactly 481 times 1.27 percent of the time. The presence of a Gaussian distribution of observations around a mean was thus, to Quetelet, a clear sign of error-ridden estimation of a mean value.

To investigate whether attributes of people in a population are similarly distributed, Quetelet analyzed the chest circumference of 5,738 Scottish soldiers, data he had obtained from an article in a Scottish medical journal (the data had likely been collected to guide tailoring of uniforms). He found that the distribution of chest sizes was also well described by a Gaussian distribution. Similarly, an analysis of the heights of French military conscripts also showed good fit to a Gaussian distribution. Such examples led Quetelet to associate such individual differences with errors. The average Scottish soldier had a chest circumference of just under forty inches. The deviations from this value seen in individual soldiers thus reflected their imperfections, their failure to match the ideal type of the Scottish soldier. As an analogy, Quetelet asks us to imagine one thousand copies being made of an ancient statue, *The Gladiator*. While the average shape of the thousand replicas may closely match the original, any individual replica is likely to have various imperfections, leading it to deviate from the true statue. Deviations of individual people from their average type can, according to Quetelet, be similarly thought of as imperfections or errors.

As I mentioned above, Quetelet's views are not consistent with modern conceptions of probability, statistics, or sociology. They reflect the conceptual confusions of early nineteenth century social science, groping toward more sophisticated understanding. Gaussian variability is no longer taken as a sign of "error," nor as evidence that the mean value has an independent existence as a natural kind. I do think, however, that Quetelet's conception is of *psychological* interest as a model of our *mental representation* of social categories. The causes of social phenomenon to Quetelet were of two sorts, those given by types (constant causes), such as *l'homme moyen*, and those given by errors (accidental causes), the failure of individuals to perfectly emulate their type. The height of a given Frenchman would, thus, be the vector sum of the height of the average Frenchman (i.e., constant cause) and the deviation of the specific individual from that average (i.e., accidental cause); the chest size of a given Scottish soldier would be the vector sum of the chest size of the average Scottish soldier and the deviation of the specific soldier from that average. As Porter writes, "Once the contribution of the constant causes was known, that of the accidental causes could be found through a process of vector subtraction" (1986, p. 56).

On this way of thinking, an individual, with all their physical characteristics, behavioral penchants, and moral proclivities is simply a vector deviation in some high-dimensional space from the average person of their type. While this may not be a useful way of thinking about actual biological or social variability, I believe it is a useful way to think about the mental representation of such variability. Quetelet's distinction between constant and accidental causes bears an interesting correspondence to the distinction between prototypes and fine-grained information drawn by Huttenlocher and colleagues (1991, 2000), discussed above. It raises the question whether the representation of a given object is *absolute* and self-contained, specifying exact values for represented dimensions, or in contrast is *relative* to a prototypical object, specifying only the ways in which the specific object differs from the prototype.

Norm-based coding of facial identity. Recent research on the visual perception of facial identity has provided intriguing evidence supporting relative representation of faces. For example, Leopold and colleagues (Leopold, O'Toole, Vetter, & Blanz, 2001) calculated the vector deviation in image space between a specific face and the average face across a number of individuals and used this deviation to create "antifaces." The antiface of an individual is a stimulus located in in exactly the opposite direction from the average face as that individual. Adaptation to an antiface produced identity-specific aftereffects. For example, adaptation to anti-Jim resulted in an average face appearing to look like Jim, whereas adaptation to a different antiface (e.g., anti-Fred) did not. A subsequent study by Rhodes and Jeffery (2006) showed that even when the perceptual distances between different faces are precisely controlled that adaptation still specifically affects the axis running through the average face. Because Jim and anti-Jim appear to be very different faces, the finding that there is a specific connection between the two suggests that they are represented as opposite poles of a single axis in "face space" (Tsao & Freiwald, 2006). Indeed, some neurons

in the temporal cortex of monkeys have been found to respond systematically to the distance between a presented face and an average face (Freiwald
& Tsao, 2010).

These results suggest that the representation of facial structure is relative,
rather than absolute. The representation of a specific face appears to be
given as the average face plus a vector deviation from that average, rather
than as an absolute specification of the shape of that individual's face.

The body image as a residual deviation from the average body. The research
described in the previous section suggested that our visual representation
of the identity of faces relies on such a relative, vector-based mechanism.
Other research has suggested that similar mechanisms operate for the visual
perception of identity from bodies (e.g., Rhodes, Jeffery, Boeing, & Calder,
2013). To my knowledge, however, no research has specifically investigated
the connection between such norm-based visual representations of faces or
bodies and the body image.

It is possible that these mechanisms are purely visual and that our body
image is an entirely separate representation specified absolutely, by a direct
representation of a three-dimensional form. I wish to suggest, in contrast, that
the body image is relative, representing the body as a vector deviation from
a representation of the average 3-D form of bodies in general, what following
Quetelet we might call *le corps moyen*, or the average body. On this view, our
own body is specified as a residual deviation from this average body, the "accidental causes" given by the vector deviation of one's body from the average.

I do not know of any data that directly indicates whether the body image
is absolute or relative. However, the idea of a relative body image has potentially interesting implications for understanding distortions of body image
in conditions such as eating disorders. For example, despite their frequent
insistence on being overweight, women with anorexia have on the whole
not been found to show different misperception of their body shape than
healthy controls (e.g., Cornelissen et al., 2013). From the perspective of relative body image, however, this pattern might result from misrepresentation
of the average body as thinner than it actually is, alongside veridical representation of one's own body, which should lead the vector deviation of the
self from the average to elongate. The insistence that they are overweight
might correspond to the length of this vector. This interpretation provides
a natural interpretation for the role of vision of bodies in mass media on
body image (e.g., Becker & Hamburg, 1996), which may alter the representation of an average body and thus lengthen the vector representing one's
own body as a deviation from this average.

Acknowledgments

The author was supported by European Research Council Starter Grant BODYBUILDING (ERC-2013-StG-336050) under the FP7.

References

Becker, A. E., & Hamburg, P. (1996). Culture, the media, and eating disorders. *Harvard Review of Psychiatry*, 4(3), 163–167.

Becker, A. E., Burwell, R. A., Gilman, S. E., Herzog, D. B., & Hamburg, P. (2002). Eating behaviours and attitudes following prolonged exposure to television among ethnic Fijian adolescent girls. *British Journal of Psychiatry*, 180(6), 509–514. doi:10.1192/bjp.180.6.509.

Brugger, P., Kollias, S. S., Müri, R. M., Crelier, G., Hepp-Reymond, M.-C., & Regard, M. (2000). Beyond re-membering: Phantom sensations of congenitally absent limbs. *Proceedings of the National Academy of Sciences of the United States of America*, 97(11), 6167–6172. doi:10.1073/pnas.100510697.

Buxbaum, L. J., & Coslett, H. B. (2001). Specialized structural descriptions for human body parts: Evidence from autotopagnosia. *Cognitive Neuropsychology*, 18(4), 289–306. doi:10.1080/02643290042000071.

Cassam, Q. (1997). *Self and world*. Oxford: Clarendon Press.

Cornelissen, K. K., Bester, A., Cairns, P., Tovée, M. J., & Cornelissen, P. L. (2015). The influence of personal BMI on body size estimations and sensitivity to body size change in anorexia spectrum disorders. *Body Image*, 13, 75–85. doi:10.1016/j.bodyim.2015.01.001.

Cornelissen, P. L., Johns, A., & Tovée, M. J. (2013). Body size over-estimation in women with anorexia nervosa is not qualitatively different from female controls. *Body Image*, 10(1), 103–111. doi:10.1016/j.bodyim.2012.09.003.

Corradi-Dell'Acqua, C., Hesse, M. D., Rumiati, R. I., & Fink, G. R. (2008). Where is a nose with respect to a foot? The left posterior parietal cortex processes spatial relationships among body parts. *Cerebral Cortex*, 18(2), 2879–2890. doi:10.1093/cercor/bhn046.

Coslett, H. B., & Lie, E. (2004). Bare hands and attention: Evidence for a tactile representation of the human body. *Neuropsychologia*, 42(14), 1865–1876. doi:10.1016/j.neuropsychologia.2004.06.002.

Coslett, H. B., Saffran, E. M., & Schwoebel, J. (2002). Knowledge of the human body: A distinct semantic domain. *Neurology*, 59(3), 357–363. doi:10.1212/WNL.59.3.357.

Derenne, J. L., & Beresin, E. V. (2006). Body image, media, and eating disorders. *Academic Psychiatry*, *30*(3), 257–261. doi:10.1176/appi.ap.30.3.257.

de Vignemont, F. (2010). Body schema and body image—pros and cons. *Neuropsychologia*, *48*, 669–680.

de Vignemont, F. (2014). Shared body representations and the "whose" system. *Neuropsychologia*, *55*, 128–136.

Field, A. E., Cheung, L., Wolf, A. M., Herzog, D. B., Gortmaker, S. L., & Colditz, G. A. (1999). Exposure to the mass media and weight concerns among girls. *Pediatrics*, *103*(3), e36.

Freiwald, W. A., & Tsao, D. Y. (2010). Functional compartmentalization and viewpoint generalization within the macaque face-processing system. *Science*, *330*(6005), 845–851. doi:10.1126/science.1194908.

Funk, M., Shiffrar, M., & Brugger, P. (2005). Hand movement observation by individuals born without hands: Phantom limb experience constrains visual limb perception. *Experimental Brain Research*, *164*(3), 341–346. doi:10.1007/s00221-005-2255-4.

Gallagher, S., Butterworth, G. E., Lew, A., & Cole, J. (1998). Hand-mouth coordination, congenital absence of limb, and evidence for innate body schemas. *Brain and Cognition*, *38*(1), 53–65. doi:10.1006/brcg.1998.1020.

Gallagher, S., & Cole, J. (1995). Body image and body schema in a deafferented subject. *Journal of Mind and Behavior*, *16*(4), 369–390.

Hamilton, K., & Waller, G. (1993). Media influences on body size estimation in anorexia and bulimia: An experimental study. *British Journal of Psychiatry*, *162*(6), 837–840. doi:10.1192/bjp.162.6.837.

Hubel, D. H., & Wiesel, T. N. (1998). Early exploration of the visual cortex. *Neuron*, *20*(3), 401–412. doi:10.1016/S0896-6273(00)80984-8.

Huttenlocher, J., Hedges, L. V., & Duncan, S. (1991). Categories and particulars: Prototype effects in estimating spatial location. *Psychological Review*, *98*(3), 352–376. doi:10.1037/0033-295X.98.3.352.

Huttenlocher, J., Hedges, L. V., & Vevea, J. L. (2000). Why do categories affect stimulus judgment? *Journal of Experimental Psychology: General*, *129*(2), 220–241. doi:10.1037/0096-3445.129.2.220.

Huttenlocher, J., Newcombe, N., & Sandberg, E. H. (1994). The coding of spatial location in young children. *Cognitive Psychology*, *27*(2), 115–147. doi:10.1006/cogp.1994.1014.

Jeannerod, M., & Pacherie, E. (2004). Agency, simulation and self-identification. *Mind & Language*, *19*(2), 113–146. doi:10.1111/j.1468-0017.2004.00251.x.

Kanwisher, N., McDermott, J., & Chun, M. M. (1997). The fusiform face area: A module in human extrastriate cortex specialized for face perception. *Journal of Neuroscience, 17*(11), 4302–4311.

Kemmerer, D., & Tranel, D. (2008). Searching for the elusive neural substrates of body part terms: A neuropsychological study. *Cognitive Neuropsychology, 25*(4), 601–629. doi:10.1080/02643290802247052.

Koffka, K. (1935). *Principles of Gestalt psychology*. London: Lund Humphries.

Kuskowska-Wolk, A., & Rössner, S. (1989). The "true" prevalence of obesity: A comparison of objective weight and height measures versus self-reported and calibrated data. *Scandinavian Journal of Primary Health Care, 7*(2), 79–82. doi:10.3109/02813438909088651.

Leopold, D. A., O'Toole, A. J., Vetter, T., & Blanz, V. (2001). Prototype-referenced shape encoding reveled by high-level aftereffects. *Nature Neuroscience, 4*(1), 89–94. doi:10.1038/82947.

Leopold, D. A., Bondar, I. V., & Giese, M. A. (2006). Norm-based face encoding by single neurons in the monkey inferotemporal cortex. *Nature, 442*(7102), 572–575. doi:10.1038/nature04951.

Longo, M. R. (2015a). Implicit and explicit body representations. *European Psychologist, 20*(1), 6–15. doi:10.1027/1016-9040/a000198.

Longo, M. R. (2015b). Intuitive anatomy: Distortions of conceptual knowledge of hand structure. *Cognition, 142*, 230–235. doi:10.1016/j.cognition.2015.05.024.

Longo, M. R. (2016). Types of body representation. In Y. Coello & M. H. Fischer (Eds.), *Foundations of embodied cognition* (pp. 117–134). New York: Routledge.

Longo, M. R. (2017). Distorted body representations in healthy cognition. *Quarterly Journal of Experimental Psychology, 70*(3), 378–388. doi:10.1080/17470218.2016.1143956.

Longo, M. R., Azañón, E., & Haggard, P. (2010). More than skin deep: Body representation beyond primary somatosensory cortex. *Neuropsychologia, 48*(3), 655–668. doi:10.1016/j.neuropsychologia.2009.08.022.

Longo, M. R., & Haggard, P. (2010). An implicit body representation underlying human position sense. *Proceedings of the National Academy of Sciences of the United States of America, 107*(26), 11727–11732. doi:10.1073/pnas.1003483107.

Longo, M. R., Long, C., & Haggard, P. (2012). Mapping the invisible hand: A body model of a phantom limb. *Psychological Science, 23*(7), 740–742. doi:10.1177/0956797612441219.

Longo, M. R., Mattioni, S., & Ganea, N. (2015). Perceptual and conceptual distortions of implicit hand maps. *Frontiers in Human Neuroscience, 9*, 656. doi:10.3389/fnhum.2015.00656.

Longo, M. R., Schüür, F., Kammers, M. P. M., Tsakiris, M., & Haggard, P. (2008). What is embodiment? A psychometric approach. *Cognition*, *107*(3), 978–998. doi: 10.1016/j.cognition.2007.12.004.

Lueck, C. J., Zeki, S., Friston, K. J., Deibar, M. P., Cope, P., Cunningham, V. J., et al. (1989). The colour centre in the cerebral cortex of man. *Nature*, *340*(6232), 386–389. doi:10.1038/340386a0.

Mancini, F., Longo, M. R., Iannetti, G. D., & Haggard, P. (2011). A supramodal representation of the body surface. *Neuropsychologia*, *49*(5), 1194–1201. doi:10.1016/j.neuro psychologia.2010.12.040.

Margolis, A. N., & Longo, M. R. (2015). Visual detail about the body modulates tactile localisation biases. *Experimental Brain Research*, *233*(2), 351–358. doi:10.1007/s00221-014-4118-3.

Medina, J., & Coslett, H. B. (2010). From maps to form to space: Touch and the body schema. *Neuropsychologia*, *48*(3), 645–654. doi:10.1016/j.neuropsychologia.2009.08.017.

Melzack, R. (1990). Phantom limbs and the concept of a neuromatrix. *Trends in Neurosciences*, *13*(3), 88–92. doi:10.1016/0166-2236(90)90179-E.

Paillard, J. (1999). Body schema and body image—A double dissociation in deafferented patients. In G. N. Gantchev, S. Mori, & J. Massion (Eds.), *Motor control: Today and tomorrow* (pp. 197–214). Sofia, Bulgaria: Academic Publishing House.

Peelen, M. V., & Downing, P. E. (2007). The neural basis of visual body perception. *Nature Reviews: Neuroscience*, *8*(8), 636–648. doi:10.1038/nrn2195.

Phillips, K. A. (2005). *The broken mirror: Understanding and treating body dysmorphic disorder*. Oxford: Oxford University Press.

Porter, T. M. (1986). *The rise of statistical thinking, 1820–1900*. Princeton, NJ: Princeton University Press.

Ramachandran, V. S., & Hirstein, W. (1998). The perception of phantom limbs: The D. O. Hebb lecture. *Brain*, *121*(9), 1603–1630. doi:10.1093/brain/121.9.1603.

Rhodes, G., & Jeffery, L. (2006). Adaptive norm-based coding of facial identity. *Vision Research*, *46*(18), 2977–2987. doi:10.1016/j.visres.2006.03.002.

Rhodes, G., Jeffery, L., Boeing, A., & Calder, A. J. (2013). Visual coding of human bodies: Perceptual aftereffects reveal norm-based, opponent coding of body identity. *Journal of Experimental Psychology: Human Perception and Performance*, *39*(2), 313–317. doi:10.1037/a0031568.

Rizzolatti, G., & Craighero, L. (2004). The mirror-neuron system. *Annual Review of Neuroscience*, *27*, 169–192. doi:10.1146/annurev.neuro.27.070203.144230.

Saadah, E. S. M., & Melzack, R. (1994). Phantom limb experiences in congenital limb-deficient adults. *Cortex, 30*(3), 479–485.

Saulton, A., Longo, M. R., Wong, H. Y., Bülthoff, H. H., & de la Rosa, S. (2016). The role of visual similarity and memory in body model distortions. *Acta Psychologica, 164*, 103–111. doi:10.1016/j.actpsy.2015.12.013.

Schwoebel, J., & Coslett, H. B. (2005). Evidence for multiple, distinct representations of the human body. *Journal of Cognitive Neuroscience, 17*(4), 543–553. doi:10.1162/0898929053467587.

Simmel, M. L. (1966). Developmental aspects of the body scheme. *Child Development, 37*(1), 83–95. doi:10.2307/1126431.

Sperry, R. W. (1968). Hemisphere deconnection and unity in conscious awareness. *American Psychologist, 23*(10), 723–733. doi:10.1037/h0026839.

Stigler, S. M. (1986). *The history of statistics: The measurement of uncertainty before 1900*. Cambridge, MA: Harvard University Press.

Treasure, J., Claudino, A. M., & Zucker, N. (2010). Eating disorders. *Lancet, 375*(9714), 583–593. doi:10.1016/S0140-6736(09)61748-7.

Treisman, A. M., & Gelade, G. A. (1980). A feature-integration theory of attention. *Cognitive Psychology, 12*(1), 97–136. doi:10.1016/0010-0285(80)90005-5.

Tsao, D., & Freiwald, W. (2006). What's so special about the average face? *Trends in Cognitive Sciences, 10*(9), 391–393. doi:10.1016/j.tics.2006.07.009.

Vetter, R. J., & Weinstein, S. (1967). The history of the phantom in congenitally absent limbs. *Neuropsychologia, 5*(4), 335–338. doi:10.1016/0028-3932(67)90005-X.

Weinstein, S., & Sersen, E. A. (1961). Phantoms in cases of congenital absence of limbs. *Neurology, 11*, 905–911.

Weinstein, S., Sersen, E. A., & Vetter, R. J. (1964). Phantoms and somatic sensation in cases of congenital aplasia. *Cortex, 1*(3), 276–290.

Zeki, S., Watson, J. D., Lueck, C. K., Friston, K. J., Kennard, C., & Frackowiak, R. S. (1991). A direct demonstration of functional specialization in human visual cortex. *Journal of Neuroscience, 11*(3), 641–649.

5   Spatial Perception and the Sense of Touch

Patrick Haggard, Tony Cheng, Brianna Beck, and Francesca Fardo

Introduction

Most animals must interact with spatially complex and dynamic environments in order to survive. For example, an animal may navigate through a forest, carefully avoiding some objects, while carefully intercepting others. This ability requires an appropriate sensory apparatus, and the cognitive capacity to interpret the afferent signals into relevant information about the spatial arrangement of its own body within the wider environment. Theoretical (Gibson, 1966; O'Regan & Noë, 2001) and experimental studies (Dupin & Wexler, 2013) have largely focused on visually guided self-motion. However, the same logic applies also to somatosensory systems. Sensory endings on the skin, and internal to the musculoskeletal system, can specify whether an object is touching the body, along with how and where it is touching. Indeed, bumping our bodies against external objects provides a primitive experiential evidence for realism about the external world. Samuel Johnson's "I refute it thus" to Bishop Berkeley comes to mind.

Here we consider the computations and representations involved in spatial perception on the skin. Classically, cognitive psychology has emphasized that somatosensory spatial information must be transformed into external spatial coordinates for the purposes of functional interaction. For example, Longo and colleagues proposed an additive model in which a stimulus is first localized on the receptor sheet of the skin, then the skin is localized on the body, and finally the body is localized in space (Longo, Mancini, & Haggard, 2015). Proprioceptive information about limb positions in space, encoded in a representation sometimes called the "body schema" (Paillard, 1999), plays a crucial role in this second transformation. Taken together, this set of computations would allow, for example, a reaching movement toward the somatosensory stimulus, as when we swat a mosquito that has alighted on the thigh or the cheek. Studies of tactile remapping suggest that the transformation from localization on the skin to localization in external space is rapid and automatic (Azañón, Camacho, & Soto-Faraco, 2010). Thus, the dominant interest in the field has been in representation of egocentric external space.

In contrast, the spatial perceptual capacities supported by the skin itself have been relatively neglected. Head and Holmes (1911) introduced the concept of a "superficial schema," which they defined as "a central mapping of somatotopic information derived from the tactile information" (Paillard, 1999). However, this concept received relatively little attention in their experimental work. They proposed two-point discrimination thresholds as a marker of the acuity of the superficial schema, but they did not otherwise describe the forms of spatial perception that the superficial schema might support. In this chapter, we aim to redress this balance by reconsidering the spatial perceptual capacities supported by the skin itself, due to the transmission of skin signals to the cortex to provide a representation of "skin space." We focus particularly on whether such a skin space could suffice for truly spatial percepts caused by tactile stimulation, logically prior to and independent of any representation of the body parts on which the skin lies, or of the position of those body parts in external space. In José Luis Bermúdez's terms (chap. 6 in this volume), we ask whether a description in terms of skin space (or S-space) may be sufficient to credit an animal with spatial somatosensory perception, in the absence of both A-location and B-location.

In developing the idea of skin space, the concept of a "sensory field" becomes important. Like most philosophers, P. F. Strawson believes that it makes sense to postulate a "visual field" for vision. Spelling out the exact nature of the visual field remains a matter of controversy (e.g., Peacocke, 1983). Strawson is more skeptical about sensory fields in other modalities, such as the auditory field and the tactile field: "Evidently the visual field is necessarily extended at any moment, and its parts must exhibit spatial relations to each other. The case of touch is less obvious: it is not, e.g., clear what one would mean by a 'tactual field'" (Strawson, 1959, p. 65). O'Shaughnessy (1989) and Martin (1992) further develop this line of thought. (For a recent discussion of the auditory field, see Soteriou, 2013.) We will come back to this toward the end of this chapter. In what follows we turn to some models of space perception developed by Jean Nicod, because they seem particularly applicable to touch.

What cognitive capacities must an organism have for us to attribute spatial perception to it? Jean Nicod (1970) imagined a creature capable of hopping a fixed distance along a manifold similar to a piano keyboard (see fig. 5.1 for an illustration). Landing on each key would produce a musical tone

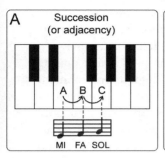 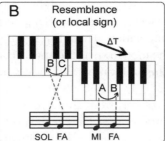 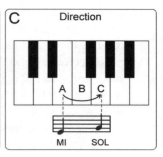

Figure 5.1

Illustration of the three primitive cognitive operations underlying the spatial perception of the world, postulated by Jean Nicod (1970). (A) The notion of *succession* refers to the cumulative counting of successive movements and allows the learning of spatial *adjacency* between A and B, B and C. (B) The notion of *resemblance* refers to the ability to learn specific associations between locations and sensory qualities (e.g., the location A is associated with the sound "MI"). This concept is similar to the *local sign* mechanism proposed by Lotze (1884). (C) Finally, the notion of *direction* allows the creature to perceive the relation between one hop and the next: whether the second hop is a repetition or a reversal of the first.

that the creature could hear. Nicod argued that, three primitive cognitive operations would suffice for this creature to have spatial perceptions of its world. First, the creature must grasp the notion of *succession* (fig. 5.1A). That is, hop B comes after hop A, but before hop C. If by cumulatively counting successive hops, the creature can represent that locations A and B are spatially adjacent, that B and C are adjacent, but that A and C are not. In essence, it perceives the relative spatial positions of locations on the keyboard via the temporal order of its own hopping movements. Second, the creature must grasp the notion of *resemblance* (fig. 5.1B). That is, if it can notice that the tone generated by the current hop is identical to a tone it has heard before, it can represent that it is in a previously visited location. In psychology, this seems to correspond to the distinctive sensory quality associated with each location, or *local sign* (Lotze, 1884). Finally, the creature must have at least a binary sense of *direction* (fig. 5.1C). In the example above, to grasp that A and C are nonadjacent, it must know whether it has changed direction between two successive hops, or not. That is, direction information is required in order to transform succession into adjacency. Succession, then, involves counting hops. Resemblance involves identifying a specific event with the outcome of a hop, and direction defines the relation between each hop and the one before it. Armed with these three primitives of succession, resemblance, and direction, the creature can proceed to compute all the key features of spatial perception, such as distance, interposition, and extrapolation. There is a striking resemblance between Nicod's creature and the modern neuroscientific concept of a rat acquiring place and grid-cell coding of location as it moves through its environment (O'Keefe, 1994). Interestingly, in Nicod's own work, succession and resemblance were handled separately from direction. Succession and resemblance were used by the creature on the piano keyboard to provide an "external" perception of space, while direction and resemblance were used by a second creature that acquires an "internal" perception of space from kinesthetic cues generated as it walks outward from a reference point, reverses its direction, and then retraces its steps. Here we have deliberately conflated Nicod's two creatures. In our view, neither creature alone would have true space perception, while a hybrid of the two would. Moreover, the three cognitive capacities do—as a matter of biological fact—tend to co-occur in mammalian brains. A discussion of the different contributions of succession, resemblance, and direction to space perception is beyond our current scope.

Sources and Organization of Afferent Information from the Skin

Individual mechanoreceptor endings and corpuscles are distributed throughout the human skin. Their density is not uniform, with the density being much higher on skin regions such as the fingertips and lips, producing the characteristic distortion of the somatosensory representation of the contralateral side of the body in the postcentral gyrus of each cerebral hemisphere (the "Penfield map," Penfield & Rasmussen, 1950). However, for our purposes, it is the regularity of receptor distribution that matters, rather than the density. The mechanoreceptors effectively cover the skin in an array of sensitive patches, which we can conceptualize as the squares of a chessboard. Each mechanoreceptor projects via an afferent neuron to the spinal cord, and thence via higher order projections neurons to the dorsal column nuclei, thalamus, and somatosensory cortex (Mountcastle, 2005). Neurons at each stage in the somatosensory pathway have a *receptive field* (RF). This term refers to the region of skin to which a neuron is responsive, in virtue of receiving afferent impulses from the mechanoreceptor located there.

We argue that the human skin can be viewed as a reversed, yet isomorphic version of Nicod's creature hopping between the keys of the piano keyboard. The RFs of cortical somatosensory neurons have the same status as the piano keyboard environment in Nicod's thought experiment, and a tactile stimulus moving across the skin has the same status as Nicod's hopping creature. The sensory apparatus is inside the creature in Nicod's case, but in the array of skin RFs in our case. Nevertheless, either arrangement has the capacity to signal succession, resemblance or local sign, and direction. Thus, the case of an animal navigating its environment, and the case of perceiving location on a sensory sheet, seem isomorphic, and epistemically equivalent, even though the representational intentionality is different in each case. That is, Nicod's creature is an object that can form a representation of its environment, while the skin is a sensing environment that can form representations of objects that encounter it.

Our view of skin space, based on an inversion of Nicod's argument is equivalent to postulating a "tactile field" defined by the array of skin RFs. To quote Haggard and Giovagnoli "the tactile field supports computation of spatial relations between individual stimulus locations, and thus underlies tactile pattern perception" (Haggard & Giovagnoli, 2011, pp. 65–66; more on this in the final section). We now describe how the array of skin RFs can underpin tactile spatial perception.

In Nicod's example, the relative position of one piano key to another is an objective spatial fact about the external world. The creature is able to learn these spatial facts because it can process information about succession, resemblance, and direction. In the case of skin RFs, it is an objective fact that two specific afferent neurons have adjacent RFs on the skin. However, the adjacency of RFs is not transparent, in the way that the successive hops of Nicod's creature may be transparent. An animal using the skin for spatial perception must somehow discover or infer that firing in two specific cortical neurons in fact refers to adjacent skin regions. Although many textbooks blandly assume that somatotopic mapping offers a sufficient explanation of spatial perception, we argue that this is not so. Rather, true spatial perception using the somatosensory system requires an additional level of representation, namely information about the relation between cortical neurons and the location of their RFs on the skin. The animal must *learn* the relation between signals arriving at the cortex and locations on the skin surface, which has classically been termed local sign (Lotze, 1884).

Classical local sign theory suggests that this relation is learned through the association between the unique sensory quality that accompanies stimulation of each RF and the orienting movements required to reach or saccade toward the location of the RF in external space. In essence, perception of space and location reduces to the movements needed to reach a target. This seems to work quite well for Nicod's creature: it learns the location of a particular key on the piano keyboard because it learns that, say, three hops in one direction are required to produce a particular tone. However, this reduction of space perception to movement coding seems to work much less well for our animal trying to establish spatial perception through the skin. In particular, I may not be able to make the relevant motor orienting response: I cannot saccade to skin locations on my lower back, and I can scratch there only with difficulty. A strict local sign theory suggests that spatial perception without (potential) orienting movement is impossible. However, spatial pattern perception on skin regions that are rarely or never targets for orienting movement can be surprisingly good (Duke, 1965).

Here, we suggest another possible mechanism that could provide information about RF locations. The statistics of natural interactions with the environment ensure that continuous movement of a stimulus across the skin is a frequent input pattern. For example, a creature that crawls or hops along the arm will stimulate successive afferent neurons in a consistent spatiotemporal pattern. A parent who strokes the arm of their infant will activate a similar pattern in the infant's brain, as will a leaf that one brushes against while walking in a forest. The consistent patterns of stimulation provided by these common events means that neurons with adjacent RFs will tend to fire in an ordered series. That is, one could learn the spatial adjacency between RFs from the temporal order of afferent signals, due to the average statistics of natural motion—rather than from the temporal order of one's own movements as in the case of Nicod's creature. Furthermore, neurons with adjacent RFs will fire in close temporal proximity, strengthening the synaptic weights between the corresponding neurons by Hebbian learning (Hebb, 1949). Lateral inhibitory mechanisms between cortical neurons further sharpen the spatial acuity of skin sensation (Laskin & Spencer, 1979). Therefore, when a stimulus moves across the skin, the pattern of information across multiple afferent neurons allows the spatial path across the skin to be perceived. Importantly, this mechanism of spatial perception does not depend on transforming the RF location into egocentric spatial coordinates. In particular, there is no need to transform skin location into an implicit egocentric orienting movement, as suggested by local sign concepts of space perception. In fact, spatial perception is possible without any spatial reference frame beyond the skin itself. This form of spatial perception is consistent with Head and Holmes's (1911) concept of a superficial schema as a central mapping of somatotopic information derived from tactile information. The view that superficial schema suffices for spatial perception contrasts strongly with the "orthodox" view that tactile stimuli are rapidly and *obligatorily* transformed into external spatial coordinates.

We have shown that core computations underlying spatial perception of the skin are consistent with the general project of sensory grounding of geometry (Nicod, 1970), with one striking difference. The striking difference between our concept of skin space and Nicod's navigating creature lies in the role of self-motion. Most accounts of sensory geometry, including Nicod's, are based on real or imaginary self-generated movement: the animal must move through the environment, or move its body parts with respect to the environment. In contrast, our concept of skin space does not seem to require this. All that is required is a natural distribution of motions of objects across the skin. These may be caused by the animal's motions relative to the environment, but they may equally be caused by motion of the environment relative to the static animal.

Testing the Idea of Skin Space

In this section we investigate whether the skin space mechanisms described above contribute to human perception. This is not straightforward: how can we know whether any particular spatial judgment arises from skin space perception alone, or also depends on transforming skin space locations into an external frame of reference such as egocentric space? How can transformation into external egocentric space be excluded? In principle, if Head and Holmes were correct in positing a superficial schema (which we take to be synonymous with our concept of skin space) distinct from the body schema, some unfortunate natural accident should have produced patients whose symptoms amount to a double dissociation. For example, a patient with damage to the superficial schema might not know the locations of stimuli on the skin, but might nevertheless be able to control orienting responses toward the location of the stimulus in external space. The "blind touch" patients described by Paillard, Michel, and Stelmach (1983) and Rossetti, Rode, and Boisson (1995) may seem to have such a superficial schema deficit. These patients appear to know the location of touches that they do not consciously perceive. The main negative symptom resulting from the putatively-damaged superficial schema might thus be the failure to perceive that they have been touched—tactile imperception. However, simply detecting touch does not involve any spatial information, so these cases cannot prove that the superficial schema is necessary for *spatial* perception. In addition, careful studies failed to confirm in healthy volunteers the dissociation between tactile detection and tactile localization observed in these neurological cases (Harris, Thein, & Clifford, 2004).

Here, we take a different approach to identify the contribution of skin space to spatial perception. Again, we begin with the isomorphism between a tactile stimulus traversing the RF array on the skin, and Nicod's creature navigating its environment. In research on animal navigation, the gold standard test that an animal forms a spatial representation of its environment, as opposed to merely orienting toward cues, is the ability to take appropriate shortcuts. The classic behavioral manifestation is a behavior known as "path integration" (Mittelstaedt & Mittelstaedt, 1980), or dead reckoning. In path integration situations, an animal moves from a home location to a new location via an indirect path, and now wishes to return home. It can, of course, retrace its steps and follow its original outward path in reverse, or it can make a straight line back toward the home location. The former behavior does not require any spatial representational ability at all: the animal could be replaying its outward movements in reverse order from a motor memory, or it could be following a sensory trail laid on its outward journey. However, the latter behavior is taken to imply that it computes the position of the home relative to the final position. It is thus able to situate locations it has visited within a map of external space, and use this map to select the optimal homing behavior. The spatial map is built-up by integrating information about the animal's current heading direction, and its self-generated movement (Etienne & Jeffery, 2004; Müller & Wehner, 1988).

We speculate that a mechanism of path integration operates in skin space (fig. 5.2). When a stimulus traces a path across the skin, knowledge of the adjacency relations for the RFs that it stimulates will suffice to compute the position of the end of the path relative to the beginning, just as the homing animal does. The problem is that other mechanisms can also calculate the homing path. For example, the animal could transform the start and end locations into egocentric external coordinates. It could then interpolate a reaching movement from the end location to the start location, and trace the direct line of the homing path. Interestingly, however, animals that perform path integration generally show a characteristic error: the homeward path shows a slight understeer, or bias toward the outward path. The reasons for this error are disputed. On one view, it results from a weighted averaging of the direction information on the outward path (Müller & Wehner, 1988). On another view, it is a strategic adaptation that minimizes the risk of missing the home location. Understeer ensures that the animal crosses its outward path on the return journey, at which point it can benefit from memory cues to ensure the final approach (Etienne & Jeffery, 2004). In any case, the understeer error is considered a universal feature of animal navigation, since it is shown by dogs, humans, rodents, and insects (fig. 5.3).

We therefore investigated whether perception of tactile spatial patterns on the human skin involved the systematic bias toward the outward path that characterizes understeer errors in path integration. The full results are reported elsewhere (Fardo, Beck, Cheng, & Haggard, in preparation).

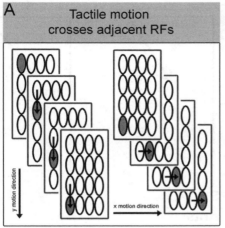
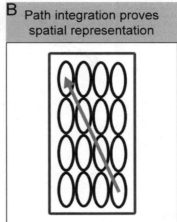

Figure 5.2

(A) Illustration of a moving stimulus in skin space (S-space). The skin surface contains a mosaic of receptive fields that are arranged like the cells of spreadsheet, or the pixels of a screen. When an object moves onto the skin, it activates a pattern of adjacent receptive fields depending on the motion direction. The central nervous system might leverage the natural statistics of adjacent RFs to represent a map of the S-space. (B) This map can support the computation of spatial relations, such as the inference of the direct path between two points via a novel route (i.e., path integration).

Here, we give a brief summary of the concept of the experiment, and its significance for the concept of skin space. Briefly, S-shaped patterns were traced on the hand dorsum of healthy participants using a haptic robot. The patterns varied randomly in their start and end locations. The S shapes consisted of a larger and a smaller convexity, and the locations of these were also randomized. A set of illustrative spatial paths are shown in figure 5.4. The participant's task was to attend to the S-shaped tactile pattern, and then, after a short delay, to point to a location on the skin exactly midway between the start and end points of the S shape just experienced. The computations involved are analogous to those of path integration by a navigating animal. Importantly, the true bisection point was never on the original S shape itself. The locations of each bisecting response were recorded and analyzed. In this task, understeer error corresponds to a constant error, or bias toward the major convexity of the S shape, since this constitutes the major deviation of the outward path. We averaged over all other factors, such as the start and end locations, direction, and location

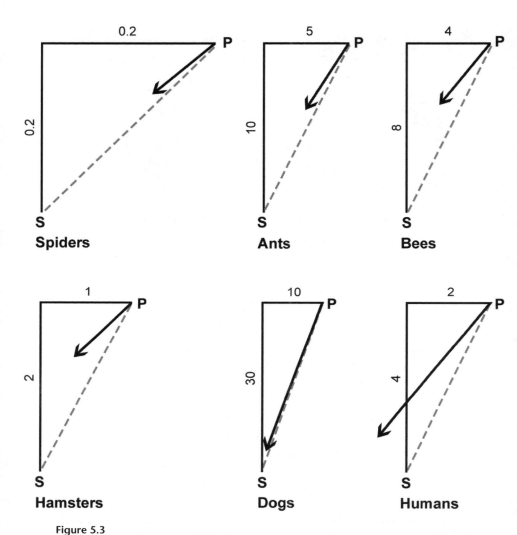

Figure 5.3
Systematic path integration errors across species, when returning from point P to the starting point S. The black L shape indicates the path travelled, while the gray dashed line represents the shortest route (ideal path) between P and S. The black arrow indicates the actual integrated path. These data suggest that the understeer error, or bias towards the outward path, is common across species. Adapted from Etienne and Jeffery (2004).

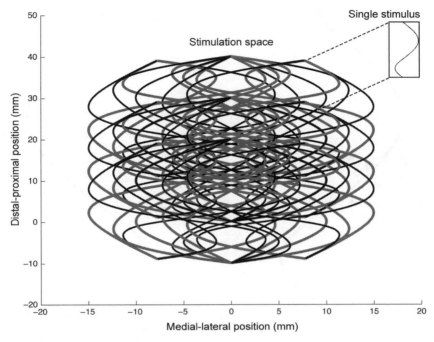

Figure 5.4
Illustration of several S-shaped paths on the dorsum of the hand. The participants' task was to attend to each point of the stimulation, and then provide a bisection judgment between the starting point and the end point of each single stimulus. Every trial was a unique path, with a variable starting point, rotatory angle, distance, and position of the biggest convexity. The large convexity was either distal-medial, distal-lateral, proximal-medial, or proximal-lateral, with equal probability.

of the major convexity. We found a small but significant overall bias toward the major convexity, indicating that the outward spatial path influenced the perceived vector between start and end points (fig. 5.5). The direction and magnitude of this error were consistent with understeer errors in path integration. We interpret this error as a consequence of using a skin space representation, based on integrating successive transitions of the stimulus across adjacent RFs, to form a spatial percept of the stimulus as a whole. Of course, this error could possibly also be explained by other factors, such as a shift of spatial attention toward the spatial center of mass of the S shape. These alternative explanations will require explicit testing in further experiments. However, the bisection error *cannot* readily be explained in terms of transformation of skin locations into egocentric external coordinates.

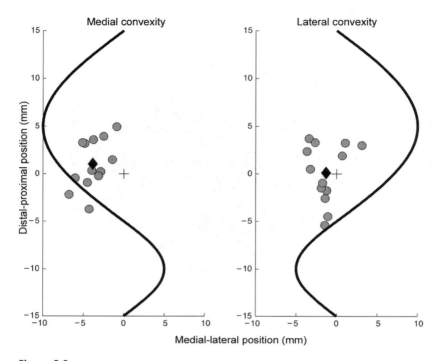

Figure 5.5
Experimental data from healthy volunteers bisecting the starting and ending point of S-shaped tactile motion stimuli. The black S shapes depict two categories of possible paths: on the left, with convexity towards the thumb (i.e., medial); on the right, with convexity towards the little finger (i.e., lateral). The crosses represent the true bisection point, while the black diamonds indicate group average actual attempts to bisection. The gray dots represent single subject actual averages. Bisection judgments were influenced by the position of the convexity. This is particularly prominent in the medial condition. Although, the judgment is not positive for all participants in the lateral condition, it is significantly shifted to the right with respect to the former condition. Note that there is an overall bias shifting the bisection points toward the radius. This has been previously reported elsewhere (Mancini et al., 2011), and could reflect bodily landmarks. Crucially, it is independent of the shape of the S stimulus.

In our data, we also found two characteristic patterns of bisection errors linked to egocentric spatial localization. We found an overall radial bias to bisect toward the radial (thumb) side of the hand. We also found an overall distal bias, shifting the bisection point away from the wrist and toward the fingertips. Both of these have been reported previously (Mancini, Longo, Iannetti, & Haggard, 2011). Importantly, they are independent of the bias induced by the S-shaped path on the skin.

Field Organization, Modality, and Perception

The notion of a tactile field has important implications for both psychological theory, and for philosophy of perception. Our starting point has been Nicod's account of space perception. His view is interestingly similar to, though not exactly the same as, P. F. Strawson's view in chapter 2 of *Individuals* (1959). There Strawson imagines a "No-Space" world. Strawson probes the plausibility of the Kantian thesis that "space is a necessary condition for objective experience" (Evans, 1980, p. 250). Strawson concludes that space or idea of space is not necessary, because a continuous "master sound" can serve as an analogy of space, though Evans (1980) found that the master sound concept was neither helpful, nor even necessary. A detailed discussion of this topic is beyond the scope of this piece. Evans instead proposed a "travel-based space." This is similar to Nicod's and our thinking (Evans, 1980, p. 255, 283) in two ways. First, both notions require movement of an observer relative to one or more environmental objects. In Evans and Nicod's formulations, the observer moves relative to objects that remain static, such as the piano keys. In our skin-space model, the stimulus object moves relative to an "environment" of sensory transducers in the skin. Crucially, we argue that these two formulations are isomorphic from the point of view of spatial perceptual ability. Therefore, the emphasis on active movement as the basis of spatial perception, though doubtless correct in specific cases such as saccadic eye movement, may not be logically necessary. Second, we emphasized the spatial adjacency of RFs as the starting point of spatial perception. As an object impinges on an ordered series of RFs, one may extract the relation between one RF and another, though not the absolute location of any RF, whether stimulated or not. However, relative RF positions may suffice for perceiving spatial patterns.

Furthermore, what we offered above can be seen as a response to Strawson on sensory fields: there is a clear sense of a tactile field that is sustained by skin space. In particular, tactile RFs form the "parts" of an extended sensory field. Not only do these parts have specific spatial relations to one another as a matter of anatomical fact, but the natural statistics of typical motions across the field allow these spatial relations to be learned, and exploited for spatial perception. Thus, postulating a tactile field not only helps in explaining relevant behavioral data, but also has a plausible physiological underpinning.

Now finally, we would like to say a bit more about the explanatory value of our concept of a tactile field defined on the skin. To reprise, the crucial explanatory power of it is to explain the relevant behavioral data. The tactile field concept has two further roles. First of all, it can help us individuate the senses: the Aristotelian conception of five senses is the traditional classification, but it has proven to be unsatisfactory for various reasons (Macpherson, 2011). Within the somatosensory system, researchers distinguish between the nociceptive system, the thermal system, and the tactile system. In this work we have shown that we need to postulate a sensory field in the tactile case. However, other studies suggest that nociceptive and thermal senses have quite different spatial properties, and may lack a field-like organizing principle (Mancini, Stainitz, Steckelmacher, Iannetti, & Haggard, 2015; Marotta, Ferrè, & Haggard, 2015). Having a sensory field or not might constitute a partial reason for discriminating between different sensory channels (Cheng, 2015), and thus provide a logical starting point for modality individuation.

Second, our field-based view of tactile object perception might be a nice supplement to the constancy-based view of object and objective perception, which has gained its currency in the recent philosophical literature (Smith, 2002; Burge, 2010). On that view, perceptual constancy is a basis of object perception. For Burge, the characteristic feature of object constancy is "a capacity to track objects perceptually—where tracking requires coordination of perception with perceptual memory and perceptual anticipation" (Burge, 2011, p. 125). Fulkerson (2014) also emphasizes the importance of object perception in the case of touch. For him, what makes touch a single sense is the way that multiple tactile sensations, or features, are bound to produce a representation of a single perceptual object. In the above discussions, we have been able to describe how people have a spatial perception of an object moving across the skin, using only the basic properties of receptors. This can be part of the explanation of perceptual constancy in touch, if we take perceptual constancy in a loose, minimal sense of spatiotemporal continuity. We have described the perception of stimuli that move continuously across the skin. We have not directly investigated whether people perceive our stimuli as one and the same object, but it seems reasonable that they do. That is, the object touching RF1 at time t1 is assumed to be the same object as that touching adjacent RF2 at time t2. Indeed, in cases of apparent tactile motion, a series of discrete tactile contacts is perceived as a continuous motion of a single stimulus (Carter, Konkle, Wang, Hayward & Moore, 2008), suggesting that spatiotemporal continuity is an important prior in tactile perception. However, this kind of spatiotemporal continuity implies a different, and perhaps thinner, notion of object constancy than may be intended by Burge. Textbook examples of perceptual constancy generally refer to basic properties of objects, such as shape, size, and color. Our view thus supplements Burge's perspective, since any constancy constraint in our approach is limited to a spatiotemporal continuity of the stimulus object. In Burge's work, the focus has generally been on vision, which affords a much richer object-based content than the passive touch studied here. If there is any perceptual constancy operating in our tactile experiments, it seems to derive from the field-like organization of the receptor-based sensory apparatus, rather than from any elaborated representation of an object having specific properties. Our approach opens the intriguing possibility that field-based organization is sufficient for the minimal form of perceptual constancy linked with spatiotemporal continuity, and that this minimal form of perceptual constancy may occur without rich representation of object properties.

Conclusions

To conclude, we have argued that some somatosensory spatial perceptual capacity may be based on skin space, rather than on the more familiar frames of reference defined by body parts, by orienting movements, or by stimulus location in external egocentric space. We do not deny that tactile information can be, and most frequently is, transformed into external spatial coordinates. However, the core features of spatial perception may be found already in the array of RFs in the skin. If correct, our position has several interesting perceptual consequences. First, it emphasizes the strong isomorphism between perceiving stimuli on the receptor surface, and perceiving one's location in the environment during navigation. Second, it replaces the motoric solution to the local sign problem with a physics-based solution, reflecting learning about spatial adjacency through natural statistics of environmental motion. Third, it implies the existence of a "tactile field" (Martin, 1992) that does not depend on the body as either volumetric object, or locus of orienting movements. It would seem fruitful to consider whether the spatial perceptual capacity that we have considered for skin might apply to other receptor surfaces, notably the retina.

Acknowledgments

P.H. acknowledges generous support from a donation by Shamil Chandaria to School of Advanced Study. This research was further supported by ERC Advanced Grant HUMVOL (agreement no. 323943). The article benefitted from P.H.'s fellowship at the Paris Institute for Advanced Studies (France), with the financial support of the French State managed by the Agence Nationale de la Recherche, program "Investissements d'avenir" (ANR-11-LABX-0027-01 Labex RFIEA+). F.F. was supported by EU FP7 Project VERE WP1 and by Novo Nordisk Foundation (no. NNF14OC0011633). B.B. was supported by an MRC grant (no. MR/M013901/1) to P.H.

We are grateful to Colin Blakemore for advice and discussion.

References

Azañón, E., Camacho, K., & Soto-Faraco, S. (2010). Tactile remapping beyond space. *European Journal of Neuroscience*, *31*(10), 1858–1867.

Burge, T. (2010). *Origins of objectivity*. Oxford: Oxford University Press.

Burge, T. (2011). Border crossings: Perceptual and post-perceptual object representation. *Behavioral and Brain Sciences*, *34*(3), 125. doi:10.1017/S0140525X10002323.

Carter, O., Konkle, T., Wang, Q., Hayward, V., & Moore, C. (2008). Tactile rivalry demonstrated with an ambiguous apparent-motion quartet. *Current Biology*, *18*(14), 1050–1054. doi:10.1016/j.cub.2008.06.027.

Cheng, T. (2015). Book review: *The first sense* [Review of the book *The First Sense: A Philosophical Study of Human Touch*, ed. M. Fulkerson]. *Frontiers in Psychology*, *6*, 1196. doi:10.3389/fpsyg.2015.01196.

Duke, J. D. (1965). Perception of finger drawings upon the body surface. *Journal of General Psychology*, *75*(2), 305–314.

Dupin, L., & Wexler, M. (2013). Motion perception by a moving observer in a three-dimensional environment. *Journal of Vision*, *13*(2). doi:10.1167/13.2.15.

Etienne, A. S., & Jeffery, K. J. (2004). Path integration in mammals. *Hippocampus*, *14*(2), 180–192. doi:10.1002/hipo.10173.

Evans, G. (1980). Things without the mind—a commentary upon chapter two of Strawson's *Individuals*. In G. Evans (Ed.), *Collected papers*. New York: Oxford University Press.

Fardo, F., Beck, B., Cheng, T., & Haggard, P. (in preparation). Mechanisms of spatial perception on the human skin. Manuscript in preparation.

Fulkerson, M. (Ed.). (2014). *The first sense: A philosophical study of human touch.* Cambridge, MA: MIT Press.

Gibson, J. J. (1966). *The senses considered as perceptual systems.* Oxford: Houghton Mifflin.

Haggard, P., & Giovagnoli, G. (2011). Spatial patterns in tactile perception: Is there a tactile field? *Acta Psychologica, 137*(1), 65–75. doi:10.1016/j.actpsy.2011.03.001.

Harris, J. A., Thein, T., & Clifford, C. W. G. (2004). Dissociating detection from localization of tactile stimuli. *Journal of Neuroscience, 24*(14), 3683–3693. doi:10.1523/JNEUROSCI.0134-04.2004.

Head, H., & Holmes, G. (1911). Sensory disturbances from cerebral lesions. *Brain, 34*(2–3), 102–254. doi:10.1093/brain/34.2-3.102.

Hebb, D. O. (1949). *The organization of behavior: A neuropsychological theory.* New York: Wiley.

Laskin, S. E., & Spencer, W. A. (1979). Cutaneous masking. II. Geometry of excitatory and inhibitory receptive fields of single units in somatosensory cortex of the cat. *Journal of Neurophysiology, 42*(4), 1061–1082.

Longo, M. R., Mancini, F., & Haggard, P. (2015). Implicit body representations and tactile spatial remapping. *Acta Psychologica, 160*, 77–87. doi:10.1016/j.actpsy.2015.07.002.

Lotze, H. (1884). *Mikrokosmos.* Leipzig: Hirzel.

Macpherson, F. (Ed.). (2011). *The senses: Classic and contemporary philosophical perspectives.* Oxford: Oxford University Press.

Mancini, F., Longo, M. R., Iannetti, G. D., & Haggard, P. (2011). A supramodal representation of the body surface. *Neuropsychologia, 49*(5), 1194–1201. doi:10.1016/j.neuropsychologia.2010.12.040.

Mancini, F., Stainitz, H., Steckelmacher, J., Iannetti, G. D., & Haggard, P. (2015). Poor judgment of distance between nociceptive stimuli. *Cognition, 143*, 41–47. doi:10.1016/j.cognition.2015.06.004.

Marotta, A., Ferrè, E. R., & Haggard, P. (2015). Transforming the thermal grill effect by crossing the fingers. *Current Biology, 25*(8), 1069–1073. doi:10.1016/j.cub.2015.02.055.

Martin, M. (1992). Sight and touch. In T. Crane (Ed.), *The contents of experience* (pp. 196–215). Cambridge: Cambridge University Press.

Mittelstaedt, M.-L., & Mittelstaedt, H. (1980). Homing by path integration in a mammal. *Naturwissenschaften, 67*(11), 566–567. doi:10.1007/BF00450672.

Mountcastle, V. B. (2005). *The sensory hand: Neural mechanisms of somatic sensation.* Cambridge, MA: Harvard University Press.

Müller, M., & Wehner, R. (1988). Path integration in desert ants, *Cataglyphis fortis*. *Proceedings of the National Academy of Sciences of the United States of America, 85*(14), 5287–5290.

Nicod, J. (1970). *Geometry and induction*. Berkeley: University of California Press.

O'Keefe, J. (1994). Cognitive maps, time and causality. In C. Peacocke (Ed.), *Objectivity, simulation, and the unity of consciousness*. Oxford: Oxford University Press.

O'Regan, J. K., & Noë, A. (2001). A sensorimotor account of vision and visual consciousness. *Behavioral and Brain Sciences, 24*(5), 939–1031. doi:10.1017/S0140525X01000115.

O'Shaughnessy, B. (1989). The sense of touch. *Australasian Journal of Philosophy, 67*(1), 37–58. doi:10.1080/00048408912343671.

Paillard, J. (1999). Body schema and body image: A double dissociation in deafferented patients. In G. N. Gantchev, S. Mori, & J. Massion (Eds.), *Motor control: Today and tomorrow*. Sofia, Bulgaria: Academic Publishing House.

Paillard, J., Michel, F., & Stelmach, G. (1983). Localization without content: A tactile analogue of "blind sight." *Archives of Neurology, 40*(9), 548–551. doi:10.1001/archneur.1983.04050080048008.

Peacocke, C. (1983). *Sense and content: Experience, thought, and their relations*. Oxford: Oxford University Press.

Penfield, W., & Boldrey, E. (1937). Somatic motor and sensory representation in the cerebral cortex of man as studied by electrical stimulation. *Brain, 60*(4), 389–443. doi:10.1093/brain/60.4.389.

Penfield, W., & Rasmussen, T. (1950). *The cerebral cortex of man: A clinical study of localization of function*. New York: Macmillan.

Rossetti, Y., Rode, G., & Boisson, D. (1995). Implicit processing of somaesthetic information: A dissociation between where and how? *Neuroreport, 6*(3), 506–510.

Smith, A. D. (2002). *The problem of perception*. Cambridge, MA: Harvard University Press.

Smythies, J. (1996). A note on the concept of the visual field in neurology, psychology, and visual neuroscience. *Perception, 25*(3), 369–371.

Soteriou, M. (2013). *The mind's construction: The ontology of mind and mental action*. Oxford: Oxford University Press.

Strawson, P. F. (1959). *Individuals: An essay in descriptive metaphysics*. London: Methuen.

II The Sense of Bodily Ownership

6 Ownership and the Space of the Body

José Luis Bermúdez

In the last twenty years a robust experimental paradigm has emerged for studying the structure of bodily experience, focusing primarily on what it is to experience one's body as one's own. As in many areas of psychology and cognitive science, induced illusions have proved highly illuminating. The initial impetus came from the rubber hand illusion (RHI) first demonstrated in Botvinick and Cohen (1998), and subsequently extended by various researchers to generate illusions of ownership at the level of the body as a whole (for reviews see Tsakiris, 2010; Serino et al., 2013; Kilteni, Maselli, Kording, & Slater, 2015). The resulting experimental paradigms and results have allowed cognitive scientists to operationalize aspects of bodily experience previously explored either purely theoretically or as distorted in neurological disorders such as unilateral spatial neglect. Experiments have focused primarily on the experience of ownership (what it is to experience one's body as one's own) and the experience of agency (what it is to experience acting with and through one's body).

However, these illusion paradigms have not directly studied one important aspect of bodily experience, namely, how the space of the body is experienced. The experienced spatiality of the body is part of what marks out our experience of our bodies as unique physical objects (Bermúdez, 1998, 2005, 2011). There is, of course, no objective difference between the space of the body and the space of the extrabodily environment. But the representation of spatial location in bodily experience is very different from the representation of spatial location in vision and other forms of exteroceptive perception. Understanding these differences is integral to understanding how bodily experience contributes to self-consciousness.

This chapter identifies some problems with how ownership is discussed in the context of bodily illusions, and then shows how those problems can be addressed through a model of the experienced space of the body. Section I briefly reviews the bodily illusions literature and its significance for cognitive science and philosophy. Section II expresses reservations with the concept of ownership in terms of which the RHI and other illusions are standardly framed. I offer three hypotheses for the source of our putative "sense of ownership." The main body of the paper focuses on the third hypothesis, which is that judgments of ownership are grounded in the distinctive way that we experience the space of the body.

I

Botvinick and Cohen (1998) introduced an experimental paradigm for inducing illusions of ownership that has been widely replicated and developed. Since 1998 over two hundred papers have been published on the RHI, in which subjects see a rubber hand being stroked while their own hand, which they cannot see, is being synchronously stroked. Subjects reliably report both feeling sensations of touch in the rubber hand and feeling that the rubber hand is their own hand. A number of studies have suggested that these subjective reports correlate reliably with behavioral measures, including:

- galvanic skin conductance response (Armel & Ramachandran, 2003);
- temperature in the stimulated hand (Moseley et al., 2008); and
- drift in the perceived location of the hand relative to the rubber hand (Tsakiris & Haggard, 2005).

The subjective experience of subjects undergoing the illusion has also been studied psychometrically with a twenty-seven-item questionnaire subsequently put through a principal component analysis (Longo, Schüür, Kammers, Tsakiris, & Haggard, 2008).

Further development of the RHI paradigm has explored the possibility of dissociating reports of ownership in the rubber hand and reports of agency with respect to the hand (Kalckert & Ehrsson, 2012); the significance of postural and anatomical congruence between the real hand and the rubber hand (Costantini & Haggard, 2007); and the possibility of eliciting the illusion without visuotactile stimulation (Kalckert & Ehrsson, 2012). In terms of understanding the mechanisms underlying the RHI, the main issue has been whether the experience of ownership is a bottom-up, stimulus-driven process—or whether it involves higher-order representations of the body, such as a long-term body image, or an occurrent postural map, or both (Tsakiris, 2010; de Vignemont, 2014). Investigations of the neural underpinnings of the experience of bodily ownership have highlighted the role of the temporal-parietal junction (Ionta, Martuzzi, Salomon, & Blanke, 2014).

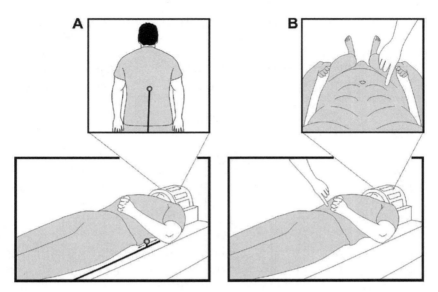

Figure 6.1
Illustration of the differences in perspective in the full body illusion (A) and the body swap illusion (B). From Serino et al. (2013).

Comparable illusions have been induced for the sense of ownership of the entire body using head-mounted displays to create a virtual reality in which subjects see the world from a different spatial perspective. The illusion has been generated from different perspectives, both third person and first person, as illustrated in figure 6.1.

In the full body illusion subjects can be brought to identify with a full body avatar that they see being stroked at a spatial location in front of them (Lenggenhager, Tadi, Metzinger, & Blanke, 2007). In the body swap illusion subjects reports a sense of ownership for a mannequin that they see being stroked in the location where they would expect their own bodies to be (Petkova & Ehrsson, 2008). An interesting phenomenon noticed in studies of the full body illusion is that the illusion persists when transposed into a third-person perspective—subjects can perceive being in front of their own bodies and even shaking hands with themselves.

One reason that the RHI and related experimental paradigms have generated such interest and excitement in the cognitive science community is that they offer a way of operationalizing and studying aspects of subjective experience that had stubbornly resisted experimental treatment in normal subjects. Previously most of what was known about bodily experience came from neuropsychological studies of disorders such as *unilateral spatial neglect* (in which neurologically damaged patients neglect one side of their bodies, and indeed one side of peripersonal and external space typically the opposite side to the lesion), *somatoparaphrenia* (in which patients report disownership of body parts, typically on the contralesional side also) and *alien hand syndrome* (in which brain-damaged subjects report that someone else is moving their hands).[1] Although the study of neuropsychological disorders has been very illuminating it has inherent disadvantages. Disorders such as somatoparaphrenia and alien hand illusion are rare. It is hard to compare across cases since there is often significant additional brain damage that makes it difficult to disentangle the relative contributions of different disorders. And the reports of patients with severe brain damage can be challenging to understand and interpret.

From a more philosophical perspective, the structure of bodily experience has been studied by philosophers working within the analytical and phenomenological traditions—in fact, this has been one of the relatively few areas where there has been productive dialog between the two traditions. Some of this work has been done, more or less, from the proverbial armchair (e.g., O'Shaughnessy, 1980). But others have engaged directly with the scientific study of the body. Merleau-Ponty (1968), for example, was very well read in the neuropsychology of his day and rested important parts of his analysis of bodily experience in *The Phenomenology of Perception* on the detailed analysis of brain-damaged patients (most famously, the German war veteran Schneider). For more recent examples see the essays in Bermúdez, Marcel, and Eilan (1995), as well as Gallagher (2005), Bermúdez (1998, 2011), and de Vignemont (2014). Many of these philosophers studying the body have converged on a small set of basic concepts and explanatory tools. These include different ways of thinking about the body image, as well as ideas of bodily ownership and bodily agency. These are precisely the notions that are operationalized and manipulated in the RHI and related bodily illusions.

II

The bodily illusions are standardly discussed as illusions of ownership—limb ownership in the case of the RHI and bodily ownership in the body swap and full body illusions. It is clear that the RHI manipulates subjects' sense of their body parts belonging to them. If the rubber hand is experienced as being part of one's body, then it is natural to describe this as the experience of "owning" the rubber hand. But ownership is a rather tenuous and metaphorical concept in this context. We do not own hands, rubber or otherwise, in the way that we own personal property. And it is unlikely that any way of unpacking the metaphor that will work for limb ownership can be applied straightforwardly to so-called bodily ownership. Intuitively one might say that to feel ownership for a limb is to experience it as connected with the rest of one's body and as a part of one. But could that be the same sense in which we might feel ownership for our bodies as a whole? What would it mean to say that one experiences one's body as a part of oneself?[2]

Certainly, it seems impossible to extend to the body as a whole a *mereological* conception of ownership, as developed in Martin (1995). Martin defines the sense of ownership as a "phenomenological quality, that the body part appears to be a part of one's body" (1995, p. 269). This is perhaps one reason that some authors have proposed an account of ownership in terms of the locus of experience (with the emphasis more on ownership of bodily experiences, rather than on ownership of specific body parts). Gallagher, for example, writes of "the sense that I am the one who is undergoing an experience. For example, the sense that my body is moving regardless of whether the movement is voluntary or involuntary" (2000, p. 15).

Thinking about ownership in terms of the locus of experience is applicable both to individual body parts and to the body as a whole. However, there is a fundamental lack of clarity in the idea of a sense of ownership, as it features in the literature. When, for example, it is said that subjects in the RHI have a sense of ownership in the rubber hand, does this mean that there is a specific feeling of ownership—a qualitative "feel" that one has in all and only those body parts that one experiences as one's own? This is how some authors have described the phenomenology of ownership (see, for example, Gallagher, 2005; de Vignemont, 2007, 2013). But I have argued elsewhere that the feeling of ownership is a philosophical fiction (Bermúdez, 2011, 2015). If there is no such specific feeling of ownership then the putative sense of ownership becomes something that itself needs to be explained, rather than a basic notion that can do explanatory work. We know that there are judgments of ownership (and judgments of disownership, for that matter, as in somatoparaphrenia). If there is a specific feeling of ownership, then those judgments can be viewed as simply reports of the feeling (or perhaps as expressions of the feeling, depending on one's view of first-person phenomenological reports). But if there is no such feeling of ownership then some account needs to be given of what those judgments are based on. This will, in effect, be a substantive account of what the sense of ownership consists in.[3]

So, when subjects report ownership (or disownership) of limbs, or of their entire bodies, what are those judgments based on? Here are three hypotheses:

(1) Judgments of ownership are based on the experienced location of sensation.
(2) Judgments of ownership are based on the experience of agency.
(3) Judgments of ownership are based on the experienced spatiality of the body.

This section explains why (1) and (2) are unconvincing. The remainder of the paper will focus on (3).[4]

The idea behind (1) is that we report ownership of those limbs and body parts where we experience sensations. This idea goes back (at least) to the seventeenth century. In his *Essay Concerning Human Understanding*, John Locke argues that our "thinking, conscious self" extends to all parts of the body "that we *feel* when they are touch'd, and are affected by, and conscious of good or harm that happens to them" (Locke, 1689/1975, Bk. II, ch. 27, §11). On this view, the body is experienced as the locus of sensation, so that judgments of ownership follow the localization of sensations.[5] One aspect of Locke's account that needs to be brought out is his stress on the dimension of concern. For Locke, to experience individual body parts and our body as a whole as parts of our "thinking, conscious self" is ipso facto to feel an immediate concern for what happens to them. This affective aspect of ownership has been highlighted by de Vignemont (in press).

However, experiencing sensations in a particular body part appears to be neither necessary nor sufficient for judgments of ownership. Somatoparaphrenia seems to show that it is not sufficient. Somatoparaphrenic patients deny ownership of a limb or even of an entire side of their body. Yet there are reports from somatoparaphrenic patients of feeling sensations in limbs that they deny are theirs (Aglioti, Smania, Manfredi, & Berlucchi, 1996; Bottini, Bisiach, Sterzi, & Vallar, 2002).[6] And there are examples from the bodily illusion literature showing that experiencing sensations in a particular body part is not required for judgments of ownership. The experiments described in Ferri, Chiarelli, Merla, Gallese, and Costantini (2013) show that the illusion can be induced by subjects seeing a rubber hand being approached, even when there is no touch (either of the rubber hand or of their own hand).

The idea that there is a connection between ownership and agency is highly intuitive, so that we experience our body and body parts as our own to the extent that we act with them, or are capable of acting with them.

Within the philosophical literature this way of thinking about judgments of ownership has typically not been distinguished from the first hypothesis. There are some good reasons for this, as will emerge in the next three paragraphs—and also some more questionable ones, connected to the postulation of a sense of agency which is claimed to be dissociable from the sense of ownership (see Gallagher, 2005, for an influential formulation). To my mind, the putative sense of agency suffers from exactly the same explanatory problems as the putative sense of ownership. In any event, setting up a dialectic on which there are distinct and separable senses of ownership and agency obscures the potential role of awareness of agency in underwriting judgments of ownership.[7]

Whereas hypothesis (1) frames the body as the locus of sensation, hypothesis (2) frames the body as the locus of action. Nonetheless, the rubber hand illusion itself shows that judgments of ownership cannot be based solely on the *experience* of acting with specific body parts, since there is no active movement in the RHI. The experience of agency cannot be a necessary condition. It may be a sufficient condition, however. Kalckert and Ehrsson (2012) showed that the RHI can be induced with active movement in the absence of sensory stimulation.

Still, hypothesis (2) seems too narrowly formulated. For one thing, focusing exclusively on the experience of agency is insufficiently distant from hypothesis (1), since a significant part of the experience of agency surely consists in kinesthetic and other bodily sensations. An alternative would be to take judgments of ownership to rest upon the capacity for agency, rather than upon the experience of agency. The guiding idea here is that the body is the physical object uniquely responsive to the will, and so we take ownership to extend to body parts that we can act with directly.

One difficulty with this proposal is that there are body parts that we judge to be our own but that we act with only in a very attenuated sense (if at all), such as the spleen or the kidney. Another, perhaps more significant challenge is operationalizing the capacity for agency, as opposed to the exercise of agency in action. What would be an adequate test of whether one experiences a body part as something that one can act with, in circumstances in which one does not actually move it? The problem is that it is not clear what would distinguish the judgment that I can act with *this* limb from the corresponding judgment of ownership (this is *my* limb)—and yet we need the former judgment to be the sort of thing that can ground the latter judgment.

A more promising approach, I think, would be to look for a phenomenon that might plausibly explain why both the experienced location of sensation and the experience of agency seem so important to judgments of ownership. This is where hypothesis (3) comes into the picture. Both forms of experience reflect the fact that we experience our bodies as distinctive physical objects. They also reflect (and possibly even contribute to) a very important source for that experienced distinctiveness, namely, the differences between how space is represented within the bounds of the body and how extrabodily space is represented—or, to put it another way, between how bodily locations are encoded and how nonbodily locations are encoded. So, the hypothesis that I will explore in this paper is that judgments of ownership track the distinctive spatiality of bodily experience.

III

This section focuses on two very general features of how bodily events are experienced. (I am understanding bodily events in a broad sense, to include sensations such as itches, pains, and so forth, as well as tactile experiences and proprioceptive/kinesthetic experiences of how one's limbs are either disposed, or moving, or both.) The first feature I call *Boundedness*.

Boundedness
Bodily events are experienced within the experienced body (a circumscribed body-shaped volume whose boundaries define the limits of the self).[8]

The body-shaped, circumscribed volume that defines the limits of the self is the experienced body. It can be, but need not be, identical to the physical body. There are many documented cases where the two diverge, and the divergence takes place in both directions. The boundaries of the bodily self in the experienced body can extend beyond the limits of the physical body. The experience of sensations in phantom limbs is a well-known example, indicating how the experienced bodily self expands to accommodate displaced sensation. Pathologies such as unilateral spatial neglect and somatoparaphrenia illustrate how the experienced body can be more restricted than the bounds of the physical body.

I should clarify how boundedness is to be understood. It is not intended as a necessary truth about human somatic experience. There seem to be counter examples in the literature. I am grateful to a referee for directing me to an interesting case presented in Cronholm (1951). Cronholm reports a phantom limb patient at the Karolinska Institute in Stockholm who appeared to be fully aware of the spatial boundaries of his *phantom* and yet who reported feeling a sensation in a region of space outside those boundaries. This case is highly unusual, but I would be surprised if it were unique. From my perspective, however, Boundedness is proposed as a general characterization of the phenomenology of bodily awareness. That it might be contravened in highly unusual circumstances is interesting, but not particularly damaging to the proposal, particularly given that boundedness does seem to be respected in the overwhelming majority of pathological cases.

In any event, boundedness captures a reciprocal, temporally extended, and plastic process. At any given moment the boundaries of the experienced body are relatively fixed. But viewed over time the experienced body is malleable and adaptable, responding to organic bodily growth, trauma, and the changing demands of movement and action. The technique of using *extended physiological proprioception* (EPP) in the design of prosthetics for amputees is an excellent illustration of the role that agency can play in redefining the limits of the experienced self. The inspiration for EPP comes from the familiar example of blind people using white canes not just as motility aids but also as tools for discovering the environment. Recognizing this type of transferred sensation as a potential tool for improving the effectiveness of prosthetic limbs, D. C. Simpson (1974) proposed EPP in the 1970s.

The basic idea of EPP is to design prostheses so that feedback information from the artificial limb is experienced proprioceptively. Agency is crucial, since the mechanism for achieving this is coupling the movement of the prosthetic with the residual movements available through the nearest intact joint so that there is a direct relation between the movement and position of the prosthetic limb and the movement and position of the anatomical joint. We can think about the movement of a prosthetic limb in input–output terms. The movement of the intact joint is the input and the new position of the prosthetic is the output. By designing the prosthetic limb so that the input and output are closely bound to each other, the output position can be sensed through proprioceptive feedback from the input movement. It appears that using the EPP technique to design prosthetic limbs improves their effectiveness (Doubler & Childress, 1984).

There are no studies that I am aware of on the subjective experience of amputees with EPP, but we can obtain guidance from qualitative studies of patients with "ordinary" prosthetics. A study of thirty-five amputees in the United Kingdom specifically explored the experience of embodiment in wearers/users of prosthetics, with many of the patients reporting their phantom limbs merging with the prosthesis (Murray, 2004). Here are some sample comments from amputees:

Participant   . . . because I don't feel as anything is really missing. So my prosthesis is "natural."

When I put on a prosthetic, the phantom becomes the prosthesis to the extent that the not-foot [phantom] is in almost the same position as the Flex-Foot [a brand of prosthesis], maybe slightly more rotated. The fit is so good, that it makes walking with the prosthesis easier because of the correspondence between the prosthetic leg and the phantom.

. . . Many amputees feel that their artificial limb is somehow part of them, a simple example of this is that I wouldn't like just anyone putting their hand on my artificial knee, even though it is not actually part of my body's flesh, it is still mine even though it's a piece of plastic and metal.

Interviewer   When you say it's part of you now, what exactly do you mean by that?

Participant   Well, to me it's as if, though I've not got my lower arm, it's as though I've got it and it's [the prosthesis] part of me now. It's as though I've got two hands, two arms.

This "merging" of phantom limbs with prostheses contrasts significantly with referred sensations in tool use and with the incorporation of tools in the body shema more generally. Here the prosthetic seems to be incorporated into the limits of the self, in the way that tools typically are not.[9]

The second general feature of how bodily events are experienced I term *Connectedness*.

Connectedness
The spatial location of a bodily event is experienced relative to the disposition of the body as a whole.

Connectedness presupposes Boundedness, but not vice versa. It is conceptually possible that we could experience bodily events within a space that defines the limits of the self and yet experience those events in isolation from everything else going on in that space. But that is not the normal phenomenology of the body. Bodily events are typically experienced relative to the background of the body as whole. In experiencing a pain in my knee, for example, I experience the pain as being in my leg, which in turn is disposed a certain way relative to my torso. My torso itself is experienced as being disposed a certain way relative to gravity and supporting surfaces. In this sense, therefore, bodily events are experienced within a holistic framework that, although sometimes recessive, is normally an ineliminable part of the content of experience. To motivate that thought, think how strange it would be to feel a sensation in your foot without having an idea of the angle of your foot relative to your lower leg, or of whether your leg is bent or straight at the knee.

The phenomena of both Boundedness and Connectedness can be readily identified in the bodily illusion experiments. So, for example, Boundedness predicts that subjects experience the rubber hand as incorporated into their own bodies—as opposed, for example, to being spatially discontinuous with their bodies. This is exactly how the phenomenology of the RHI is described by the subjects reviewed in Longo et al. (2008). Moreover, as Longo and colleagues observe, the rubber hand is typically experienced as displacing the subject's real hand. It is very rare for subjects in RHI experiments to report experiencing the rubber hand as a third, supernumerary hand (although see Ehrsson, 2009, for a version of the RHI in which healthy subjects seem to report experiencing two right hands). Interestingly, in the so-called invisible hand illusion, where referred sensations are elicited by stroking empty space, subjects report feeling the referred sensations in a hand that they cannot see, rather than outside the body (Gutersdam, Gentile, & Ehrsson, 2013).

As this indicates, bodily awareness can only be manipulated within certain, structural limits. One limiting factor is what is sometimes called the long-term body image (O'Shaughnessy, 1980, 1995)—an implicit understanding of the large-scale, structural properties of the body (such as the property of having no more than two hands). A number of studies have shown that the RHI is constrained by factors of anatomical plausibility. The illusion is extinguished, for example, when the rubber hand is of a different laterality from the subject's own hand (Tsakiris & Haggard, 2005). This is another Boundedness effect.

Manipulations of the RHI paradigm also reveal Connectedness effects. Most significantly, postural mismatches can extinguish the illusion. The difference between a postural mismatch and an anatomical mismatch is important. In both cases the manipulation extinguishes the illusion by, in effect, revealing it to be impossible for the subject to be the owner of the rubber hand. This comes about because the rubber hand is placed in a position that conflicts with subjects' knowledge of their own bodies and how they are disposed. As we have seen the knowledge engaged in Boundedness effects is general knowledge of the structure of the body. In cases of postural mismatch, in contrast, the rubber hand is (as it were) anatomically viable. But it just couldn't be part of the subject's body because the disposition of the rubber hand is inconsistent with the subject's knowledge of how his actual hand and arm are disposed. Tsakiris and Haggard (2005), for example, established that the illusion disappears if the rubber hand is oriented at a ninety-degree angle to the subject's actual hand. The angle of the rubber hand rules out its being attached to the subject's wrist and arm. This is a Connectedness effect, because if the position of the hand were not coded relative to the position of the wrist, and so on, there would be no inconsistency.

There are clear connections between, on the one hand, Boundedness and Connectedness and, on the other, the experienced location of sensation (hypothesis 1) and the experience of agency (hypothesis 2). One reason the experienced location of sensations seems so important for ownership is that (*per* Boundedness) sensations are typically experienced within the limits of the bodily self. Likewise for the experience of agency, which is standardly enabled by the experience of a connected and bounded body.[10] Boundedness and Connectedness are more general aspects of the phenomenology of bodily awareness, however. Letting them carry the explanatory weight allows us to think of judgments of ownership as multifactorial. The experience of agency and the experienced location of sensations both play a role in grounding judgments of agency. In the next section we will see that both Boundedness and Connectedness are themselves ultimately grounded in certain very basic features of the spatiality of bodily experience.

IV

How is the space of the body represented? The general topic of somatic spatial representation has seen rapidly increasing attention from psychologists and neuroscientists over the last three decades. Researchers have pursued a number of different, but overlapping, questions highly germane to the discussion in earlier sections of bodily illusions and the phenomenology of bodily awareness, but the two lines of research do not always map cleanly and directly onto each other. The principal focus of research into bodily illusions is on how we experience our bodies as our own. The principal focus of research into the neuroscience of spatial representation has been on how the brain encodes information about the body and about the location of objects in the immediate distal environment to allow reaching and other motor behaviors. Of course, it is hard to imagine that the way in which we experience our bodies is not at least partially determined by how the brain encodes spatial information, but the fact remains that these are two different questions. This section disentangles some of these issues.

One much discussed issue is how peripersonal space is represented. Peripersonal space is standardly defined as the area of space around the body that is within reach—as opposed to extrapersonal space, which is out of reach. Whereas information about extrapersonal space comes primarily through vision, with contributions from audition and smell, awareness of peripersonal space is much more multimodal. An elegant illustration of the difference between peripersonal and extrapersonal space comes from experiments on patients with unilateral spatial neglect. Neglect patients typically make significant errors when asked to bisect lines—since they neglect (typically) the left side of space they will place the midpoint of the line far to the right of the true midpoint. Since these bisection tasks involve drawing a line they take place within peripersonal space. However, Halligan and Marshall (1991) showed that a neglect patient with right hemisphere damage after a stroke, despite having the standard deficit when asked to *draw* a bisecting line, showed no deficit when asked to use a laser pointer to bisect a line in extrapersonal space.

There is considerable consensus that the representation of peripersonal space engages multiple frames of reference, depending on the relevant modality (Holmes & Spence, 2004; Battaglia-Mayer, Caminiti, Lacquaniti, & Zago, 2003). Information from vision is standardly represented in retinotopic coordinates (coordinates centered on the retina), while auditory and olfactory information is coded in head-centered coordinates (Cohen & Anderson, 2002). Moreover, neuron recordings in macaque monkeys have identified arm-centered receptive fields in the premotor cortex (Graziano, Yap, & Gross, 1994). These receptive fields move when the arm moves, rather than when the eyes move. So, the representation of peripersonal space is multilevel and varies according to modality and context.

Moreover, Noel, Pfeiffer, Blanke, and Serino (2015) have shown that in the full body illusion peripersonal space shifts to being centered at the location of the virtual body. However, one cannot draw direct conclusions about how the spatiality of the body is experienced from representations of peripersonal space. It is true that if a receptive field moves with the location of the arm, then the nervous system must have some way of keeping track of where the arm is. But it is perfectly possible, given the design of the studies, that the location of the arm is tracked visually, relative to a retinotopic reference frame. This would tell us nothing about how the body is experienced "from the inside" through bodily sensations, proprioception, and kinesthesis. And even if the location of the arm were tracked "from the inside," the question is still wide open as to the frame of reference relative to which this tracking takes place.

The question of how somatosensory spatial information is integrated with visual information has been prominent in studies of reaching. Successful reaching depends upon calibrating the represented location of the target with the represented starting point of the hand, to allow both the initial aiming and online monitoring and correction of the movement. There is evidence from psychophysics that successful reaching depends upon remapping the target location from a retinotopic coordinate system into body-centered or hand-centered frames of reference, or both (Soechting & Flanders, 1989a, 1989b). Such remapping would plausibly make the calibration easier. But, as with the representation of peripersonal space, it does not really help with the question we are interested in. Exactly the same question arises. To say that a target location is relative to a hand-centered frame of reference just means that target location is coded on a coordinate system whose origin is some designated point in the hand. But that doesn't tell us how the nervous system encodes the location of the center of the coordinate system—let alone how the location of the hand is experienced "from the inside" relative to the rest of the body.

What is needed to complement ongoing research into how peripersonal space and reaching movements are neutrally encoded is a model of how normal subjects experience the space of the body. Such a model obviously needs to be consistent with the existing experimental literature, but also needs to go further in two key respects. First, it needs to focus on the phenomenological aspect of spatial awareness of the body. That is, on how subjects are conscious of bodily space—on what it is to experience a bodily sensation at a particular bodily location, for example, or how the layout of the body is presented in somatosensory experience. Second, it needs to explain why our experience of our own bodies has the properties of Boundedness and Connectedness.

V

The first issue that arises in modeling the spatial content of bodily awareness is determining a frame of reference and corresponding coordinate system. This section introduces two possible approaches.

The first approach is in essence a direct continuation of the modeling strategies discussed in the previous section in the context of peripersonal space and reaching. We looked at a number of different reference frames—retinotopic, head-centered, or centered on specific body parts such as the hand. These are all standard Cartesian frames of reference with three axes. What distinguishes them is the point each takes as its origin. A natural extension of this approach would be to conceptualize the space of the body in a Cartesian frame with three axes, corresponding to the frontal, sagittal, and transverse planes. A plausible candidate for the origin of the coordinate system would be the body's center of mass.

So, on this modeling strategy, to experience a bodily event at a particular bodily location is to experience it at a certain point (x, y, z) in a space whose origin is the body's center of mass, where that point is given in terms of its distance from the origin on each of the three axes. A variant (probably more plausible) would be to use a spherical coordinate system, generalizing two-dimensional polar coordinates, rather than Cartesian coordinates, so that the sensation is given as located at a point (r, θ, φ) where r is the radial distance from body's center of mass; θ is the polar angle (measured from a fixed zenith in the vertical direction opposite the pull of gravity); and φ the azimuth angle (measured from a fixed direction on a plane orthogonal to the zenith, and so at right angles to the pull of gravity). Cartesian and spherical coordinate systems are interconvertible, of course.

One advantage of this approach is that it allows the space of the body to be mapped straightforwardly onto peripersonal space. A target location perceived in hand-centered coordinates in peripersonal space can equally be described in Cartesian or spherical coordinates relative to an origin in the body's center of mass. And so for example, it is computationally easy to plot the displacement required to move the hand from its current location to the target location, as well as to monitor the movement and adjust while it is in progress.

On the other hand, though, the approach has difficulty doing justice to how we actually experience our bodies. For one thing, as I have pointed out in previous work, our experience of our own bodies does not typically present a particular point as a privileged origin so that we experience particular bodily locations as being nearer than or further away from that origin (Bermúdez, 1998, 2005, 2011). In fact, it is not clear that the concepts *nearer than* or *further away from* have any applicability to the space of bodily experience. These comparative concepts have an implicit self-reference built into them, unless some other object is explicitly given as a reference point. To say that one thing is nearer than another is typically to say that it is nearer to *me*. Within a visual perspective this makes perfectly good sense, since the structure of the visual field implicitly defines a point that can serve as me for the purposes of comparison. But bodily awareness is not like this. The body's center of mass is important, of course, for balance, and so more generally for movement, but not in a way that makes it a candidate for calibrating distance and direction. And there is no other point in the body that can count as me relative to the rest of the body in the same way that the origin of the visual field counts as me relative to objects in the distal environment. So comparisons of distance and direction really only make sense in special circumstances (talking to the doctor, for example).

A second problem with the standard approach comes with accommodating Boundedness and Connectedness. According to Boundedness, bodily events are experienced within the experienced body (a circumscribed body-shaped volume whose boundaries define the limits of the self). So, from the perspective of conscious bodily experience, there is a marked distinction between bodily space and peripersonal space. Within the total volume of space defined by the limits of peripersonal space, those points that fall within the perceived space of the body are experientially privileged. They are, as Locke would put it, part of the conscious self. Yet this distinction is not at all captured within the model under consideration. Within the context of a frame of reference centered on the body's center of mass, the space defined is completely homogenous. There is no distinction between a point that falls within the perceived space of the body and one that does not—between a point that falls within my left forearm, for example, and a point that is three inches to the right in extrapersonal space. The standard approach would admittedly allow bodily boundaries to be defined, but this would be (as it were) a purely geometrical way of marking the difference between bodily space and peripersonal space. It would not in any sense capture how the space of the body is experientially privileged.

The standard approach fares no better with Connectedness. According to Connectedness, the spatial location of a bodily event is experienced relative to the disposition of the body as a whole. It follows that experienced locations within bodily space are not experienced in isolation. So, when we experience our foot flexed at a certain angle we experience that flexing of the ankle relative to the disposition of the foot, the knee, and the hip, for example. That is to say, bodily experience is both relational and holistic. In contrast, spatial locations on the standard approach are purely particularist. A bodily location is given as a triple of numbers, either (x, y, z) or (r, θ, φ). The coding of the location carries no information about what is going on elsewhere in the body.

For these reasons I have proposed a different model for thinking about how the space of the body is represented in conscious bodily experience. A starting point for the model is a distinction between two different ways of thinking about bodily location. We can think about a given bodily location in a way that abstracts from the disposition at a time of the body as a whole. So, for example, we might think about an itch being located at the front of the shin. This is a location that the itch has as long as it endures, irrespective of whether or not the shin moves. Alternatively one might think of the itch in a way that takes into account what the rest of the body is doing. In previous work I have termed these A-location and B-location respectively (Bermúdez, 1998, 2005, 2011).

A-location (1)
The location of a bodily event in a specific body part relative to an abstract map of the body, without taking into account the current position of the body.

B-location (1)
The location of a bodily event in a specific body part relative to the current position of relevant body parts.

So, for example, if I have a pain in the middle finger of my left hand and then contract my bicep to raise my left hand by six inches, then the A-location of my pain remains unchanged, while the B-location changes. The A-location remains unchanged because the pain is still in the middle finger of my left hand. The B-location is different, however, because my left hand is now at a different angle relative to my elbow. Both A-location and B-location are body relative. If I move six feet to the left and then stand as I am standing here, the pain in the middle finger of my left hand will still have the same A-location and B-location.

The idea, therefore, is that we experience a given bodily event at a specific A-location and B-location. A-location and B-location are not independent of each other—two different aspects of a single type of experience rather than two different ways of experiencing bodily events. The A-location dimension of bodily experience does justice to Boundedness, while the B-location dimension speaks more to Connectedness. If we typically experience a bodily event at a specific A-location then it follows automatically that we experience it within the experienced body, because A-locations can only fall within the perceived limits of the body. By the same token, if we typically experience a bodily event at a specific B-location, then we gain immediate insight into the relation between that bodily event and the overall disposition of the body.[11]

Of course, the explanatory value of this model depends upon giving a substantive account of A-location and B-location. In particular, we need an account of how the body is represented in somatosensory experience that will explain how and why we experience bodily events at specific A-locations and B-locations. I offer such an account in the next and final section.

VI

Extending Bermúdez (1998) and subsequent papers (2005, 2011) the previous section offered a general account of how the space of the body is represented in experience. This section offers a more detailed account that develops insights from two approaches to modeling the body—in biomechanics and robotics, on the one hand, and in Marr and Nishihara's (1978) model of object recognition on the other.

The model proposed in *The Paradox of Self-Consciousness* starts from how the body is articulated as a relatively immoveable torso connected by joints to moveable body parts. These joints range in size and scope from the knee and the neck, at one extreme, to the joints in fingers and toes, at the other. Joints afford the possibility of moving the body parts that they connect. There are around 230 joints in the human body, differing in the types of movement that they allow and in the degrees of freedom that they offer. The hip, for example, operates on all three planes and allows six different types of movement (abduction, adduction, extension, flexion, horizontal abduction, and horizontal adduction). The knee; like many of the finger joints, allows only flexion and extension in a single plane.

Joints provide the fixed points relative to which particular A-locations and B-locations can be specified.

A-location (2)
A particular bodily A-location is experienced in a given body part and specified relative to the joint immediately controlling the movement of that body part.

So, for example, an itch in the palm of my hand is experienced in the palm of my hand and its location is specified relative to the wrist, since the wrist immediately controls the movement of the palm of my hand (as opposed to the elbow and shoulder, whose control is mediate rather than immediate).

B-location (2)
A particular B-location is a given A-location oriented in a certain way relative to the rest of the body. It is specified recursively relative to the joints that lie between it and the immoveable torso.

The B-location of the itch in the palm of my hand is its A-location, supplemented by specifying the angles of the wrist relative to the forearm, the elbow relative to the upper arm, and the shoulder relative to the torso.[12]

To flesh this general model out further we can draw on two different but complementary approaches to modeling the body. The first comes from biomechanics and robotics, where the body is typically modeled as a system of rigid links connected by mechanical joints. Kinesiologists and roboticists have developed sophisticated tools for representing both

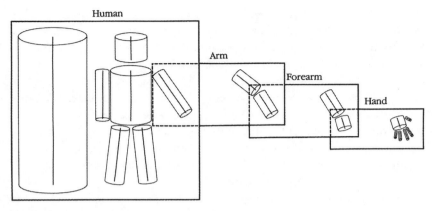

Figure 6.2
Marr and Nishihara's model of the human body as a hierarchy of generalized cones.
From Marr and Nishihara (1978).

bodily position at a time and movement over time in terms of the angles
of the relevant joints (see, e.g., a standard biomechanics textbook such as
Hall, 2014).

The second derives from Marr and Nishihara's model of object recognition in terms of matching three-dimensional object representations derived
from vision with a stored catalog of 3-D representations (Marr & Nishihara
1978). Objects are represented schematically as complexes of generalized
cones (surfaces generated by moving a cross-section along an axis, maintaining its shape but possibly varying its size). The human body is represented as a hierarchy of generalized cones, as depicted in figure 6.2.

The suggestion I will develop is that *within bodily experience* the human
body is represented in terms of generalized cones. This approach has two
very significant advantages.

First, it allows us to fill in a gap in the general models of the body in
biomechanics and robotics. Understandably, given what they are trying
to achieve, kinesiologists and roboticists typically abstract away from the
details of what goes on inside the limbs. From the perspective of studying
human movement or programming artificial movement it makes perfectly
good sense to treat limbs as rigid links with no intrinsic properties. When
studying the experienced space of the body, however, we obviously need
tools for describing the location of bodily events that take place inside limbs.
Modeling limbs as generalized cones allows us to do this in a way that is
faithful to the anatomy of the body.

Second, if we think of limbs as generalized cones then we can use a cylindrical coordinate system, somewhat similar to the spherical coordinate system discussed earlier. Identifying a cylindrical coordinate system involves identifying an origin at the intersection of the longitudinal axis (along the cylinder's axis of symmetry) and a reference plane orthogonal to the longitudinal axis, with a specified reference direction. The location of a point x in the cylinder is given by the triple (ρ, φ, z) where (ρ, φ) are in effect the polar coordinates of x on the plane that passes through x and is parallel to the reference plane and z is the distance from the origin to x along the longitudinal axis. As mentioned earlier, this is just one example of a number of interconvertible coordinate systems.

So, my proposal is that the space of the body is experienced relative to a model of body as a hierarchy of generalized cones linked by mechanical joints. Specifically, the hypotheses that I am making for A-location and B-location are as follows.

First,

A-location (3)
The A-location of a bodily event in a given limb is given in a cylindrical coordinate system whose origin is at the midpoint (center of mass) of the joint immediately controlling the position of that limb.

The subject's awareness of the large-scale structure of her body (e.g., what O'Shaughnessy, 1980 termed the "long-term body image") in effect fixes the surface and volume of the cylinder, thus defining the potential bodily space within which bodily events can be experienced. In most normal cases, of course, there will be a close map between the physical boundaries of the body and the cylinder thus defined. But it is perfectly conceivable that a cylinder should be defined with its origin at the tip of an amputation. This seems to be what is happening when amputees feel sensations in prosthetic limbs, as discussed earlier in the context of extended physiological proprioception.

Second,

B-location (3)
The B-location of a bodily event in a given limb is given by supplementing its A-location with a chain of relative joint angles that collectively specify the location of the given limb relative to the immoveable torso.

I am using the term "joint angle" as shorthand for whatever information is required to specify the disposition of a joint. It is likely, of course, to involve more than one coordinate, but no joint requires more than six (corresponding to the maximum number of degrees of freedom—three rotational and three translational). The degree of complexity will increase, however, when chains of joint angles are considered.

VII

To recap, experiments on bodily illusions raise important questions about what it is to experience one's body as one's own. Philosophers and cognitive scientists often refer to a sense of ownership that extends both to individual body parts and to the body as a whole. I do not find that this approach has much explanatory power and proposed investigating the complex phenomenon of ownership by looking at the grounds for judgments of ownership. After discounting the idea that there is a specific feeling of ownership, three hypotheses emerged.

(1) Judgments of ownership are based on the experienced location of sensation.
(2) Judgments of ownership are based on the experience of agency.
(3) Judgments of ownership are based on the experienced spatiality of the body.

Hypotheses (1) and (2) give an important part of the overall picture, but I argued that neither is fully explanatory on its own. Hypothesis (3) identifies a phenomenon that is more fundamental, since both experiencing agency and experiencing sensations take place relative to experiencing the distinctive space of the body.

In developing hypothesis (3) I began with two large-scale features of the phenomenology of bodily awareness. According to Boundedness, bodily events are experienced within a circumscribed body-shaped volume whose boundaries define the limits of the self, while according to Connectedness, the spatial location of a bodily event is experienced relative to the disposition of the body as a whole. Developing an account of the spatiality of bodily experience that does justice to Boundedness and Connectedness took us to the idea that bodily events are experienced in terms of A-location and B-location, which I then glossed through combining biomechanical models of the body as rigid links connected by mechanical joints with the picture of the body loosely derived from Marr and Nishihara's (1978) model of object recognition. The space of the body is experienced, I suggest, relative to a model of the body as a hierarchy of generalized cones linked by mechanical joints.

Circling back, therefore, to the starting point of the paper, my main proposal is that the judgments of ownership that we make about our bodies and body parts are ultimately grounded in the fact that we experience the space of the body in this distinctive way that differs fundamentally from how we experience extrabodily events, even those in peripersonal space. With this proposal in view let me end by identifying some important open questions for future work.

• How should the account of spatial content proposed in terms of A-location and B-location be developed into a full account of the content of bodily experiences?
• How should we spell out in detail the inferential or quasi-inferential relations in which bodily experiences stand to judgments of agency?
• How do those inferential or quasi-inferential relations compare to the relations between "ordinary" perceptual experiences and perceptual judgments?
• How should the account be extended to cases of *disownership*, as occur for example in somatoparaphrenia and other disorders?
• Can a parallel explanatory strategy to that proposed here for the "sense of ownership" be extended to the putative "sense of agency"?
• If so, what role does the distinctive spatiality of bodily experience play in underwriting judgments of agency?

Acknowledgments

I am very grateful to the editors and to two anonymous referees for probing and helpful comments; to Patrick Haggard and Tony Cheng for their commentary at the December 2015 Copenhagen workshop and in this volume; and to the other participants at the Copenhagen workshop.

Notes

1. For reviews see Corbetta and Shulman (2011) (spatial neglect), Vallar and Ronchi (2009) (somatoparaphrenia), and Scepkowski and Cronin-Golomb (2003) (alien hand syndrome).

2. For discussion at the neural level of the relation between ownership of the whole body and ownership of particular body parts see Petkova et al. (2011) and Gentile, Björnsdotter, Petkova, Abdulkarim, and Ehrsson (2015).

3. For a broadly similar overall strategy see Alsmith (2015), although he develops an account of judgments of ownership rather different from that proposed here. Alsmith's account of the RHI in terms of spontaneous imagining has some plausibility, but it is unclear how it would extend to nonillusory judgments of ownership.

4. The difference between (1) and (3) will become clear in section 4, but in brief the distinction is this: To base a judgment of ownership on the experienced location of sensation is to say that you take to be your own the body parts in which you feel sensations. In contrast, to base a judgment of ownership on the experienced spatiality of the body is to base it on the distinctive way in which bodily locations are experienced relative to how nonbodily locations are experienced.

5. For more recent discussions see Cassam (1995, 1997), and Hamilton (2013).

6. It may be that what somatoparaphrenic patients are denying is concern or care for the relevant body parts, rather than that those body parts are their own, which might suggest that bodily location and concern are not as inextricably connected as Locke (and others) have thought. It is rarely straightforward to interpret the reports of patients with somatoparaphrenia and comparable disorders.

7. But see Tsakiris, Prabhu, and Haggard (2006) for empirical explorations in the context of the RHI.

8. Cf. Martin (1995). According to Martin, it is a distinctive feature of the phenomenology of the body that "in having bodily sensations, it appears to one as if whatever one is aware of through having such sensations is a part of one's body" (1995, p. 269). This is a clear statement of what I am calling Boundedness (and he uses that very term at p. 271). Martin describes this phenomenological feature as a sense of ownership. For reasons indicated above I do not find this terminology very helpful. Moreover, he does not provide an explicit account of what grounds this phenomenological feature, which he seems to treat more as an explanandum than as an explanans (entirely appropriately, given his broader philosophical aims in that paper). Accordingly, I did not include his position as one of the three hypotheses about the grounds of judgments of ownership considered above.

9. For further discussion of tools and bodily awareness, see de Vignemont and Farnè (2010).

10. I am focusing here on what might be termed direct agency. There are also cases where subjects have an indirect experience of agency (as might be experienced by drone pilots and other remote-tool users) that do not seem to involve an experience of a connected and bounded body.

11. B-location does not immediately yield Connectedness in its entirety, however, due to the restriction to *relevant* body parts. Thanks to Adrian Alsmith for pressing me here.

12. In the case of bodily events taking place in the torso A-location and B-location will coincide. Localization in the torso has not been as well studied as in bodily extremities, such as the fingers and hands. But see Van Erp (2008) for a study indicating that stimulus locations on the torso may be coded in polar coordinates centered on the body's center of gravity. Van Erp suggests that, in order to compensate

for constant distortion of the skin surface as the torso flexes and moves, the angular component of the polar coordinate is more salient than the distance component. As he puts it, as long as we move our hand in the correct direction we will hit the stinging mosquito sooner or later.

References

Aglioti, S., Smania, N., Manfredi, M., & Berlucchi, G. (1996). Disownership of left hand and objects related to it in a patient with right brain damage. *Neuroreport, 8*(1), 293–296.

Alsmith, A. (2015). Mental activity and the sense of ownership. *Review of Philosophy and Psychology, 6*(4), 881–896. doi:10.1007/s13164-014-0208-1.

Armel, K. C., & Ramachandran, V. S. (2003). Projecting sensations to external objects: Evidence from skin conductance response. *Proceedings of the Royal Society, Series B: Biological Sciences, 270*(1523), 1499–1506. doi:10.1098/rspb.2003.2364.

Battaglia-Mayer, A., Caminiti, R., Lacquaniti, F., & Zago, M. (2003). Multiple levels of representation of reaching in the parieto-frontal network. *Cerebral Cortex, 13*(10), 1009–1022. doi:10.1093/cercor/13.10.1009.

Bermúdez, J. L. (1998). *The paradox of self-consciousness*. Cambridge, MA: MIT Press.

Bermúdez, J. L. (2005). The phenomenology of bodily awareness. In D. W. Smith & A. L. Thomasson (Eds.), *Phenomenology and philosophy of mind* (pp. 295–316). New York: Oxford University Press.

Bermúdez, J. L. (2011). Bodily awareness and self-consciousness. In S. Gallagher (Ed.), *Oxford handbook of the self* (pp. 157–179). Oxford: Oxford University Press; 10.1093/oxfordhb/9780199548019.003.0007.

Bermúdez, J. L. (2015). Bodily ownership, bodily awareness and knowledge without observation. *Analysis, 75*(1), 37–45. doi:10.1093/analys/anu119.

Bermúdez, J. L., Marcel, A. J., & Eilan, N. (Eds.). (1995). *The body and the self*. Cambridge, MA: MIT Press.

Bottini, G., Bisiach, E., Sterzi, R., & Vallar, G. (2002). Feeling touches in someone else's hand. *Neuroreport, 13*(2), 249–252.

Botvinick, M., & Cohen, J. (1998). Rubber hand "feel" touch that eyes see. *Nature, 391*(6669), 756. doi:10.1038/35784.

Cassam, Q. (1995). Introspection and bodily self-ascription. In J. L. Bermúdez, A. J. Marcel, & N. M. Eilan (Eds.), *The body and the self* (pp. 311–336). Cambridge, MA: MIT Press.

Cassam, Q. (1997). *Self and world*. Oxford: Oxford University Press.

Cohen, Y. E., & Andersen, R. A. (2002). A common reference frame for movement plans in the posterior parietal cortex. *Nature Reviews: Neuroscience, 3*, 553–562.

Corbetta, M., & Shulman, G. (2011). Spatial neglect and attention networks. *Annual Review of Neuroscience, 34*, 569–599. doi:10.1146/annurev-neuro-061010-113731.

Costantini, M., & Haggard, P. (2007). The rubber hand illusion: Sensitivity and reference frame for body ownership. *Consciousness and Cognition, 16*(2), 229–240. doi:10.1016/j.concog.2007.01.001.

Cronholm, B. (1951). Phantom limbs in amputees: A study of changes in the integration of centripetal impulses with special reference to referred sensations. *Acta Psychiatrica et Neurologica Scandinavica, 72*(Suppl.), 1–310.

de Vignemont, F. (2007). Habeas corpus: The sense of ownership of one's own body. *Mind & Language, 22*(4), 427–449. doi:10.1111/j.1468-0017.2007.00315.x.

de Vignemont, F. (2013). The mark of bodily ownership. *Analysis, 73*(40), 643–651. doi:10.1093/analys/ant080.

de Vignemont, F. (2014). A multimodal conception of bodily awareness. *Mind, 123*(492), 989–1020. doi:10.1093/mind/fzu089.

de Vignemont, F. (in press). *Mind the body*. Oxford: Oxford University Press.

de Vignemont, F., & Farnè, A. (2010). Widening the body to rubber hands and tools: What's the difference? (Incorporer des objets et des membres factices: Quelle différence?). *Revue de Neuropsychologie, 2*(3), 203–211. doi:10.3917/rne.023.0203.

Doubler, J. A., & Childress, D. S. (1984). An analysis of extended physiological proprioception as a prosthesis-control technique. *Journal of Rehabilitation Research and Development, 21*(1), 5–18.

Ehrsson, H. H. (2009). How many arms make a pair? Perceptual illusion of having an additional limb. *Perception, 38*(2), 310–312. doi:10.1068/p6304.

Ferri, F., Chiarelli, A. M., Merla, A., Gallese, V., & Costantini, M. (2013). The body beyond the body: Expectation of a sensory event is enough to induce ownership over a fake hand. *Proceedings of the Royal Society, Series B: Biological Sciences, 280*(1765), 20131140. doi:10.1098/rspb.2013.1140.

Gallagher, S. (2000). Philosophical conceptions of the self: Implications for cognitive science. *Trends in Cognitive Sciences, 4*(1), 14–21. doi:10.1016/S1364-6613(99)01417-5.

Gallagher, S. (2005). *How the body shapes the mind*. New York: Oxford University Press.

Gentile, G., Björnsdotter, M., Petkova, V. I., Abdulkarim, Z., & Ehrsson, H. H. (2015). Patterns of neural activity in the human ventral premotor cortex reflect a whole-body multisensory percept. *NeuroImage, 109*, 328–340. doi:10.1016/j.neuroimage.2015.01.008.

Graziano, M. S. A., Yap, G. S., & Gross, C. G. (1994). Coding of visual space by pre-motor neurons. *Science, 266*(5187), 1054–1057.

Gutersdam, A., Gentile, G., & Ehrsson, H. H. (2013). The invisible hand illusion: Multisensory integration leads to the embodiment of a discrete volume of empty space. *Journal of Cognitive Neuroscience, 25*(7), 1078–1099. doi:10.1162/jocn_a_00393.

Hall, S. (2014). *Basic biomechanics* (7th ed.). New York: McGraw Hill.

Halligan, P. W., & Marshall, J. C. (1991). Left neglect for near but not far space in man. *Nature, 350*(6318), 498–500. doi:10.1038/350498a0.

Hamilton, A. (2013). *The self in question: Memory, the body, and self-consciousness.* Basingstoke: Palgrave Macmillan.

Holmes, N. P., & Spence, C. (2004). The body schema and the multisensory re presentation(s) of peripersonal space. *Cognitive Processing, 5*(2), 94–105. doi:10.1007/s10339-004-0013-3.

Ionta, S., Martuzzi, R., Salomon, R., & Blanke, O. (2014). The brain network reflecting bodily self-consciousness: A functional connectivity study. *Social Cognitive and Affective Neuroscience, 9*(12), 1904–1913. doi:10.1093/scan/nst185.

Kalckert, A., & Ehrsson, H. H. (2012). Moving a rubber hand that feels like your own: A dissociation of ownership and agency. *Frontiers in Human Neuroscience, 6*, 40. doi:10.3389/fnhum.2012.00040.

Kilteni, K., Maselli, A., Kording, K. P., & Slater, M. (2015). Over my fake body: Body ownership illusions for studying the multisensory basis of own-body perception. *Frontiers in Human Neuroscience, 9*, 141. doi:10.3389/fnhum.2015.00141.

Lenggenhager, B., Tadi, T., Metzinger, T., & Blanke, O. (2007). Video ergo sum: Manipulating bodily self-consciousness. *Science, 317*(5841), 1096–1099. doi:10.1126/science.1143439.

Locke, J. (1975). In P. H. Nidditch (Ed.), *An essay concerning human understanding.* Oxford: Clarendon Press. (1698).

Longo, M., Schüür, F., Kammers, M. P. M., Tsakiris, M., & Haggard, P. (2008). What is embodiment? A psychometric approach. *Cognition, 107*(3), 978–998. doi:10.1016/j.cognition.2007.12.004.

Marr, D., & Nishihara, H. K. (1978). Representation and recognition of the spatial organization of three-dimensional shapes. *Proceedings of the Royal Society of London, 200*(1140), 269–294. doi:10.1098/rspb.1978.0020.

Martin, M. (1995). Bodily awareness: A sense of ownership. In J. L. Bermúdez, A. J. Marcel, & N. Eilan (Eds.), *The body and the self* (pp. 267–289). Cambridge, MA: MIT Press.

Merleau-Ponty, M. (1968). *The phenomenology of perception.* London: Routledge.

Moseley, G. L., Olthof, N., Venema, A., Don, S., Wijers, M., Gallace, A., et al. (2008). Psychologically induced cooling of a specific body part caused by the illusory ownership of an artificial counterpart. *Proceedings of the National Academy of Sciences of the United States of America, 105*(35), 13169–13173. doi:10.1073/pnas.0803768105.

Murray, C. D. (2004). An interpretative phenomenological analysis of the embodiment of artificial limbs. *Disability and Rehabilitation, 26*(16), 963–973. doi:10.1080/09638280410001696764.

Noel, J.-P., Pfeiffer, C., Blanke, O., & Serino, A. (2015). Peripersonal space as the space of the bodily self. *Cognition, 144,* 49–57. doi:10.1016/j.cognition.2015.07.012.

O'Shaughnessy, B. (1980). *The will: A dual aspect theory.* Cambridge: Cambridge University Press.

O'Shaughnessy, B. (1995). Proprioception and the body image. In J. L. Bermúdez, A. J. Marcel, & N. Eilan (Eds.), *The body and the self* (pp. 175–203). Cambridge, MA: MIT Press.

Petkova, V. I., & Ehrsson, H. H. (2008). If I were you: Perceptual illusion of body swapping. *PLoS One, 3*(12), e3832. doi:10.1371/journal.pone.0003832.

Petkova, V. I., Björnsdotter, M., Gentile, B., Jonsson, T., Li, T.-Q., & Ehrsson, H. H. (2011). From part- to whole-body ownership in the multisensory brain. *Current Biology, 21*(13), 1118–1122. doi:10.1016/j.cub.2011.05.022.

Scepkowski, L. A., & Cronin-Golomb, A. (2003). The alien hand: Cases, categorizations, and anatomical correlates. *Behavioral and Cognitive Neuroscience Reviews, 2*(4), 261–277.

Serino, A., Alsmith, A., Costantini, M., Mandrigin, A., Tajadura-Jimenez, A., & Lopez, C. (2013). Bodily ownership and self-location: Components of bodily self-consciousness. *Consciousness and Cognition, 22*(4), 1239–1252. doi:10.1016/j.concog.2013.08.013.

Simpson, D. C. (1974). The choice of control system for the multimovement prosthesis: Extended physiological proprioception (EPP). In P. Herberts, R. Kadefors, R. Magnusson, & I. Petyersen (Eds.), *The control of upper-extremity prostheses and orthoses* (pp. 146–150). Springfield, IL: Charles C. Thomas.

Soechting, J. F., & Flanders, M. (1989a). Sensorimotor representations for pointing to targets in three-dimensional space. *Journal of Neurophysiology, 62*(2), 582–594.

Soechting, J. F., & Flanders, M. (1989b). Errors in pointing are due to approximations in sensorimotor transformations. *Journal of Neurophysiology, 62,* 595–608.

Tsakiris, M. (2010). My body in the brain: A neurocognitive model of body-ownership. *Neuropsychologia, 48*(3), 703–712. doi:10.1016/j.neuropsychologia.2009.09.034.

Tsakiris, M., & Haggard, P. (2005). The rubber hand illusion revisited: Visuotactile integration and self-attribution. *Journal of Experimental Psychology, 31*(1), 80–91. doi:10 .1037/0096-1523.31.1.80.

Tsakiris, M., Prabhu, G., & Haggard, P. (2006). Having a body versus moving your body: How agency structures body-ownership. *Consciousness and Cognition, 15*(2), 423–432. doi:10.1016/j.concog.2005.09.004.

Vallar, G., & Ronchi, R. (2009). Somatoparaphrenia: A bodily delusion. A review of the neuropsychological literature. *Experimental Brain Research, 192*(3), 533–551. doi:10.1007/s00221-008-1562-y.

van Erp, J. B. F. (2008). Absolute localization of vibrotactile stimuli on the torso. *Perception & Psychophysics, 70*(6), 1016–1023. doi:10.3758/PP.70.6.1016.

7   Deflationary Accounts of the Sense of Ownership

Shaun Gallagher

The concepts of sense of agency (SA) and sense of ownership (SO) have figured in definitions of the minimal self, and have been put to productive use in experimental science (most famously in the literature on the rubber hand illusion) and in psychiatry. But they have also become controversial in philosophy of mind. Philosophers have challenged the terminology, the distinction, and even the existence of the putative experiences that these terms signify. In this chapter I want first of all to offer some clarifications about the meaning of these concepts, and then focus specifically on the sense of ownership in relation to bodily awareness.

Specifically I want to consider the deflationary account of the sense of ownership offered by Michael Martin (1995) and José Louis Bermúdez (2011). On the deflationary account, the sense of ownership is something intrinsic to bodily awareness, rather than some additional quality. I will argue that, notwithstanding arguments to the contrary, the phenomenological account of the sense of ownership in terms of a prereflective self-awareness fits with this deflationary account. In contrast to the deflationary account, however, the phenomenological account suggests that, rather than perception of the veridical objective body, bodily awareness is primarily awareness of the lived body, which may include things like phantom limbs and prosthetics. Finally, despite a conceptual distinction between sense of ownership and sense of agency, this does not preclude the fact that these experiences are usually integrated and not easily distinguishable. Understanding how they integrate and extend to action makes the deflationary explanation more complex and nuanced, and suggests its importance for enactivist accounts of embodied perception.

Some Preliminaries

I'll start with a simple and brief review of some distinctions that can be found running across philosophical, experimental, and psychiatric contexts. The

Table 7.1 Prereflective and reflective levels

Experience	Prereflective	Reflective judgment
Ownership (subjectivity, my-ness, mineness, or ownness)	Sense of ownership (SO)—the prereflective *experience* that I am the one moving (or keeping still) or thinking, and so on.	*Attribution/judgment of ownership*, or attribution of subjectivity (Graham & Stephens, 1994)—the reflective (retrospective) realization or judgment that I am the one who moved or had a specific thought.
Agency (authorship)	*Sense of agency* (SA)—as I act or think, the prereflective *experience* that I am the cause/initiator of my action or thinking, and have some control over it.	*Attribution/judgment of agency*—the reflective (retrospective) attribution or *judgment* that an action or a thought was caused by me.

first is the aforementioned distinction between SA and SO. In the 1990s, in many writings about self and schizophrenic delusional symptoms, for example, the distinction between SA and SO remained implicit (e.g., Campbell, 1999; Frith, 1992; Gallagher & Marcel, 1999; Marcel, 2003). Stephens and Graham (2000, drawing on their own earlier work, Graham & Stephens, 1994) and Gallagher (2000) proposed a more explicit set of distinctions that included both reflective and prereflective experiences that can be mapped out as in table 7.1 (see Gallagher, 2015).

The terminology varies from one theorist to another, including use of terms such as "authorship" for agency, "subjectivity" for ownership, and so on. Synofzik, Vosgerau, and Newen (2008) clarified the important difference between feeling/experiencing and judging, which is also reflected in the distinction between prereflective sense and reflective attribution of agency and ownership. I'll continue to use the abbreviations SA and SO to signify the prereflective (or first-order) feeling or experience of agency and ownership, respectively.

SA and SO may be difficult to distinguish in typical intentional action where they are well integrated and perhaps experientially indistinct. In the example of involuntary movement, however, the two come apart. In reflex movement or a case where someone pushes me or manipulates my body, I lack SA for the initial movement, although I still have a sense that the movement is mine in the sense that it is happening to me—it is my body that is moving. At least on one interpretation, ceteris paribus, my reflective judgment would reflect that situation and attribute ownership but not agency.

Concerning the phrase "sense of ownership," especially with reference to one's body, a number of theorists have rightly pointed out that "ownership" may not be the right term, and is certainly an overly strong term to signify the experience at stake. "Ownership" typically applies to things, objects, or property and tends to signify a legal claim about such property. One's body, however, is not a piece of property, and we are not in this kind of relationship of ownership to our own body. Thus Bermúdez suggests that "ownership is a rather tenuous and metaphorical concept in this context. We do not own hands, rubber or otherwise, in the way that we own personal property" (this volume).[1] It is certainly true that this is a problem with the term "ownership" as it is applied in the phenomenological sense to the body. We find the phrase "sense of ownership" in use, however, at least from the mid-1990s, for example in Michael Martin's (1995) essay "Bodily Awareness: A Sense of Ownership," in *The Body and the Self*. As far as I can tell, this is the first use of this phrase in the sense that Martin defined it, as the "phenomenological quality, that [a] body part appears to be part of one's body" (Martin 1995, p. 269; see also Martin 1992).[2] Phenomenologists, in the philosophical tradition following Husserl, and in the phenomenological psychiatry tradition following Jaspers, avoid the term "ownership," and instead use the term "mineness" (see, e.g., Hopkins 1993). I take the term "mineness" as used by phenomenologists and the term "ownership" in the discussions that follow Martin, to be equivalent, and for my purposes I'll stay with the term "ownership" as it continues in current philosophical and scientific usage.

The sense of ownership, however, seemingly applies not only to one's body, taken as a whole, but also to body parts (e.g., my hand), to bodily sensations (e.g., my pain), and in addition, to actions, to thoughts, and most basically to experiences. One important question in this regard is whether the concept means the same thing when it is used to refer to these different phenomena. Although, in this chapter, I will focus on the issue of SO as it is involved in bodily awareness, this question is still relevant. Bermúdez makes this clear with respect to applying the concept of SO, which he considers metaphorical, to the body as a whole in contrast to a body part:

> It is unlikely that any way of unpacking the metaphor that will work for limb ownership can be straightforwardly applied to so-called bodily ownership. Intuitively one might say that to feel ownership for a limb is to experience it as con-

nected with the rest of one's body and as a part of one. But could that be the same sense in which we might feel ownership for our bodies as a whole? What would it mean to say that one experiences one's body as a part of oneself? (Bermúdez, this volume)

Whether SO can apply in the same way to these different phenomena, or not, will depend on how we conceive or define it. If one defines it as involving some kind of connectedness, as Bermúdez suggests seems intuitive, then it's a puzzle how it can apply to the body as a whole and not just to a part of the body. To what is the body as a whole connected?

The Phenomenological Sense of Body Ownership

Rather than defining SO in terms of connectedness, let's consider Martin's (1995) definition, which is also taken up by Bermúdez (this volume). For Martin, SO is defined in terms of spatial boundaries, so that "when one feels a sensation, one thereby feels as if something is occurring within one's body" (Martin, 1995, p. 267). This also allows one to talk about ownership for parts of one's body: "in having bodily sensations, it appears to one as if whatever one is aware of through having such sensation is a part of one's body. . . . This phenomenological quality, that the body part appears to be part of one's body—call this *a sense of ownership*—is itself in need of further elucidation" (Martin, 1995, p. 269). The awareness involved in that sensory experience is, according to Martin, a perceptual awareness. The sensory awareness is a perception of a part of my body, and the experience includes SO for that part. SO is further elucidated in terms of that which occurs within the boundaries of my body. Specifically it is the fact that the sensation (whether proprioceptive, nociceptive, or any modality of bodily sensation) has a location, which is the quality of falling within one's apparent body boundary. This is what accounts for SO. This is not a matter of explicit judgment, as if I were experiencing a free-floating sensation concerning which I needed to judge its spatial location as falling within my body boundaries. Rather, as Martin argues, its apparent location is an intrinsic feature of the sensation itself, at least for any sensation that possesses a felt location. SO, apparent ownership, is not a quality in addition to other qualities of experience (e.g., apparent location), but "already inherent within them" (Martin, 1995, p. 278).

Bermúdez (this volume) follows Martin in thinking that the body boundary (or "boundedness") is important: "Bodily events are experienced within the experienced body (a circumscribed body-shaped volume whose boundaries define the limits of the self)." If one accepts this, one can then add connectedness ("the spatial location of a bodily event is experienced relative to the disposition of the body as a whole") to get a more complete conception of the experienced spatiality of the body.

Along with Martin, Bermúdez rejects the idea that SO is a special additional sense over and above these other qualities. He rejects the idea that there is "a specific feeling of ownership—a qualitative 'feel' that one has in all and only those body parts that one experiences as one's own." According to Bermúdez (2011), SO conceived in this "inflationary" way, is a philosophical fiction. Although one does experience a sense of body boundedness and connectedness, one does not experience, in addition, SO as a separate and independent feeling. Bermúdez thus denies that there is a positive first-order (nonobservational) phenomenology of ownership or feeling of "mineness." In contrast to this "inflationary" conception, which he attributes to phenomenologists such as Merleau-Ponty (Bermúdez also cites Gallagher, 2005; de Vignemont, 2007, 2013) he offers a deflationary account. "On a deflationary conception of ownership the sense of ownership consists, first, in certain facts about the phenomenology of bodily sensations and, second, in certain fairly obvious judgments about the body (which we can term judgments of ownership)" (Bermúdez, 2011, p. 162). The idea, as I understand it, is that something like an explicit experience of ownership only comes up when we turn our reflective attention to our bodily experience and attribute that experience to ourselves. But that involves adding something that's not there to begin with. "There are facts about the phenomenology of bodily awareness (about position sense, movement sense, and interoception) and there are judgments of ownership, but there is no additional feeling of ownership" (Bermúdez, 2011, p. 166).

Whereas it is possible to read Martin as positing a feeling of ownership that is inherent, implicit, or intrinsic to sensations located in or on one's body—although not as an additional or separable quality—Bermúdez seemingly denies that there is anything like an inherent SO (see, e.g., de Vignemont, 2013). In this respect, there are only bodily sensations and a reflective judgment or attribution of ownership. I'll argue that what Bermúdez refers to as an inflationary conception of SO is not essentially different from what Martin defines in terms of an inherent (but not additional) feeling that sensations are of one's body, which I'll paraphrase in the following way: SO consists of a certain intrinsic aspect of the phenomenology of bodily awareness. To say that it is an intrinsic aspect is to agree that it is not an additional or independent feeling, but rather, a sense "already inherent within" the phenomenology of bodily sensations. On the phenomenological view, and in contrast to Bermúdez, this intrinsic aspect is "prereflective" in the sense that one has this intrinsic experience of ownership without having to make a reflective judgment about ownership.

Let me point out that Bermúdez may have been misled by the wording of a claim that I made, and which he quotes.

> In non-observational self-awareness I do not require the mediation of a perception or judgment to recognize myself as myself. I do not need to reflectively ascertain that my body is mine, or that it is *my* body that is in pain or that it is experiencing pleasure. In normal experience, this knowledge is already built into the structure of experience. (Gallagher, 2005, p. 29; quoted in Bermúdez, 2011, p. 162)

Bermúdez emphasizes the last sentence and seems to take the phrase "this knowledge" in a stronger fashion than I intended it. I admit that "knowledge" might have been the wrong term to use here. By "this knowledge" I did not mean the sort of knowledge one has by reflective judgment; I meant a nonobservational awareness—something akin to what Bermúdez (2015), following Anscombe, calls "knowledge without observation." This is a prereflective awareness that is built into (not something separate and distinct from) the structure of precisely the experience I have of my body or of a sensation that is located in my body. I think that this is consistent with a deflationary account. At the same time, however, this means that there is a positive, even if intrinsic or integrated, experience of mineness (SO) in my bodily awareness. This is also what Dokic (2003) claims in an account that Bermúdez identifies as deflationary. "Bodily experience gives us a *sense of ownership.* . . . The very idea of *feeling* a pain in a limb which does not seem to be ours is difficult to frame, perhaps unintelligible" (Dokic, 2003, p. 325).

Frédérique de Vignemont (2007) offers the example in which you experience SO for your hand when another person touches it, in a way that you do not feel SO for the touching hand. According to Bermúdez, this is nothing more than experiencing sensations at the location of your hand. Still, your experience of it is as of *your* hand, and even if the "yourness" or "ownness" is implicit or intrinsic to the experience of the touch, it is nonetheless part of that experience. I'll come back to this example below to suggest that there is something more going on in this experience.

Using phenomenological terminology, I've suggested that SO involves a *prereflective* self-awareness, a notion that is sometimes regarded as mysterious jargon by some philosophers of mind. Let me start with a description that comes from someone who is in mainstream analytic philosophy of mind.

[Consider] the case of thinking about *x* or attending to *x*. In the process of thinking about *x* there is already an implicit awareness that one is thinking about *x*. There is no need for reflection here, for taking a step back from thinking about *x* in order to examine it. . . . When we are thinking about *x*, the mind is focused on *x*, not on our thinking of *x*. Nevertheless, the process of thinking about *x* carries with it a nonreflective self-awareness. (Goldman, 1970, p. 96)

Phenomenologists generalize this idea; they take it to apply to consciousness in general—including, not just thinking or attending, but also bodily awareness (Gallagher & Zahavi, 2015). How is SO related to prereflective self-awareness?

Bermúdez appeals to Anscombe's notion of "knowledge without observation" to make the point that we don't have proprioception and kinesthesia, and then, on that basis, make a judgment about body position or movement. He quotes Anscombe (1962), who considers the expression "sensation of X" and distinguishes between the idea that "of X" signifies the sensation content or something that always goes with it, and provides the example of the sensation of going down in a lift. Does the phrase "the sensation of going down in a lift" (1962, p. 56) signify the feeling I have of an upward feeling in my stomach (the internal description or content of the sensation) or the event of going down in an elevator (the external accompaniment). I think that Goldman's description of prereflective self-awareness can apply here. In the process of having the sensation of going down in the lift, I can focus on going down in the lift (that external accompaniment or event which is the intentional object of my perception), or I can focus on the internal upward feeling in my stomach; but even if I focus on going down in the lift, that focus carries with it a nonreflective (nonobservational) awareness of my phenomenal experience (the sensation content), which implicitly includes the sense that this is happening to me—that is, a nonreflective self-awareness that, roughly, it is *my* stomach that is moving upward, or perhaps something more indeterminate, but nonetheless, an experience in or of *my* body.

Anscombe and Bermúdez are right to say that things are not always so unambiguous with proprioception, kinesthesia, and vestibular sensations; such experiences usually underdetermine the sense of how one's body is configured. They nonetheless do indicate that however it may be configured, it is *one's own* body that is at stake. Again, however, this can be read in the deflationary way, so that there is no "perfectly determinate 'quale' associated with the feeling of myness'" (Bermúdez, 2011, p. 165) independent of the proprioceptive and kinesthetic sensations. SO is not a separate quality, like the experienced quality of boundedness; it is, rather, an intrinsic aspect of any quality that is part of bodily awareness.

Bermúdez doesn't deny that we can have a proprioceptive and kinesthetic awareness of our bodily (and limb) posture and movement. Such sensory experiences are part of what gives us a sense of boundedness and connectedness "from the inside." The sense of boundedness or of connectedness, however, may be even more underdetermined than SO. There is a more or less integrated pattern of experience in which proprioceptive/kinesthetic awareness includes an intrinsic experience that it is *my own* body that is positioned such and such, or moving so and so.

Veridicality

There are two further points that can help us understand the sense of ownership. The first, a distinction between the objective body and the lived body, derives from a phenomenological approach to questions of embodiment. The second emphasizes an enactivist approach to perception (see the next section). The first point concerns an issue that is related to SO and is brought out by Martin in his discussion of veridicality.

Martin discusses the case of feeling a sensation of pain in a phantom limb. In objective terms, this sensation falls outside of the real boundaries of the physical body, since the limb is no longer there. For Martin (1995, p. 275) this means that to at least some degree the sensation is illusory. The pain is true enough, but it is illusory to the extent that it seems to be in a part of the body that is no longer there. It's not that the pain itself is an illusion (any more than the referred pain of myocardial ischemia, which might appear in the left arm, is an illusion); its location is not veridical. The measure of veridicality here is the objective body. If the limb is objectively or physically not there, then there is nothing in that location to perceive. One can also think of other cases, such as the rubber hand illusion (RHI) (Botvinick & Cohen, 1998; Tsakiris, 2016), and experiments with robots (Cole, Sacks, & Waterman, 2000) in which subjects come to feel sensations in the rubber hand or in the robotic hand.[3] Such experiences may involve SO for the phantom, the rubber hand, or the robot hand, but if SO depends on the location of the sensation being within the boundary of the objective body, then we should say that the SO is also illusory. On the one hand, that may be right, if the measure of illusion is tied to the objective body. Accordingly, for example, the RHI is defined as an illusion.

On the other hand, one may ask whether this understanding doesn't privilege what Anscombe called the external accompaniment, that is, the intentional object of perception—in this case, the body as object, which is typically where we experience our sensations as apparently located. But isn't the sensation content (as Anscombe called it) of pain in the phantom (which is a case of referred pain) more or less the same as when experiencing the sensation as located in our existing limb? The experience of, for example, the phantom, rubber hand, or robot hand is illusory with respect to the objective body, but it still involves an experience of SO. One can think differently about this in terms of the phenomenological conception of the lived body, the body as it is experienced, the agentive body that can extend to include prosthetics and phantoms, as well as rubber and robot hands. Part of the measure of the lived body is the fact that SO extends along the same lines to include prosthetics, etc.

De Vignemont notes that some amputees experience their prosthetic limb as belonging to their body; others do not. She suggests that the difference is a difference in the SO. Bermúdez, however, wants to know where this "feeling of myness" is located, and he lists three possibilities: (1) in the prosthesis; (2) at a determinate location elsewhere in the body; (3) or it might be a "nonlocalizable" feeling. He rejects all three possibilities. This way of asking the question, however, raises an issue similar to the one Bermúdez raises about how connectedness could apply to the body as a whole. The issue here is how ownership could be experienced for the limb or body part itself if it is an intrinsic experience of a sensation located within the limb. We surely want to say that SO applies pervasively to the sensation (this is my experience, my pain, etc.) and the body part (this is my arm), as well as to the body as a whole (this is my body). There is a problem only if we think of location in terms of falling within *objectively defined* boundaries of the physical body, and of all sensations as discrete experiences. Proprioception and kinesthesia, for example, are relational rather than discrete. On the proprioceptive map, my arm, for example, is located always in relation to the other parts of my body, and the experience of a discrete sensation, the pain of a pin prick, for example, typically includes proprioceptive awareness of where on my body it is experienced. Proprioception maps my *lived* body rather than objective space. It's neither egocentric nor third-person allocentric; rather, it is a non-perspectival awareness of one's body (Gallagher, 2003). Bermúdez himself notes a "fundamental disanalogy between the bodily space of proprioception and the egocentric space of perception and action. . . . In contrast with vision, audition, and the other canonically exteroceptive modalities, there are certain spatial notions that do not seem to be applicable to somatic proprioception" (1998, pp. 152–153).

Still, if one considers the prosthesis as part of one's lived body, one might think that the feeling is in the prosthesis. Bermúdez rejects this idea because "feelings and sensations are experienced only within the confines of the body" (Bermúdez, 2011, p. 164). In this he differs from Martin who allows the possibility of feeling sensations "to be located in regions that fall outside of the actual limits of the [objective] body" (Martin, 1995, p. 278), although Martin would call these experiences illusions rather than perceptions. If the SO is an intrinsic aspect of a certain localized sensation, however, as the deflationary account suggests, then it could be in the prosthesis just to the extent that one could feel a sensation in that part of the lived body. Given evidence from classic examples of things like the blind man's cane (Head, 1920; Merleau-Ponty, 2012), and the RHI (see de Vignemont, 2013), at the very least it seems possible that one could experience SO in the prosthesis, which has the same or similar sensation content as a sensation located in the confines of the objective body. It is illusory only in the sense that it would not literally be within the confines of the objective body. But one can still maintain that SO, even in this case, is an aspect intrinsic to other sensory experiences, since one does experience apparent location, and perhaps an extended apparent boundedness and connectedness with respect to the lived body. In this regard we can still accept the idea that apparent ownership is not "a quality additional to the other qualities of experience but as somehow already inherent within them," but reject what Martin identifies as a corollary of this view, namely that "bodily awareness is primarily awareness of one's physical [i.e., objective] body, and awareness of body parts only in as much as they are parts of that body" (1995, p. 278). The phenomenological corollary is rather that bodily awareness is primarily awareness of one's lived body.[4]

Integrating Ownership and Agency

In this section I want to push the deflationary idea that SO is an inherent, implicit, or intrinsic aspect of bodily awareness a bit further, and specifically in an enactivist direction. It will be easier to do this by staying with Martin's idea that bodily awareness is perceptual (but see note 5), and for the sake of argument I'll adopt that view.

First, let me say that I agree with de Vignemont (2014) that bodily awareness is multimodal (see e.g., Gallagher, 2005; Tsakiris, 2016). I am not as concerned as she is in regard to the lack of reliability or precision of proprioception or the other sense modalities. Indeed, proprioception never functions just by itself, and reliability should be measured in terms of the whole system and its integrated functioning. Moreover, if we consider reliability pragmatically—and not just epistemologically—proprioception, functioning along with other modalities (touch, vision, etc.), provides a pragmatic bodily awareness related primarily to the subject's action. The fact that it does not give me a precise sense of my bodily posture or shape or boundaries as I am lying in bed or am not moving, in contrast to when I am moving, is fine since I don't usually need high precision in such circumstances. Even in regard to action, I do not always need precise information about body boundary or limb location; pragmatic estimates are good enough in most cases, and we get more precision when needed via the mix of senses. We don't need the precision of a global positioning system for action. What is at stake, in regard to proprioception and bodily awareness more generally, is not precise information about objective posture or limb location. Indeed, the kind of prereflective awareness of one's body provided by proprioception and the other senses is attenuated and not overly precise for a reason. The attenuation would be a "flaw" (de Vignemont, 2014, p. 998) only if one assumed that proprioception was supposed to deliver precise awareness of the objective body.

The enactivist point in this is that bodily experience, in the form of proprioception, kinesthesia, interoception, and so on, is action oriented. If we are to consider it a form of perception, it is a form of enactive perception which serves our different ways of coping with the environment. In this respect I want to return to the idea expressed in the first section, that in typical, everyday experience, SO may be difficult to distinguish from the sense of agency; in typical intentional action SO and SA are well integrated and perhaps experientially indistinct. I think this fact is consistent with the deflated account of SO. A similar account can be offered for SA. Langland-Hassan (2008), for example, suggests that the phenomenology of agency is "one that is embedded in all first order sensory and proprioceptive phenomenology as diachronic, action-sensitive patterns of information; it does not stand apart from them as an inscrutable emotion" (2008, p. 392). This is also consistent with an embodied enactivist conception of SA (see Buhrmann & Di Paolo, 2015; Gallagher 2012, 2013).

Maintaining the focus on SO, I want to clarify this enactivist point by returning to an example mentioned earlier. This is the example given by de Vignemont (2007). You experience SO for your hand when another person touches it, in a way that you do not feel SO for the touching hand. For Bermúdez this is nothing more than experiencing sensations at the location of your hand.[5] It nonetheless involves SO integrated with this tactile-proprioceptive experience—an experience of the hand as *your* hand. I now want to suggest that there is something more in this experience than just experiencing sensations at the location of your hand and SO for that hand. In this regard, Merleau-Ponty's well known example of one hand touching another, as an example of what he calls "reversibility," can help to show that there is a potential for action (something action oriented) in the experience of my hand being touched, and not just an experience of bodily location.

Merleau-Ponty's example is first of all about my own two hands. If I use my right hand to touch my left hand, there is the immediate possibility of a reversibility—that my right hand touching can immediately become the touched; and my left hand touched can immediately become the touching. If the touching–touched is in some objective sense simultaneous, in terms of our single-minded attention it is not, but involves a dynamic sequential reversibility, not unlike the reversing of the Necker cube in vision, but one that can be easily done at will (Merleau-Ponty, 1968, p. 141). My attention can go back and forth between touching and being touched, attempting to capture a structure that is prereflectively already established at the sensory level. Each hand, whether touching or being touched holds a relation to action, something actualized in the case of touching, but only potential in the case of being touched. Even as my one hand is touched, it holds a certain power for touching which could reverse the action.

This is the case whether it is my own hand touching my other hand, or, as in de Vignemont's example, someone else's hand touching mine.[6] In the sensation of being touched there is, along with a sense of location and boundary, and the implicit SO that comes along with this, a sense of agency to the extent that I have control over the reversibility—in effect, to the extent that I can immediately turn the being touched into an act of touching. This sense of agency, tied to my potentiality for action, just to the extent that it is *my* hand that is involved, is integrated with SO. We can clearly see in the one hand, whether it is touched by ourselves, or by another, an interweaving of the sensory-motor, and of the senses of agency and ownership, in the action-orientation of our body.

Given that the whole body can move and can touch or be touched, this applies not just to hands. Likewise, this is not just about proprioception. A pain in my leg can define what I can and cannot do and can diminish my sense of agency. Interoceptive aspects of hunger or fatigue may do the same. Proprioception, however, is important not only for registering the location or position sense of my body. Proprioception plays a role in motor control, and without proprioception we lose control over our body, and this can diminish my sense of agency as well.[7] Eilan, Marcel, and Bermúdez capture this idea when they state: "one of the features distinguishing our relation to our own bodies from our relations to other physical objects is the fact that we can act directly with our bodies" (1995, p. 21). The point to be made here is that this difference shows up in our bodily awareness as an integration of SA and SO.

Conclusion

I conclude by summarizing the three points for which I argued.

First, the phenomenological account of SO in terms of a prereflective self-awareness fits the conception of a deflationary (rather than inflationary) account. It takes SO to be something intrinsic to bodily awareness, not some additional feeling that would be independent of proprioception or awareness of the location of a sensation. Nonetheless, one can still speak of SO as a positive aspect of experience, something that is manifest in bodily awareness.

Second, I've argued that bodily awareness is primarily awareness of the lived body. Questions about the veridicality of such experiences use a different measure—namely, the objective body—and seemingly discount SO for those things that are not part of the objective body. From this perspective, SO for a phantom or a prosthetic is an illusion. Outside of a narrow philosophical concern, however, it is more productive to consider SO in pragmatic contexts and in regard to questions that concern the lived body. In this regard, just as phantom pain is a very real phenomenon, the fact that it is *my* pain seems equally as significant. And if the SO is part of an experience that allows me to have more control over my prosthetic limb, whether its epistemic status involves perception or illusion is not so significant.

Third, in any particular case of bodily awareness, the action-oriented dynamics among position sense (proprioception), kinesthesia, vestibular, and other interoceptive sensations, include an integrated, intrinsic sense of ownership and sense of agency where SO and SA are not easily distinguishable. This reinforces a point that remains important even in the project of making clear distinctions between the sense of agency and the sense of ownership, and understanding how they integrate and extend to action. This makes the deflationary account somewhat more complex and nuanced, and suggests its importance for enactivist accounts of embodied perception.

Acknowledgments

The author acknowledges the support of the Humboldt Foundation's Anneliese Maier Research Award, and the Australian Research Council

(ARC) project DP170102987, Minds in Skilled Performance at the University of Wollongong.

Notes

1. In the specific sense that this term is meant in the literature we are considering here, this is correct. There are contexts, however, in which the concept of legal ownership of one's body is discussed. Petchesky (1995) for example, traces the use of the concept of body ownership through a number of legal and historical contexts, and discusses a "shift in the early-modern European origins of ideas about owning one's body" which has less to do with property rights in an economic sense and more to do with claims about protecting "one's sexuality and personal security from arbitrary invasion" (Petchesky, 1995, p. 390). One finds evidence of this in the Reformed Consistory of Geneva which documents a legal defense in 1568 where a woman claims that as Paris belongs to the King, *"mon corps est a moy!"* (Petchesky, 1995, p. 391). More recently the notion of body ownership in this sense has been redeployed in feminist discussions (e.g., Pateman, 1988). Clearly, however, this does not indicate anything about the phenomenological conception of SO.

2. A specific phenomenological use of the phrase "sense of ownership" was already in use in contexts that involved education and psychoanalysis (e.g., Glodis & Blasi, 1993, who discussed "the sense of ownership of personal experience" that they found in Mann, 1991; and Lefebvre, 1988 who discusses "a loss of sense of ownership of the psyche and soma" in psychoanalytic contexts).

3. Also, possibly, tools (see e.g., Maravita & Iriki, 2004), prosthetics (see e.g., Marasco, Kim, Colgate, Peshkin, & Kuiken, 2011), or even the bodies of others (see the notion of the joint body schema, Soliman & Glenberg, 2014), which involves an expanded peripersonal space that redefines the experiential boundaries of one's body. See Holmes and Spence (2006) for review.

4. I think one could go further and challenge the idea that bodily awareness of this sort is necessarily perceptual. For an argument that supports the idea that it is nonperceptual awareness, see Gallagher (2003).

5. "Do we need a feeling of myness to explain what is going on when I feel the pressure of someone else's hand upon mine? If we do, then we need it to explain what is going on when I feel the pressure of the table on my hand. But I am not sure that we have anything here beyond the descriptive fact emphasized in the deflationary conception of ownership—namely, that sensations are typically experienced within the confines of the body" (Bermúdez 2011, p. 163).

6. With some modification, Merleau-Ponty too extends this reversibility to the case when I touch your hand, you touch mine, or both: "when touching the hand of another, would I not touch in it the same power to espouse the things that I have

touched in my own?" (Merleau-Ponty, 1968, p. 141). He suggests that "the handshake too is reversible; I can feel myself touched as well and at the same time as touching" (1968, p. 142).

7. This is seen in the case of I. W. who lost proprioception and the sense of touch below the neck. With the loss of proprioception he lost control of his movement, and until he learned a new way to control his movement he experienced a diminishment in SA (Cole, 1995; Cole & Paillard, 1995; Gallagher & Cole, 1995). Not only is proprioception confirmatory of movement as sensory feedback, but motor control processes involving forward models anticipate proprioceptive consequences of movement (Lau, Rogers, Haggard, & Passingham, 2004; Lau & Passingham, 2007; Haggard, Aschersleben, Gehrke, & Prinz, 2002; Haggard & Eimer, 1999; Haggard & Magno, 1999); there also may be preparatory preaction activation of the proprioceptive system (Lethin, 2008). See also Legrand (2006).

References

Anscombe, G. E. M. (1962). On sensations of position. *Analysis, 22*(3), 55–58. doi:10.2307/3326426.

Bermúdez, J. L. (2011). Bodily awareness and self-consciousness. In S. Gallagher (Ed.), *Oxford handbook of the self* (pp. 157–179). Oxford: Oxford University Press. doi: 10.1093/oxfordhb/9780199548019.003.0007.

Bermúdez, J. L. (2015). Bodily ownership, bodily awareness and knowledge without observation. *Analysis, 75*(1), 37–45. doi:10.1093/analys/anu119.

Botvinick, M., & Cohen, J. (1998). Rubber hand "feel" touch that eyes see. *Nature, 391*(6669), 756. doi:10.1038/35784.

Buhrmann, T., & Di Paolo, E. (2015). The sense of agency—a phenomenological consequence of enacting sensorimotor schemes. *Phenomenology and the Cognitive Sciences.* doi:10.1007/s11097-015-9446-7.

Campbell, J. (1999). Schizophrenia, the space of reasons and thinking as a motor process. *Monist, 82*(4), 609–625.

Cole, J. (1995). *Pride and a daily marathon.* Cambridge, MA: MIT Press.

Cole, J., & Paillard, J. (1995). Living without touch and peripheral information about body position and movement: Studies with deafferented subjects. In J. L. Bermúdez, A. Marcel, & N. Eilan (Eds.), *The body and the self* (pp. 245–266). Cambridge, MA: MIT Press.

Cole, J., Sacks, O., & Waterman, I. (2000). On the immunity principle: A view from a robot. *Trends in Cognitive Sciences, 4*(5), 167. doi:10.1016/S1364-6613(00)01459-5.

de Vignemont, F. (2007). Habeas corpus: The sense of ownership of one's own body. *Mind & Language, 22*(4), 427–449. doi:10.1111/j.1468-0017.2007.00315.x.

de Vignemont, F. (2013). The mark of bodily ownership. *Analysis, 73*(4), 643–651. doi:10.1093/analys/ant080.

de Vignemont, F. (2014). A multimodal conception of bodily awareness. *Mind, 123*(492), 989–1020. doi:10.1093/mind/fzu089.

Dokic, J. (2003). The sense of ownership: An analogy between sensation and action. In J. Roessler & N. Eilan (Eds.), *Agency and self-awareness* (pp. 321–344). Oxford: Oxford University Press.

Eilan, N., Marcel, A. J., & Bermúdez, J. L. (1995). Self-consciousness and the body: An interdisciplinary introduction. In J. L. Bermúdez, A. Marcel, & N. Eilan (Eds.), *The body and the self* (pp. 1–28). Cambridge, MA: MIT Press.

Frith, C. D. (1992). *The cognitive neuropsychology of schizophrenia*. Hillsdale, NJ: Erlbaum.

Gallagher, S. (2000). Philosophical conceptions of the self: Implications for cognitive science. *Trends in Cognitive Sciences, 4*(1), 14–21. doi:10.1016/S1364-6613(99)01417-5.

Gallagher, S. (2003). Bodily self-awareness and object-perception. *Theoria et Historia Scientiarum, 7*(1), 53–68.

Gallagher, S. (2005). *How the body shapes the mind*. Oxford: Oxford University Press.

Gallagher, S. (2012). Multiple aspects in the sense of agency. *New Ideas in Psychology, 30*(1), 15–31. doi:10.1016/j.newideapsych.2010.03.003.

Gallagher, S. (2013). Ambiguity in the sense of agency. In A. Clark, J. Kiverstein, & T. Vierkant (Eds.), *Decomposing the will* (pp. 118–135). Oxford: Oxford University Press.

Gallagher, S. (2015). Relations between agency and ownership in the case of schizophrenic thought insertion. *Review of Philosophy and Psychology, 6*(4), 865–879. doi: 10.1007/s13164-014-0222-3.

Gallagher, S., & Cole, J. (1995). Body schema and body image in a deafferented subject. *Journal of Mind and Behavior, 16*(4), 369–390.

Gallagher, S., & Marcel, A. J. (1999). The self in contextualized action. *Journal of Consciousness Studies, 6*(4), 4–30.

Gallagher, S., & Zahavi, D. (2015). Phenomenological approaches to self-consciousness. In E. N. Zalta (Ed.), *The Stanford encyclopedia of philosophy*. Retrieved from http://plato.stanford.edu/archives/spr2015/entries/self-consciousness-phenomenological/.

Glodis, K. A., & Blasi, A. (1993). The sense of self and identity among adolescents and adults. *Journal of Adolescent Research, 8*(4), 356–380. doi:10.1177/074355489384002.

Goldman, A. (1970). *A theory of human action*. New York: Prentice-Hall.

Graham, G., & Stephens, G. L. (1994). Mind and mine. In G. Graham & G. L. Stephens (Eds.), *Philosophical psychopathology* (pp. 91–109). Cambridge, MA: MIT Press.

Haggard, P., Aschersleben, G., Gehrke, J., & Prinz, W. (2002). Action, binding and awareness. In W. Prinz & B. Hommel (Eds.), *Common mechanisms in perception and action* (pp. 266–285). Oxford: Oxford University Press.

Haggard, P., & Eimer, M. (1999). On the relation between brain potentials and the awareness of voluntary movements. *Experimental Brain Research, 126*(1), 128–133. doi:10.1007/s002210050722.

Haggard, P., & Magno, E. (1999). Localising awareness of action with transcranial magnetic stimulation. *Experimental Brain Research, 127*(1), 102–107. doi:10.1007/s002210050778.

Head, H. (1920). *Studies in neurology, in two volumes.* New York: Oxford University Press.

Holmes, N. P., & Spence, C. (2006). Beyond the body schema: Visual, prosthetic and technological contributions to bodily perception and awareness. In G. Knoblich, I. M. Thornton, M. Grosjean, & M. Shiffrar (Eds.), *Human body perception from the inside out* (pp. 15–64). Oxford: Oxford University Press.

Hopkins, B. C. (1993). The eidetic structure of subjectless, egoless, and selfless transcendental reflection. In P. Blosser, E. Shimomissé, L. Embree, & H. Kojima (Eds.), *Japanese and Western phenomenology* (pp. 69–80). Dordrecht: Springer.

Langland-Hassan, P. (2008). Fractured phenomenologies: Thought insertion, inner speech, and the puzzle of extraneity. *Mind & Language, 23*(4), 369–401. doi:10.1111/j.1468-0017.2008.00348.x.

Lau, H. C., Rogers, R. D., Haggard, P., & Passingham, R. E. (2004). Attention to intention. *Science, 303*(5661), 1208–1210. doi:10.1126/science.1090973.

Lau, H. C., & Passingham, R. E. (2007). Unconscious activation of the cognitive control system in the human prefrontal cortex. *Journal of Neuroscience, 27*(21), 5805–5811. doi:10.1523/JNEUROSCI.4335-06.2007.

Lefebvre, P. (1988). The psychoanalysis of a patient with ulcerative colitis: The impact of fantasy, affect, and the intensity of drives on the outcome of treatment. *International Journal of Psycho-Analysis, 69*(1), 43–53.

Legrand, D. (2006). The bodily self: The sensori-motor roots of pre-reflective self-consciousness. *Phenomenology and the Cognitive Sciences, 5*(1), 89–118. doi:10.1007/s11097-005-9015-6.

Lethin, A. (2008). Anticipating sensitizes the body. *Phenomenology and the Cognitive Sciences, 7*(2), 279–300. doi:10.1007/s11097-007-9054-2.

Mann, D. W. (1991). Ownership: A pathography of the self. *British Journal of Medical Psychology*, *64*(3), 211–223.

Marasco, P. D., Kim, K., Colgate, J. E., Peshkin, M. A., & Kuiken, T. A. (2011). Robotic touch shifts perception of embodiment to a prosthesis in targeted reinnervation amputees. *Brain*, *134*(3), 747–758. doi:10.1093/brain/awq361.

Maravita, A., & Iriki, A. (2004). Tools for the body (schema). *Trends in Cognitive Sciences*, *8*(2), 79–86.

Marcel, A. (2003). The sense of agency: Awareness and ownership of action. In J. Roessler & N. Eilan (Eds.), *Agency and self-awareness* (pp. 48–93). Oxford: Oxford University Press.

Martin, M. G. F. (1992). Sight and touch. In T. Crane (Ed.), *The content of experience* (pp. 199–201). Cambridge: Cambridge University Press.

Martin, M. G. F. (1995). Bodily awareness: A sense of ownership. In J. L. Bermúdez, T. Marcel, & N. Eilan (Eds.), *The body and the self* ((pp. 267–289). Cambridge, MA: MIT Press.

Merleau-Ponty, M. (2012). *Phenomenology of perception* (D. A. Landes, Trans.). New York: Routledge.

Merleau-Ponty, M. (1968). *The visible and the invisible: Followed by working notes* (A. Lingis, Trans.). Evanston, IL: Northwestern University Press.

Pateman, C. (1988). *The sexual contract*. Cambridge: Polity Press.

Petchesky, R. P. (1995). The body as property: A feminist re-vision. In F. D. Ginsburg & R. Rapp (Eds.), *Conceiving the new world order: The global politics of reproduction* (pp. 323–345). Berkeley: University of California Press.

Soliman, T., & Glenberg, A. M. (2014). The embodiment of culture. In L. Shapiro (Ed.), *The Routledge handbook of embodied cognition* (pp. 207–219). London: Routledge.

Stephens, G. L., & Graham, G. (2000). *When self-consciousness breaks: Alien voices and inserted thoughts*. Cambridge, MA: MIT Press.

Synofzik, M., Vosgerau, G., & Newen, A. (2008). I move, therefore I am: A new theoretical framework to investigate agency and ownership. *Consciousness and Cognition*, *17*(2), 411–424. doi:10.1016/j.concog.2008.03.008.

Tsakiris, M. (2016). The multisensory basis of the self: From body to identity to others. *Quarterly Journal of Experimental Psychology*, *70*(4), 597–609. doi:10.1080/1747 0218.2016.1181768.

8 From Pathological Embodiment to a Model for Body Awareness

Francesca Garbarini, Lorenzo Pia, Carlotta Fossataro, and Anna Berti

1 When Your Hand Becomes My Hand: A Monothematic Delusion of Body Ownership in Brain-Damage Patients

In the last twenty years, converging multidisciplinary approaches have considered the sense of body ownership, described as the feeling that my body (in all its parts) belongs to me, as a fundamental component of self-consciousness (for review, see Blanke, Slater, & Serino, 2015). In the present chapter we try to understand how body awareness is constructed in the normally functioning brain by taking a neuropsychological perspective, studying patients in whom, after focal brain damage, the sense of body ownership is dramatically impaired. In particular, we review a series of studies related to a recently described pathological form of embodiment, in which limbs belonging to other people are felt as a part of the patient's body, with the aim of discussing possible implications of this disorder for a theoretical model of body ownership.

In brain-damaged patients with motor and somatosensory impairments, body awareness deficits are often observed. Patients may perceive a sense of strangeness toward a contralesional limb that can be felt as separated from the patient's body. This disorder is a disturbance called somatoparaphrenia,[1] characterized by a strong sense of disownership, in which patients believe that the contralesional limbs do not belong to their own body but to another person (Vallar & Ronchi, 2009).

We recently observed a converse pattern of delusional behavior in which brain-damaged patients do not explicitly deny the ownership of their contralesional limb (as in somatoparaphrenia), but on the contrary, claim that the examiner's hand is their own hand whenever it is located in a body-congruent position, aligned with the patient's shoulder (Fossataro, Gindri, Mezzanato, Pia, & Garbarini, 2016; Garbarini et al., 2013; Garbarini, Fornia, et al., 2014; Garbarini, Fossataro, et al., 2015; Pia, Garbarini, Fossataro, Fornia, & Berti,

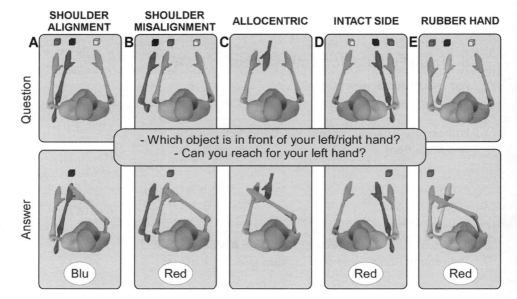

Figure 8.1

Embodiment evaluation: An alien left arm (the examiner's arm) was positioned on the table in four different conditions: (A) *alien-congruent condition*: the alien arm (in gray) was located in the constralesional space, aligned with the patient's shoulder, in a congruent position with respect to the patient's contralesional arm and perceived in egocentric perspective; (B) *alien-noncongruent condition*: the alien arm (in gray) was misaligned with the patient's shoulder; (C) *alien-allocentric condition*: the alien arm (in gray) was placed in a congruent position with respect to the patient's contralesional arm, as in (A) but perceived in an allocentric perspective, that is, facing the patient; (D) *intact side*: the alien arm (in gray) was located in the intact ipsilesional body side; (E) *rubber hand condition*: the alien arm (in light yellow) was a rubber hand instead of the examiner's arm (as in the other conditions). Patient was asked: (1) to count how many hands and objects were on the table; (2) to reach his or her own hemiplegic hand with his or her own nonplegic ipsilesional hand; and (3) to identify his or her own hand on the basis of the color of the object facing the hand. In all conditions the patient counts three objects (blue, red, and green) and three hands (question 1). In (A) (lower part) patient reaches the alien hand (the gray one) (question 2) and identifies his or her own hand as the one in front of the blue cube (question 3); in (B) (lower part) patient correctly reaches his or her own hand (the pink one) (question 2) and identifies it as the one facing the red cube (question 3); in (C) (lower part) patient correctly reaches his or her own hand (question 2); in (D) (lower part) patient correctly identifies his or her own hand (the pink one) as the one facing the red cube (question 3); in (E) (lower part) patient correctly reaches his or her own hand (the pink one) (question 2) and identifies it as the one facing the red cube (question 3). Adapted from Garbarini, Fossataro, Berti, Gindri, Romano, Pia, . . . Neppi-Modona (2015). © 2014 by Elsevier Ltd. Adapted with permission.

2013). To observe this phenomenon, the coexperimenter must place his or her hand on the table next to the patient's contralesional affected hand, internally positioned with respect to it and aligned with the patient's trunk midline. When the examiner asks the patient to identify his or her own affected hand, either by reaching to it with his or her intact hand or by naming a colored object in front of it, the patient systematically identifies the examiner's hand as his or her own (see fig. 8.1).

Moreover, objects different from a real hand do not elicit this behavior, which we will call "pathological embodiment." Therefore, in order for pathological embodiment to occur, it is necessary that the alien hand is a human hand (the coexperimenter's hand), located in the contralesional space, aligned with the patient's shoulder and perceived in egocentric perspective (fig. 8.1, panel A). In this condition, patients also treat and care for the experimenter's left arm as if it were their own. Because of this pathological embodiment, we named them E+ patients (control patients, without pathological embodiment, were named E–). By contrast, pathological embodiment does not occur in the following control conditions: when the alien hand is misaligned with the patient's shoulder (fig. 8.1, panel B); when the alien hand is perceived in allocentric perspective (fig. 8.1, panel C); when the alien hand is positioned in the intact ipsilesional body side (fig. 8.1, panel D); and when the alien hand is the rubber hand usually employed during the rubber hand illusion (see below) procedure (fig. 8.1, panel E).

In the last four years, we evaluated about ninety cerebrovascular patients, with either motor deficits or sensory deficits (or both) of contralesional upper limbs, in the subacute or chronic phase of the illness (Fossataro et al., 2016; Garbarini et al., 2013; Garbarini, Fornia, et al., 2014; Garbarini, Fossataro, et al., 2015; Pia et al., 2013). In this sample, 40 percent of patients showed pathological embodiment. Patients entered the studies only if they did not show any severe general cognitive or linguistic impairment. For this reason, we tested more right than left brain-damaged patients. Although it seems that pathological embodiment is more common after right than after left brain damage, the right limb embodiment after left brain damage, when present, is completely comparable to the left limb embodiment after right brain damage. This datum, while needing further investigation on a larger sample of patients, seems to suggest the presence of a right hemisphere dominance in construction of the sense of body ownership rather than an absolute lateralization of this function in the right hemisphere (see also Tsakiris, Costantini, & Haggard, 2008). Considering the E+ patients' neurological characteristics, pathological embodiment seems to be strongly associated to severe primary (motor, tactile, and proprioceptive) deficits. However, the motor deficits' severity is equally represented in the E+ and E– groups. On the contrary, the presence of tactile and proprioceptive deficits is more common in the E+ group. Other neuropsychological deficits, such as extrapersonal and personal neglect (Bottini et al., 2009), seem to be more present in the E+ group. However, none of these deficits alone can explain pathological embodiment because we have found a few important double dissociations between embodiment, neglect, and primary sensory-motor deficits.

It is important to note that at the time of testing, E+ patients usually do not show any explicit form of disownership; they never spontaneously report delusional beliefs about the contralesional body parts. Accordingly, when only their left hand is present, they correctly identify it as their own left hand. However, when both their own and an alien hand are present, they not only misidentify the alien hand as their own, but they also identify their own left hand as alien, affirming that it belongs to someone else, thus showing, only in this specific condition, an explicit sense of disownership. This suggests that the two delusional behaviors (disownership of the own hand and ownership of an alien hand) may coexist in the same patients, further suggesting that these two forms of body unawareness lay on a continuum, possibly characterizing different phases (acute, subacute, and chronic) of the disease or different intensity of the deficit. Furthermore, the E+ patients' lesion patterns seem consistent with those described in previous studies on neural correlates of the delusion of disownership (Fossataro et al., 2016; Gandola et al., 2012; Garbarini et al., 2013).

2   The Pathological Embodiment of Another Person's Hand Has Direct Consequences for Patients' Representations

Converging experimental evidence shows that the E+ patients' belief that the alien hand belongs to themselves is not a mere verbal confabulation (i.e., a left hemisphere telling stories to rationalize absent or wrong information coming from the right hemisphere), but instead, reflects an embodiment mechanism able to alter the patients' motor and somatosensory representations and to trigger the same physiological parameters as the real body (Fossataro et al., 2016; Garbarini et al., 2013; Garbarini, Fornia, et al., 2014; Garbarini, Fossataro, et al., 2015; Pia et al., 2013). Broadly speaking, this means that this delusion of body ownership can meet the criteria of a recently proposed definition of the embodiment concept, claiming that others' body parts can be considered as fully embodied, "if and only if," as in these patients, "some properties of them are processed in the same way as the properties of one's own body" (de Vignemont, 2011).

2.1 Motor Consequences

One of the most counterintuitive observations related to E+ patients' behavior is that pathological embodiment occurs not only with a static alien hand, but also when movements are present. Indeed, when the alien hand (i.e., the examiner's hand) moves, patients claim that they are moving their own (paralyzed) hand. We reasoned that if this false belief reflects an actual incorporation of the alien hand into the patients' body representations, then this should specifically and selectively affect the E+ patients' (but not E– patients') motor programs. To test this prediction, we (Garbarini et al., 2013) employed a modified version of a circles–lines task, known to induce bimanual motor effects in healthy subjects (Franz, Zelaznik, & McCabe, 1991). The circles–lines task can be used as an effective tool to investigate motor and bodily consequences of altered awareness in pathological conditions (Garbarini & Pia, 2013). In the classical version of the paradigm, when people have to draw lines with one hand while drawing circles with the other hand, each movement interferes with the other one and both trajectories tend to become ovals (i.e., the circles tend to become lines and the lines tend to become circles), that is, a bimanual coupling effect (Franz et al., 1991; Garbarini, Rabuffetti, Piedimonte, Solito, & Berti, 2015; Garbarini et al., 2012, 2013; Garbarini, D'Agata, et al., 2014; Piedimonte, Garbarini, Rabuffetti, Pia, & Berti, 2014). In E+ patients, a modified version was used in which patients were asked "to try" to perform the bimanual circles–lines task with both hands. However, due to the left limb paralysis, they only performed vertical lines with their right intact hand. The crucial aspect of this paradigm is that, while the patient starts to draw lines with his or her right hand, the examiner's left hand starts to draw circles, acting either in egocentric or in allocentric perspective (Garbarini et al., 2013). The experiment results (fig. 8.2) showed that when E+ patients in the egocentric (and not in allocentric) condition misidentified the alien hand as their own, a clear coupling effect was found (i.e., the lines drawn by the E+ patients' intact hand became ovalized, as in normal individuals actually performing the bimanual task). On the contrary, in the same condition, neither healthy controls nor hemiplegic patients without pathological embodiment showed any coupling effect, suggesting that simply looking at a hand drawing circles is not sufficient to induce line ovalization.

These findings suggest that in E+ patients, the delusion of ownership arises from an abnormal embodiment process that automatically triggers

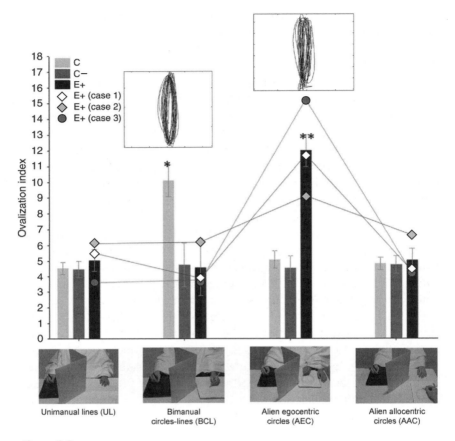

Figure 8.2
Ovalization results for the patients and controls: Bar plots show the Ovalization Index mean values (with standard error) for each group—controls (C), E–, and E+ patients—in each condition. Different lines show the individual mean values for each E+ patient (as single case) in each condition. * P < 0.01; ** P < 0.001. The two boxes at the top of the figure show examples of right hand ovalization in one control subject performing BCL-c and in one E+ patient performing AEC-c. Adapted from Garbarini, Pia, Piedimonte, Rabuffetti, Gindri, and Berti (2013). © 2013 by Elsevier Ltd. Adapted with permission.

the intention-programming processes for the own hand. More generally, they suggest a presence of a hierarchic order where the sense of body ownership has an impact on the motor awareness (E+ patients, usually aware of their motor impairment, were convinced that their left hand was moving) and the sense of agency (E+ patients ascribed the alien movements to themselves), by directly modulating action execution (E+ patients showed an interference coupling effect very similar to those found in healthy subjects actually performing bimanual circles–lines task).

2.2 Sensory Consequences

During clinical evaluation of the E+ patients, a very surprising behavior was documented in the sensory domain. When we applied stimuli to the alien hand, E+ patients reported feeling those stimuli on their own hand. In a first study, we tested E+ and E– patients, as well as healthy controls, with a pinprick protocol to assess pain perception (Pia et al., 2013). In the own hand condition, participants placed their arms on a table (no alien hand was present) and the hand dorsum (either of the right or of the left hand) was stimulated. In the alien hand condition, the coexperimenter's left or right arm was placed alongside the participants' left or right arm, respectively, and the left or right coexperimenter's hand dorsum was stimulated. In both conditions, participants had to rate the perceived sensation on a zero-to-five-point Likert scale. Results showed that healthy controls and E– patients gave scores higher than zero only when their own hands were stimulated. On the contrary, E+ patients gave scores higher than zero both when their own hands (left or right) were stimulated and when the coexperimenter's left (embodied) hand, but not the right (not embodied) hand, was stimulated, thus suggesting a phenomenal experience of the stimuli delivered to someone else's hand. It is important to note that there were some differences in the patients' behavior, which were found to depend on the E+ patients' somatosensory capacities. When patients could feel sensation on their own hand (spared tactile/nociceptive sensibility) or when they were not aware that they could not feel any stimulation on their own hand (anosognosia for hemianesthesia), they reported to experience noxious stimuli on the left alien hand. On the contrary, when patients were aware that they could not feel any tactile/nociceptive stimulation on their own hand (hemianesthesia without anosognosia), they did not experience noxious stimuli on the left alien hand, coherently with their normal sensory awareness. This means that the belief that the subjects have about their sensory abilities is transferred to the alien hand, once it is embodied.

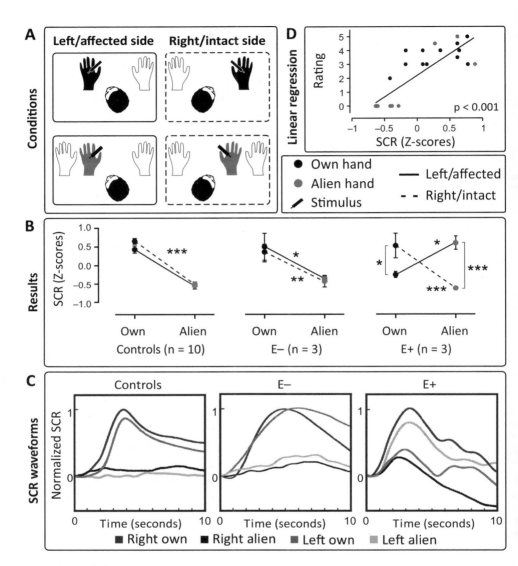

Figure 8.3

Experimental task and SCR results: (A) Experimental task. In the "own" conditions, participants placed their arms on a table and either the right or the left hand dorsum was stimulated. In the "alien" conditions, the coexperimenter's arm was placed alongside the participants' arm, either on the right or on the left body side, and the coexperimenter's hand dorsum was stimulated. A sequence of five stimulations per each condition was repeated twice in a counterbalanced order (ABCD-DCBA). (B) SCR ANOVA results. Graphs show the peak to peak SCR mean values expressed in Z-scores (with standard errors) for the Controls group (n = 10) and for the two

In a subsequent study (Garbarini, Fornia, et al., 2014), we examined whether such subjective experience of pain has an electrophysiological counterpart. Six right brain-damaged patients without sensory loss (three E+, three E–) and ten healthy controls were administered the same previously mentioned nociceptive stimulation protocol while recording skin conductance response (SCR), known to detect arousal response to expected noxious stimuli. The results showed that, in control subjects, the SCR was evoked only when they received stimuli, and reported feeling pain, on their own hands. As for the E+ patients, SCR comparable to that found for the own intact hand was also found for the alien hand, but only when the patients believed that it was their own hand and claimed to feel pain on it (i.e., when it was located on the affected side, in a body-congruent position). See details in figure 8.3. Interestingly, E+ patients also showed, for the own affected hand, lower SCR values with respect to the own intact and alien embodied hand. This suggests that, when the alien limb is present, although E+ patients usually do not deny that the affected hand belonged to their body (i.e., they do not show somatoparaphrenia), they disowned the affected hand both explicitly (verbal report) and implicitly (reduced SCR). Interestingly, the same observation has been reported in somatoparaphrenic patients, who show a reduced SCR when threatening stimuli approach their own, contralesional, hand they explicitly consider as not belonging to themselves (Romano, Gandola, Bottini, & Maravita, 2014). According to the above mentioned clinical and anatomical considerations, this physiological data also suggests the existence of a link between the two body ownership pathologies. Taken together, these behavioral and physiological findings suggest that the sensory stimuli delivered to the alien, embodied hand are processed in the same way as the ones delivered to the subject's own hand (de Vignemont, 2011).

Spatial consequences

It is well known that active tool use can change the spatial relations between the body and the external space (Berti & Frassinetti, 2000; Berti, Smania, &

Figure 8.3 (continued)
groups of patients without (E–; n = 3) or with (E+; n = 3) the pathological embodiment. * P < 0.01; ** P < 0.001; *** P < 0.0001. (C) Examples of SCR waveforms. An example of the SCR waveform was shown for each group (Controls, E–, E+), normalizing raw data and averaging all the trials (n = 10) for each condition. (D) Linear regression "rating by SCR" results. The mean SCR (expressed in Z-scores) value was used as an independent variable to predict the perceived sensation scores reported by the patients on a zero-to-five Likert scale. Adapted from Garbarini, Fornia, Fossataro, Pia, Gindri, and Berti (2014). © 2014 by Elsevier Ltd. Adapted with permission.

Allport, 2001; Giglia et al., 2015) so that far space can be remapped as near. This happens because the tool is incorporated into the body representation, and the personal space dimension is, therefore, extended (Maravita & Iriki, 2004). Previous evidence in normal subjects has demonstrated that active tool use modulates the representation of related body parts. It has been shown that participants estimate the midpoint of their forearm to be more distally located after a fifteen minute training with a tool sixty centimeters long, as compared to a pretraining condition (Sposito, Bolognini, Vallar, & Maravita, 2012). Reasoning on this evidence, we asked whether, in E+ patients, the alien limb could be so deeply embedded within the patient's body schema to affect the perceived extension of the own corresponding hand, thus showing spatial remapping after tool use (Garbarini, Fossataro, et al., 2015).

In our experiment (Garbarini, Fossataro, et al., 2015), healthy subjects were tested in three different conditions. They were either asked to actually perform the tool-use training with their own arm (action condition) or to observe an alien arm (the examiner's arm) performing the tool-use training, while holding (observation with-tool condition) or not (observation without-tool condition) a similar tool. According to Sposito and colleagues (2012), we found an overestimation of the forearm length only after active tool-use training (action condition). We were also interested in verifying if this overestimation effect could be induced by simply observing an alien arm performing the tool-use training. According to Costantini and colleagues (2011), a difference between the observation with-tool and without-tool conditions had to be expected. However, in our data, we did not find any significant remapping effect during observation.

As far as patients are concerned, in our experiment (Garbarini, Fossataro, et al., 2015) they were asked to try to perform the tool-use training with their own (paralyzed) limb, while the alien arm performed the tool-use training acting either in the E+ position, where pathological embodiment systematically occurs, or in the E– position, where this pathological embodiment does not occur. The crucial aspect of this experiment is that, although the task implied the observation of an alien arm performing the training, it was proposed as an active task, where hemiplegic patients were asked to try to perform the required movements with their plegic arm. The results (fig. 8.4) showed that, in the E+ position, when patients truly believed to be actually performing the task with their own arm, they showed an overestimation of their forearm length in the post-training phase with respect to the pretraining phase (similarly to healthy subjects actually performing the task in the active condition). Conversely, in the

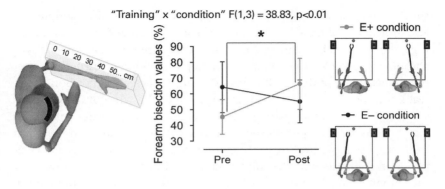

Figure 8.4
Tool-use experimental task and results: Bisection task: (right side) schematic aerial view of the experimental setting depicting the forearm bisection procedure. The arm lied inside a translucent Plexiglas parallelepiped to avoid tactile feedback could be either the left or the right arm, depending on the body side where embodiment occurred. The numbers on top represent the paper ruler used to calculate the subjective midpoint in centimeters. The forearm arm was always the left arm. Tool-use training: (left side) the training was performed by the examiner's (alien) arm (in dark gray). The alien arm could act (a) in a position more proximal to the patient's trunk midline (E+ condition, upper right) where embodiment occurs, or (b) in a more distal position (E– condition, lower right), where embodiment does not occur and patients correctly acknowledge that the alien arm belongs to the examiner. The task was performed on the patients' contralesional side. ANOVA results: (center) Graphic representation of patients' mean forearm bisection values (in percent) in the pretraining (PRE) and in the post-training phase (POST) during the left or right arm E+ condition (in red) and the left or right arm E– condition (in blue). ***$P < .0001$; **$P < .001$; *$P < .01$. Adapted from Garbarini et al. (2015). Adapted with permission.

E– condition, when patients were aware of not performing the task with their own arm, they did not show any overestimation of their forearm length, similar to healthy subjects performing the task in the observation condition. These findings strongly support the view that the sense of body ownership modulates the sensory map of action-related body parts.

3   Differences and Similarities between Pathological Embodiment and the Rubber Hand Illusion

Within cognitive neuroscience, the extensive literature on the rubber hand illusion (RHI) (Botvinick & Cohen, 1998; Ehrsson, Spence, & Passingham, 2004; Moseley et al., 2008; Tsakiris & Haggard, 2005; Tsakiris, 2010) suggests that the sense of body ownership can be successfully manipulated also in healthy subjects. During the classic experimental procedure, watching a rubber hand being touched, while one's unseen hand is touched synchronously, can lead to qualitative (the reported sense of ownership over the rubber hand) and quantitative (a shift in the perceived position of the real hand toward the fake hand) modulation of the sense of body ownership, so that the rubber hand is embodied and the real hand is subject to a sort of disembodiment. Recently, a new motor version of the RHI has been proposed: controlling for the temporal congruence between participants' movements and the model hand, an illusion of ownership over the moving model hand arises, without any kind of tactile stimulation. Converging evidence (Hegedüs et al., 2014; Kalckert & Ehrsson, 2012) show that, irrespective of the stimulation modality (either sensory or motor), this body ownership alteration presumably depends on the multisensory integration processes arising within a frontoparietal network, where the ventral premotor cortex seems to play a crucial role (Blanke et al., 2015). The illusory mechanism is interpreted in terms of visual capture of tactile (motor) sensation that leads to changes in proprioception. In other words, the proprioceptive location information of one's own hand is overwritten on the visual information about the location of the rubber hand.

Because the subject's hand-centered reference frame shifts toward the rubber hand during the illusion, it has been proposed that, as a consequence, the real hand is subject to a sort of disembodiment (Ehrsson et al., 2004). Consistently, a decrease in the temperature of the real hand has also been described (Moseley et al., 2008). Moreover, it has been demonstrated that cooling down the subject's hand increases the strength of the RHI, while warming the hand decreases it (Kammers, Rose, & Haggard, 2011). However, other studies are quite critical of this disembodiment claim. Rohde and colleagues (Rohde, Wold, Karnath, & Ernst, 2013) found that hand cooling can be present in both experimental (synchronous) and control (asynchronous) conditions, thus suggesting that it is not a reliable correlate of the subjective feeling of hand disownership in the RHI. Furthermore, Folegatti and colleagues (Folegatti, de Vignemont, Pavani, Rossetti, & Farnè, 2009) proposed that somatosensory changes observed in the participants' hand while experiencing the RHI can be explained by crossmodal mismatch between the seen and felt position of the hand and are not necessarily a signature of disownership.

In order for the RHI to occur, several constraints have to be met (Tsakiris, 2010; for review, see Blanke et al., 2015): peripersonal space (PPS) constraints (i.e., the rubber hand has to be placed close to the body, within the PPS); postural and perspectival constraints (i.e., the rubber hand has to be placed in a compatible body posture and perceived in first-person perspective); body-related visual information constraints (i.e., the rubber hand has to be shaped in the form of a human hand). It has been demonstrated that the RHI does not arise when the fake hand is placed in a third-person perspective or in a noncompatible posture, nor when it is substituted with neutral objects (Costantini & Haggard, 2007; Ehrsson et al., 2004; Tsakiris & Haggard, 2005). Accordingly, similar constraints characterize the pathological embodiment observed in our patients, which occurs only if the alien hand is a natural hand (and not a neutral object) and is located in postural congruent position within the patient's PPS (fig. 8.1, panel A). Taken together, this evidence suggests that, in order for the embodiment to occur, both in RHI and E+ patients, bottom-up multisensory integration processes (Armel & Ramachandran, 2003; Makin, Holmes, & Ehrsson, 2008) are not sufficient, but instead, preexisting body representations, containing

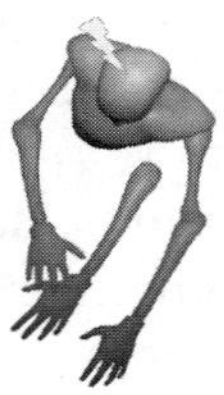	E+ Patients vs RHI	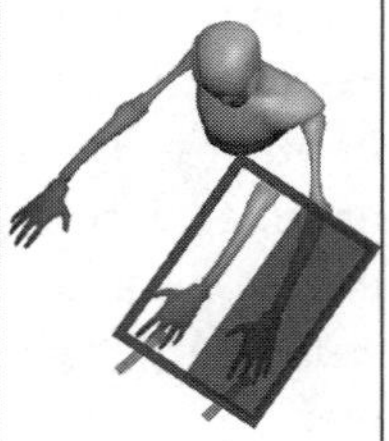
✓	Peripersonal space (PPS) constraints	✓
✓	Postural and proprioceptive constraints	✓
✓	Body-related visual information constraints	✓
✗	Experimental procedure	✓
✓	Brain damage	✗
✗	Artificial hand	✓
✓	Conscious belief	✗

Figure 8.5
E+ patient versus RHI: The table shows similarities and differences between E+ patients (on the left side) and RHI experimental procedure (in the right side). The checkmarks represent what is able (the "x" what is not) to induce embodiment over a fake hand, depending on the pathological (E+ patients) or experimental (RHI) condition.

information about what can be potentially included in one's own body according to specific constraints, are necessary (Tsakiris et al., 2008; Tsakiris & Haggard, 2005).

However, although pathological embodiment relies on similar constraints as those present in the RHI, there are several differences between the altered body ownership during the RHI and the abnormal body ownership in E+ patients (fig. 8.5). First of all, the body-related visual information constraint implies that a prosthetic, humanlike plastic hand can be successfully employed during the RHI. In E+ patients, this constraint is more strict and only a real human hand is able to induce pathological embodiment, suggesting that a preexisting distinction between biological and artificial categories (Kriegeskorte et al., 2008; Mazzoni, Brunel, Cavallari, Logothetis, & Panzeri, 2011; Mazzoni, 2015) is spared in our patients and plays an important role in the construction of body ownership. Note that while in the RHI subjects always know that the rubber hand is not their real hand, in the E+ condition patients really believe that the alien hand belongs to themselves. Furthermore, in E+ patients, pathological embodiment is a consequence of brain lesions and it is spontaneous and not induced by an experimental procedure that manipulates different sources of stimulation. In other words, no concurrent tactile stimuli are delivered on the patient's hand, as during the RHI, but the simple vision of the alien hand induces pathological embodiment. The dominance of vision over other somatosensory information has already been demonstrated within other experimental conditions. During a modified version of the RHI, using either a mirror illusion (Holmes, Snijders, & Spence, 2006) or a laser on the rubber hand (Durgin, Evans, Dunphy, Klostermann, & Simmons, 2007), proprioceptive drift and referred tactile sensations can be induced by the sole vision of the rubber hand. In addition, during immersive virtual reality experimental procedures, the view of a realistic, life-sized virtual human body, exactly in the same location and posture as the subject's physical body (Slater, Spanlang, Sanchez-Vives, & Blanke, 2010), is able to induce a full body illusion (Lenggenhager, Tadi, Metzinger, & Blanke, 2007; Van der Hoort, Guterstam, & Ehrsson, 2011). However, as already mentioned, the crucial difference between these perceptual experiences induced by vision and the pathological delusion of ownership in E+ patients is that only the latter produces a false belief over the hand ownership, while in the former, the subjects are always aware of the illusory nature of the perceptual experience.

4   Toward a Model of Body Ownership

Several influential models of body ownership (Apps & Tsakiris, 2014; Blanke, 2012; Limanowski & Blankenburg, 2013; Makin et al., 2008; Moseley, Gallace, & Spence, 2012; Tsakiris, 2010; for review, see Blanke et al., 2015), exist in the literature and they are largely based on evidence coming from the RHI. Almost all the interpretations of the RHI effects assume, as a necessary condition, the principle of multisensory integration (MSI). MSI is a bottom-up process in which sensory inputs, originally processed in sensory-dependent reference frames (e.g., visual stimuli in eye centered; auditory stimuli in head centered; tactile stimuli in skin centered), are realigned and integrated into a common reference frame based on proprioceptive inputs (e.g., in monkeys: Graziano, Cooke, & Taylor, 2000; Graziano, 1999; in humans: Ehrsson et al., 2004; Makin et al., 2008). As extensively explained above, in the RHI procedure, viewing a fake hand being touched in synchrony with tactile sensation on the real unseen hand generates a conflict between visual, tactile, and proprioceptive inputs. The brain, by means of multimodal neurons in the premotor and parietal areas (e.g., Graziano et al., 2000; Graziano, 1999), solves the conflict realigning the tactile and proprioceptive inputs based on the visual inputs.

However, in the RHI interpretations, clear differences emerge when taking into account a possible role of top-down processes. Some models (Armel & Ramachandran, 2003; Makin et al., 2008), for instance, claimed that MSI is sufficient to generate the illusion. This, in turn, predicts the illusory effects under a wide range of visual conditions as incongruent positions with respect to the body schema or a different identity. On the contrary, Tsakiris and colleagues (Tsakiris et al., 2008; Tsakiris & Haggard, 2005), suggest that such a bottom-up process must be necessarily compared to preexisting body representation (PEBR), containing information about what can be potentially included in one's own body according to specific constraints (PPS constraints; postural and perspective constraints; body-related visual information constraints) (Tsakiris, 2010; for review, see Blanke et al., 2015). This latter interpretation is in-line with data showing that the illusion does not arise when the rubber hand is not congruent with the participant's hand in terms of identity (e.g., neutral objects) or body postures (e.g., third-person perspective) (Costantini & Haggard, 2007; Ehrsson et al., 2004; Tsakiris & Haggard, 2005).

Coming back to the pathological context described here, we know from the control conditions of the E+ patients' clinical evaluation (fig. 8.1), that the typical constraints of the PEBR have to be met in order for pathological embodiment to occur (i.e., alien hands perceived in not congruent position or not aligned with the patient's shoulder are not embodied). Thus, we can assume that the PEBR system is spared in E+ patients. On the contrary, clinical considerations suggest that in E+ patients, the MSI cannot be fed in the correct way because of the severity of the primary somatosensory deficit. Also anatomical considerations seem to suggest that E+ patients may have problems with the MSI. The lesion studies of E+ patients (Fossataro et al., 2016; Garbarini et al., 2013) show a specific subcortical involvement of the periventricular white matter (mainly involving the corona radiata), where all the ascending (sensory) and descending (motor) pathways to and from the cortex are contained. This lesion pattern is compatible with the severity of the primary deficit affecting E+ patients and suggests that the MSI cannot be correctly fed. Furthermore, one lesion study (Pia et al., under review) also shows a specific cortical lesion, involving the premotor cortex (PMC) that has been described as a crucial brain center for multisensory integration, both in monkeys (Graziano, 1999) and in humans (Ehrsson et al., 2004; Makin et al., 2008). This PMC lesion can lead, in E+ patients, to a specific deficit at the level of MSI. Thus, E+ patients are not able to recognize their own hand based on the information coming from MSI system, either because the tactile and proprioceptive information is prevented or because the PMC is damaged. In this view, PMC has a crucial role in veridical and nonveridical body ownership construction. However, we propose that a damaged, not-fed MSI might be a necessary, but insufficient, condition in order for pathological embodiment to occur. Indeed, we have E– cases with severe tactile and proprioceptive deficits, leading to a not-fed (empty) MSI, with spared body ownership. These E– cases with "empty" MSI can immediately recognize the subject's own and the alien hand due to the perceptive details (the color of the skin, the age, the dimension, etc.), of the hand. In other words, they discriminate between self and others' body using what we can call a perceptual self-identity (PSI) system, where perceptual (primarily visual) body identity details are stored (Limanowski & Blankenburg, 2015a; Myers & Sowden, 2008; Peelen & Downing, 2007; Wold, Limanowski, Walter, & Blankenburg, 2014). On the contrary, E+ patients seem to completely ignore information coming from PSI. Indeed, they are not able to note the identity details of the hand and they cannot visually discriminate between the own and the alien hand, although both hands are visible on the table. Thus, for the E+ patients, we need to assume a deficit at the level of PSI. It is important to note that Tsakiris (2010) did not distinguish between PEBR and PSI, mainly because in the RHI there is overwhelming evidence suggesting that physical dissimilarity between one's own body and foreign body parts does not really matter. However, what emerges from our neuropsychological data is that, when motor, tactile, and proprioceptive information are lost because of the brain lesion, some patients (E–) are still able to use these perceptual details in order to discriminate between self and other body parts, while other patients (E+) completely ignore them and fail in self and other body discrimination. Thus, outside the context of the RHI, perceptual details seem to be relevant for body ownership.

We can speculate that some visual-related areas involved in body part recognition, such as the lateral occipitotemporal cortex (LOC) or extrastriate body area (EBA), or both (Limanowski & Blankenburg, 2015b), need to functionally work with the PMC—involved in multisensory integration—in order to discriminate between self and other body part. A functional coupling between EBA and ventral PMC has recently been described during RHI (Limanowski & Blankenburg, 2015a). In E+ patients, the absence of functional connectivity between PMC and EBA can potentially explain the PSI deficit shown by E+ patients. In E+ patients, a specific impairment related to the visual recognition of the body self, as well as its neurofunctional correlate, could be investigated by means of an experimental paradigm designed to explore the ability to discriminate between self and other people's hands (Ferri, Frassinetti, Ardizzi, Costantini, & Gallese, 2012; Frassinetti, Maini, Romualdi, Galante, & Avanzi, 2008).

Thus, in normal conditions, a veridical body awareness emerges from the comparison between PEBR (containing the representations of the features that can be potentially included in one's own body), PSI (where body identity details are stored), and MSI (where inputs coming from different modalities are realigned in a unique reference frame). This veridical body awareness not only allows the discrimination between the subject's own and the other person's body, but it is also crucial to formulate predictions about the somatosensory and the motor consequences related to what has been recognized as the own body.

On the contrary, in the pathological condition, the PEBR predictions cannot be compared to the PSI and the MSI information (both systems are damaged in E+ patients). As a result, PEBR, spared in E+ patients, works alone and assumes a dominant role. Thus, each stimulus, matching the constraints of the preexisting body representation, is considered as a part of the subject's own body (i.e., it is embodied). As a consequence, what is lost in E+ is the possibility of rejecting a stimulus matching the PEBR constraints as "other's body." Based on this nonveridical body awareness, E+ patients formulate motor and sensory predictions on the alien body they believe is their own.

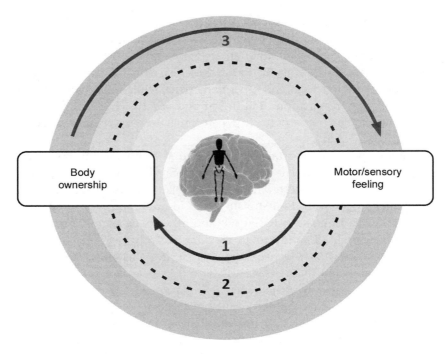

Figure 8.6
The Euthyphro dilemma of body ownership: The model describes the possible cause–
effect relationship between body ownership and the motor and sensory feelings.

What can pathological embodiment tell us about the interaction between
body ownership and somatosensory and motor systems? More specifically,
how can we explain the motor and sensory conscious experience that
patients report when the alien hand is moving or when it is stimulated? As
suggested by Frédérique de Vignemont (personal communication), alternative possibilities can be considered. In the famous dilemma, found in Pla-
to's dialogue *Euthyphro*, Socrates asks Euthyphro, "Is the pious loved by the
gods because it is pious, or is it pious because it is loved by the gods?" (10a).
According to de Vignemont's suggestion, we can apply this dilemma to our
context: "Do I feel this body moving (or perceiving sensation) because I
believe it to be mine? Or do I believe it to be mine because I feel it moving
(or perceiving sensation)?" This line of reasoning leads to the formulation
of three alternative models (fig. 8.6).

According to a first model, in E+ patients, abnormal motor and sensory
feelings, while patients observe an alien hand moving or being touched,

generate an abnormal body ownership. As mentioned above, during the RHI, tactile or motor (Hegedüs et al., 2014; Kalckert & Ehrsson, 2012) synchronous stimulation can induce the illusory experience of feeling sensations on the fake hand or of moving it. Thus, it is true that motor and sensory feelings can be sufficient in order to alter the body ownership in healthy subjects, who, nevertheless, are always aware of the illusory nature of the perceptual experience. However, in the pathological context, motor and sensory feelings are not necessary for establishing the E+ patients' false belief over the hand ownership. Indeed, in the basic evaluation, pathological embodiment is tested in static conditions, where the alien hand is not touched and it is not moving. This means that this first model is falsified by E+ patients' data, because we do not need motor and sensory feelings in order for the body ownership to occur.

In a second model, patients can independently experience either abnormal motor and sensory feelings or abnormal body ownership. According to this model, a double dissociation between these two pathological aspects is predicted. In a different pathological context, synesthetic people, probably due to an atypical functioning of the mirror-touch system (Blakemore, Bristow, Bird, Frith, & Ward, 2005), can experience tactile sensations in a given body part simply by looking at another person being touched on the same part. It has been proposed that, in synesthetic people, the abnormal sensory feelings are accompanied by an alteration of the self–other discrimination system (for review, see Banissy & Ward, 2013). Although this alteration does not lead to an actual misattribution of the other body parts to the self, as in E+ patients, a greater illusory experience, compared to healthy controls, has been described during different experimental manipulations of body ownership, such as RHI (Aimola Davies & White, 2013) and enfacement illusion (Maister, Banissy, & Tsakiris, 2013). According to this association between motor and sensory feelings and body ownership, shown in mirror-touch synesthesia, E+ patients' data suggest, in a complementary way, that when the alien hand is moving or being touched, motor and sensory feelings always accompany the abnormal sense of body ownership. In other words, when E+ patients believe that the alien hand is their own hand, they always show objective consequences in motor, sensory, and spatial domains. Thus, both mirror-touch synesthesia and pathological embodiment falsify the second model, predicting a dissociation between motor and sensory feelings and body ownership.

According to a third model, the one we propose, body ownership over the alien hand generates motor and sensory feelings while patients observe the alien hand moving or being touched. We can speculate that body ownership exerts a top-down modulation on motor and sensory cortical areas, known to be activated by vision, by means of mirror-like mechanisms, when subjects observe other bodies moving or being touched (Bonini, 2016; Keysers & Gazzola, 2009). Normal body ownership, discriminating between self and other's body, can either upregulate the sensory motor cortical activity, in order to bind conscious experience to the own body, or downregulate the cortical activity, in order to avoid conscious experience for the events occurring on the others' bodies. Pathological body ownership, in which the discrimination between oneself and another body is absent, can only upregulate the sensory motor cortical activity, binding conscious experience to both oneself and the other's body. According to the classical neuropsychological inference, this suggests the existence, in the normal functioning of the human brain, of a specific neural process that binds self-awareness to one's own body, as opposed to other bodies.

Notes

1. According to Vallar and Ronchi (2009) somatoparaphrenia is a clinically infrequent, but not negligible, symptom following brain damage. For instance, in a study by Baier and Karnath (2008) eleven out of seventy-nine acute stroke right brain-damaged patients exhibited abnormal attitudes toward their left affected limbs. It is interesting to note that somatoparaphrenia is more common in acute than in sub-acute and chronic patients, indeed in our sample of subacute and chronic patients only one out of ninety patients showed somatoparaphrenia (Pia et al., under review).

References

Aimola Davies, A. M., & White, R. C. (2013). A sensational illusion: Vision-touch synaesthesia and the rubber hand paradigm. *Cortex*, *49*(3), 806–818. doi:10.1016/j .cortex.2012.01.007.

Apps, M. A. J., & Tsakiris, M. (2014). The free-energy self: A predictive coding account of self-recognition. *Neuroscience and Biobehavioral Reviews*, *41*, 85–97. doi:10.1016/j .neubiorev.2013.01.029.

Armel, K. C., & Ramachandran, V. S. (2003). Projecting sensations to external objects: Evidence from skin conductance response. *Proceedings. Biological Sciences*, *270*(1523), 1499–1506. doi:10.1098/rspb.2003.2364.

Baier, B., & Karnath, H.-O. (2008). Tight link between our sense of limb ownership and self-awareness of actions. *Stroke*, *39*(2), 486–488. doi:10.1161/STROKEAHA .107.495606.

Banissy, M. J., & Ward, J. (2013). Mechanisms of self-other representations and vicarious experiences of touch in mirror-touch synesthesia. *Frontiers in Human Neuroscience, 7,* 112. doi:10.3389/fnhum.2013.00112.

Berti, A., & Frassinetti, F. (2000). When far becomes near: Remapping of space by tool use. *Journal of Cognitive Neuroscience, 12*(3), 415–420. doi:10.1162/08989 2900562237.

Berti, A., Smania, N., & Allport, A. (2001). Coding of far and near space in neglect patients. *NeuroImage, 14*(1), S98–S102. doi:10.1006/nimg.2001.0815.

Blakemore, S.-J., Bristow, D., Bird, G., Frith, C., & Ward, J. (2005). Somatosensory activations during the observation of touch and a case of vision-touch synaesthesia. *Brain, 128*(7), 1571–1583. doi:10.1093/brain/awh500.

Blanke, O. (2012). Multisensory brain mechanisms of bodily self-consciousness. *Nature Reviews: Neuroscience, 13*(8), 556–571. doi:10.1038/nrn3292.

Blanke, O., Slater, M., & Serino, A. (2015). Behavioral, neural, and computational principles of bodily self-consciousness. *Neuron, 88*(1), 145–166. doi:10.1016/j.neuron .2015.09.029.

Bonini, L. (2016). The extended mirror neuron network: Anatomy, origin, and functions. *Neuroscientist, 23*(1). doi:10.1177/1073858415626400.

Bottini, G., Sedda, A., Ferrè, E. R., Invernizzi, P., Gandola, M., & Paulesu, E. (2009). Productive symptoms in right brain damage. *Current Opinion in Neurology, 22*(6), 589–593. doi:10.1097/WCO.0b013e328332c71d.

Botvinick, M., & Cohen, J. (1998). Rubber hands "feel" touch that eyes see. *Nature, 391*(6669), 756. doi:10.1038/35784.

Costantini, M., Ambrosini, E., Sinigaglia, C., & Gallese, V. (2011). Tool-use observation makes far objects ready-to-hand. *Neuropsychologia, 49*(9), 2658–2663. doi: 10.1016/j.neuropsychologia.2011.05.013.

Costantini, M., & Haggard, P. (2007). The rubber hand illusion: Sensitivity and reference frame for body ownership. *Consciousness and Cognition, 16*(2), 229–240. doi:10.1016/j.concog.2007.01.001.

de Vignemont, F. (2011). Embodiment, ownership and disownership. *Consciousness and Cognition, 20*(1), 82–93. doi:10.1016/j.concog.2010.09.004.

Durgin, F. H., Evans, L., Dunphy, N., Klostermann, S., & Simmons, K. (2007). Rubber hands feel the touch of light. *Psychological Science, 18*(2), 152–157. doi:10.1111/j.1467-9280.2007.01865.x.

Ehrsson, H. H., Spence, C., & Passingham, R. E. (2004). That's my hand! Activity in premotor cortex reflects feeling of ownership of a limb. *Science, 305*(5685), 875–877. doi:10.1126/science.1097011.

Ferri, F., Frassinetti, F., Ardizzi, M., Costantini, M., & Gallese, V. (2012). A sensorimotor network for the bodily self. *Journal of Cognitive Neuroscience, 24*(7), 1584–1595. doi:10.1162/jocn_a_00230.

Folegatti, A., de Vignemont, F., Pavani, F., Rossetti, Y., & Farnè, A. (2009). Losing one's hand: Visual-proprioceptive conflict affects touch perception. *PLoS One, 4*(9), e6920. doi:10.1371/journal.pone.0006920.

Fossataro, C., Gindri, P., Mezzanato, T., Pia, L., & Garbarini, F. (2016). Bodily ownership modulation in defensive responses: Physiological evidence in brain-damaged patients with pathological embodiment of other's body parts. *Scientific Reports, 6,* 27737. doi:10.1038/srep27737.

Franz, E. A., Zelaznik, H. N., & McCabe, G. (1991). Spatial topological constraints in a bimanual task. *Acta Psychologica, 77*(2), 137–151. doi:10.1016/0001-6918(91)90028-X.

Frassinetti, F., Maini, M., Romualdi, S., Galante, E., & Avanzi, S. (2008). Is it mine? Hemispheric asymmetries in corporeal self-recognition. *Journal of Cognitive Neuroscience, 20*(8), 1507–1516. doi:10.1162/jocn.2008.20067.

Gandola, M., Invernizzi, P., Sedda, A., Ferrè, E. R., Sterzi, R., Sberna, M., et al. (2012). An anatomical account of somatoparaphrenia. *Cortex, 48*(9), 1165–1178. doi: 10.1016/j.cortex.2011.06.012.

Garbarini, F., D'Agata, F., Piedimonte, A., Sacco, K., Rabuffetti, M., Tam, F., et al. (2014). Drawing lines while imagining circles: Neural basis of the bimanual coupling effect during motor execution and motor imagery. *NeuroImage, 88,* 100–112. doi:10.1016/j.neuroimage.2013.10.061.

Garbarini, F., Fornia, L., Fossataro, C., Pia, L., Gindri, P., & Berti, A. (2014). Embodiment of others' hands elicits arousal responses similar to one's own hands. *Current Biology, 24*(16), R738–R739. doi:10.1016/j.cub.2014.07.023.

Garbarini, F., Fossataro, C., Berti, A., Gindri, P., Romano, D., Pia, L., et al. (2015). When your arm becomes mine: Pathological embodiment of alien limbs using tools modulates own body representation. *Neuropsychologia, 70,* 402–413. doi:10.1016/j .neuropsychologia.2014.11.008.

Garbarini, F., & Pia, L. (2013). Bimanual coupling paradigm as an effective tool to investigate productive behaviors in motor and body awareness impairments. *Frontiers in Human Neuroscience, 7,* 737. doi:10.3389/fnhum.2013.00737.

Garbarini, F., Pia, L., Piedimonte, A., Rabuffetti, M., Gindri, P., & Berti, A. (2013). Embodiment of an alien hand interferes with intact-hand movements. *Current Biology, 23*(2), R57–R58. doi:10.1016/j.cub.2012.12.003.

Garbarini, F., Rabuffetti, M., Piedimonte, A., Pia, L., Ferrarin, M., Frassinetti, F., et al. (2012). "Moving" a paralysed hand: Bimanual coupling effect in patients with anosognosia for hemiplegia. *Brain, 135*(Pt 5), 1486–1497. doi:10.1093/brain/aws015.

Garbarini, F., Rabuffetti, M., Piedimonte, A., Solito, G., & Berti, A. (2015). Bimanual coupling effects during arm immobilization and passive movements. *Human Movement Science*, *41*, 114–126. doi:10.1016/j.humov.2015.03.003.

Giglia, G., Pia, L., Folegatti, A., Puma, A., Fierro, B., Cosentino, G., et al. (2015). Far space remapping by tool use: A rTMS study over the right posterior parietal cortex. *Brain Stimulation*, *8*(4), 795–800. doi:10.1016/j.brs.2015.01.412.

Graziano, M. S. (1999). Where is my arm? The relative role of vision and proprioception in the neuronal representation of limb position. *Proceedings of the National Academy of Sciences of the United States of America*, *96*(18), 10418–10421. doi:10.1073/pnas.96.18.10418.

Graziano, M. S., Cooke, D. F., & Taylor, C. S. (2000). Coding the location of the arm by sight. *Science*, *290*(5497), 1782–1786. doi:10.1126/science.290.5497.1782.

Hegedüs, G., Darnai, G., Szolcsányi, T., Feldmann, Á., Janszky, J., & Kállai, J. (2014). The rubber hand illusion increases heat pain threshold. *European Journal of Pain*, *18*(8), 1173–1181. doi:10.1002/j.1532-2149.2014.00466.x.

Holmes, N. P., Snijders, H. J., & Spence, C. (2006). Reaching with alien limbs: Visual exposure to prosthetic hands in a mirror biases proprioception without accompanying illusions of ownership. *Perception & Psychophysics*, *68*(4), 685–701. doi:10.3758/BF03208768.

Kalckert, A., & Ehrsson, H. H. (2012). Moving a rubber hand that feels like your own: A dissociation of ownership and agency. *Frontiers in Human Neuroscience*, *6*, 40. doi:10.3389/fnhum.2012.00040.

Kammers, M. P. M., Rose, K., & Haggard, P. (2011). Feeling numb: Temperature, but not thermal pain, modulates feeling of body ownership. *Neuropsychologia*, *49*(5), 1316–1321. doi:10.1016/j.neuropsychologia.2011.02.039.

Keysers, C., & Gazzola, V. (2009). Expanding the mirror: Vicarious activity for actions, emotions, and sensations. *Current Opinion in Neurobiology*, *19*(6), 666–671. doi:10.1016/j.conb.2009.10.006.

Kriegeskorte, N., Mur, M., Ruff, D. A., Kiani, R., Bodurka, J., Esteky, H.,. . . Bandettini, P. A. (2008). Matching categorical object representations in inferior temporal cortex of man and monkey. *Neuron*, *60*(6), 1126–1141. doi:10.1016/j.neuron.2008.10.043.

Lenggenhager, B., Tadi, T., Metzinger, T., & Blanke, O. (2007). Video ergo sum: Manipulating bodily self-consciousness. *Science*, *317*(5841), 1096–1099. doi:10.1126/science.1143439.

Limanowski, J., & Blankenburg, F. (2013). Minimal self-models and the free energy principle. *Frontiers in Human Neuroscience*, *7*, 547. doi:10.3389/fnhum.2013.00547.

Limanowski, J., & Blankenburg, F. (2015a). Network activity underlying the illusory self-attribution of a dummy arm. *Human Brain Mapping*, *36*(6), 2284–2304. doi:10.1002/hbm.22770.

Limanowski, J., & Blankenburg, F. (2015b). That's not quite me: Limb ownership encoding in the brain. *Social Cognitive and Affective Neuroscience*, *11*(7), 1130–1140. doi:10.1093/scan/nsv079.

Maister, L., Banissy, M. J., & Tsakiris, M. (2013). Mirror-touch synaesthesia changes representations of self-identity. *Neuropsychologia*, *51*(5), 802–808. doi:10.1016/j.neuro psychologia.2013.01.020.

Makin, T. R., Holmes, N. P., & Ehrsson, H. H. (2008). On the other hand: Dummy hands and peripersonal space. *Behavioural Brain Research*, *191*(1), 1–10. doi:10.1016/j .bbr.2008.02.041.

Maravita, A., & Iriki, A. (2004). Tools for the body (schema). *Trends in Cognitive Sciences*, *8*(2), 79–86. doi:10.1016/j.tics.2003.12.008.

Mazzoni, A. (2015, November). Neural coding mechanisms of artificial and naturalistic sensory stimuli. Paper presented at the Twenty-Third National Congress of the Italian Society of Psychophysiology. Abstract retrieved from http://www.ledonline.it /NeuropsychologicalTrends/.

Mazzoni, A., Brunel, N., Cavallari, S., Logothetis, N. K., & Panzeri, S. (2011). Cortical dynamics during naturalistic sensory stimulations: Experiments and models. *Journal of Physiology, Paris*, *105*(1–3), 2–15. doi:10.1016/j.jphysparis.2011.07.014.

Moseley, G. L., Gallace, A., & Spence, C. (2012). Bodily illusions in health and disease: Physiological and clinical perspectives and the concept of a cortical "body matrix." *Neuroscience and Biobehavioral Reviews*, *36*(1), 34–46. doi:10.1016/j.neubiorev .2011.03.013.

Moseley, G. L., Olthof, N., Venema, A., Don, S., Wijers, M., Gallace, A., et al. (2008). Psychologically induced cooling of a specific body part caused by the illusory ownership of an artificial counterpart. *Proceedings of the National Academy of Sciences of the United States of America*, *105*(35), 13169–13173. doi:10.1073/pnas .0803768105.

Myers, A., & Sowden, P. T. (2008). Your hand or mine? The extrastriate body area. *NeuroImage*, *42*(4), 1669–1677. doi:10.1016/j.neuroimage.2008.05.045.

Peelen, M. V., & Downing, P. E. (2007). The neural basis of visual body perception. *Nature Reviews: Neuroscience*, *8*(8), 636–648. doi:10.1038/nrn2195.

Pia, L., Garbarini, F., Fossataro, C., Fornia, L., & Berti, A. (2013). Pain and body awareness: Evidence from brain-damaged patients with delusional body ownership. *Frontiers in Human Neuroscience*, *7*, 298. doi:10.3389/fnhum.2013.00298.

Piedimonte, A., Garbarini, F., Rabuffetti, M., Pia, L., & Berti, A. (2014). Executed and imagined bimanual movements: A study across different ages. *Developmental Psychology, 50*(4), 1073–1080. doi:10.1037/a0034482.

Rohde, M., Wold, A., Karnath, H.-O., & Ernst, M. O. (2013). The human touch: Skin temperature during the rubber hand illusion in manual and automated stroking procedures. *PLoS One, 8*(11), e80688. doi:10.1371/journal.pone.0080688.

Romano, D., Gandola, M., Bottini, G., & Maravita, A. (2014). Arousal responses to noxious stimuli in somatoparaphrenia and anosognosia: Clues to body awareness. *Brain, 137*(4), 1213–1223. doi:10.1093/brain/awu009.

Slater, M., Spanlang, B., Sanchez-Vives, M. V., & Blanke, O. (2010). First person experience of body transfer in virtual reality. *PLoS One, 5*(5), e10564. doi:10.1371/journal.pone.0010564.

Sposito, A., Bolognini, N., Vallar, G., & Maravita, A. (2012). Extension of perceived arm length following tool-use: Clues to plasticity of body metrics. *Neuropsychologia, 50*(9), 2187–2194. doi:10.1016/j.neuropsychologia.2012.05.022.

Tsakiris, M. (2010). My body in the brain: A neurocognitive model of body-ownership. *Neuropsychologia, 48*(3), 703–712. doi:10.1016/j.neuropsychologia.2009.09.034.

Tsakiris, M., Costantini, M., & Haggard, P. (2008). The role of the right temporo-parietal junction in maintaining a coherent sense of one's body. *Neuropsychologia, 46*(12), 3014–3018. doi:10.1016/j.neuropsychologia.2008.06.004.

Tsakiris, M., & Haggard, P. (2005). The rubber hand illusion revisited: Visuotactile integration and self-attribution. *Journal of Experimental Psychology: Human Perception and Performance, 31*(1), 80–91. doi:10.1037/0096-1523.31.1.80.

Vallar, G., & Ronchi, R. (2009). Somatoparaphrenia: A body delusion. A review of the neuropsychological literature. *Experimental Brain Research, 192*(3), 533–551. doi:10.1007/s00221-008-1562-y.

van der Hoort, B., Guterstam, A., & Ehrsson, H. H. (2011). Being Barbie: The size of one's own body determines the perceived size of the world. *PLoS One, 6*(5), e20195. doi:10.1371/journal.pone.0020195.

Wold, A., Limanowski, J., Walter, H., & Blankenburg, F. (2014). Proprioceptive drift in the rubber hand illusion is intensified following 1 Hz TMS of the left EBA. *Frontiers in Human Neuroscience, 8*, 390. doi:10.3389/fnhum.2014.00390.

9 Mineness First: Three Challenges to the Recent Theories of the Sense of Bodily Ownership

Alexandre Billon

When I walk, when I laugh, when I sing, when I fall and feel pain in my hand, I am immediately aware of my limbs *as my own*. This "sense of ownership" is so intimate indeed, that it seems impossible to question that these limbs that I feel are really mine. Why is that so? Where does such a sense of ownership come from and what makes it so intimate? A simple "deflationary" answer, which Bermúdez (this volume) traces back to Locke, is that because my bodily sensations necessarily represent *my* bodily parts, it suffices to be aware of one's bodily sensation to be aware of the bodily parts in which it falls as one's own. I would thus be aware of a limb as mine provided that I have bodily sensations in it, or more rigorously, provided that it falls within the limits of my bodily sensations' spatial content.

At the turn of the eighteenth century, the Lockean, deflationary view of the sense of bodily ownership was criticized by a group of French philosophers and physiologists known as the Ideologists. The latter explicitly agreed with Locke that my body is, by nature, the locus of my bodily sensations. They took it, however, that even if my bodily sensations necessarily represent *my* bodily parts, they need not represent these *as mine*. They accordingly tried to complement the Lockean view by accounting for what presents the bodily parts I feel, and the bodily sensations I feel in it, as mine. Destutt de Tracy famously argued that the answer laid in "the faculty of will" which is "the origin of the idea of the self":

> The idea of ownership can only appear in a being gifted with will and . . . it necessarily and inevitably appears in such a being, and in all its plenitude, for as soon as this individual knows his self or his moral person, and his capacity for enjoying, suffering and acting, necessarily this self is the exclusive owner of this body it animates, these organs he moves, of all their faculties their forces and the effects they produce, for all this finishes and starts with this self, exists only through him, is moved only by its actions, and no other moral person can use these same

instruments, nor be affected in the same way by their effect. (Tracy, 1800, IV-§11; cf. also Tracy,1800, I-§7)

According to the Tracyan, nondeflationary view, I am aware of a body part as mine *only if the bodily sensations I feel in it are independently marked as mine*. One problem for such a view is that it posits a mark of ownership whose nature is unclear. For Tracy, the mark of ownership is grounded on "the will," by which he meant agency, the sense of agency, and affectivity—and which he would ultimately construe as a form of sixth sense. A contemporary of Tracy, Cabanis, would argue that at a deeper level, the mark of mineness stems from "organic" or "internal impressions," a set of largely implicit visceral sensations constituting an implicit background feeling of bodily existence, and that would later be called *cenesthetic*. Heirs of Tracy and Cabanis such as Biran, Ribot, Taine, or even Bergson would disentangle the many aspects of Tracy's "will" and put forward various dissenting views on the mark of mineness, explaining it in either sensory, sensorimotor, interoceptive, or affective terms. Even if it did not totally settle them, it is fair to say that the discovery and the careful study of a pathological condition known as "depersonalization" eventually simplified these debates, ruling out many views of the sense of bodily ownership. It even suggested that the mark of mineness might be psychologically primitive, that is, not reducible to psychological (as opposed to purely neurophysiological) features (Dugas & Moutier, 1911).

Although there has been a recent renewal of interest in the study of the sense of bodily ownership, depersonalization has still been largely ignored by contemporary researchers. This is unfortunate since recent theories of the sense of bodily ownership interestingly mirror the older ones, and the objections raised against these are still relevant today. In this chapter I will argue that depersonalization raises three challenges for contemporary theories. These challenges thwart all these theories and suggest that the sense of bodily ownership hinges on a phenomenal mark of mineness that cannot be accounted for in terms of our sensory, interoceptive, agentive, cognitive, or affective dispositions and that is psychologically primitive. In short: that mineness is first.

In what follows, I will present the leading theories of the sense of bodily ownership. Given the scope of this chapter, this presentation will remain quite cursory and it will focus on the most popular theories (section 1). I will then describe depersonalization (section 2) and put forward three challenges that it raises against theories of self-awareness (section 3). My conclusion will favor theories that posit a psychologically primitive mark of mineness (section 4).

1   Contemporary Theories of the Sense of Bodily Ownership

As I use the term, the sense of bodily ownership is the awareness of our limbs and bodily parts *as our own*. The sense of bodily ownership is the kind of awareness reflected in standard first-personal judgments of ownership, such as "this is my hand." Even though on many theories it also justifies these judgments and fixes the reference of "my hand," it is just defined as a form of *awareness*. Finally, even though the terminology "sense of ownership" is in this respect unfortunate—I would have called it bodily self-awareness if the expression were not often used to mean something else—I do not want to suggest that there must be a significant analogy between the sense of ownership and sense perception or that the sense of ownership should necessarily involve a "feeling."

The debate on the sense of bodily ownership has made a remarkable comeback these last twenty years. The different protagonists of this debate come from different fields or subfields, with different terminologies and it is not always totally clear that they really talk about the same phenomenon. Yet I think it is possible to outline a rough typology of the most popular theories at stake.

First, we can still distinguish between deflationary and nondeflationary theories of the sense of bodily ownership. In a paper that has largely framed the contemporary debate, Martin (1995) has for example defended a paradigmatic deflationary theory. According to him, the sense of bodily ownership (i) is grounded on the spatial content of my bodily sensations and (ii) does not involve a specific mark of mineness. In response, de Vignemont (2007, 2013) has put forward some influential arguments against Martin's theory, contributing to a revival of the nondeflationary theories. The debate between de Vignemont and Martin bears on both (i) and (ii): She argues both that the spatial content of sensations is not sufficient to explain the sense of bodily ownership (against [i]), and that a mark of mineness is required for that (against [ii]). For simplicity, I will suppose that it is (ii), rather than (i), that defines the deflationary position. Deflationists deny, but nondeflationists accept, the existence of a mark of mineness. The latter, it should be emphasized, is supposed to make a *phenomenal* difference and it is in that sense conscious, but it need not be, on modern nondeflationary theories, a discrete experience or quale that could be had in isolation.

De Vignemont's master argument relies on somatoparaphrenia, a fascinating neurological condition in which bodily self-awareness seems to err. Patients suffering from somatoparaphrenia can misattribute one of their limbs to someone else. The alien limb is normally paralyzed and patients do not feel any sensations in it. In some rare cases, however (I know only of four), the patient can correctly report sensations in the disowned limb. In such cases, it seems that patients have normal bodily sensations in a limb without bodily self-awareness for that limb. This suggests that Martin's deflationary theory is wrong and that there must exist an extra mark of mineness accounting for the sense of bodily ownership in conjunction with the spatial content of bodily sensations.

This modern vindication of the nondeflationary theories is not totally unproblematic though. First, it relies on a description of the relevant cases that is not uncontroversial. It might be wondered for example whether the reports of patients suffering from somatoparaphrenia should be taken seriously. These patients are delusional and according to some views of delusions, for example, delusional reports are meaningless and do not express propositions (cf. Berrios, 1991). It might also be wondered whether the bodily sensations of these patients really have a normal spatial content.

A second problem for holders of the nondeflationary view is that they need to elucidate the nature of this mark of mineness, which they posit and that deflationists eliminate, and which is arguably quite elusive. Most researchers agree that it should be reduced to more basic psychological features but their proposed analyses diverge importantly. In fact, virtually every aspect of the mind has be invoked to explain this mark of ownership.

Sensory views: Although he has expressed some sympathy for the deflationary theory in some earlier writings (it is in fact he who christened it "deflationary"), I take Bermúdez (this volume) to endorse an austere brand of nondeflationism to the effect that there is a mark of mineness, but (i) the latter is not a discrete quale, and (ii) it can be explained in mere sensory terms. According to Bermúdez (this volume) mineness hinges on the peculiar spatial format of bodily sensations: a bodily part is marked as mine, roughly, if its sensations are experienced within the experienced body (something he calls "boundedness") and if their locations are experienced relative to the disposition of the body as a whole (something he calls "connectedness").

Sensorimotor views: de Vignemont (2007) has hinted at a *sensorimotor or agency view*, to the effect that a bodily sensation is marked as mine if it falls within my *body schema*. As I understand it, the view is that a given bodily sensation will be marked as mine if it is properly connected to my action dispositions, that is, if it is poised to be used directly for action.

Interoceptive views: There has also been a revival of the old "cenesthetic" view, originated in Cabanis, Ribot, James, and Séglas, to the effect that a sensation is marked as mine if it is properly integrated with a certain set of interoceptive signals (Damasio, 1999). Seth (2013) has recently updated the interoceptive view, embedding it into a predictive coding framework. According to him, the brain actively infers "which signals are most likely to be 'me'" on the basis of statistical correlations between interoceptive and exteroceptive signals. Such an active inference would explain and modulate the mark of mineness (which he calls "the experience of body ownership").

Affectivity views: In her most recent writings, de Vignemont (this volume) has put forward an affective, *narcissistic view* to the effect that a bodily sensation is marked as mine if it falls within my "protective body schema," that is, the body I care for in a special, protective way, the body that has a distinctive "narcissistic" quality.

Cognitive views: At the other end of the spectrum, cognitive views claim that the sense of bodily ownership is grounded in certain cognitive states. Alsmith (2015) has claimed that some cognitive states are necessary for the sense of bodily ownership and that they play a decisive role in the modulation of the sense of bodily ownership. On Alsmith's view, whether I feel a given limb as mine, for example, depends and whether I judge—or even, in some cases, merely imagine—that it is mine. Although Alsmith refrains from making explicit explanatory claims, it is natural to read him as holding a cognitive view, and it is hard to figure out what other kind of explanation he could invoke once he has granted such an important role to cognitive attitudes.[1,2]

In fairness, all these views are not inconsistent with each other. The current interoceptive views are usually considered as affectivity views as well, its proponents assimilating interoceptive feelings to emotions. Likewise, Bermúdez's (this volume) sensory view is consistent with the agency view, as it stresses that the spatial format of bodily representations makes them poised to be used for actions planning and control. There is still however much disagreement, and many reasons to expect future advances in the characterization of the mark of ownership.

Among the reductionist views listed above, we can also distinguish between those invoking a purely objective *analysans*, and those invoking a subjective, experiential one. For example, while some sensorimotor theories might analyze the mark of mineness in terms of purely objective sensorimotor abilities, others might invoke sensorimotor experiences as well. Although this distinction is seldom made—and it is not always easy to discern whether a given reductive theory is meant to be subjective or objective—it shall prove quite useful in what follows.

Finally, we can oppose these reductionist views to a primitivist one, which would construe the mark of mineness as psychologically primitive, that is as irreducible to more basic psychological features (but only reducible to neurophysiological features).

2 Depersonalization

We have seen that de Vignemont argues against the deflationary view by appeal to the case of somatoparaphrenia. "Depersonalization" is another pathological condition that consists in a deep modification of the way things appear to a subject, leading him to feel estranged from his body, his actions, his thoughts, his mind, and even from himself. Although there are subclinical forms of depersonalization or proto-depersonalization characterized by mild or short-lived feelings, depersonalization can be intense, pervasive, and debilitating, leading the subject to seek medical help. Unlike patients suffering from somatoparaphrenia, depersonalized patients are not however generally delusional: their reality testing is intact and they take great care not to take their strange impressions at face value.

In what follows, I will focus on such cases of severe (but nondelusional) depersonalization and argue that they constitute a fruitful probe for current theories of the sense of bodily ownership.[3]

Depersonalized patients typically report feeling estranged from their body. This alienation usually involves the impression of not owning some of one's bodily parts. The third item of the Cambridge Depersonalization Scale (a questionnaire that has become the gold standard for assessing depersonalization) thus reads "Parts of my body feel as if they didn't belong to me."[4]

Patients can in fact complain of feeling their *whole body* as alien:

> I do not feel I have a body. When I look down I see my legs and body but it feels as if it was not there. When I move I see the movements as I move, but I am not there with the movements. I am walking up the stairs, I see my legs and hear footsteps and feel the muscles but it feels as if I have no body; I am not there. (Dugas & Moutier, 1911, p. 28, my translation)

When they feel like not owning their whole body patients can also report feeling outside of their body or seeing themselves from outside:

> I feel like a robot, like I am listening to someone else talking, like I am looking at myself from the outside, but it is not another voice or body, it is mine, it is me, it

just doesn't feel like it. . . . I spend all day trying to figure it out. Maybe I am too analytical. Nothing makes it better but being with other people makes it worse. (Baker et al., 2003, p. 431)

Depersonalized patients do not, however, just suffer from an altered sense of bodily ownership—awareness of their *bodily parts as theirs*—they seem to have an impaired awareness of their *bodily sensations* too. Many spontaneously describe themselves as not feeling any bodily sensations in certain parts of their body ("the top of my head is popping and buzzing and then it seems to go all numb," Shorvon, 1946, p. 42) or even in their whole body ("he claims he has lost all sensibility," Janet, 1908, my translation) and they can touch or hurt themselves in order to feel something. A patient of Leroy's thus kept touching and pinching every part of her body:

She did not feel anything, or rather, she did not feel anything as she used to, so she had to touch herself. . . . "When I wash myself, she said, my hand is insensitive. . . . Yesterday when I kissed my daughter, it didn't do me anything, my lips did not feel anything. . . . My eyelids [she explained that she used to touch them every morning] are insensitive. . . . It is like a big void in my back, she says, while touching her spine, I do not feel 'my back.'". . . Touching her left side she said: "it is like insensitive." (Leroy, 1901, pp. 520–521, my translation)

Reports and behaviors such as these led early researchers to suppose that these patients really were anesthetized. However clinical examinations generally revealed no sensory alteration whatsoever (Leroy, 1901; Janet, 1928). Conversely, in spite of a few exceptions (e.g., Oliver Sacks's Christina, see Sacks, 1985, pp. 31–32), deafferentation, or wide bodily anesthesia, are not generally accompanied by depersonalization (Janet, 1928).

The problem with these patients' bodily sensations seems to be in fact a problem of the sense of ownership for sensations—the awareness of one's sensations as one's own—rather than of *awareness* proper. When the patient says he does not feel sensations in his back, for example, the problem seems to be that although he feels these sensations, he does not feel them *as his*, or to put it differently, that it does not seem to him that *he himself* feels these sensations. If we call *sense of mental ownership* our awareness of our mental states as our own we can say that patients have an impaired sense of mental ownership for some of their bodily sensations. This is indeed what some patients say. Thus, Janet's patient mentioned above, who claimed to have lost "all sensibility" immediately explains: "it is not me who feels. I am not interested in what I appear to be feeling, it is somebody else who feels mechanically" (Janet, 1908, p. 515, my translation). Similarly, a patient of Mayer-Gross says: "I feel pains in my chest, but they seem to belong to someone else, not to me" (Mayer-Gross, 1935, p. 114).[5] Unlike anesthesia, an altered sense of mental ownership for bodily sensations has indeed made it to the Cambridge Depersonalization Scale, whose seventeenth item reads: "When a part of my body hurts, I feel so detached from the pain that it feels as if it were somebody else's pain."

The disturbance of the sense of mental ownership in depersonalization is not however restricted to bodily sensations. It can affect emotions, memories, imaginings, perceptions, and any other kind of mental states. Patients can deny that all such states seem to be theirs to them. Depersonalization can moreover affect the awareness of our actions as our own—something often called *the sense of agency*—patients often complaining that their actions seem alien (not theirs) and mechanical (see Billon, forthcoming, for an overview). Finally, it is arguable that in extreme cases, the patient's awareness of her- or himself as "I"—call it *the sense of oneself*—gets impaired as well: some patients are inclined not to use the first person and talk about themselves as if they had only an external, third-person access to themselves (see Billon, in press). If we call "forms of *self-awareness*" the sense of ownership, agency, and oneself, we can say, to sum up, that depersonalization involves disorders of all forms of self-awareness.[6]

The discovery of depersonalization, at the turn of the nineteenth century, elicited numerous debates on the nature of the sense of bodily ownership, mental ownership, agency, and oneself, debates that largely echo contemporary controversies. It was globally agreed that depersonalization was at least in part a problem of the sense of bodily ownership and that the explanation of depersonalization would give us insights on the grounds of the sense of bodily ownership, and of self-awareness in general. The idea was that what is altered in depersonalization is what explains our normal self-awareness.

In the seminal monograph he coauthored with Moutier, Dugas—the French philosopher who coined the term "depersonalization"—put forward a series of arguments for what we might call a primitivist, nondeflationary theory of self-awareness and depersonalization. According to this theory, the sense of bodily ownership does not reduce to the spatial content of our bodily sensations but involves an extra mark of mineness, which normally accompanies all mental states, explains self-awareness in general, and would be altered in depersonalization. This extra mark of mineness is moreover primitive in that it does not reduce to the available reductive theories purporting to account for it in terms of sensory capacities, cenesthesia (interoception), agency, or affectivity.

In what follows I would like to revive some of these arguments and show their relevance for the current debate on the sense of bodily ownership. I will argue that the study of depersonalization raises three challenges for current theories of the sense of bodily ownership that tend to favor the more primitivist, nondeflationary theories on the market.

3   Three Challenges

I will now argue that depersonalization raises three different challenges for current theories of the sense of bodily ownership. The first, *centrality challenge*, hinges on the fact that most current theories do not readily generalize to explain other forms of self-awareness (the sense of mental ownership, agency, and oneself), but that they should, as depersonalization is a unified pathology that can affect all these forms of self-awareness. The second, *dissociation challenge*, targets these theories that predict that a certain capacity should be impaired when the sense of bodily ownership is impaired, while this capacity is in fact intact among depersonalized patients. The final, *grounding challenge*, shows moreover that many of the theories, which do indeed make verified predictions concerning depersonalization, can however be ruled out as wrong or merely incidental by considerations of fundamentality.

3.1   The Centrality Challenge

Most current theories ground the sense of bodily ownership on something that cannot readily explain other forms of self-awareness as well (the sense of mental ownership, agency, and oneself). We can call them *modular*. Martin's deflationary theory explains the sense of bodily ownership in terms of the spatial content of bodily sensations, and it is unclear how such a theory could explain the sense of mental ownership of bodily sensations, let alone that of thoughts with no spatial content such as "thinking is difficult." The same goes for de Vignemont's (2007) body schema theory, de Vignemont's (2016) more recent narcissistic account, or Bermúdez's (this volume) bodily spatiality theories. All these theories were framed for the sense of bodily ownership and they do not generalize in any obvious way to other forms of self-awareness (the sense of mental ownership, agency, and oneself). We can contrast modular theories with *central* theories of the sense of bodily ownership. The latter explain the sense of bodily ownership in terms of something that can readily explain other forms of self-awareness.[7]

The simplest central theory, or theory schema, claims that all our conscious mental states normally have a phenomenal mark of mineness, and that:

• I have a sense of mental ownership for a mental state when it has this mark of mineness.
• I have a sense of bodily ownership for a bodily part when the sensations I feel in it have this mark of mineness.
• I have a sense of agency for an action if I have a sense of mental ownership for the intention in action that drives it, that is, if the latter has this mark of mineness.
• I have a sense of myself as long as I have a sense of ownership for some of my mental states.
• And the mark of mineness posited here is always of the same kind (for bodily sensations, intentions in action and for all mental states).[8]

We can call this central theory the *central mineness view*. I have suggested elsewhere that the mark of mineness might be identified with what is often called the subjective character or the "meishness" of experience (Levine, 2001; Kriegel, 2009): a mental state is marked as mine if it has a subjective character (Billon, 2015). This goes some way toward specifying this theory schema. However, there are many accounts of the subjective character,[9] and many accounts of its role with regard to consciousness—Does it explain it? Does it necessarily accompany all conscious states? As such, this "central mineness view" is accordingly still quite schematic.[10]

Cognitive views, such as the view suggested by Alsmith (2015), constitute another example of central theories. According to these views, whether a mental state or an action seems to be mine to me depends on some cognitive attitude bearing on that mental state.[11]

The difference between central theories and modular theories is that the former posit a common ground for all forms of self-awareness. Unlike modular theories, they can accordingly explain how all forms of self-awareness might come and go together without invoking a pure coincidence. Of course, central theories do not imply that all forms of self-awareness should *always* come and go together. A central theory explaining the sense of agency and the sense of bodily ownership by a common ground C can allow that the sense of agency breaks down while the sense of bodily ownership is intact, by arguing, for example, that C grounds the sense of agency through the intermediary ground X and grounds the sense of bodily ownership through another intermediary ground Y. In such a case, if X but not Y

breaks down, then the sense of agency but not the sense of bodily ownership will break down.

Now the interesting thing with depersonalization is that it is a global
disorder: it is not, as we have seen, a merely bodily disorder and it can
affect all forms of self-awareness. Given that depersonalization is a single
psychological entity, it should receive a unified explanation, from which
it follows that there should be a single explanation for all the disorders of
self-awareness involved in depersonalization, and hence for all the forms
of self-awareness that are disordered in depersonalization.[12] Let C be this
central explanans of all forms of self-awareness, and let Mbo be a purported
modular explanans of the sense of bodily ownership. Either C does not
explain Mbo and then the latter cannot explain the sense of bodily ownership after all. Or C does explain Mbo, and Mbo can explain the sense of
bodily ownership, but it is at best an incidental, nonfundamental explanation: what explains the sense of bodily ownership, is at the bottom, C, not
Mbo. Modular accounts of the sense of bodily ownership are either wrong,
then, or incidental.

The global character of the disorders of self-awareness in depersonalization, and the unified character of this pathology thus threatens the classical
theories of the sense of bodily ownership, which are modular, and supports
central views such as the "central mineness view."

One way to resist this objection would be to deny that depersonalization
really is unified. Some have questioned whether depersonalization is a *specific* condition (as opposed to one present in almost every psychiatric condition, like anxiety), or that it is a *discrete* condition (as opposed to a part
of, or a prodrome of another condition). I believe such doubts should have
been cleared by recent epidemiological studies on large samples (Simeon
et al., 2008; Baker et al., 2003; see Sierra, 2009, pp. 1–6), and recent brain-
imaging studies separating the correlates of depersonalization and of other
disorders (Lemche et al., 2013). In any case, they do not threaten the claim
that depersonalization is a *single* syndrome. The only researcher I know
who has questioned this orthodox claim is Sacco (2010). He has denied that
depersonalization/derealization disorder is "unidimensional in nature" on
the grounds that (i) it can be induced by different "precipitating causes" (he
cites for example epilepsy, drug use, meditation, vertigo, major life stress,
self-focus, etc.), (ii) it can have different "affective implications" (some
subjects having nonpathological depersonalization-like experience find
it in fact pleasant), and (iii) an influential theory explains it in biological
terms (Sierra & Berrios, 1998) while another explains it in cognitive terms
(Hunter, Phillips, Chalder, Sierra, & David, 2003). First, it should be noticed

that Sacco does not focus, as we have, on pathological forms of depersonalization. By "depersonalization/derealization disorder"[13] he means a much wider class including what he calls "normal depersonalization" (short-lived or mild, nonpathological episodes of depersonalization-like experiences), and he explicitly agrees that pathological depersonalization has much less diverse precipitating causes and affective implications. So even if (i–ii) threatened the unity of "depersonalization/derealization disorder," it is not clear that it would threaten the unity of depersonalization in the narrower sense used here. Moreover, in the sense in which he uses these terms, "precipitating causes" of X are just distal causes of X, and "affective implications" of X are the ways a subject can emotionally appraise it. Accordingly, their multiplicity is simply irrelevant with respect to the unity of X. Consider for example a burn: it can be "precipitated" by friction, heat, chemicals, and radiation, and it can be extremely distressing or quite indifferent depending on its severity, yet it is a single medical entity. In order to show that depersonalization is disunited, Sacco would have to show that its various "precipitating causes" in fact cause different things, things whose nature should be explained differently. Now (iii) might have shown this if the two cited theories of depersonalization were both true *and* inconsistent with each other. I see no reason, however, to suppose that this is the case (the point of cognitive neuropsychology is precisely to unify neurophysiological and cognitive explanations and Sierra has in fact endorsed both theories). Finally there is positive reason to think that depersonalization is psychologically unified. First, as Sacco recognizes, it is phenomenologically unified. More importantly, there is evidence that depersonalization is both biologically and cognitively unified as well, as witnessed, for example by the relative success of the neuropsychological model put forward by Sierra and David (2011). I have argued elsewhere that all cases of depersonalization could be construed as variations in intensity and extension of a single (neuropsychologically grounded) phenomenological alteration (Billon, forthcoming).

Another way to resist this objection would be to argue that the sense of bodily ownership grounds all other forms of self-awareness and that *any* explanation of the sense of bodily ownership is accordingly (trivially) central rather than modular. However, there are patients suffering from depersonalization who display an impaired sense of bodily ownership without an impaired sense of ownership for mental states others than bodily sensations and without an impaired sense of themselves. This implies that the sense of bodily ownership cannot ground these two other forms of self-awareness and that its explanation cannot be central.

3.2 The Dissociation Challenge

A theory of the sense of bodily ownership purports to explain the sense of bodily ownership in terms of a certain state of an *explanans*. It predicts that *an alteration of the sense of bodily ownership should be accompanied by a similar alteration of the state of that explanans*. The second challenge raised by depersonalization comes from the fact that except for their altered self-awareness, patients suffering from depersonalization seem intriguingly normal. They accordingly show that an alteration of the sense of bodily ownership can be dissociated from many factors purportedly explaining it.

Martin's deflationary theory and other sensory theories

This dissociation challenge for example thwarts Martin's deflationary theory and all theories, deflationary or not, which appeal to the spatial content of sensations.

The first explanations of depersonalization—an explanation put forward by Krishaber (1873), Taine (1873), and the founder of French scientific psychology Ribot (1883)—appealed exclusively to distorted sensations. Taine (1873) for example believed that the patient's sensations were so altered that they involved a radical discontinuity in his psychic life, and that, "like a caterpillar who has become a butterfly" he could not recognize himself anymore. These sensory theories relied mainly on the patients' subjective reports of sensory distortions. The latter, we have seen can complain of feeling anesthetized. They can likewise say that they are blind, or that they cannot see depth and colors. Less commonly, they can claim to feel as if some of their bodily parts grew larger or smaller. Even if some patients might indeed suffer from objective sensory impairments (some patients of Krishaber's seem to have suffered from diplopia and vertigo), this seems rather anecdotal. Clinical examination revealed that patients do not generally show any objective sensory impairment, having intact discriminative capacities (Janet, 1928, pp. 40, 63–64). As we have seen, claims of apparent anesthesia seem to express a lack of sense of mental ownership for the corresponding sensations. Claims of color blindness and stereo blindness are often prefaced by an "as if" and are usually considered metaphorical as well (Dugas & Moutier, 1911). The lack of depth might indeed refer to a—very commonly felt—lack of presence or reality, and the lack of color to a—very commonly felt as well—lack of emotional valence.

The rebuttal of sensory theories of depersonalization thwarts all brands of sensory theories of the sense of bodily ownership, and in particular Martin's deflationary theory, which appeals to the spatial content of sensations. As I understand it, Martin's theory predicts that the spatial content of patients' bodily sensations should be abnormal. I am not sure what the abnormality should consist in, maybe the bodily sensations of the disowned limb should represent some events as situated far away, disconnected from the rest of the body. Maybe they should be altogether absent. In any case, nothing indicates *any* abnormality in the spatial content of patients' sensations. The objection here is somehow similar to de Vignemont's objection from somatoparaphrenia. There are important differences though. First, cases of depersonalization are much more common than cases of somatoparaphrenia with conscious sensations in the disowned limb. Second, depersonalized patients are not generally delusional. Third, there is very good evidence that their bodily sensations are intact and have a perfectly normal spatial content. This, I believe, reinforces her case against Martin's theory.

Interoceptive theories

It was suggested that even if the patients' five senses and proprioception are intact, they might suffer from an alteration of cenesthesia, which has generally been construed as interoception (e.g. by Deny and by Camus), to which some, such as Foerster and Storch, added the vestibular system and muscle proprioception (cf. Dugas & Moutier [1911] and Hesnard [1909]). However, here again, no alteration was significant enough to be detected by clinical examination. For example, although they can complain of not feeling hunger and thirst, patients seem to have a interoceptive abilities, as witnessed by their normal bowel and bladder function as well as their normal gag reflexes (Janet, 1928, pp. 40, 63–64). This has been confirmed experimentally very recently: Michal et al. (2014) compared twenty-four depersonalized patients to twenty-six normal controls and noticed that despite their impaired bodily self-awareness, the patients' interoceptive abilities (as measured by heartbeat discrimination tasks, which are known to be a reliable indicator of general interoceptive abilities), were perfectly normal. They concluded to a "striking discrepancy of anomalous body experiences with normal interoceptive accuracy in depersonalization-derealization disorder."[14]

Just as it undermines the old "cenesthetic" theories of the sense of bodily ownership (and self-awareness in general), this rebuttal of the interoceptive theories of depersonalization undermines the recent interoceptive theories of the sense of bodily ownership such as Damasio (1999) or Dolan (1999), and Seth (2013). The latter, for example, explain the sense of bodily ownership in terms of the correlation between interoceptive and exteroceptive signals, and they wrongly predict that such signals should be distorted in depersonalization.

Sensorimotor theories

The same dissociation threatens what we might call sensorimotor theories: those that appeal not only to sensations, but also to their connection with bodily movements and actions. In a few paragraphs devoted to depersonalization, Bergson (1896) for example speculated that the sense of the reality of the self and of the external world stemmed from the connection of our sensations with action, connections which anchor them in the present, and the actual (you cannot act on the past or on the merely possible).[15] He suggested that such a connection was lost in depersonalization. It is true that some patients can report feeling as if they move or walk strangely. A patient of Krishaber's, reported by Hesnard, thus "had the impression that the ground was soft and moving, and that her legs were alien to her body" (Hesnard, 1909, p. 66; see also Sierra, 2009, p. 31). Some also feel like they're not in a position to accomplish actions with their alien body, and express surprise or amazement as they do accomplish them. A patient of Hesnard thus describes his feelings while shopping:

> I watch me acting as I would watch someone else. My voice, my gestures and my computations seem to me like things combined in advance, that I would have decided but that I would not be accomplishing. . . . I make no effort to accomplish these automatic gestures but I never do the wrong things. *This is what amazes me. I leave the shop and I wonder: will I have the strength and the precision to get out? I will fall, as I make no effort to walk.* . . . *And yet I walk.* (1909, p. 117, my translation, emphasis added)

There is however ample clinical evidence that such subjective complaints are not accompanied by any objective motor control problem (Janet, 1901, p. 490, 1928, pp. 40, 63–64). The most thorough experiment testing the sensorimotor capacities of depersonalized patients was conducted by Cappon and Banks (1965). They used an instrument constituted by riders moving on various rods, which they could manipulate to indicate their perceived body length, thickness, width, and position. The instrument could be used visually and (in the absence of visual cues) kinesthetically. In both cases, the error, latency, and variability of the subjects' performances were measured. Despite the bodily complaints of depersonalized patients, and despite the fact that such complaints did occur during the test phase as well, Cappon and Banks failed to differentiate patients from matched controls on all measures, both in normal conditions and in disturbing conditions meant to impede bodily perception and to induce depersonalization crises (caloric stimulation, repeated rotations on a chair, sensory deprivation, and sleep deprivation). This strongly suggests that depersonalized patients have no motor problem.

As Sierra puts it, commenting on Capon and Banks' experiments, "perceptual distortions affecting 'body image' do not seem accompanied by corresponding changes in body schema (defined as unconscious postural and body adjustments regarding motor behaviour)" (Sierra, 2009, p. 31).[16]

These objections against the sensorimotor theories of depersonalization are ipso facto objections against the corresponding sensorimotor theories of the sense of bodily ownership. They threaten, in particular, de Vignemont's (2007) body schema theory of the sense of bodily ownership. According to de Vignemont's (2007) body schema theory, I am aware of a limb as mine if I have in it sensations that fall within my body schema. This theory predicts that someone whose sense of bodily ownership is impaired should have an impaired body schema, or else sensations with an impaired spatial content. Depersonalized patients, however, have none of these.[17]

But Capon and Banks's (1965) experiments also seem relevant for certain sensory theories of depersonalization. Take Martin's (1995) deflationary theory, which predicts that the spatial content of patients' sensations should be abnormal, or Bermúdez's (this volume) bodily spatiality theory, which predicts that patients should experience some of their bodily events as not within the experienced body (boundedness), or as not located relative to the disposition of the body as a whole (connectedness). I find it hard to understand how patients could get normal results on all the tests of bodily perceptions designed by Cappon and Banks if such predictions were verified. It should be noted, moreover, that some patients in fact disown their *whole* body. The patients' body's spatiality and spatial sensory contents are not only objectively quite normal, they also seem, I believe, quite normal to them. Their problem is just that this otherwise normal body does not seem to be theirs to them. The problem is not internal to their body: it bears on the way their body is related to them.

Cognitive theories

It was very early acknowledged that depersonalized patients do not generally have any cognitive dysfunction, and cognitive theories of depersonalization have been quite rare. Depersonalized patients are not delusional and their rationality seems perfectly intact. Recent studies have confirmed that their intelligence, memory, high-level attention, and executive functioning are normal (Simeon & Abugel, 2006, p. 99). Patients were only found slightly differing from controls in some very specific aspects of low-level attention and memory implied in tasks involving great perceptual overload (Guralnik, Schmeidler, & Simeon, 2000; Guralnik, Giesbrecht, Knutelska, Sirroff, & Simeon, 2007). It is true that patients can show a form of hyerreflexity or heightened self-observation and become obsessed with their own thoughts (Sierra 2009, p. 31). This, however, seems to be an understandable consequence of the disorders of self-awareness rather than a cause of their condition.

The normal cognitive functioning of depersonalized patients challenges cognitive views, such as the one suggested by Alsmith (2015). According to these views the sense of bodily ownership is grounded in certain cognitive states. These theories should predict that deficits of the sense of bodily ownership should occur when subjects have an abnormal cognitive functioning, be it because it is intrinsically abnormal or because it is hindered by an abnormal environment. Now given that depersonalized patients can have a distorted sense of bodily ownership in normal environmental conditions and that their intrinsic cognitive functioning is normal, they can be counted as evidence against cognitive views.[18]

3.3   The Grounding Challenge

The *dissociation challenge* targets theories of depersonalization and of the sense of bodily ownership explaining them in terms of a factor that remains normal in depersonalization. Many reductive theories of the sense of bodily ownership and depersonalization appeal to an explanans that is also altered on depersonalization and are accordingly not threatened by the dissociation challenge. Some theories appeal to affectivity, and affectivity is indeed abnormal among depersonalized patients. Some sensorimotor theories might invoke not only objective motor control, but agentive *experiences* as well, (or even the sense of agency) which are indeed abnormal in depersonalization. Instead of objective interoceptive capacities, some interoceptive, cenesthetic theories, might likewise invoke interoceptive *experiences*, which are also abnormal. Affectivity theories and those theories invoking agentive experience and interoceptive experiences theories might not be independent of each other (on many views of emotions, affectivity essentially involves agentive or interoceptive experiences). They are all *subjective theories*: they invoke experiences—that do indeed seem abnormal in depersonalized patients—over and above objective capacities and dispositions—which seem normal in depersonalization. Unlike their objective counterparts, these subjective theories are accordingly immune to the dissociation challenge. A partisan of one of the objective theories we have reviewed before might thus be tempted to adopt the corresponding subjective theory, or even claim that he had such a theory in mind all along. We shall see, however, that these subjective theories are thwarted by a more subtle challenge devised by Dugas and Moutier (1911)—call it "the grounding challenge."

Affectivity theories

To get the general form of this challenge, it is better to consider an example. Many depersonalized patients complain of feeling nothing, of having no emotions, or only attenuated ones, and can claim, as a result not to care about anything anymore. Here is for example the testimony of Claire, a patient of Janet:

> Emotions stop, they do not develop, they get lost and do not reach me, a thing that should have frightened me let me calm, I cannot feel afraid, I have too much calm; I can still feel joys and pains but they are attenuated. . . . This is what I am sorry for. I do not have a heart anymore. Sometimes it wakes up, and then if falls back again. (Janet, 1903, p. 301)

It was very early considered that this affective flattening was a key element in depersonalization.[19] In the seminal paper in which he coined the term depersonalization, Dugas (1898) in fact argued that the affective attenuation afflicting depersonalized patients were evidence that the self and its self-awareness are grounded in affectivity. He concluded:

> The self is essentially the being that vibrates, that feels moved, and not the one that acts or thinks, apathy [in the sense of a lack of affect] is really the loss of the sense of the self. (Dugas, 1898, p. 507; translations from the French are mine)

This line of thought, whose conclusion is interestingly echoed by recent neuroscientific works (Panksepp, 1998; Northoff & Panksepp, 2008; Damasio, 2003), was pursued and deepened by many researchers in France and Germany, most notably by Lipps (1902) and Oesterreich (1908). Dugas, however, progressively abandoned this affective view of depersonalization and self-awareness. He noticed that the affectivity problem of depersonalized subjects was indeed of a very specific sort. Just like patients who complain of feeling no sensations do not really seem anesthetized, patients who report missing or attenuated emotions generally seem normal from a third-person point of view. Janet's patient Claire, quoted above, for example ends the description of her flattened emotional life by acknowledging that it can be hard to believe her:

> You do not want to believe that I have no heart, I look just like a loving daughter. Deep down nothing matters to me, I do not wish to be cured, I would like to be very sad. I would like to be deeply moved, to suffer a lot: being so quiet, so calm, frightens me. (Janet, 1903, p. 301, my translation)

As Schilder observed, even if in depersonalized patients

> the emotions . . . undergo marked alteration. Patients complain that that they are capable of experiencing neither pain or pleasure; love and hate have perished with them. . . . The objective examination of such patients reveals not only an intact sensory apparatus, but also an intact emotional apparatus. All these pa-

tients exhibit natural affective reactions in their facial expressions, attitudes, etc.; so that it is impossible to assume that they are incapable of emotional response. (Schilder 1935, quoted by Sierra, 2009, p. 26)

The following reports give us an idea of the patients' strange and dissonant condition:

I only feel anger from the outside, by its physiological reactions. (Dugas & Moutier, 1911, p. 121)

I am afraid for my thoughts, for my brain, which I do not master anymore, but deep down, I do not know whether I am afraid. . . . It would be better to have a genuine fear. (Dugas & Moutier, 1911, p. 124)

I do not care about anything . . . I look at my hands that are writing this text. How curious! They are still interested in some things. (Dugas & Moutier, 1911, p. 127)

It was painful and my arm felt like withdrawing, but it was not a genuine pain, it was a pain that did not reach the soul. . . . It is a pain, if you want, but the surface of my skin is miles away from my brain, and I do not know whether I am suffering. (Janet, 1928, p. 65)

What happens, it seems, is not so much that the patient has no emotional responses or importantly attenuated ones. Rather he does not, or not clearly, feel them as his own. It seems to him, to put it differently, that he does not *himself* have, or clearly have, emotions. His emotional responses are there, but lacking their normal sense of mental ownership, they do not reach him and are somehow alienated.

This does not mean, it should be emphasized, that the subject's emotions are normal. Indeed, it is arguable that to be afraid necessarily implies feeling (oneself) endangered, to be angry necessarily involves feeling (oneself) offended, and so on, and more broadly, that to have an emotion necessarily involves feeling (oneself) concerned by something. If that is so, whatever the patients' objective emotional responses might be, a lack of sense of mental ownership will indeed entail an alteration of emotions. Moreover, it is doubtful that the objective emotional response of the patients is perfectly normal. After all, the subjects objectively report blunted or alienated emotions, and this is abnormal. My point is only that these alterations correspond to, or should be explained by an alteration of the sense of mental ownership for emotions and its biological correlates.[20]

These observations, to the effect that emotions are only altered in virtue of their lack of normal sense of ownership, led Dugas to abandon his former affectivity theory and to conclude that:

Depersonalization is not uniquely the loss of feeling [*la perte du sentiment*] as it affects the feeling itself. . . . Emotions get detached and alienated from the self;

they do not hence constitute, by themselves the material or the substance of the self. Depersonalization implies deaffectualization but does not reduce to it. (Dugas & Moutier, 1911, p. 144)[21]

As I understand it, Dugas and Moutier's objection is that:

1. The patients' emotions are only altered in virtue of lacking the normal sense of mental ownership that usually accompanies them (the patient's deaffectualization is merely a lack of sense of mental ownership for emotions).
2. The same explanans (call it E) must explain both the lack of a normal sense of mental ownership for emotions (i.e., deaffectualization), and the other aspects of depersonalization such as the lack of a normal sense of mental ownership of other mental states, the lack of a normal sense of bodily ownership, agency, and oneself.
3. So it is E, not deaffectualization, that is the proper explanation of depersonalization.

We have already defended (1). (2) follows from the fact that deaffectualization is a disorder of the sense of ownership, and as we have used the term, more broadly of *self-awareness*, which is entailed by (1)—and from the fact that all things being equal, disorders of the same kind should receive a unified explanation. (3) follows from (1) and (2).

Notice that the fact that it is E, not deaffectualization, that is the proper explanation of depersonalization might still leave an important role for deaffectualization. Deaffectualization might for example explain all the other aspects of depersonalization and count as somehow explaining depersonalization. It might thus explain the disorders of the sense of bodily ownership, agency, and oneself, and even those of the sense of mental ownership for mental states other than emotions (the disorders of the sense of mental ownership for emotions *constitute* deaffectualization). But even then, it would be an incidental, nonfundamental explanation. An explanation that does not go deep enough, deep into the ground explanans E. Deaffectualization is a disorder of self-awareness for emotions that is explained by E, and unlike E, it could only be an incidental, nonfundamental explanation of other disorders of self-awareness.

For all we know, moreover, deaffectualization might also only share a common ground (E) with other aspects of depersonalization. In that case, it would not contribute to explain these other symptoms at all.

Dugas and Moutier (1911) appealed to an objection of this form against the leading affectivity theories of depersonalization and self-awareness of their time, but also against the "cenesthetic" theories, which invoked altered interoceptive experiences, also known as "organic sensations." They argued that "[the depersonalized] patient feels alien to his visceral sensations like he feels alien to his visual sensations" and that "organic sensations are sensations like others; they must, like others, be attached to the self" (Dugas & Moutier, 1911, p. 38). What explains our normal sense of bodily ownership will not accordingly be our normal interoceptive experiences but rather what explains that we have self-awareness for them (we are aware of them as our own), and for other experiences and actions. This objection, or objection schema, generalizes mutatis mutandis to all theories of depersonalization and the sense of bodily ownership (or even self-awareness in general) that invoke a factor Mbo which is abnormal in depersonalization, but whose abnormality just consists in a lack of self-awareness for Mbo, that is, in the fact that Mbo does not seem to be his to the subject. It strongly suggests that in such cases, there will be a factor accounting both for our normal sense of bodily ownership and for our Mbo-cum-normal-self-awareness, and that the purported explanation of the sense of bodily ownership by Mbo will be at best incidental (or worse, simply wrong). Such an objection schema, I take it, thwarts recent theories of the sense of bodily ownership that appeal to affectivity, such as de Vignemont's (2016) narcissistic theory. Remember that de Vignemont's (2016) theory claims my body is where I feel sensations marked as mine and that a sensation is marked as mine if it falls within my "protective body schema," the body which has an affective, narcissistic quality in virtue of which I am concerned for it in a specific, protective way. Now, it is true that the depersonalized patient's body often has an abnormal narcissistic quality. Their body seems alien to them, and they can express a certain lack of care for it. However, just like the depersonalized patient's affectivity is only abnormal in that it is alienated—the patient lacks self-awareness for it—their body's narcissistic quality is only abnormal in that it is alienated, the patient lacking self-awareness or ownership for it. There is still indeed a form of self-concern for the body lurking. The body is still protecting itself. Thus when Janet inflicts a painful stimulus to Laetitia, his patient, he notices that her protective reflexes are still there and her arm does withdraw. But the self-concern is alienated. It is the body's rather than the subject's self-concern. It is a self-concern for which the subject lacks self-awareness or ownership. This is why, as we have seen, after receiving a painful stimulus on her hand Laetitia says: "It was painful and *my arm felt like withdrawing*, but it was not a genuine pain" (Janet, 1928, pp. 65-66, emphasis added). Similarly, it is why Dugas and Moutier's patient Lucile seems to acknowledge that her body is still concerned by the things around her, but disavows this concern: "I look at my hands that are writing this text," she says, "How curious! They are still interested in some things" (Dugas & Moutier, 1911, p. 127).[22]

Conclusion

I have presented three challenges raised by depersonalization to recent—and not so recent—theories of the sense of bodily ownership. The *dissociation challenge* threatens objective sensory, interoceptive, and sensorimotor theories as well as cognitive theories. The *grounding challenge* threatens affectivity theories and the subjective versions of the sensorimotor and interoceptive theories—versions that invoke feelings of agency or interoception in supplement to objective capacities. I have argued that these two challenges accordingly threaten Martin's deflationary theory, Bermúdez's sensory theory, de Vignemont's sensory theory and her later affectivity theory, Damasio's and Seth's interoceptive theories, as well as Alsmith's cognitive theory. I have also argued that all these theories, except for Alsmith's cognitive theory, are thwarted by *the centrality challenge*. Finally, I have claimed that this last challenge naturally suggests a theory to the effect that that all my mental states have a mark of mineness that tags them as mine, and that grounds all forms of self-awareness, including the sense of bodily ownership. The mark of mineness of my bodily sensations, which accounts for my sense of bodily ownership, cannot moreover be accounted for by the leading theories of the sense of bodily ownership. It does not reduce to sensory, interoceptive, sensorimotor, or affective dispositions. All this suggests that this mark of mineness cannot be accounted for in psychological terms, and that it is, in this sense, primitive.

Notes

1. Alsmith's (2015) view is, strictly speaking, neutral on the deflationary/nondeflationary debate. Yet, it is consistent with the nondeflationary view and could be used to account for the mark of mineness.

2. I thank Adrian Alsmith for helpful discussions on his view.

3. Even though it is has been the subject of a regained interest in the last twenty years, depersonalization has never been more studied than during the last quarter of the nineteenth century and the first quarter of the twentieth century, during the golden age of French clinical psychology. Psychologists of that time also had an obvious interest in the "phenomenological" or descriptive aspects of psychopathology, and they explicitly tried to get an understanding of the sense of bodily ownership and self-awareness in general from the study of depersonalization. I will accordingly allow myself to quote them extensively.

4. "I could look down at my hands and see them writing," explains a patient of Shorvon's (1946, p. 42) in a very typical report, "but they don't seem to belong to me."

5. Sollier likewise reports a patient whose "pain sense is singularly dulled" in that "when she is pricked she says the effect upon her is as if it were being done to another person, although her tactile sense is preserved" (Sollier, 1907, p. 3).

6. Depersonalization is also commonly associated with derealization (the impression that the world is unreal) and detemporalization (the impression that time is unreal or lacks some of its central properties), but it can occur without the latter disorders. See Simeon et al. (2008); see Sierra et al. (2005) for a study of 394 patients and 138 patients respectively; and Sierra, Lopera et al. (2002).

7. The distinction between central and modular theories corresponds roughly to Alsmith's (2015) distinction between conservative (local) and liberal views on ownership.

8. Ribot (1883) endorsed such a theory and analyzed the mark of mineness ("*la marque personnelle*") in cenesthetic terms.

9. On some accounts the subjective character rests on a form of higher-order representation of that state (Rosenthal, 2005), or on a same-order representation of that state (Kriegel, 2009); on other accounts it is a feature of the mode rather than of the content of our experiences (Henry, 1990); on yet others it is a primitive and unanalyzable phenomenal feature (see Billon, forthcoming, for an overview of extant theories of the subjective character).

10. The central mineness view also presupposes a rich view of phenomenality, to the effect that our conscious mental states and intentions in action are normally part of experiences, which might not be totally uncontroversial and will be denied by foes of "cognitive phenomenology." I thank José Luis Bermúdez for pressing me on this point.

11. Notice that the cognitive views are different with the central mineness view, but they are consistent with it, as one might argue that whether a state X comes with a mark of mineness depends on a cognitive attitude toward X.

12. More precisely, the unified explanation of a psychological entity consisting in a series of disorders of psychological function F1 . . . Fn should appeal to a single factor F, whose abnormal condition C*, explain the disorders of F1 . . . Fn. Moreover, if the abnormal condition C* of F explains the disorders of F1 . . . Fn, its normal condition C should explain their normal functioning.

13. The term "depersonalization/derealization disorder" is a bit slippery as it now refers to the DSM-V's compartment for nondelusional depersonalization, when it is not caused by drugs and does not occur within the course of another mental disorder.

14. The same year, the same journal published a paper with contradictory results (Sedeño et al., 2014), but the latter only tested *one* depersonalized subject.

15. "The past is only idea," said Bergson (1896), "the present is sensorimotor."

16. Of course it is still possible the depersonalized patients sensorimotor capacities differ from normal subjects in ways that that could not be discovered using Cappon and Banks's (1965) methodology or clinical observation. However these ways will have to be so subtle that it makes it quite dubious that they might explain the impaired sense of bodily ownership rather than be explained by it.

17. It should be emphasized that the fact that the sense of bodily ownership can be impaired without altering motor control does not mean that the sense of bodily ownership or the mark of mineness have no causal influence on action. Depersonalized patients' impaired sense of bodily ownership indeed makes them do all sorts of things, such as reporting feeling some of their bodily parts as alien, seeking medical help, or even trying to self-inflict pains in order to check that they can feel pain normally, and so on. I thank Frédérique de Vignemont for pressing me on that point.

18. It is true that cognitive views also predict that patients should have abnormal cognitive attitudes toward their disowned limbs, such as judgments of disownership, and that this prediction is verified. This prediction, however, is made by virtually all theories of the sense of bodily ownership and it cannot accordingly count as evidence for cognitive views against other views.

19. Some authors, such as Deny, Camus, and Sollier, endorsed a Jamesian view of emotion and identified this affective flattening to a "cenesthetic" distortion.

20. Depersonalized patients also display a reduction (and prolonged latency) of their skin conductance response to unpleasant pictures (Sierra, Senior et al., 2002), and facial expressions of disgust (Sierra et al., 2006), as well as "abnormal decreases in limbic activity to increasingly intense emotional expressions, and increases in dorsal prefrontal cortical activity to emotionally arousing stimuli" (Lemche et al., 2007, p. 473). Here again, I would suggest that these alterations correspond to, or should be explained by an alteration of the sense of mental ownership for emotions and its biological correlates.

21. Hesnard (1909, p. 227) outlines a similar objection against affectivity theories of depersonalization.

22. Similar objections could be addressed to subjective sensorimotor theories, which invoke the experience of agency over and above the objective sensorimotor abilities. Such a theory would be immune to the dissociation challenge, but it would succumb to the grounding challenge. The patients' agency is indeed only altered in virtue of a lack of sense of agency (self-awareness for actions). As the reader would have understood by now, the grounding challenge can similarly target subjective interoceptive theories.

References

Alsmith, A. (2015). Mental activity and the sense of ownership. *Review of Philosophy and Psychology*, *6*(4), 881–896. doi:10.1007/s13164-014-0208-1.

Baker, D., Hunter, E., Lawrence, E., Medford, N., Patel, M., Senior, C., et al. (2003). Depersonalisation disorder: Clinical features of 204 cases. *British Journal of Psychiatry*, *182*(5), 428–433. doi:10.1192/bjp.182.5.428.

Bergson, H. (1896). *Matière et mémoire*. Paris: PUF.

Bermúdez. (2011). Bodily awareness and self-consciousness. In S. Gallagher (Ed.), *Oxford handbook of the self* (pp. 157–179). Oxford: Oxford University Press.

Bermúdez, J. L. (2015). Bodily ownership, bodily awareness and knowledge without observation. *Analysis*, *75*(1), 37–45. doi:10.1093/analys/anu119.

Berrios, G. (1991). Delusions as "wrong beliefs": A conceptual history. *British Journal of Psychiatry. Supplement*, *159*(14), 6–13.

Billon, A. (2015). Why are we certain that we exist? *Philosophy and Phenomenological Research*, *91*(3), 723–759. doi:10.1111/phpr.12113.

Billon, A. (forthcoming). What is it like to lack subjective character? Depersonalization as a probe on the scope, function, and nature of subjective character. In M. Garcia-Carpintero & M. Guillot (Eds.), *The Sense of Mineness*. Oxford: Oxford University Press.

Billon, A. (in press). Basic self-awareness: Lessons from the real world. *European Journal of Philosophy*. doi:10.1111/ejop.12168.

Cappon, D., & Banks, R. (1965). Orientational perception: II. Body perception in depersonalization. *Archives of General Psychiatry*, *13*(4), 375–379. doi:10.1001/archpsyc.1965.01730040085012.

Damasio, A. (1999). *The feeling of what happens: Body and emotion in the making of consciousness*. New York: Harcourt Brace.

Damasio, A. (2003). Feelings of emotion and the self. *Annals of the New York Academy of Sciences*, *1001*(1), 253–261.

de Vignemont, F. (2013). The mark of bodily ownership. *Analysis*, *73*(4), 643–651.

de Vignemont, F. (2016). *A narcissistic conception of the sense of bodily ownership*. Unpublished MS.

Dilthey, W. (2010). The origin of our belief in the reality of the external world and its justification (1890; M. Aue, Trans.). In R. A. Makkreel & F. Rodi (Eds.), *Wilhelm Dilthey: Selected works* (Vol. 2): *Understanding the human world*. Princeton, NJ: Princeton University Press.

Dolan, R. J. (1999). Feeling the neurobiological self [Review of the book *The feeling of what happens: Body and emotion in the making of consciousness*, by A. Damasio]. *Nature*, *401*(6756), 847–848. doi:10.1038/44690.

Dugas, L. (1898). Un cas de d epersonnalisation. *Revue Philosophique de la France et de L'etranger*, *45*, 500–507.

Dugas, L., & Moutier, F. (1911). *La dépersonnalisation*. Paris: Félix Alcan. http://www .biusante.parisdescartes.fr/histmed/medica/cote?79749.

Guralnik, O., Giesbrecht, T., Knutelska, M., Sirroff, B., & Simeon, D. (2007). Cognitive functioning in depersonalization disorder. *Journal of Nervous and Mental Disease*, *195*(12), 983–988. doi:10.1097/NMD.0b013e31815c19cd.

Guralnik, O., Schmeidler, J., & Simeon, D. (2000). Feeling unreal: Cognitive processes in depersonalization. *American Journal of Psychiatry*, *157*(1), 103–109. doi:10.1176/ ajp.157.1.103.

Henry, M. (1990). *Phénoménologie matérielle*. Paris: PUF.

Hesnard, A. (1909). *Les troubles de la personnalité: Dans les états d'asthénie psychique: Étude de psychologie clinique*. Paris: Félix Alcan.

Hunter, E. C., Phillips, M. L., Chalder, T., Sierra, M., & David, A. S. (2003). Depersonalisation disorder: A cognitive-behavioural conceptualisation. *Behaviour Research and Therapy*, *41*(12), 1451–1467. doi:10.1016/S0005-7967(03)00066-4.

Janet, P. (1903). *Les obsessions et la psychasthénie* (Vol. *2*). Paris: Félix Alcan.

Janet, P. (1908). Le sentiment de dèpersonnalisation. *Journal de Psychologie Normale et Pathologique*, *5*, 514–516.

Janet, P. (1928). De l'angoisse à l'extase (Vol. *2*). *Les sentiments fondamentaux*. Paris: Félix Alcan.

Kriegel, U. (2009). *Subjective consciousness: A self-representational theory*. Oxford: Oxford University Press.

Krishaber, M. (1873). *De la névropathie cérébro-cardiaque*. Paris: Masson.

Lemche, E., Surguladze, S. A., Brammer, M. J., Phillips, M. L., Sierra, M., & David, A. S., et al. (2013). Dissociable brain correlates for depression, anxiety, dissociation, and somatization in depersonalization-derealization disorder. *CNS Spectrums*, *21*(1), 35–42. doi:10.1017/S1092852913000588.

Lemche, E., Surguladze, S. A., Giampietro, V. P., Anilkumar, A., Brammer, M. J., Sierra, M., et al. (2007). Limbic and prefrontal responses to facial emotion expressions in depersonalization. *Neuroreport*, *18*(5), 473–477. doi:10.1097/WNR.0b013e328057deb3.

Leroy, E.-B. (1901). Sur l'illusion dite dépersonnalisation. *L'Année Psychologique*, *8*(1), 519–522.

Levine, J. (2001). *Purple haze: The puzzle of consciousness* (Vol. 6). Oxford: Oxford University Press.

Lipps, T. (1902). *Einheiten und relationen: Eine skizze zur psychologie der apperzeption.* Leipzig: Barth.

Martin, M. G. F. (1995). Bodily awareness: A sense of ownership. In J. L. Bermúdez, T. Marcel, & N. Eilan (Eds.), *The body and the self* (pp. 267–289). Cambridge, MA: MIT Press.

Mayer-Gross, W. (1935). On depersonalization. *British Journal of Medical Psychology, 15*(2), 103–126. doi:10.1111/j.2044-8341.1935.tb01140.x.

Michal, M., Reuchlein, B., Adler, J., Reiner, I., Beutel, M. E., & Vögele, C., et al. (2014). Striking discrepancy of anomalous body experiences with normal interoceptive accuracy in depersonalization-derealization disorder. *PLoS One, 9*(2), e89823. doi:10.1371/journal.pone.0089823.

Northoff, G., & Panksepp, J. (2008). The trans-species concept of self and the subcortical—cortical midline system. *Trends in Cognitive Sciences, 12*(7), 259–264. doi:10.1016/j.tics.2008.04.007.

Oesterreich, K. (1908). *Die Entfremdung der Wahrnehmungswelt und die Depersonalisation in der Psychasthenie.* Leipzig: Verlag Barth.

Panksepp, J. (1998). The periconscious substrates of consciousness: Affective states and the evolutionary origins of the self. *Journal of Consciousness Studies, 5*(5–6), 556–582.

Ribot, T. (1883). *Les maladies de la personnalité.* Paris: Félix Alcan.

Rosenthal, D. M. (2005). *Consciousness and mind.* Oxford: Oxford University Press.

Sacco, R. G. (2010). The circumplex structure of depersonalization/derealization. *International Journal of Psychological Studies, 2*(2), 26–40. doi:10.5539/ijps.v2n2p26.

Sacks, O. (1985). *The man who mistook his wife for a hat: And other clinical tales.* New York: Summit Books.

Schilder, P. (1935). *The image and appearance of the human body.* London: Kegan Paul.

Sedeño, L., Couto, B., Melloni, M., Canales-Johnson, A., Yoris, A., Baez, S., et al. (2014). How do you feel when you can't feel your body? interoception, functional connectivity and emotional processing in depersonalization-derealization disorder. *PLoS One, 9*(6), e98769. doi:10.1371/journal.pone.0098769.

Seth, A. K. (2013). Interoceptive inference, emotion, and the embodied self. *Trends in Cognitive Sciences, 17*(11), 565–573. doi:10.1016/j.tics.2013.09.007.

Shorvon, H. J. (1946). The depersonalization syndrome. *Proceedings of the Royal Society of Medicine, 39*(12), 779–791.

Sierra, M. (2009). *Depersonalization: A new look at a neglected syndrome*. Cambridge: Cambridge University Press.

Sierra, M., Baker, D., Medford, N., & David, A. S. (2005). Unpacking the depersonalization syndrome: An exploratory factor analysis on the Cambridge Depersonalization Scale. *Psychological Medicine, 35*(10), 1523–1532.

Sierra, M., & Berrios, G. E. (1998). Depersonalization: Neurobiological perspectives. *Biological Psychiatry, 44*(9), 898–908. doi:10.1016/S0006-3223(98)00015-8.

Sierra, M., & David, A. S. (2011). Depersonalization: A selective impairment of self-awareness. *Consciousness and Cognition, 20*(1), 99–108. doi:10.1016/j.concog .2010.10.018.

Sierra, M., Lopera, F., Lambert, M., Phillips, M., & David, A. (2002). Separating depersonalisation and derealisation: The relevance of the "lesion method." *Journal of Neurology, Neurosurgery, and Psychiatry, 72*(4), 530–532. doi:10.1136/jnnp.72.4.530.

Sierra, M., Senior, C., Dalton, J., McDonough, M., Bond, A., Phillips, M. L., et al. (2002). Autonomic response in depersonalization disorder. *Archives of General Psychiatry, 59*(9), 833–838. doi:10.1001/archpsyc.59.9.833.

Sierra, M., Senior, C., Phillips, M. L., & David, A. S. (2006). Autonomic response in the perception of disgust and happiness in depersonalization disorder. *Psychiatry Research, 145*(2), 225–231. doi:10.1016/j.psychres.2005.05.022.

Simeon, D., & Abugel, J. (2006). *Feeling unreal: Depersonalization disorder and the loss of the self*. Oxford: Oxford University Press.

Simeon, D., Kozin, D. S., Segal, K., Lerch, B., Dujour, R., & Giesbrecht, T. (2008). De-constructing depersonalization: Further evidence for symptom clusters. *Psychiatry Research, 157*(1–3), 303–306. doi:10.1016/j.psychres.2007.07.007.

Sollier, P. (1907). On certain cenesthetic disturbances with particular reference to cerebral cenesthetic disturbances as primary manifestations of a modification of the personality. *Journal of Abnormal Psychology, 2*(1), 1–8. doi:10.1037/h0073962.

Taine, H. (1873). Note sur la formation de l'idée de moi. In H. Taine (Ed.), *L'intelligence* (pp. 465–474). Paris: Hachette.

Tracy, D. de (1800). *Projet d'éléments d'idéologie à l'usage des écoles centrales de la République française*. Paris: Pierre Didot.

10   Agency and Bodily Ownership: The Bodyguard Hypothesis

Frédérique de Vignemont

When I report, "I am raising my arm," there are two occurrences of the first-person pronoun: at the level of the agentive experience (*I* am raising my arm), and at the level of the body part that is moving (*my arm* is raising). The first expresses the sense of agency. The second expresses a sense of bodily ownership. The question that I want to raise here is how one should understand the relationship between these two types of self-awareness. The point is not to reduce the latter to the former: one can be aware of one's body as one's own while one remains still or during passive movements for which one experiences no sense of agency. Still there may be a sense in which bodily control, which is at the core of the sense of agency, contributes to the sense of bodily ownership too. The challenge is to assess in what manner.

According to an agentive conception of the sense of ownership, the body that we experience as our own is the body that we represent as being under our control. In 2007, I defended a version of this conception (de Vignemont, 2007). More specifically, I argued that the body schema, defined as a specific type of body representation that is action-oriented, grounds the sense of bodily ownership, and that its disruption causes disownership syndromes. However, such an agentive conception faces a number of difficulties that cannot be solved without further refinements. After highlighting the complexity of the relationship between bodily control and the sense of bodily ownership, I will argue in favor of a specific type of body schema, whose function is to protect the body. I will then defend what I call the bodyguard hypothesis by showing how the protective body schema can account for the first-personal character of the sense of bodily ownership. I will finally offer some speculation about the functional role of the sense of bodily ownership.

1   An Agentive Mark of the Sense of Bodily Ownership?

> We posit that the potentiality for action of our bodily self is a necessary condi-
> tion to accomplish the sense of body ownership we normally entertain. (Gallese
> & Sinigaglia, 2010, p. 751)

> The body is a unity of actions, and if a part of the body is split off from action, it
> becomes "alien" and not felt as part of the body. (Sacks, 1984, p. 166)

As illustrated by these quotations, many theories appeal to the notion of
action in relation to the sense of ownership, and even more of disownership (Davies, Coltheart, Langdon, & Breen, 2001; Dieguez & Annoni,
2013; Gallese & Sinigaglia, 2010; de Vignemont, 2007; Baier & Karnath,
2008; Aymerich-Franch & Ganesh, 2016). But is our ability to control our
body a necessary condition for the sense of bodily ownership: does one
experience a body part as one's own only if one can control it? And is it a
sufficient condition: does one's ability to control a body part entail that one
experiences it as one's own?

The fact is that disownership syndromes often involve some more or
less extreme motor impairment. This is especially salient in the case of
the neurological condition of somatoparaphrenia. Patients suffering from
somatoparaphrenia deny ownership of their left arm and can even attribute
the so-called "alien" hand to another person. Their sense of disownership
cannot be explained by their numbness: some patients can still feel tactile
and painful sensations to be located in their "alien" hand. Instead it may
be explained by their lack of control: most of them are paralyzed, and those
who are not suffer from the anarchic hand sign (i.e., the limb seems to have
a will of its own). Patients actually frequently complain about the useless-
ness of their "alien" limb: "It is this damned hand. . . . It doesn't want to
do anything, it doesn't help me. It betrays me" (Cogliano, Crisci, Conson,
Grossi, & Trojano, 2012, p. 766). One may then be tempted to account for
their sense of disownership as follows:

> The patient with somatoparaphrenia is no longer able to move her paralysed
> limb, which is at odds with her prior experience of her limb. This generates the
> thought that the limb cannot be hers: it is an alien limb. This initial thought
> is then accepted uncritically as true. (Rahmanovic, Barnier, Cox, Langdon, &
> Coltheart, 2012, p. 39)

The case of deafferented patients, who have lost proprioceptive and tactile
signals from most of their body, is also interesting. At the beginning of their
disease, when they had not learned yet to control their body by exploiting

visual information, they could report feeling alienated from their body. But as soon as they regained control over their body, they regained a sense of bodily ownership (Gallagher & Cole, 1995). Likewise, amputees who have been transplanted another person's hands experience the new hands as their own only when they can control them (after eighteen months), and not earlier when they gain sensations in them (after six months) (Farnè, Roy, Giraux, Dubernard, & Sirigu, 2002):

Journalist: When did you really appropriate these hands?

Denis Chatelier: When the first phalanges started to move, when I was able to eat again with a fork. Then, I said: "Here are my hands." Now I'm completely normal.[1]

Finally, the importance of control is confirmed by illusions of ownership in virtual reality environments: controlling a virtual avatar can make one experience the avatar's body as one's own (e.g., Slater, Perez-Marcos, Ehrsson, & Sanchez-Vives, 2008).

At this point, one might simply object that bodily control cannot be essential to the sense of bodily ownership given the number of individuals who are paralyzed and who still experience their body as their own. Indeed disownership syndromes are very rare, whereas paralysis is not, and most patients that are paralyzed do not experience disownership.[2] Hence, the loss of control cannot be sufficient for the loss of the sense of bodily ownership. This first objection invites us to propose two alternative agentive proposals.

The first proposal appeals to *agentive feelings* to account for the sense of bodily ownership. On this view, the body that I experience as my own is the body that I *feel* that I can control. However, this proposal is both too conservative and too liberal. It is too conservative because it cannot account for cases of individuals who feel they cannot control their limbs and still experience them as their own. I have mentioned patients who are paralyzed, but one could also point to schizophrenic patients with delusions of control and to patients with "pure" anarchic hand: they feel that their limbs do not obey them but they still experience them as their own. On the other hand, this proposal is too liberal because the fact that one feels that one can move a limb does not ensure that one experiences it as one's own. This is clearly demonstrated by patients with somatoparaphrenia, who can be unaware of their paralysis (i.e., anosognosia for hemiplegia): they erroneously feel that they can control their paralyzed "alien" hand and yet they do not experience it as their own.

There is, however, a different version of the agentive conception that does not appeal to agentive feelings, but only to *sensorimotor* body representations: it is both necessary and sufficient for a body part to be incorporated in the body schema for one to experience it as one's own (de Vignemont, 2007). The body schema is a specific kind of representation of the body that is dedicated to action: it carries information about the bodily parameters that are required to plan and to guide bodily movements, such as posture, strength, limb size, and so forth (de Vignemont, 2010). It represents the various parts of the body that are under control, and thus it can misrepresent them. It can thus be dissociated from actual motor capacity. Consequently, the body schema can still include legs that are actually paralyzed. It can also be dissociated from the conscious experience that one has of one's motor abilities. In anosognosia for hemiplegia, for example, the sensorimotor representation of the paralyzed side of the body is disrupted, and yet patients still feel that they can move it. This sensorimotor proposal can thus avoid what appeared as fatal objections to other agentive proposals. As such, it is more promising, but does it really work? I will now focus on two arguments that could be made against it, one based on the rubber hand illusion (RHI), and the other based on tool use. They will show that we need to refine our agentive conception and our definition of the body schema even more.

2   From the Rubber Hand Illusion to Tool Use

If the body schema grounds the sense of bodily ownership, then action planning, which is based on it, should be modified by the incorporation of extraneous body parts and by the exclusion of one's body parts. If the agentive conception is true, one should thus expect specific motor correlates to the sense of ownership and of disownership.

Let us first consider the sense of disownership. According to the agentive conception, it should be accompanied by the inability to correctly control the limb that has been excluded from the body schema. Such a prediction is confirmed by a study using hypnosis. In this study, one group received a suggestion about their loss of bodily control: "Whenever I tap my pen like this *[tap pen three times on table]*, this arm *[touch targeted arm]* will feel paralysed" (Rahmanovic et al., 2012, p. 45). Although some members of this group felt paralyzed and behaved as if they were paralyzed, they did not report disownership experiences. This confirms what we already know from paralyzed patients, who continue to experience their body as their own. What is more interesting is the second type of suggestion that another group of participants received, which was explicitly about disownership: "Whenever I tap my pen like this *[tap pen three times on table]*, this arm *[touch targeted arm]* will feel that it belongs to someone else" (Rahmanovic et al., 2012, p. 45). This suggestion successfully induced disownership. Interestingly, it also induced as much paralysis as the paralysis suggestion. Hence, paralysis not only can cause an experience of disownership (as in somatoparaphrenia), but it also can be its collateral damage.

Let us now consider the motor correlates of the sense of bodily ownership. The agentive conception predicts that action planning, which is based on the body schema, should be modified by the incorporation of extraneous body parts, such as a rubber hand. However, this is not the case. In the classic setup of the rubber hand illusion, one sits with one's arm hidden behind a screen, while fixating on a rubber hand presented in one's bodily alignment; when the rubber hand is stroked in synchrony with one's hand, one reports feeling touch to be located on the rubber hand and feeling the rubber hand as if it were one's hand (Botvinick & Cohen, 1998). The RHI is a purely sensory illusion, at least in its original setting: participants have no control over the rubber hand, nor do they report feeling control over it (Longo et al., 2008). It then comes as no surprise that action planning can be impervious to the embodiment of the rubber hand. In one study, participants were asked to grasp the hand that was touched with their opposite hand, but although they judged the stimulated hand to be at a location close to the location of the rubber hand, their movement itself was not influenced by the illusion (Kammers, de Vignemont, Verhagen, & Dijkerman, 2009): the motor system did not take the location of the rubber hand as a starting parameter when planning reaching and grasping movements.[3] A critic of the agentive conception may then argue that this result suffices to show that the body schema does not ground the sense of bodily ownership. The objection runs as follows: (i) motor immunity to the illusion shows that the rubber hand is left out of the body schema that guides the movements; (ii) yet participants report ownership over it; (iii) thus, it is false that one experiences as one's own only body parts that are represented in the body schema.

Another objection against the agentive conception, which works as a mirror objection to the objection from the RHI, derives from tool use: whereas one feels the rubber hand as part of one's body although it does not seem to be incorporated in the body schema, one does not feel tools as parts of one's body although they seem to be incorporated in the body schema. Tools can indeed be motorically embodied to such an extent that after tool use, one programs one's movements as if one were still holding the tool, even for actions that have never been performed with it. Let me for instance mention the following study by Cardinali and colleagues (2009). Participants first repetitively used a long mechanical grabber to grasp objects. They were then asked to reach and grasp objects with their hand alone, but the kinematics of their movements was significantly modified, as if their arm were longer than before using the grabber. Moreover, this effect of extension was generalized to other movements, such as pointing on top of objects, although they were never performed with the grabber. Finally, after using the grabber, participants localized touches delivered on the middle fingertip and elbow of their tool use arm as if they were farther apart: they perceived their arm as being longer. These results indicate that the body schema was updated during tool use, integrating the grabber. The critical question is why one generally experiences no ownership for tools. As Botvinick notes,

> From this finding, we would predict that tools are represented as belonging to the bodily self. However, although this may be true in some weak sense, the feeling of ownership that we have for our bodies clearly does not extend to, for example, the fork we use at dinner. (2004, p. 783)

The objection runs as follows: (i) tools are included in the body schema that guides reaching and pointing movements; (ii) yet participants report no ownership over them; (iii) thus, it is false that one experiences as one's own any body parts that are represented in the body schema. One might be tempted to reply that the body schema can make us feel an object as part of our body only if the object looks like a body part (De Preester & Tsakiris, 2009). In other words, if tools are not experienced as parts of our body, it is because they do not look bodily. Some studies have indeed shown that one cannot induce the RHI for a wooden object that does not look like a hand, such as a rectangular block (Tsakiris, Carpenter, James, & Fotopoulou, 2010). However, other studies have found the opposite results (Ma & Hommel, 2015). It is difficult to precisely fix at which point an object starts counting as being bodily shaped. Furthermore, even when tools are completely hand shaped, as it is the case for prostheses, amputees have still difficulties appropriating them.

Should one simply give up the agentive conception? I do not think so. We simply need a more refined account of the notion of body schema. More specifically, I will argue that there is an equivocation of the term, which can refer to two distinct types of sensorimotor body representations.

3   The Duality of Body Schema

Let us consider again the RHI. It is true that one can experience a rubber hand as part of one's body while failing to plan one's movements on the basis of its location. However, the movements that are tested with the RHI are only goal-directed instrumental movements such as pointing and grasping, and there is a different range of movements that is worth exploring, namely *defensive movements*. Physiological response to threat has indeed become the main implicit measure of the RHI: it has been repeatedly shown that participants react when the rubber hand is threatened, but only when they report it as their own after synchronous stroking, and the strength of their reaction (i.e., physiological arousal measured by their skin conductance response) is correlated with their ownership rating in questionnaires (e.g., Ehrsson, Wiech, Weiskopf, Dolan, & Passingham, 2007). This protective response, which one normally has for one's own body, can be revealed also at the motor level. In one study, participants were in an immersive virtual reality environment, which induced them to feel ownership over a virtual hand. The virtual hand was then attacked with a knife. Although participants were instructed not to move, their event-related brain potentials revealed that the more they experienced the virtual hand as their own, the more the perception of threat induced a response in the motor cortex (Gonzalez-Franco, Peck, Rodríguez-Fornells, & Slater, 2013). Roughly speaking, when one observes the rubber hand that one experiences as one's own being threatened, one automatically withdraws one's hand. This finding suggests that the RHI has a specific type of agentive mark in the context of self-defense.

Let us now reconsider the objection from tool use. More than a century ago in his satirical novel *Erewhon, or Over the Range*, Samuel Butler created a character who denied any significant difference between tools and limbs: "We do not use our own limbs other than as machines; and a leg is only a much better wooden leg than any one can manufacture" (Butler, 1872, p. 219). Why then, does one experience no sense of ownership toward tools most of the time, even when they look like a body part? It may be because contrary to what Butler's character assumed, we use our own limbs other than as machines. More specifically, we protect them other than as machines: "the target of the actions may be located well within reach, but a tool is chosen as a substitute for the upper limb in order to avoid harm" (Povinelli, Reaux, & Frey, 2010, p 244). This hypothesis has been tested by Povinelli and colleagues (2010) on chimpanzees. Chimpanzees had the choice between using their hand or a tool to open a box. It has been found that they removed the cover of the box with their hand when they perceived that it contained food and with the tool when they perceived the object in the box as potentially dangerous.

More generally, we use tools in harmful situations in which we would not use our limbs and we can easily put them at risk as long as there is no risk for our body. If we protected tools as we protect our limbs we would not be able to use them as extensively as we do and the range of our actions would be far more limited: we could no longer stoke the hot embers of a fire or stir a pot of boiling soup. This claim does not contradict the fact that we protect tools and react if they are threatened or damaged. We actually need to keep them in good shape in order to be able to use them. Nonetheless, their significance is not of the same kind as the significance of our own body and it is likely that their protection is subserved by different mechanisms than bodily protection.

We thus have a double dissociation: the rubber hand is incorporated for planning protective movements but not instrumental ones, whereas tools are incorporated for planning instrumental movements but not protective ones. I propose that there are two kinds of body schema that underlie these distinct types of actions. The *working body schema* consists in a sensorimotor representation of the body used for acting on the world, for grasping, exploring, manipulating, and so forth. Most literature in neuropsychology and in cognitive neuroscience has focused its interest exclusively on this notion, but there is another type of sensorimotor representation of the body that one should not neglect, which is involved in avoiding predators and obstacles, namely, the *protective body schema*. One does not defend one's biological body; one defends the body that one takes oneself to have and the protective body schema, like any representation, can misrepresent one's biological body and include a rubber hand, for instance. Although rarely mentioned in the literature on body representations, this notion of body schema can be found in the literature on pain:

> There's a body schema representation which is primarily concerned with *protective* action: that is, one which maps out parts of our bodies that we should pay special attention to, avoid using, keep from contacting things, and so on. Call this a *defensive representation* of the body: it shows which parts of the body are in need of which sorts of defense. (Klein, 2015a, p. 94)

The notion of a distinctive space to defend can also be found in the literature on *peripersonal space* (i.e., space immediately surrounding the body). It was first described by the Swiss biologist Heini Hediger (1955), the director of the Zurich zoo, who noted that animals do not process space uniformly:

they flee at a specific distance from a predator (i.e., flight distance) and they do not tolerate the proximity even of their conspecifics (i.e., personal distance). Electrophysiological studies on monkeys have confirmed that stimuli close to the body can elicit avoidance responses (Graziano & Gross, 1993). In humans, it was also found that peripersonal space is represented in a specific way compared to far space (Brozzoli, Makin, Cardinali, Holmes, & Farnè, 2012). For example, human participants lean away from a visible object, and, when walking through a doorway they tilt their shoulders to protect their body from hitting the doorframe. Other defensive behaviors require no action at all, such as freezing or playing dead. For example, an intense sound near the hand can cause a defensive-like freeze response (Avenanti, Annela, & Serino, 2012), resembling that observed during the presentation of noxious stimuli or potential threats (Cantello, Civardi, Cavalli, Varrasi, & Vicentini, 2000). Peripersonal space can then be conceived as a spatial margin of safety, which requires appropriate actions if it is invaded. What the protective function of peripersonal space highlights is the fact that the body matters for survival. It has a special significance for the organism's evolutionary needs. Because of this significance, there is a specific representation of the body to fix what is to be protected, namely, the protective body schema, which is the anchor of the peripersonal margin of safety. The function of the protective body schema is thus both to draw the boundary of the territory to defend, and to guide how to best defend it. And what better defense than to directly connect what is to be protected and how to protect it with no intermediary, no additional processing? One can then directly translate what happens to one's body to appropriate actions. Hence, the protective body schema represents both the body to guard and the bodyguard. Let us now see how the sense of bodily ownership arises from such a body schema.

4   The Bodyguard Hypothesis

The spatial content of bodily experiences is structured by representations of the enduring properties of the body, such as its configuration and its metrics. These representations play the role of spatial frames of reference for bodily sensations. What I propose is that one of the reference frames of bodily experiences is given by the protective body schema. For example, if a spider crawls on my hand, I feel its contact as being located at the basis of my thumb within the frame of the body to protect. This in turn can trigger my hand to withdraw.

In virtue of their protective frame of reference, one may then claim that the function of bodily experiences qualify as being *narcissistic*. I am not claiming that they involve a kind of self-love that eventually ends badly. Instead, I use the notion of narcissism partly in the same way as Akins (1996) does in her analysis of the function of sensory systems. On her view, narcissistic perception is not about what is perceived, but about the impact of what is perceived for the subject. It aims at securing what is best for the organism. For instance, she notes that thermal sensations do not covary with external temperature, but rather indicate what is dangerous or safe for the body given its thermal needs. The felt temperature degree is one thing, but its localization is another, and it is there that the protective body schema intervenes. It informs the brain about the potential relevance of the location of the sensation for the organism's needs. Thanks to their protective reference frame, bodily experiences are thus not simply about the body; they are about the body that has an evolutionary significance for the organism. They involve the awareness of the body as having a special import for the self.

The narcissistic quality of bodily experiences is something over and above the sensory phenomenology of bodily experience. It cannot be reduced to the sensory recognition of bodily properties, but involves autonomic responses. It should thus be conceived of in affective terms. To explore this specific affective phenomenology, I will take as a starting point a more "familiar" affective feeling, namely, the feeling of familiarity. When I see my students entering the classroom, my visual experience is about their faces that have a special significance for me. The phenomenology of my experience includes both the visual phenomenology of the shape of their faces and an affective phenomenology of the personal significance of their faces. Likewise, I suggest that the phenomenology of my bodily experiences is dual: it normally includes both the tactile phenomenology of the pressure on my hand and an affective phenomenology of the evolutionary significance of this body part. Hence, it is not only that bodily boundaries can have a specific type of evolutionary significance and that the boundaries that have such significance are represented in the protective body schema. It is also that it *feels* something specific when one is aware of this significance in the same way as it feels something specific when one sees a person that one knows. This affective phenomenology, which arises from the protective frame of reference of bodily experiences, constitutes the sense of bodily ownership.[4]

We can now formulate the following hypothesis:

The bodyguard hypothesis: One experiences as one's own any body parts that are incorporated in the protective body schema.

Given the suite of cognitive capacities that human beings normally have, the protective body map grounds the sense of bodily ownership. The bodyguard hypothesis falls in line with the general agentive conception because it posits a sensorimotor representation at the core of the sense of bodily ownership, but it includes a new dimension, namely, an affective one.

Now the question is whether the bodyguard hypothesis can account for the first-personal character of the sense of bodily ownership in a satisfactory way, that is, for the fact that the phenomenology of bodily ownership normally grounds self-ascriptive judgments (e.g., this is my own body). It might indeed seem that the bodyguard hypothesis faces a version of the classic Euthyphro dilemma. Socrates noted that an action is just because it pleases the gods, but the action pleases the gods because it is just. Similarly, it might seem that I experience my body as my own because of its special value for me but this specific body is valuable for me in virtue of being experienced as my own. Put it another way, if the protective body schema represents one's body qua one's own, then it can account for the first-personal character of the sense of bodily ownership, but it does so "by taking for granted the notion of ownership by a subject, rather than by offering some kind of reductive explanation of the notion" (Peacocke, 2015, p. 174).

Let us first make clear that the bodyguard hypothesis assumes only that the function of the protective body schema is to represent the boundaries of the body that matters for survival; it does not assume that it represents the boundaries of the body that matters for survival qua one's own, even in a nonconceptual way. This distinction is important if one wants to block the risk of circularity denounced by Peacocke. But then one may wonder what is at the origin of the first-personal dimension of the sense of bodily ownership: how am I aware that this hand is *mine*? In order to answer this question, I will go back to Akins's notion of narcissism. Indeed, what better reference than narcissism to eke out self-referentiality? According to Akins, perception is always shaped by the following narcissistic question: "But how does this all relate to ME?" (Akins, 1996, p. 345). On her view, this question does not only affect the content of my experiences, filtering only what is relevant to me. It also marks the structure, or the format, of my experiences, like a signature: "by asking the narcissistic question, the *form* of the answer is compromised: it always has a self-[c]entered glow" (Akins, 1996, p. 345).

This self-centeredness calls to mind perspectival experiences. For instance, when I see the pen on the left, my egocentric experience is centered on me. Egocentric phenomenology can refer to the self more or less implicitly (on the left or on my left), but in any case it can ground self-locating beliefs of the type "the pen is on my left" (see Alsmith, this volume). Likewise, I propose that under normal circumstances bodily experiences present the body in its narcissistic relation to the self: I am aware of the evolutionary significance of this body part *for me*.[5] Most of the time, the reference to the self is only implicit (i.e., the body that matters). This explains why the phenomenology of bodily ownership is generally dim and elusive. Still in some contexts, when there is uncertainty for example, the phenomenology of bodily ownership explicitly refers to the self (i.e., the body that matters *to me*). In any case, it can ground self-ascriptive bodily judgments of the type "this is my body."

One prediction based on this view is that general disruption of self-awareness should lead to disruption of the sense of bodily ownership even if the protective body schema is intact because patients would lose the ability to be aware of the significance of the body *for them*. This prediction seems to be confirmed by depersonalization disorder (see Billon, this volume). Patients with depersonalization feel detached from their bodily sensations and feel as if their body did not belong to them, "I can sit looking at my foot or my hand and not feel like they are mine" (Sierra, 2009, p. 27). For instance, they can feel pain and they have protective behaviors like withdrawing, but they experience pain as if they were not concerned (Janet, 1928). A patient with depersonalization reports: "it is as if I don't care, as if it was somebody else's pain" (Sierra, 2009, p. 49). As Klein notes, the patient is like the man to whom a policeman shouts, "Stop or I'll shoot!" (2015b, p. 510), without recognizing that the command is addressed to him. I thus suggest that patients with depersonalization have at least a partially preserved protective body schema, but they are no longer aware of the significance of their body for themselves because they have a more general deficit of self-awareness. Consequently, they feel as if their body were not their own.

5   The Function of the Sense of Bodily Ownership

The notion of narcissistic quality provides us insight about the first-personal dimension of the sense of bodily ownership. It also sheds light on its functional role. According to Akins, narcissistic perception is in direct relation to action: "No matter what else the senses do, in the end, they must inform movement or action" (Akins, 1996, p. 352). For example, to perceive the temperature of the bath as being burning hot is to inform us that we should remove our hand. If the sense of bodily ownership consists in the narcissistic quality of bodily experiences, as I assume, then its functional role must also be to inform movement and action, and more specifically protective movements and actions.

However, it is important to avoid oversimplification. Here is what the bodyguard hypothesis does *not* claim: The body that one protects is the body that one experiences as one's own. Since one protects many things besides one's body and since one does not always protect one's body, this view is indeed clearly untenable. Like any other behavior, protective behaviors can result from complex decision-making processes, involving a variety of beliefs, desires, emotions, moral considerations, and so forth. As Helm notes about caring:

> This is not to deny that someone who genuinely cares may in some cases be distracted by other things that are more important. . . . What is required, however, is a consistent pattern of attending to the relevant object: in short, a kind of *vigilance* for what happens or might well happen to it. (Helm, 2008, p. 22)

There are thus many situations in which we do not protect our body and yet still feel it as our own. It can simply be because we are paralyzed. Or it can be for selfish reasons, such as pleasure in extreme sports. It can also be for altruistic reasons, such as the desire to save the nation at war. However, even if the soldier is ready to sacrifice himself, it is highly likely that he pays extreme attention to the immediate environment and that he is ready to react in case of threat. Otherwise, he would be a bad soldier, of little use for the nation.

But how should one interpret the case of individuals who consistently fail to protect their body? If their protective body schema is impaired, the bodyguard hypothesis must predict that such individuals should experience no sense of bodily ownership. And indeed this seems to be the case, at least in somatoparaphrenia. Many patients with somatoparaphrenia often try to get rid of their "alien" limb and they display misoplegia (i.e., dislike of one's body) and self-inflicted injuries. One patient, for example, claimed: "Yes, please take it away . . . I don't care about its destiny as it is not mine" (Gandola et al., 2012, p. 1176). Another patient said: "I got to get rid of them. . . . Put them in a garbage" (Feinberg, 2009, p. 15). Finally, when their "alien" hand is threatened, they do not react, as shown by the following study. Somatoparaphrenic patients saw either a cotton swab or a needle approaching either their right hand, which they felt as their own, or their left hand, which they felt as "alien" (Romano, Gandola, Bottini, & Maravita, 2014). The experimenter then analyzed their physiological level of arousal measured by their skin conductance response (SCR). We know that seeing our body threatened normally induces an increase of our SCR and indeed when the needle approached the right hand, the SCR increased, as expected. But when the needle approached the left "alien" hand, there was no modification of the SCR.

These findings are in line with the bodyguard hypothesis: the lack of bodily ownership correlates with the lack of bodily protection. However, this correlation does not always seem to hold. For instance, patients with amygdala lesion do not experience fear: S. M., the most studied of these patients, was threatened several times in her life, including by a man who wanted to stab her, but she did not react (Tranel & Damasio, 1989). Similar lack of protective behavior can be found in patients with pain asymbolia: asymbolic patients seem to be in pain insofar as they are able to judge the location and the intensity of painful stimuli, but they do not try to avoid them and do not realize when something is threatening them (Grahek, 2001). What is interesting with these two types of patients is that they seem to show no bodily protection, and yet, as far as I know, they report no sense of disownership. Do they invalidate the bodyguard hypothesis? As said earlier, there are many reasons one may have for not protecting one's body besides impaired protective body schema, and one of them is faulty evaluation of danger. What is interesting is that the patients' affective attitude toward danger is not simply neutral. Actually, it has been found that S. M. shows increased arousal under threat (Tranel & Damasio, 1989). This might indicate that at some basic level, she still cares about her body or more simply, that she is interested by what is happening. But in both interpretations, she is not indifferent. And she does not merely fail to run away from danger, she is actually eager to face it: once when she saw a snake, she did not only fail to run away, she actually grasped it. Likewise, patients with pain asymbolia expose themselves to danger almost with a smile: "On occasion, the patient willingly offered his hands for pain testing and laughed during stimulation" (Berthier, Starkstein, & Leiguarda, 1988, p. 42). The fact that they seem to enjoy painful stimulations to some extent or look for danger indicates that they are *misevaluating* what is going on.

All together, these findings are consistent with the bodyguard hypothesis. They further highlight the motivational role of the protective body schema. But the crucial question is whether the sense of bodily ownership itself plays a motivational role. Arguably, an organism that has a protective body schema but that is not aware of the evolutionary significance of its body will well survive. If so, the sense of bodily ownership is merely epiphenomenal, and only its ground—namely the protective body schema—contributes to bodily protection.

However, I want to propose that there might be a specific role that the sense of bodily ownership can play in humans. This is the role of practical authority. In order to defend this view, I base my discussion on Klein's (2015a) imperativist theory of pain. Klein aims to explain how pains motivate us to act and how they justify our actions. On his view, pains are intentional states whose content is imperative: they consist in bodily commands. As he notes, however, we humans do not accept and obey all commands. We do so only when we accept the source of the command as having the right authority: acknowledging the practical authority of the source suffices to motivate and to give us reason to act. Klein then argues that in the case of pain the body constitutes our practical authority. By recognizing the authority of the body, we are bound to at least consider the actions that will keep us alive:

> We accept our bodies, I suggest, as minimal practical authorities. Our body commands us to protect a certain part. Because we accept our body as a practical authority, that command gives us reason to act—regardless of what else we'd want to do and regardless of what else we know. (Klein, 2015a, p. 80)

What is interesting for the prospect of our discussion of the sense of bodily ownership is the reason for which we accept our bodies as authorities. According to Klein, this is not simply a brute biological fact; we accept it because we have a long-standing attitude of caring about our bodies:

> Of course, we accept our bodies as authorities for good reason. Our body is important to us. We care about it. We are in bad shape if it doesn't work. We cease to exist when it does. If we regarded the body as something less than a minimal practical authority, then we would still have reasons to act in ways that promoted bodily integrity. But we would also be free to accept or ignore those reasons as we please. If we did that, then we'd probably screw it up. (Klein, 2015a, p. 81)

The notion of bodily care, however, raises a number of difficulties (de Vignemont, 2015). I suggest replacing it by the notion of narcissistic significance: we accept this specific body as a practical authority because we are aware of its special significance for us. Roughly speaking, it is because I experience the body that commands me as my own that I obey it. The function of the sense of bodily ownership is thus to provide me reason to accept this specific body as a practical authority.

Conclusion

The bodyguard hypothesis solves the difficulties that a more general agentive conception faces, while doing justice to the intuition that the sense of bodily ownership is intimately related to action. We can now reply to the following questions:

• *What grounds the sense of bodily ownership?* The sense of bodily ownership is grounded in the spatial frame of reference of bodily experience that is provided by a specific type of body schema, namely, the protective body schema.
• *What does it mean to feel one's body as one's own?* Feeling one's body as one's own is to experience a specific type of affective phenomenology that can be described in narcissistic terms. It expresses the awareness of the significance of the body for the subject.
• *What is the function of the sense of bodily ownership?* The sense of bodily ownership plays a motivational role for self-protection. More specifically, it provides us a reason to accept our body as a minimal practical authority to which we should obey.

Notes

1. "L'important: jouer avec mes enfants," *Le Matin*, August 26, 2008, my translation.

2. Burin and colleagues (2015) found that paralyzed patients had a stronger RHI when their affected hand was stroked than healthy participants. They concluded that the patients had a diminished sense of ownership for their paralyzed hand. These results, however, are difficult to interpret because the same patients had no RHI whatsoever when their nonaffected hand was stroked. This can hardly be explained by a diminished sense of ownership of the paralyzed hand. Hence, there might be a more general disruption, which was responsible both for the stronger RHI on the affected side, and the lack of RHI on the nonaffected side.

3. Still it is worth noting that in other situations the way that one moves one's hand is affected by the posture of the rubber hand when one experiences it as one's own (e.g., Kammers, Kootker, Hogendoorn, & Dijkerman, 2010).

4. More on the phenomenology of bodily ownership in de Vignemont (forthcoming).

5. There is a difference between egocentric experiences and narcissistic feelings: in egocentric experiences the notion of selfhood is minimal and involves only a mere point in time and space, while it seems that narcissistic significance involves an enduring self (survival matters only if one lasts over time).

References

Akins, K. (1996). Of sensory systems and the "aboutness" of mental states. *Journal of Philosophy, 93*(7), 337–372. doi:10.2307/2941125.

Avenanti, A., Annela, L., & Serino, A. (2012). Suppression of premotor cortex disrupts motor coding of peripersonal space. *NeuroImage, 63*(1), 281–288. doi:10.1016/j.neuroimage.2012.06.063.

Aymerich-Franch, L., & Ganesh, G. (2016). The role of *functionality* in the body model for self-attribution. *Neuroscience Research, 104*, 31–37. doi:10.1016/j.neures.2015.11.001.

Baier, B., & Karnath, H. O. (2008). Tight link between our sense of limb ownership and self-awareness of actions. *Stroke, 39*(2), 486–488. doi:10.1161/STROKEAHA.107.495606.

Berthier, M., Starkstein, S., & Leiguarda, R. (1988). Asymbolia for pain: A sensory-limbic disconnection syndrome. *Annals of Neurology, 24*(1), 41–49. doi:10.1002/ana.410240109.

Botvinick, M. (2004). Probing the neural basis of body ownership. *Science, 305*(5685), 782–783. doi:10.1126/science.1101836.

Botvinick, M., & Cohen, J. (1998). Rubber hands "feel" touch that eyes see. *Nature, 391*(6669), 756. doi:10.1038/35784.

Brozzoli, C., Makin, T. R., Cardinali, L., Holmes, N. P., & Farnè, A. (2012). Peripersonal space: A multisensory interface for body–object interactions. In M. M. Murray & M. T. Wallace (Eds.), *The neural bases of multisensory processes*. Boca Raton, FL: CRC Press.

Burin, D., Livelli, A., Garbarini, F., Fossataro, C., Folegatti, A., Gindri, P., et al. (2015). Are movements necessary for the sense of body ownership? Evidence from the rubber hand illusion in pure hemiplegic patients. *PLoS One, 10*(3), e0117155. doi:10.1371/journal.pone.0117155.

Butler, S. (1872). *Erewhon, or Over the range* (2nd ed.). London: Trübner.

Cantello, R., Civardi, C., Cavalli, A., Varrasi, C., & Vicentini, R. (2000). Effects of a photic input on the human cortico-motoneuron connection. *Clinical Neurophysiology, 111*(11), 1981–1989. doi:10.1016/S1388-2457(00)00431-4.

Cardinali, L., Frassinetti, F., Brozzoli, C., Urquizar, C., Roy, A. C., & Farnè, A. (2009). Tool-use induces morphological updating of the body schema. *Current Biology, 19*(12), R478–R479. doi:10.1016/j.cub.2009.05.009.

Cogliano, R., Crisci, C., Conson, M., Grossi, D., & Trojano, L. (2012). Chronic somatoparaphrenia: A follow-up study on two clinical cases. *Cortex, 48*(6), 758–767. doi:10.1016/j.cortex.2011.08.008.

Davies, M., Coltheart, M., Langdon, R., & Breen, N. (2001). Monothematic delusions: Towards a two-factor account. *Philosophy, Psychiatry, & Psychology, 8*(2), 133–158. doi:10.1353/ppp.2001.0007.

Dieguez, S., & Annoni, J.-M. (2013). Asomatognosia: Disorders of the bodily self. In O. Godefroy (Ed.), *The behavioral and cognitive neurology of stroke* (2nd ed., pp. 170–192). New York: Cambridge University Press.

de Preester, H., & Tsakiris, M. (2009). Body-extension versus body incorporation: Is there a need for a body-model? *Phenomenology and the Cognitive Sciences, 8*(3), 307–319. doi:10.1007/s11097-009-9121-y.

de Vignemont, F. (2007). Habeas Corpus: The sense of ownership of one's own body. *Mind & Language, 22*(4), 447–449.

de Vignemont, F. (2010). Body schema and body image: Pros and cons. *Neuropsychologia, 48*(3), 669–680.

de Vignemont, F. (2015). Pain and bodily care: Whose body matters? *Australasian Journal of Philosophy, 93*(3), 542–560.

de Vignemont, F. (forthcoming). *Mind the body.* Oxford: Oxford University Press.

Ehrsson, H. H., Wiech, K., Weiskopf, N., Dolan, R. J., & Passingham, R. E. (2007). Threatening a rubber hand that you feel is yours elicits a cortical anxiety response. *Proceedings of the National Academy of Sciences of the United States of America, 104*(23), 9828–9833. doi:10.1073/pnas.0610011104.

Farnè, A., Roy, A. C., Giraux, P., Dubernard, J. M., & Sirigu, A. (2002). Face or hand, not both: Perceptual correlates of reafferentation in a former amputee. *Current Biology, 12*(15), 1342–1346. doi:10.1016/S0960-9822(02)01018-7.

Feinberg, T. E. (2009). *From axons to identity: Neurological explorations of the nature of the self.* New York: Norton.

Gallagher, S., & Cole, J. (1995). Body schema and body image in a deafferented subject. *Journal of Mind and Behavior, 16*(4), 369–390.

Gallese, V., & Sinigaglia, C. (2010). The bodily self as power for action. *Neuropsychologia, 48*(3), 746–755. doi:10.1016/j.neuropsychologia.2009.09.038.

Gandola, M., Invernizzi, P., Sedda, A., Ferrè, E. R., Sterzi, R., & Sberna, M., . . . Bottini, G. (2012). An anatomical account of somatoparaphrenia. *Cortex, 48*(9), 1165–1178. doi:10.1016/j.cortex.2011.06.012.

González-Franco, M., Peck, T. C., Rodríguez-Fornells, A., & Slater, M. (2013). A threat to a virtual hand elicits motor cortex activation. *Experimental Brain Research, 232*(3), 875–887. doi:10.1007/s00221-013-3800-1.

Grahek, N. (2001). *Feeling pain and being in pain* (2nd ed.). Cambridge, MA: MIT Press.

Graziano, M. S. A., & Gross, C. G. (1993). A bimodal map of space: Somatosensory receptive fields in the macaque putamen with corresponding visual receptive fields. *Experimental Brain Research, 97*(1), 96–109. doi:10.1007/BF00228820.

Hediger, H. (1955). *Psychologie des animaux au zoo et au cirque*. Paris: René Julliard.

Helm, B. W. (2002). Felt evaluations: A theory of pleasure and pain. *American Philosophical Quarterly*, *39*(1), 13–30.

Helm, B. W. (2008). Plural agents. *Noûs*, *42*(1), 17–49.

Janet, P. (1928). De l'angoisse à l'extase (Vol. 2). *Les sentiments fondamentaux*. Paris: Alcan.

Kammers, M. P., de Vignemont, F., Verhagen, L., & Dijkerman, H. C. (2009). The rubber hand illusion in action. *Neuropsychologia*, *47*(1), 204–211. doi:10.1016/j.neuropsychologia.2008.07.028.

Kammers, M. P., Kootker, J. A., Hogendoorn, H., & Dijkerman, H. C. (2010). How many motoric body representations can we grasp? *Experimental Brain Research*, *202*(1), 203–212. doi:10.1007/s00221-009-2124-7.

Klein, C. (2015a). *When the body commands*. Cambridge, MA: MIT Press.

Klein, C. (2015b). What pain asymbolia really shows. *Mind*, *124*(494), 493–516. doi:10.1093/mind/fzu185.

Longo, M. R., Schüür, F., Kammers, M. P., Tsakiris, M., & Haggard, P. (2008). What is embodiment? A psychometric approach. *Cognition*, *107*, 978–998.

Peacocke, C. (2015). Perception and the first person. In M. Matthen (Ed.), *The Oxford handbook of philosophy of perception* (pp. 168–180). Oxford: Oxford University Press; 10.1093/oxfordhb/9780199600472.013.022.

Povinelli, D. J., Reaux, J. E., & Frey, S. H. (2010). Chimpanzees' context-dependent tool use provides evidence for separable representations of hand and tool even during active use within peripersonal space. *Neuropsychologia*, *48*(1), 243–247. doi:10.1016/j.neuropsychologia.2009.09.010.

Rahmanovic, A., Barnier, A. J., Cox, R. E., Langdon, R. A., & Coltheart, M. (2012). "That's not my arm": A hypnotic analogue of somatoparaphrenia. *Cognitive Neuropsychiatry*, *17*(1), 36–63. doi:10.1080/13546805.2011.564925.

Romano, D., Gandola, M., Bottini, G., & Maravita, A. (2014). Arousal responses to noxious stimuli in somatoparaphrenia and anosognosia: Clues to body awareness. *Brain*, *137*(4), 1213–1223. doi:10.1093/brain/awu009.

Sacks, O. (1984). *A leg to stand on*. London: Picador.

Sierra, M. (2009). *Depersonalization: A new look at a neglected syndrome*. Cambridge: Cambridge University Press.

Slater, M., Perez-Marcos, D., Ehrsson, H. H., & Sanchez-Vives, M. V. (2008). Towards a digital body: The virtual arm illusion. *Frontiers in Human Neuroscience*, *2*(6). doi:10.3389/neuro.09.006.2008.

Tranel, D., & Damasio, H. (1989). Intact electrodermal skin conductance responses after bilateral amygdala damage. *Neuropsychologia, 27*(4), 381–390. doi:10.1016/0028-3932(89)90046-8.

Tsakiris, M., Carpenter, L., James, D., & Fotopoulou, A. (2010). Hands only illusion: Multisensory integration elicits sense of ownership for body parts but not for non-corporeal objects. *Experimental Brain Research, 204*(3), 343–352. doi:10.1007/s00221-009-2039-3.

III   The Self Represented

11 Sight and the Body

Louise Richardson

I

The five familiar senses are capacities for *exteroceptive* perceptual awareness. That is, they are capacities for the perception of things external to our bodies. We can of course see—for instance—our own bodies, but when we do our visual experience is not special: when seen, the body is for us an object like any other.

Bodily awareness is a capacity[1] for *nonexteroceptive* perceptual awareness: a capacity for the perception of one's body. And when one is aware of one's body in the bodily mode one's experience *is* special. We are each aware of our own body in a way in which we are aware of nothing else: from the inside. "From the inside" might be used to capture more than one distinctive feature of bodily awareness. Here, I will use it to pick out bodily awareness's spatial character, which is quite different to that of exteroceptive perceptual experience. When I see, hear, touch, taste, or smell some object it seems to me as if the location of the object is distinct from the location from which it is perceived.[2] For example, when I look at my pencil it seems to be *there*, where *there* is a place distinct from the place—*here*—from which I am aware of it. This here–there distinction constitutes sight's perspectival spatial character, and that of other forms of exteroceptive perceptual awareness. Bodily awareness lacks the perspectival spatial character of exteroceptive awareness. When I have a headache, the pain seems to be in my head, but there is no distinct location or place from which I am aware of the pain.

My concern in this chapter is with whether, in order to accommodate the perspectival character of exteroceptive awareness—and in particular, that of visual awareness—we should accept the following:

Visual bodily awareness claim (VBA): when absent from the visual field, one's body is visually perceptually represented from the inside in normal visual experience.

Visual perceptual representation of the body would be from the inside if, like bodily awareness, it lacked sight's perspectival character. That would be the case if, for instance, in seeing my pencil *there* I were also visually aware of my body *here*, and there was no further location or place from which I am visually aware of my body. I say more about what is meant by "visually perceptually represented" later.

At first glance, VBA might look too implausible to consider. It might seem a condition on perceptual representation of an object being visual that the object is in the visual field. However, there are prima facie reasons to take VBA seriously. First, sight's perspectival spatial character, as we said above, consists in there being a here–there distinction present in visual perceptual experience. This distinction is clearly visual: it would falsify the phenomenology to explain it wholly in terms of, say, proprioceptive experience. Second, one typically knows that the location from which one sees—*here*—is occupied, and that it is occupied by one's body. It does not seem unreasonable to say that this is something one knows "by looking" even when one's body is outside the visual field.[3]

Hence, there are reasons to accept:

Bodily spatial relations claim (BSR): seen things are in normal visual experience visually perceptually represented as spatially related to one's body, which is visually perceptually represented from the inside.

If BSR is true then so is VBA. Or at least, BSR entails VBA if we assume that one's body can be wholly out of view, in normal visual experience, and that when it is, sight does not lose its normal perspectival character. Not everyone is willing to make this assumption. For example, José Bermúdez (2000, chap. 5)—after Gibson—suggests that the body is nearly always in the visual field. It is also his view that on those rare occasions when the body is out of view, such as when looking through binoculars, the perspectival character of visual experience changes.[4] Agreeing with this claim about seeing through binoculars would be one way of arguing that one does not need to accept VBA in order to accommodate sight's perspectival character. However, it is just as difficult to know whether we should accept that the perspectival character of visual experience changes when looking through binoculars as it is to know whether VBA is true. So it is worth considering whether one can argue for the same conclusion (i.e., that one does not need to accept VBA in order to accommodate sight's perspectival character) in a different way. That's what I try to do in this chapter.

In the next section I will provide some reasons for thinking that we should care whether BSR and thus—given the above assumption—VBA is true. In sections III and IV I will discuss how these claims might be defended and then, in section V, I will suggest that one particularly promising-looking defensive strategy fails and in sections VI and VII I draw conclusions.

First though, three notes that should make what follows clearer:

(1) My concern in this chapter is with the content of visual perceptual experience, considered as a personal-level mental item. It is thus of a piece with other attempts to address questions about the admissible contents of perceptual experience. When, for instance, Clare Batty (2009, p. 323) considers whether ordinary objects or merely their odors are olfactorily perceived, she is asking about the representational content of olfactory experience: a personal-level state of the subject. Similarly, when Susanna Siegel (2006) asks whether the property of being a pine tree figures in the content of visual experience she, again, is concerned with the representational contents of personal-level perceptual experiences. These are not questions about what is represented in the subpersonal states of the perceptual system that enable perceptual experience, though, of course, considerations about what is represented subpersonally may be called upon in arguing for claims about personal-level content. Likewise, BSR and VBA are not claims about what is represented subpersonally. It may be that information about the body, or receptors or mechanisms dedicated to the harvesting of such information, play a role, perhaps an essential role, in enabling visual perception. If this is the case, it does not speak *directly* to the truth of BSR and VBA.

(2) I use "representation" throughout what follows but do not intend to commit to a representational or intentional theory of perception. One could perhaps rephrase what follows without using this term but I've found that difficult, which may be revealing.[5]

(3) By "visual perceptual representation" in BSR and VBA I mean a kind of perceptual contact with the body that is nonepistemic in the same sense as Dretske's nonepistemic seeing (1969, chap. 2). Visual perceptual representation of the body referred to in BSR and VBA does not require the having of a belief or other cognitive attitude with the body in its content. BSR and VBA are not made true by it being the case that one epistemically sees, or "sees that" the pencil is in front of and at a short distance from one's body, as one undoubtedly does.

II

It is always reasonable to ask why we should be interested in some philosophical claim about which we are asked to think, although where the claim is the subject of ongoing philosophical debate one may sometimes refrain from answering. It is particularly pressing that we consider the value of philosophical attention to BSR and VBA then, since they do not seem to have been much considered. The lack of attention to BSR and VBA might be thought to suggest that they are either extremely implausible (notwithstanding the straightforward reasons to accept them mentioned in the previous section) or of little interest.

Despite there being little philosophical debate about them there are at least two reasons to be interested in BSR and VBA. The first is that considering them does contribute to ongoing philosophical discussion even if they are not themselves much or at all discussed. Some philosophers have endorsed a claim related to VBA that we might call the "visual self-awareness claim" or VSA. According to VSA the *self* figures in visual perceptual content despite being outside the visual field. For some of these philosophers it is important that we add that that the self in question is the *bodily* self.[6] One thing that is puzzling about VBA is something it shares with VSA. Namely, in order to endorse VBA or VSA one must accept that something— the body, the self, perhaps the bodily self—can be visually perceptually represented despite being outside the visual field. This claim about the literal extent of our visual representational capacities is far from obviously true: we should think carefully about whether to accept it and considering BSR and VBA allows us to do so, undistracted.

This is because VSA involves an additional and understandably distracting source of puzzlement that VBA does not involve. Namely, in order to endorse VSA one must accept that the self can figure in the content of visual experience. This "self-regarding" aspect of VSA has understandably taken center stage in its consideration. After all, this aspect of VSA has been, for some, the source of its interest: if the self can figure in the content of perceptual experience then, or so it might seem, there will be a primitive form of self-consciousness that might help us to understand its less primitive forms. So, where philosophers are concerned with VSA, the natural focus of enquiry would be on identifying criteria for self-awareness and considering whether sight can meet them. Focusing on VBA instead (in our case, via BSR) allows us to set aside such issues and think instead about the puzzling idea of visual perceptual representation short of being seen. In what follows, I will mean by "visual perceptual representation short of being seen" just that kind of visual perceptual contact with things one can have, if BSR and VBA are true, with things outside of the visual field. Of course, "visual perceptual representation short of being seen" could also be used to describe other things, such as hallucination, but I am not using the expression in that way here.

A second reason to be interested in the truth of BSR and VBA is that there is a theoretical purpose that they might serve: namely, they bring along with them a way of spelling out of what it is to be "implicit in experience." The need for such spelling-out can be seen if we consider a view that is inconsistent with BSR. John Campbell has argued that in order to specify the spatial content of perceptual experience we need only monadic and not relational spatial notions. Relational spatial notions are two-place, such as those used when we say "the pen is to the left of the apple" or "the table is below the cup." Monadic spatial notions are one-place, such as those used when we say "the pen is to the left" or "the table is below" (Campbell, 2002, p. 184). One of Campbell's reasons for thinking that we only need monadic spatial notions to specify spatial content is that, as he puts it, a creature's vision does not "make explicit the spatial relations things bear to it; it is not always itself an object in its own visual field" (Campbell, 2002, p. 184). I assume that the latter clause in this quotation is intended as a spelling out of the former: in that a creature is not always an object in its own visual field, visual experience does not make explicit the spatial relations that things bear to it. Similarly, Martin suggests, citing Campbell, that the place from which one sees or that which occupies this place is not "explicitly marked as an element of the presentation" (Martin, 2002, p. 409).

To say that some item x is not "explicitly marked" or that relations to it are not "made explicit" suggests what? It suggests most obviously that x is in some sense *implicit* in experience. Otherwise, why not say simply that x does not figure in experience? Why bother with the denial of explicitness? We may reasonably interpret Campbell then as saying that seen things *are* visually represented as spatially related to something, but that thing is *only implicit* in experience. And as we have seen, it seems as if part of what drives Campbell to say that this thing is merely implicit in experience is that it is not always in the visual field. Plausible though this claim may be, "implicit in experience" is left mysterious on Campbell's view. This is where BSR and VBA come in, potentially. BSR and VBA give us a way of spelling out "implicit in experience" because, as we have seen, they bring along with them the idea of visual perceptual representation short of being seen. This kind of visual perceptual contact with things outside the visual field, overlooked by Campbell, might allow us to understand "implicit in experience." This gives us reason to think about whether BSR and VBA are true, as I do here.

This way of motivating considering BSR and VBA will succeed only if there is any sense to be made of this idea of visual perceptual representation short of being seen. Suppose we identify a set of individually necessary, jointly sufficient conditions for seeing an object o. The most obvious way to make sense of the idea of something being visually perceptually represented but not seen is as meeting all of these bar one, namely, being in the visual field. Take the following individually necessary, jointly sufficient conditions:

(1) o causes an experience;
(2) the temporal properties of the experience are determined by those of the things perceived;
(3) o makes the right kind of difference to the phenomenal character of the experience;
(4) o makes the right kind of difference to the visual phenomenal character of the experience; and
(5) o is in the visual field.

I am not in the business of defending these conditions here: we just need a reasonably plausible account to work with. Condition 1 should be uncontroversial, so long as we are sufficiently ecumenical about "causes an experience." Conditions 2 and 3 say more about the kind of difference an object must make to a perceptual representation in order for that representation to count as *perceptual*. Condition 2 is required to differentiate perceptual representation from experiential memory. As Matthew Soteriou puts it:

> Any successful perception of the world depends upon the occurrence of perceptual experiences whose inception and duration are causally determined by the temporal locations of events involving the items perceived. (2011, p. 199)

We need condition 3 to differentiate things that are perceptually represented from things that, as we might put it, *merely* play a causal role in experience, while meeting conditions 1 and 2. For example, if a puppeteer manipulates an object in your environment, such as a marionette on the stage of a puppet theater, then the puppeteer might meet conditions 1 and 2. Yet it seems wrong to say that the puppeteer figures in the content of your perceptual experience. The expression "the right kind of difference" will be left unanalyzed, here. Suffice it to say the puppeteer does not make the right kind of difference.

Condition 4 can be added if we are to have in play a notion of *visual* perceptual representation short of being seen. It is not, of course, uncontroversial that visual phenomenal character is that which makes a representation of *o* visual. However, condition 4 is the right condition for our purposes. This is because on other standard criteria for individuating vision and the other senses, the representation of the body mentioned in BSR and VBA could not be visual. This representation is not of color, so would not be visual by a "properties" criterion. It is not produced by light, so would not be visual by a "proximal stimulus" criterion. It is not produced via accredited visual channels: one does not visually perceptually represent one's body from the inside via light from one's body reaching one's retina. This is an obstacle to counting the representation as visual by a "sense organ" criterion.[7] Condition 4 is chosen to give VBA and BSR a chance of being true. I won't say anything here about what makes phenomenal character visual nor about what making the right kind of difference to visual phenomenal character might be. It seems right to say that not everything that makes a difference to visual phenomenal character is visually represented, but the fact that it is hard to know what more to say poses no problem unique to the project undertaken here.

We can say then that there is visual perceptual representation short of being seen where conditions 1 to 4 are met while 5 is not. Further reason to think that we can make sense of this idea comes from the fact that, as Schwenkler suggests, we might already have to accept it in order to accommodate a range of "'amodal perception' phenomena that are quite common characteristics of visual experience" (Schwenkler, 2014, p. 151). When, for example, visual perceptual experience represents occluded parts of objects and parts of objects that fall outside of the visual field, conditions 1 to 4 might be met while 5 is not. We can then make sense of the idea of visual perceptual representation short of being seen that BSR and VBA require.

Let's sum up where we've got to so far. We are concerned with whether the body always figures in visual experience (VBA) because things always visually seem to be spatially related to the body (BSR) even when the body is wholly outside the visual field. In this section, I have argued that this is a question worth answering, because (a) asking it brings to the fore the idea of being visually perceptually represented without being seen, an idea that is required by holders of other views that are the subject of ongoing philosophical debate, and (b) because this phenomena—of visual perceptual representation short of being seen—might provide a promising way of spelling out the idea of things that are "implicit in experience," an idea that, I have suggested, needs spelling out.

In the next two sections I consider how the truth of BSR and thus VBA might be defended.

III

As I said in section 1, my question is about the admissible contents of perceptual experience. Philosophers have used many different methods to answer questions like this. For example, they have considered the nature of perceptual processing and argued that the best or only way to make sense of this processing is as functioning to enable the perception of some property F or object o (Nudds, 2009). They have considered subjects with certain deficits (such as associative agnosia) and argued that to explain the difference between those subjects and those who do not have those deficits, we need to accept that the experiences the latter group of subjects represent o's or F's (Bayne, 2009). Another approach involves arguing from the phenomenal character of experience. In some cases, the appeal to phenomenal character is direct: one might argue, for example, that we are directly aware of material objects rather than sense-data because when you reflect on your visual experience, all you find are those material objects: you do not find the sense-data and this gives us a (defeasible) reason to think they are not among the objects of awareness (Martin 2002, p. 381).

A direct appeal to phenomenal character looks hopeless here. There is an incontrovertible item of relevant visual phenomenology in the offing: the here–there distinction constitutive of sight's perspectival spatial character. But merely attending to this item of phenomenology does not tell me whether it constitutes visual perceptual representation of my body from the inside. There are, however, less direct ways to use the phenomenal character of experience to answer questions about its content.

One approach is the method of phenomenal contrast (Siegel, 2006). I will consider John Schwenkler's attempt to use this method to defend VSA in the next section. A different approach depends on accepting a not uncontroversial thesis about the nature of sensory imagination. According to this Dependency Thesis, to sensorially imagine an o (for example, to visualize it) is to imagine perceiving an o: in the case of visualization, it is to imagine seeing it. If the Dependency Thesis is true then as Joel Smith puts it, "the content of sensory imagination mirrors the content of experience" (Smith 2006, p. 57), and we can use sensory imagination's mirroring qualities to test claims about the content of perception. Smith uses this method to test the claim that the self is represented in the content of bodily experience (VSA). If the self were represented in the content of bodily experience and the Dependency Thesis were true then when I imagine having a headache, I should, thereby, imagine myself having the headache. Smith argues that this is not what we find and thus that bodily awareness is not awareness of the self.

We might hope to use the same method to test BSR/VBA. Visualize an apple. If the Dependency Thesis is true, you should be imagining seeing an apple. Try to make this a visual experience you might have with your body wholly out of view: suppose the apple is on a high shelf that you are looking up at. If BSR and VBA are true you should be imagining an experience in which your body is visually perceptually represented. Are you? In my own case, I don't know how to answer: we don't seem to have got any further than we do by merely reflecting directly on phenomenal character. Perhaps looking more at the details of Smith's argument will help move us on. Smith's imaginative task is to imagine being Napoleon in pain. He concludes:

> When I imagine being Napoleon having a pain, the very same piece of sensory imagination would serve equally well to imagine being Goldilocks having a pain. The difference between the two is a difference in what is suppositionally imagined, i.e. whose experience it is. (Smith, 2006, p. 57)

This suggests that what we need to determine is whether the same piece of visual sensory imagination would serve equally well in a case of imagining oneself looking at something and a case of imagining something bodiless looking at something. If the Dependency Thesis is true and so are BSR/VBA then we should find a difference in these two imaginings.

There are at least two problems with this strategy. The first is that the Dependency Thesis, on the truth of which it relies, is controversial (see, for example, Noordhof, 2002). And while there are some reasons to accept the Dependency Thesis for all modalities (Smith, 2006, pp. 52–54), Smith's argument relies on the Dependency Thesis being especially plausible in the case of imagined bodily sensations. We, of course, are interested not in sensory imagination in the bodily mode but in visualizing. The second problem arises even if we accept the Dependency Thesis for visualizing. The problem is that supposing it is even possible to imagine being something bodiless looking at an apple, it is far from clear how we are to know that we have done so successfully. I might set out, in different circumstances, to imagine being a ghost by visualizing scared people running from me. But the visual experience I employ in this case may be, so far as I can know, not an experience that a bodiless creature could enjoy. The same goes for the experience I employ in attempting to imagine being a bodiless thing by visualizing an apple. In the next section I turn to the other way of using the phenomenal character of experience indirectly to answer questions about its content: the phenomenal contrast argument.

IV

To use a phenomenal contrast argument to defend the claim that some object *o* or property *F* figures in the representational content of experience in some modality, one starts with a pair of cases in which two subjects, or the same subject over time, have or has experiences that differ. Then, one argues that the best explanation of the difference requires us to accept that the *o* or *F* in question figures in the representational content of experience in the relevant modality.

In his 2014 paper, John Schwenkler is primarily interested in explaining how it is that visual experience enables self-locating thought, which is to say, how I can tell "by looking" that, for example, I am to the left of my office window. Schwenkler uses a phenomenal contrast argument to defend the claim that I can tell this by looking because the self figures in visual perceptual content. Thus, Schwenkler defends VSA. However, as will shortly be made clear, Schwenkler is interested in the visual representation of the location, movement (and lack of movement) of the perceiver's body, so it is reasonable to assume that the self he has in mind is bodily or embodied: which is to say, it just is the body, experienced in some special first-personal way. So, though Schwenkler's concern is with VSA, if his argument succeeds, VBA is true also. Furthermore, if Schwenkler's argument succeeds, VBA is true in virtue of BSR: Schwenkler's target is the view of Campbell and others, mentioned above, that to specify the spatial content of perceptual experience we need only use monadic spatial notions. He calls this the *minimal view*.

To explain Schwenkler's argument it is necessary, first, to introduce what is known as the visual illusion of self-motion or vection, though it should not be assumed at the outset that the illusion is properly described as visual, if by that we mean that the illusory representation is a visual one. Rather, that is part of what the argument is intended to establish. To induce the illusion, a subject is placed inside a large, floorless drum on the inside of which are painted vertical stripes. The drum is rotated counterclockwise, around the stationary subject. Initially, it seems to the subject that the drum is rotating around them, and that they are stationary. Call this veridical experience, as Schwenkler does, *V*. After a short time, things change: it seems to the subject as if the drum is stationary and that they, the subject, are rotating clockwise inside it. Call this illusory experience, as Schwenkler does, *I*. *V* and *I* are the pair of cases from which Schwenkler's phenomenal contrast argument proceeds.

For clarity, I present Schwenkler's argument by employing the structure of Susanna Siegel's phenomenal contrast argument for "thesis K," the claim that high-level properties can figure in the content if visual perceptual experience (Siegel, 2006). Laid out in this way, one can see that the structure of the argument involves two stages. First (premise 0) the claim that V and I differ in some way, which ought to be uncontroversial. Second, a series of steps (P1 to P4) each of which rule out some explanation of 0 so that only one remains:

0. The overall experience of the subject of V differs from the overall experience of the subject of I.

P1. If the overall experience of the subject of V differs from the overall experience of the subject of I then there is a difference in the *sensory* experiences of the subjects of V and I.

P2. If there is a difference in the sensory experiences of the subjects of V and I it is a difference in the *visual* experiences (V-VE and I-VE) of the subjects of V and I.

P3. If there is a difference in V-VE and I-VE then those experiences differ *in representational content*.

P4. If V-VE and I-VE differ in representational content this difference is a difference in whether the (bodily) self is represented as moving.

P1 rules out that 0 is explained by a difference in the nonsensory states of the subjects of V and I, such as their beliefs. P2 rules out that 0 is explained by a difference in their subjects' nonvisual experiences, such as their proprioceptive experiences. P3 rules out that 0 is explained by a nonrepresentational difference between their subjects' visual experiences and P4 rules out that the difference is representational and visual, but not a matter of whether the subject is represented as moving in I-VE and stationary in V-VE.

If the argument is successful then we can conclude that the (bodily) self is represented in the content of visual experience in I and V. Since the (bodily) self is not in the subject's visual field, we can furthermore conclude that in these experiences, the (bodily) self is visually perceptually represented but not seen. This does not yet give us VSA or VBA, claims about what is represented in normal visual experience generally. However, we can reach a general claim from here quite easily. As Schwenkler points out

> it would be wrong to think that the contrived nature of this particular setup, or the fact that experience I is illusory rather than veridical, means that it should be dismissed as somehow exceptional. Rather, illusions of vection simply bring into stark relief a very widespread phenomenon, which is an essential characteristic of our ability to perceive the world veridically. (Schwenkler, 2014, p. 144)

So, if the argument is successful we can conclude that VSA, and, given the remarks made at the beginning of this section, VBA, are true, and true in virtue of BSR.

The defender of the minimal view, Schwenkler's opponent, can avoid these conclusions by rejecting one of the premises of the phenomenal contrast argument. Schwenkler argues that this cannot be done, for each of P1 to P4. One premise that it seems natural to question is P2. It might be thought that 0 can be explained by a difference in the proprioceptive/kinesthetic experiences of the subjects of V and I. On this view, in V the subject proprioceptively seems to be stationary while the drum visually seems to move, and in I the subject proprioceptively seems to move while the drum visually seems to be stationary.

Schwenkler provides two arguments for rejecting this anti-P2 view, while allowing, as one must, that there are also differences in the nonvisual sensory phenomenology of the subjects of V and I. He argues that if it were not the case that the subjects of V and I also had different visual experiences (V-VE and I-VE) then their overall experiences, V and I, would exhibit cross-modal disunity or discordance. And that is not what we find (Schwenkler, 2014, p. 147). Call this the unity argument. He also argues that the illusion of vection is "more vivid visually than in other modalities" (Schwenkler, 2014, p. 148). One reason to accept this, he suggests, is that one can undermine such illusions by focusing on one's nonvisual experiences. This, he goes on to say, may be because the other nonvisual aspects of I are the result of its visual aspect: "the fact that one's own apparent motion is experienced visually" (Schwenkler, 2014, p. 148). Call this the vividness argument.

The vividness argument, as Schwenkler admits, is unlikely to convince his opponent. It is an empirical question whether one can undermine the illusion of vection by focusing on one's nonvisual sensory experiences and possible to deny that the illusion is most compelling visually. The unity argument is also problematic. Suppose one proprioceptively experiences clockwise rotation in I. There will only be discordance in I, one's overall experience, if one's visual experience, as it were, speaks to one's location. But this is precisely what Schwenkler's opponent (and the defender of the minimal view) denies. They can say instead that visual experience is simply silent on the question of one's own movement: a visual experience I have when I move through my environment, and one I have when my environment moves around me can be, on this view, identical. If this is right then the rejection of P2 would not entail any disunity in the subject of I's overall experience (which is to say, in I). The unity argument, then, will not work unless one already agrees that the (bodily) self is represented in visual experience.

Now this is not to say that 0 is not to be explained at least in part in terms of the visual experiences of the subjects of V and I. I will in the next section offer an alternative on which it is to be thus explained. However, what the preceding discussion suggests is that acceptance of P2 will be difficult to motivate in advance of an account of what the difference between V-VE and I-VE might be, which considerably reduces the force of the argument in which it is a premise.

V

How might the visual experiences of the subjects of V and I differ, if not in whether the subject seems to be moving? Here is one suggestion: in V, the subject's visual field seems to remain stationary while its occupants pass through it. In I, in contrast, the occupants of the visual field seem to be stationary while the visual field itself seems to move. If this were right, then we could allow that the explanation of the difference between V and I lies in the difference between V-VE and I-VE, without endorsing BSR or VBA. In this section I expand on this suggestion and argue that it should be understood as a rejection of P3 of Schwenkler's argument.

To reject P3 one needs to accept that there are some phenomenal features of perceptual experiences that are not representational features—features in virtue of which an experience represents what it does. Christopher Peacocke's sensational properties are one kind of nonrepresentational feature. They are called for, according to Peacocke, to explain facts such as the following: when you see two trees of the same size, one further away than the other, they are represented in the content of your visual experience as being the same size. Nevertheless, there is a respect in which the nearer tree also seems to take up more space than the one that is further away, though it is not represented as being larger. What explains this, according to Peacocke, are the nonrepresentational sensational properties of the experience. The tree that is nearer to you has larger "size in the visual field" than the tree that is further from you and this is a nonrepresentational, sensational feature of your experience of the trees (Peacocke, 1983, p. 12).

Schwenkler offers his opponent the idea that just as there can be "size in the visual field" so too there can be "movement" in the visual field. The defender of the minimal view can then attempt to explain the difference between I and V in terms of this sensational feature. They can say, that is, that the difference between the two is a "purely qualitative difference deriving from the changing positions of things in the visual field" (Schwenkler, 2014, p. 149). Schwenkler argues that this appeal to sensational properties will not work: in both I-VE and V-VE there will be movement in the visual field in this sense. Furthermore, the notion of sensational properties is controversial. For example, pure Intentionalists (those who would argue that all the phenomenal features of perceptual experience are representational features) argue that the two trees case mentioned above can be explained in terms of representational features. (See, for instance, Tye, 1991, p. 130.)

Peacocke's sensational properties are not the only nonrepresentational features of perceptual experience to which Schwenkler's opponent might appeal in order to reject P3. And there are notions of the visual field other than Peacocke's. Another kind of nonrepresentational, phenomenal feature of perceptual experience is the *structural feature* which, as I and others have argued, is that in virtue of which vision has a field in Mike Martin's sense.[8] "Visual field," as Peacocke uses the term, seems to refer, as Christopher Hill puts it, to "an internal mental entity of some sort" (2009, p. 60). There is a visual field in Martin's sense, in contrast, in that in some respect a cone-shaped region of *physical* space figures in visual experience. The cone-shaped region has its apex about where your eyes are and its base way off in front. To find its other boundaries, locate those places where one can no longer see an object that would be seen were it in the center of the field.

One might be tempted to think of the boundaries of the visual field as the edges of something like an object, namely a chunk of physical space. Likewise, one might be tempted to think that we are aware of them in the way in which we are aware of the edges of objects within the visual field. However, this cannot be right. When we are aware of the edges of objects within the visual field we are aware of the space beyond those objects' edges. I am aware of my pencil as bounded in a space of which I am also— in some respect—visually aware. We are not visually aware of the space beyond the boundaries of the visual field in this same way. Furthermore, if we "shrink" the visual field by, for instance, closing an eye, it does not visually seem as if any object or chunk of stuff has changed shape or been made smaller. Just as tellingly, space simply does not come in chunks with edges to which we could be perceptually sensitive as we are sensitive to the edges of the objects of which we are aware.

We should accept then that the boundaries of the visual field are not the edges of something like an object and that we are not aware of them in the way in which we would be aware of such edges. What then are the boundaries of the visual field? It should not be controversial to say that they are the boundaries beyond which I cannot see. We should also accept, I think, that we aware of these boundaries as being just that: awareness of the boundaries of my visual field presents itself, as it were, as a matter of my only being able to see so far. When an object passes through my visual field, as when my cat walks across my desk, she seems, as she passes beyond the rightmost boundary of the field, to have gone out of view. In other words, in being aware of the boundaries of the visual field I am aware that I am limited sensorially, and in particular, visually. A corollary of this is that the space within these boundaries seems to be a space within which I can see things: within which things are visible. Where no visible thing is present in some part of this region, the space seems empty: empty, that is, of visible things. For our purposes here, that should be enough to make clear Martin's notion of the visual field: it is a region of space that figures in experience as a space within which things can be seen, and vision's having this field is explained by the fact that, in visual experience, we are aware of our own visual sensory limitations.

So far, it might seem as if nothing we have said calls for any nonrepresentational features of experience. One might agree that visual experience involves a Martin-style visual field as described so far and say: every normal visual experience perceptually represents the perceiver's visual sensory limitations and, as corollary, the space they delimit as a space within which things can be seen. Alternatively, one might say that the features in virtue of which vision has its field are structural rather than representational features of experience (see references in note 8 below). The presence in experience of one's visual sensory limitations and the space they delimit is a matter of the form rather than the content of experience.

That this nonrepresentational view is plausible can be seen by thinking about sight's oft noted transparency. When you try to attend to your experience, so it is said, your efforts are thwarted: your attention passes straight through to the worldly objects of awareness and their properties that it represents. Martin introduces this Transparency Thesis with the following example: when, in looking at a lavender bush, I turn my attention to my visual experience of the lavender bush, the bush is not replaced as the focus of attention (2002, p. 380). Martin's way of putting the point brings out that the force of the Transparency Thesis is not that one cannot attend to one's visual experience, but that one can only attend to it by attending to its objects. Thus, if there are nonrepresentational features of experience then, since experience is transparent, we will discover them by attending to the worldly objects of awareness and their properties.

Now, think about how we attend to those aspects of experience constitutive of the visual field. We attend to them by attending to the worldly objects of awareness and their properties. For instance, in order to reflect upon the left-most boundary of my visual field, I direct my attention to the objects on my far left, either while trying not to change the field by moving my eyes, head, or body, or by moving my head and reflecting on how this changes how things seem to me. And how things seem to me is that more objects, or more parts of objects, come into view. Furthermore, the objects to my far left, in the example, are not replaced as the center of my attention when I reflect upon the left-most boundary of my visual field.

The likely etiology of the presence in experience of our visual sensory limitations and the space they delimit also speaks in favor of thinking of this as a matter of experience's form or structure rather than its content, at least if that content is *perceptual*. Recall, from section 2, our conditions (1 to 5) on seeing and (1 to 4) on visual perceptual representation, and in particular condition 2. If something present in experience is represented perceptually, then your experience of it is the result of ongoing sensitivity to its presence and absence, and some properties of it, over time. The presence in experience of the region of space that the visual field delimits is not like this—we are not sensitive to the region of space in this way and there is no reason why we would be, given that regions of space are invariantly present. Soteriou suggests instead that the presence of this space in experience should be thought of as a matter of one's perceptual system making a presupposition about the presence of a region of space, to which it is not causally sensitive, "in representing the contingent aspects of the environment to which it is causally sensitive" (Soteriou, 2011, p. 201). In that the perceptual system that enables experience makes this presupposition, our experience takes on an invariant form or structure that it would not otherwise have.[9]

There are also reasons to want to avoid building the visual field into the representational content of experience, and thus to favor the structural view just sketched. If we did try to build the visual field into the content of experience, we would not (or not merely) be accepting a very *liberal* account of perception's representational content. There are lots of objects present in our environment and they have lots of different properties. The dispute between liberals and conservatives about perceptual content is about which of these can be perceived, and in particular about the properties that can figure in perceptual experience (Bayne, 2009). Just low-level properties such as colors and shapes? Or high-level properties such as the property of being a pipe or a pine tree or angry? A defender of a liberal account will not balk at the idea that such properties of things in our immediate environment can be seen. To say that our visual sensory limitations, and the space they delimit as a space within which things can be seen, figure in the content of visual perceptual experience, is to depart from what is usually thought to be the case, *beyond liberality*. It is to say not that high-level properties of objects in our environment figure in experience. Instead, it is to say in part that notions that are themselves experiential ("seen," "visible") can figure in normal visual experience's representational content.

With the structural account of the visual field thus motivated, we can return to and refine the suggestion, made at the beginning of this section, about how the visual experiences of the subjects of *V* and *I* differ, if not in whether the subject seems to be moving. The suggestion was that what seems to move in *I* and not in *V* is not the perceiver's body but their visual field. This, we can now see, is not quite right. In *I*, I have a visual experience, *I-VE*, in which my surroundings do not appear to be moving but in which, at the right hand boundary of my visual field, I seem to be able to see successively more, while on the left, I seem to be able to see successively less far. This, like the "pseudomovement" exhibited in LED light displays, is something that we would naturally describe as movement but which does not in fact involve anything changing its location. In *V*, in contrast, I have a visual experience, *V-VE*, in which my surroundings do appear to be moving, thereby passing into the field on the right and out again on the left.

That there can be a difference between the phenomenology of something moving into my visual field under its own steam, and something coming into view as the result of my moving and thus changing the region of space that the field delimits is borne out by simple experiments. For example, hold your hand behind you and then sweep it forward in an arc around your body until it comes into view. Then, hold your hand behind you and turn your head until you see it. The visual experiences you have will be different. Among the differences between them will be that in the former your hand seems to move and thereby come into view, while in the latter it seems to come into view without moving.

If this suggestion is accepted, then whatever other differences there might be between *V* and *I* there is also a difference between their subjects' visual experiences. This difference is, I have argued, nonrepresentational. It is not a matter of what experience represents nor, thus, of whether it represents the body, the self, or the bodily self. This alternative explanation of the difference between *V* and *I* undermines Schwenkler's argument, construed as a defense of VBA.

VI

It would be hasty to conclude from this that VBA is false, for a number of reasons. First, while I hope I have said enough to make this explanation a plausible alternative to Schwenkler's I'm not sure I can claim to have given a *better* explanation, and there may be other explanations that the reader considers equally plausible and which I have not ruled out. Second, it may be that VBA is made true by something other than BSR.[10] I say nothing about that possibility here. We have been concerned with the claim that we need VBA to capture the perspectival character of visual perceptual experience (i.e., that it is made true by BSR). VBA may be required to capture other aspects of visual experience. Third, I have not ruled out there being other examples from which a phenomenal contrast argument similar to Schwenkler's might take off, and which might be more successful in establishing BSR and VBA. The force of this third point should not be overstated. As we said above, *I-VE* and *V-VE* are in relevant respects, typical visual experiences. Thus, if we don't need BSR and thus VBA to explain them, that does give us some reason to think that we don't need them to explain the perspectival spatial character of visual experience more generally. Nevertheless, there are some cases that we should address, of which the following two examples are representative:

Example 1

A: An experience in which it seems to the subject that the train they are on is moving and that the train at the neighboring platform is stationary. (In fact, the reverse is true.)

B: An experience in which it seems to the subject that the train they are on is stationary and that the train at the neighboring platform is moving. (As is in fact the case.)[11]

On the face of it, it seems as if the explanation of the difference between *V* and *I* given in section V could be used here, too. In *A*, supposing the train seems to be moving forward, you will seem to be seeing successively more ahead and successively less behind. The neighboring train will seem to be stationary, and yet parts of it that weren't in view will now seem to be. However, what if one is seated in such a way that the other train does not seem to pass in or out of one's visual field at its boundaries, because as you are seated and oriented what is at those boundaries are just parts of the walls of the train you are on? (I am imagining a case in which you are seated by a small window. Most of your visual field is occupied by the train you are on, and the window frames just a small portion of the neighboring train.) What should one say, then? Presuming that the illusion would persist in such a case, this could be explained straightforwardly as an illusion of induced motion, in which two objects—the train one is on and the neighboring train—change their relative locations but one misrepresents which of the objects has in fact moved. Another illusion of the same kind occurs when the moon illusorily seems to move in relation to the clouds that, as a matter of fact, are moving across the sky (Goldstein, 2010, p. 181).

Example 2

C: The experience of a subject looking straight ahead at Buckingham Palace.

D: The experience of a subject looking at Buckingham Palace with her "face still towards" it but with her body "turned towards a point on the right" (Peacocke, 1992, p. 106).

According to Peacocke, in D "the Palace is experienced as being off to one side from the direction of straight ahead – even if the view remains exactly the same as in the first case" (Peacocke, 1992, p. 106). The strategy invoked in section 5 to explain the difference between V and I cannot obviously be used to explain any difference between C and D. According to Peacocke, we need to give a set of labeled axes in giving the content of visual experience. The origin of the axes might be the center of the chest, the "axes given by the directions back/front, left/right and up/down with respect to that centre" (Peacocke, 1992, p. 106). This set of labeled axes captures, on his view, the distinction between C and D. There are two reasons to think that Peacocke's account of this example shouldn't lead us to accept BSR and thus VBA.

First, it is, I think, far from obvious that there is any difference in visual phenomenology between C and D. I said in section 4 that it is difficult to motivate acceptance of the claim that there is a visual difference between V and I in advance of an account of what that visual difference might be. The same is true of C and D. This doesn't mean that it is not the case that appeal to a set of labeled axes are required to give the content of visual experience. But it does mean that Peacocke's argument for the need to appeal to such axes from the claim that there is a difference in visual phenomenology between C and D will have limited force.

Second, even if we accept that there is a difference in phenomenology between C and D and that it should be explained in Peacocke's way, it's not clear that this would entail that BSR and VBA are true. Peacocke himself notes that

> to say that bodily parts are mentioned in the labeling of the axes is not to imply that the bodily parts are given to the subject is some visual or other sensory manner. . . . The nature of the way in which bodily parts are given when they are appropriate labels for the axes is actually an issue of considerable interest. (1992, p. 106)

By Peacocke's own lights then, the way in which the body or its parts show up in visual experience is left open by his account. As such, whether his account requires that we accept BSR and VBA is also left open.

VII

I have argued that we do not need to accept BSR and VBA in order to accommodate the perspectival spatial character of visual perceptual experience. Thus we do not have this reason, at least, to think that sight, like bodily awareness, represents the body "from the inside." In section II we considered two reasons for being interested in BSR and VBA. First, we said that focus on these claims would allow us to home in on and assess the idea of things being visually perceptually represented but not seen. Thus far, anyway, it turns out that we do not need any such idea. Second, we said BSR and VBA might help us to spell out the idea that certain things, such as the subject of visual perceptual experience, are "implicit in experience." If the argument of this chapter is accepted, some other way of spelling out "implicit in experience" will be required. Two possibilities come to mind, both of which will have to be developed elsewhere.

When one sees, say, a pencil, and it seems to be *there* and thereby in some spatial relation to *here*, you have both a visual experience of the pencil, *there*, and a proprioceptive experience of one's body, *here*. According to Merleau-Ponty, these experiences—and modality-specific experiences in general—should be considered abstractions from a whole which is, as it were, greater than the sum of its parts. (See Hass, 2008, pp. 45–51, for discussion.) It may be that when taken in abstraction from this whole, there is no way to capture the sense in which, as one sees the pencil, it seems to be spatially related to the body. This is one sense in which the body is only implicit in that visual abstraction.[12]

Second, the structural features we have appealed to may themselves yield a notion of "implicit in experience." As we have seen, in order to capture the phenomenological aspects of visual experience in virtue of which vision has a field, we need to mention, for example, the perceiver's own visual sensory limitations. We might say that something is implicit in experience to the extent that mention of it is needed to explain some aspect of phenomenal character, despite the fact that it is not perceptually represented. Appeal to structural features explains how and why there are some things that are, in this second way, merely implicit in experience.

Acknowledgments

I am grateful to audiences at Leeds and Stirling, the Mind and Reason group at York, and The Body and the Self Revisited workshop in Copenhagen for much helpful discussion. Special thanks to Alisa Mandrigin, Adrian Alsmith, and Keith Allen for more specific guidance.

Notes

1. Or capaci*ties*. Whether bodily awareness is one capacity or several need not concern us here.

2. Richardson (2013) defends smell's exteroceptivity.

3. It is less plausible that "here" is visually represented as occupied by a sense organ or body part. While it might be reasonable to believe that I can tell "by looking" that my body is to the left of my office window there seems no reason to believe that I can tell, in the same way, how my body's parts are arranged or what parts it has. Thank you to Alisa Mandrigin for pushing me on this point.

4. I am very grateful to José Bermúdez for making this suggestion at the workshop in Copenhagen organized by this volume's editors.

5. BSR and VBA might provide a special problem for a Naïve Realist. If one thinks of perception as fundamentally the obtaining of a state with representational—perhaps propositional—content, one has made room, in principle, for all sorts of things to figure in that content, including one's body when it is outside the visual field. We understand what it is to have a state that represents, say, that the pencil is in front of my body: we can have beliefs or make judgments with these contents. But if one thinks that, at bottom, perception is a special kind of relation, things are not so straightforward. One would not then have the same way of making sense of the truth of BSR and VBA.

6. For example, Cassam (1997), Bermúdez (2000, 2011), and Schwenkler (2014). Alsmith (this volume) argues against the claim that visual experience locates the bodily self and in favor of an agentive account.

7. See, for example, Macpherson (2011).

8. Martin's notion of the visual field appears in three of his works (1992, 1993, 1995). It is discussed in detail in Soteriou (2011, 2013, chap. 5) and Richardson (2010, 2014). As Soteriou construes the notion of structural features, they have their home in a Relationalist or Naïve Realist theory of perception. I set this aside, here.

9. Although cf. Mac Cumhaill (2015).

10. See, for example, Alsmith's agentive account (this volume), on which perceptual experience represents objects as the focus of its subject's possible action, and thereby the subject's (bodily) self as located.

11. Thanks to the audience at a visiting speaker seminar at Stirling for very helpful discussion of this example and to Alisa Mandrigin for helping me to see what to say about it.

12. Of course, the body may be said to figure in visual experience implicitly or explicitly in other ways too, on Merleau-Ponty's view.

References

Batty, C. (2009). What's that smell? *Southern Journal of Philosophy, 47*(4), 321–348. doi:10.1111/j.2041-6962.2009.tb00164.x.

Bayne, T. (2009). Perception and the reach of phenomenal content. *Philosophical Quarterly, 59*(236), 385–404. doi:10.1111/j.1467-9213.2009.631.x.

Bermúdez, J. L. (2011). Bodily awareness and self-consciousness. In S. Gallagher (Ed.), *The Oxford handbook of the self.* Oxford: Oxford University Press. doi:10.1093/oxfordhb/9780199548019.003.0007.

Bermúdez, J. L. (2000). *The paradox of self-consciousness.* Cambridge, MA: MIT Press.

Campbell, J. (2002). *Reference and consciousness.* Oxford: Oxford University Press.

Cassam, Q. (1997). *Self and world.* Oxford: Oxford University Press.

Dretske, F. (1969). *Seeing and knowing.* Chicago: Chicago University Press.

Goldstein, E. B. (2010). *Sensation and perception* (8th International Edition). Belmont, CA: Wadsworth.

Hass, L. (2008). *Merleau-Ponty's philosophy.* Bloomington, IN: Indiana University Press.

Hill, C. S. (2009). *Consciousness.* Cambridge: Cambridge University Press.

Mac Cumhaill, C. (2015). Perceiving immaterial paths. *Philosophy and Phenomenological Research, 90*(3), 687–715. doi:10.1111/phpr.12037.

Macpherson, F. (2011). Taxonomising the senses. *Philosophical Studies, 153*(1), 123–142. doi:10.1007/s11098-010-9643-8.

Martin, M. G. F. (2002). The transparency of experience. *Mind & Language, 17*(4), 376–425. doi:10.1111/1468-0017.00205.

Martin, M. G. F. (1995). Bodily awareness: A sense of ownership. In J. L. Bermúdez, A. J. Marcel, & N. M. Eilan (Eds.), *The body and the self* (pp. 267–289). Cambridge, MA: MIT Press.

Martin, M. G. F. (1993). Sense modalities and spatial properties. In N. Eilan, R. McCarthy, & B. Brewer (Eds.), *Spatial representation*. Oxford: Oxford University Press.

Martin, M. G. F. (1992). Sight and touch. In T. Crane (Ed.), *The contents of experience* (pp. 196–215). New York: Cambridge University Press.

Noordhof, P. (2002). Imagining objects and imagining experiences. *Mind & Language*, *17*(4), 426–455. doi:10.1111/1468-0017.00206.

Nudds, M. (2009). Sounds and space. In M. Nudds & C. O'Callaghan (Eds.), *Sounds and perception: New philosophical essays* (pp. 69–96). Oxford: Oxford University Press.

Peacocke, C. (1992). Scenarios, concepts and perception. In T. Crane (Ed.), *The contents of experience* (pp. 105–135). Cambridge: Cambridge University Press.

Peacocke, C. (1983). *Sense and content: Experience, thought, and their relations*. Oxford: Oxford University Press.

Richardson, L. (2014). Space, time and Molyneux's question. *Ratio*, *27*(4), 483–505. doi:10.1111/rati.12081.

Richardson, L. (2013). Sniffing and smelling. *Philosophical Studies*, *162*(2), 401–419. doi:10.1007/s11098-011-9774-6.

Richardson, L. (2010). Seeing empty space. *European Journal of Philosophy*, *18*(2), 227–243. doi:10.1111/j.1468-0378.2008.00341.x.

Schwenkler, J. (2014). Vision, self-location, and the phenomenology of the "point of view." *Noûs*, *48*(1), 137–155. doi:10.1111/j.1468-0068.2012.00871.x.

Siegel, S. (2006). Which properties are represented in perception? In T. S. Gendler & J. Hawthorne (Eds.), *Perceptual experience* (pp. 481–503). Oxford: Oxford University Press.

Smith, J. (2006). Bodily awareness, imagination, and the self. *European Journal of Philosophy*, *14*(1), 49–68. doi:10.1111/j.1468-0378.2006.00243.x.

Soteriou, M. (2013). *The mind's construction: The ontology of mind and mental action*. Oxford: Oxford University Press.

Soteriou, M. (2011). The perception of absence, space, and time. In J. Roessler, H. Lerman, & N. Eilan (Eds.), *Perception, causation, and objectivity* (pp. 181–206). Oxford: Oxford University Press.

Tye, M. (1991). *The imagery debate*. Cambridge, MA: MIT Press.

12   Perspectival Structure and Agentive Self-Location

Adrian J. T. Alsmith

1   Introduction

Perceptual experience is perspectivally structured. Perceptual experience is self-locating. Failure to distinguish these claims masks a significant issue dividing accounts of spatial self-consciousness. Perceptual experience is perspectivally structured, in the sense relevant here, when that which is perceived is experienced from somewhere. If perceptual experience can have this kind of structure without being self-locating, then one must go beyond the structure of perceptual experience itself in giving an account of how we are able to think of ourselves as part of the world we perceive. Conversely, if it cannot be perspectivally structured without being self-locating, then one need not go beyond the structure of perceptual experience to give such an account.

Accounts of the former kind have in common the idea that "experience alone is powerless to place its subject with respect to its objects" (Brewer, 1992, p. 26). But there is room for variation in what provides the missing ingredient. Here we can paint a broad-strokes distinction between intellectual accounts and agentive accounts of spatial self-consciousness. Intellectual accounts, such as those held by Campbell (1994) and Evans (1982), hold that thoughts about one's location require an appropriate conception of oneself as a spatiotemporal being. Agentive accounts, such as those proposed by Brewer (1992) and Schellenberg (2007), appeal to the idea that one acts upon objects from one's location in explanation of how an experience can represent oneself as located.[1]

My aim here is to show the merits of an agentive account by developing its resources further than has been previously achieved. I will not do so by discussing intellectual accounts in much detail. Rather, the main contrast will be with views that hold that perceptual experience itself *is* sufficient to place its subject with respect to its objects. In a generalized form we may call it the perspectival self-location thesis (PST).

PST: If an experience is perspectival, then it represents its subject's location.

Against this, I will defend what I will call the agentive self-location thesis (AST).

AST: If an experience represents an object as the focus of its subject's possible action, then it represents its subject's location.

Some remarks are in order to give context to these two theses. Each provides a basis for an account of how perceptual experience can represent its subject's location. On the assumption that all perceptual experience is perspectival, then PST straightforwardly undermines any motivation for AST. For if PST were true, then the perspectival structure of perceptual experience alone would be sufficient for a subject to have thoughts about her location. Any appeal to one's agency to account for the latter would then be redundant.

Note also that neither is concerned with what is minimally necessary for a subject to represent her location. Indeed, it may be plausible to think that the conditional in PST only holds for subjects already independently capable of self-representation of some kind. This restriction is certainly built into AST, where the antecedent involves experience representing an object as the focus of *its subject's* possible action. Perhaps a less restrictive thesis could be formulated and defended. However, my interest here is not to provide an account of how subjects come to represent themselves in the most fundamental respect, whatever that might be, but rather with how they come to represent themselves in relation to the world that they perceive. The idea that the relationship between perception and action is essential to the most basic emergence of self-consciousness is one that I find attractive, but it is not one that I will defend here.[2]

The rest of the discussion proceeds as follows.

Section 2 groups and discusses two ways in which perceptual experiences are often described as perspectival. Section 3 introduces the general idea of a perceptual experience having self-locating content. It also provides an interpretation of PST according to which perceptual experiences are self-locating in virtue of representing the location of a perspective as the location of the subject.

The next two sections build a case against PST. Section 4 provides arguments from the cases of film experience and visualization, to show that experiences can be structured around the location of a perspective without requiring that location to be represented as the subject's. Further consideration of these cases in section 5 reveals that there are various ways in which we can individuate perspectives independently of the subject's location. It is then argued that even if being perspectivally structured were sufficient for an experience to represent the location of a perspective within the subject's body, this would not be sufficient for representing the subject's location.

The final two sections respectively aim to develop AST as an alternative to PST and show its capacity to accommodate relevant aspects of the unity of perceptual experience. Section 6 presents the basic commitments of AST, shows why it requires an account of the unity of the body in action, and provides such an account. Finally, section 7 argues that AST is better placed than PST to capture a sense in which we are conscious of ourselves as singly located, precisely because of its central appeal to the notion of a unified body.

2 Perspectival Structure

Experiences are perspectival when they instantiate certain kinds of structure. There are two kinds of perspectival structure commonly recognized to obtain in perceptual experience. The first is what I will label a *limitation structure*. The second is what I will label an *egocentric structure*.

Limitation structure is characterized by certain sensory limitations.[3] One of these is that things are only perceptible if they are within a certain bounded region at a time. Thus the visual field or field of view is horizontally and vertically limited such that one can only see objects within those limits. Another limitation is that an object falling within the bounds of the visual field may not be seen, or some of its parts may not be seen, due to the fact that opaque surfaces occlude one another. Occlusion is a limitation characterizing the visibility of objects experienced as three-dimensional.[4] This is in slight tension with a historically popular view, according to which the appearance of objects in the visual field is limited to a two-dimensional structure that gives only the impression of depth.[5] According to this characterization, strictly speaking, the objects of perceptual experience appear in graphical perspective. Their size and shape are as of a two-dimensional projection, in which the lines of projection run through an image plane to a single point. Tensions aside, we can recognize the kernel of truth common among these descriptions, which is that each putative limitation is such relative to a particular location. This is variously called the origin, point of observation, point of view, or more simply the perspective of the experience in question.

The other kind of structure, egocentric structure, concerns the systematic organization of the experienced locations of objects within an egocentric frame of reference. Locations in an egocentric frame of reference are assigned relative to a single point. This point is typically at the intersection of three orthogonal axes, each of which may be labeled according to canonical egocentric directions such as leftward, upward, forward, and so on.[6] The general structure admits of static and dynamic species. Sometimes, one might need to only specify the synchronic spatial organization of a subject's experience: some things are experienced as nearby, others far away, some of these seem straight ahead, others to the left or to the right, and so on. But for other cases, a diachronic specification of the subject's experience is required, such as when things are seen as coming closer, moving leftward, and so on. When the content of experience is described as egocentric, or egocentrically organized, what is typically meant is that it is structured in one of these two ways.

If an experience has either a limitation structure or an egocentric structure, or both (as is usually the case), then it is perspectival in the sense relevant here. Vision is the paradigm for perspectivally structured perceptual experience, so naturally this form of perceptual experience will be our principal focus. But the same structures might be thought to obtain in experiences in other sensory modalities, or indeed, as I will suggest in a later section, in sensory imagery. What I will assume, in any case, is that any form of experience that instantiates either form of structure described above is then a form of perspectival experience.

3   Perspectival Self-Location

It is fairly common to think that an ordinary episode of human visual experience will be sufficient for its subject to form a judgment about her location.[7] Glibly put, you can judge where you are just by looking at something. This fact (as I will assume it is) admits of a variety of explanations. For instance, one might hold that in order to judge that, for example, I am in front of a door, "something more than the *sheer* [perceptual] awareness is called for: the perceptual state must occur in the context of other kinds of knowledge and understanding [involved in conceiving herself as] a persisting subject of experience" (Evans, 1982, p. 232). Christopher Peacocke expresses a somewhat contrasting set of intuitions as follows:

> Consider . . . the everyday case in which a person forms a belief with the content
> 'I am in front of a door', and does so for the reason that he sees a door ahead of
> him. His visual experience represents him as bearing a certain spatial relation to

the door . . . taking his experience at face value, he would judge that he is in front of a door. (Peacocke, 2001, pp. 215–216)

An experience represents its subject's location when its content includes a spatial relation between the subject and the object of the experience. It includes a relation of the kind aRx, where a refers to the object of experience, x to the subject of the experience, and R to the spatial relation between them. In representing R, the content specifies the relative location of each relatum as represented by the experience. One of these, the subject, is picked out by x in a manner distinctive of first-personal contents, in that it cannot fail to refer to the subject (Shoemaker, 1968). If visual experiences have such contents, then they suffice for a certain class of first-person thoughts, namely thoughts about one's location.

Recall the perspectival self-location thesis (PST).

PST: If an experience is perspectival, then it represents its subject's location.

PST is a thesis about the conditions under which an experience can have self-locating content. It is most plausible as a thesis about perceptual experience, holding that the perspectival structure of perceptual experience is sufficient for it to represent one's location. A natural explanation then follows for the sufficiency of perceptual experience in forming thoughts about one's location. One might come to think that one is somewhere just by looking at something, just because one sees that thing from somewhere—somewhere which one represents as one's own location.

Now, as noted in the introduction, the idea that perceptual experience is self-locating is rarely distinguished from the idea that perceptual experience is perspectivally structured.[8] In some cases this may be due to an error of conflation, or the distinction lacking relative importance; in other cases, such a verdict seems less plausible, for example:

Simply in virtue of its perspectival character, visual experience can include the location of the perceiver among its face value contents. (Schwenkler, 2014, p. 139)

Perceptual content. . . . can vary along a *perspectival* dimension, in regard to how things *look* (or appear) from the vantage point of the perceiver. . . . This corresponds to the fact that perception is, at once, a way of keeping track of how things are, and also of our relation to the world. Perception is thus world-directed and self-directed. (Noë, 2004, p. 168)

[In] egocentric spatial perception the objects of perception are experienced as standing in spatial relations to the perceiver. . . . Egocentric spatial perception can therefore be described as self-locating. (Cassam, 1997, pp. 52–53)

Plausibly, remarks like these are not mere conflations, rather they involve a suppressed assumption that the perspectival structure of an experience implies that it has self-locating content; in short, PST. We can most readily make sense of this if we characterize perspectivally structured experiences as representing relations between objects and the locations of subjects. Perspectival structures, on this gloss, involve a relation between an object and the perspective from which the object is experienced, where the location of the latter is represented as the location of the subject. Call this claim *perspectival identity*: for a perceptually represented object a, a spatial relation R, a subject x at location l_x and a perspective p at location l_p, a perceptual experience represents aRx just because it represents aRp and l_p is represented as l_x.

Two comments on this claim are in order before moving on. First, not everyone agrees with the characterization of perspectival structure involved here: Campbell (1994, p. 119) affirms that visual experience is perspectivally structured, but denies that it must then include relations such as R; Perry (1986, pp. 137–138) denies that visual experience requires "any idea or representation" of oneself.[9] But note that we can grant that perspectival structures are relational, without then accepting perspectival identity. So, *pace* Campbell and Perry, let us say that any instance of limitation-structured or egocentric-structured content in perceptual experience specifies aRp. For even if we grant this, it is an open question whether the experience ·represents aRx.

Second, it is sometimes argued that if the location of the perspective, l_p, is represented in the experience, it is not itself perceived. That is, it is not represented in just the same way as other objects, rather it is represented by means of representing those objects within a perspectival structure.

> [The perspectival aspect of] how things are presented as being does not turn up in experience as a point of view being an explicit element of how things are presented as being, with the relations of the objects perceived being marked relative to it. . . . Rather, the point of view from which one perceives is marked in one's visual experience through it being the point to which the objects perceived are presented—if one can fix the location of those objects, one [can] thereby determine the location of the point of view. (Martin, 2002, pp. 409–410)

In these remarks, I think, is the basic truth that if objects and their parts are consistently represented in a perspectival structure there will be a single location relative to which they are arranged in that structure. Hence, the structure itself is sufficient to determine l_p. The views attributed to Campbell and Perry above amount to a simple denial that from the fact that the

l_p can be determined in this way one can infer that the experience implicitly represents it, let alone l_x. But others have taken just the opposite lesson: that although l_p does not figure in the explicit content of the experience, it figures implicitly just in so far as the experience presents objects in a manner that is perspectivally structured.[10] This dispute is interesting and important, but for a separate occasion. For the sake of the present discussion, I will assume that the content of perspectivally structured experience is relational, such that it represents objects in relation to an implicitly represented particular location, l_p. The question that concerns us is whether, if one represents objects in this way, one then represents l_x.

4   The View from Elsewhere

A central difficulty in entertaining the thought that PST is false is that there may be some inherent difficulty in extricating the idea that experience can be perspectival from the idea that an experience can represent its subject's location. The aim of this section is to provide the basis for this conceptual distinction. I will raise two cases in which, I argue, it is plausible to think that a subject can be aware of the fact that they are experiencing a scene from elsewhere, that is, from somewhere that they are not. Consideration of these cases thus removes a certain motivation for PST. For it reveals the sheer fact that a subject's experience of something is from somewhere is not itself sufficient for the subject to represent that location as their location.[11]

For the first case, consider Campbell's observations on "the position of someone watching a film" (Campbell, 1994, p. 120). Call our film-watcher Johanna. Johanna may "watch as the camera pans and swoops and tracks" without being forced "at any level, to use the first person in responding to the film" (Campbell, 1994, p. 120). Here is what I take to be just right about this. Film is a medium for the presentation of perspectival images of scenes. Film images can and typically do have both *limitation structure* and *egocentric structure*. Johanna's film experience, her experience of a filmed scene through film images, will also be structured in these ways. Unless one is involved in the creation of the film, the filmed scene will typically not be anywhere in one's whereabouts. Hence, Johanna can experience a filmed scene that is not itself in her locale and be aware of this fact. And given that she is aware of this fact, ex hypothesi we then have no reason to think that Johanna would represent the perspective from which she experiences the filmed scene as where she herself is located. Film experience thus seems to be a candidate case in which one can experience something from elsewhere, without representing oneself as being in that location.

For the second, consider Bernardo, who sits at home visualizing a bottle floating in outer space. He imagines it rotating end over end along its sagittal plane. The occlusion and exposure of the bottle's visible surfaces are characterized by a *limitation structure*, as perhaps is the appearance of its size and shape; the positions and directions of parts of the bottle are characterized by an *egocentric structure*. Accordingly, his experience of the imagined bottle is perspectival. Yet he does not imagine where the bottle is located relative to where he is sitting. In supposing the bottle to be located somewhere in outer space, he merely supposes it to be in that kind of environment, rather than anywhere in particular. Bernardo's experience of the bottle seems then to be another case in which someone can experience something from somewhere that they are not, without representing themselves as being in that location.

A defender of PST might insist that in such cases we must think that the subject would misrepresent or imaginatively represent their location as the location of the perspective in question. But that seems to be more than is required for the experience to be structured around a perspective. Certainly there are cinematographic devices that do facilitate the viewer's identification of the perspective of the camera with their own perspective, such as, for instance, the "point of view shot" But this, I take it, is the exception rather than the rule. The vast majority of film images, despite being perspectivally structured, can present a filmed scene as such without the subject locating themselves anywhere in relation to it, or indeed anywhere in particular.

Similarly, the perspectival structure of a visualization need not intrinsically involve the subject representing herself as located relative to the visualized object. Bernardo might experience the very same imagery when he supposes that his nemesis, Giorgio, is floating in space, looking at a bottle rotating in front of him. Bernardo would then imagine how the bottle would look from where he imagines Giorgio to be located.[12] Indeed, even if there must be a subject to the imagined experience, this does not itself require that it be anyone in particular. All it requires is someone, some nameless entity for all that Bernardo cares, being in the right kind of relation to the imagined object. If that is right, then this subject does not play any role significantly different from the perspective according to which the visualization is structured. Whatever the entity required, we have no motivation for the view that we must think that Bernardo represents himself as located where it is.

Neither of these cases constitute knockdown arguments against PST, in part because neither of these cases is straightforwardly a case of perceptual experience. But they do serve to illustrate the core conceptual distinction between perspectivally structured experience and the subject's representation of her location. For what they describe is a case in which the location of a perspective around which an experience may be structured and the subject's representation of their own location can conceivably come apart.

5   Locating Perspectives and Locating Subjects

Another kind of motivation for PST might be that it is difficult to think of how we might individuate the location of a perspective independently of a subject experiencing something from that perspective. However, my treatment of the above cases suggests that we ought to be able to do this. In this section, I will draw out some principles for how we can individuate the locations of perspectives and subjects independently. This will both remove a further motivation for PST and reveal certain difficulties a proponent of that thesis would face in providing an account of how they are connected.

Let me first set aside one common respect in which location of the perspective itself might be individuated in both of the two cases discussed in the previous section. Common to both cases is that the subject experiences an image; thus the structure of the experienced image itself might provide an individuating condition. The principle here, briefly discussed at the end of section 3 in the context of some quoted remarks made by Martin, is that the experienced image being perspectivally structured implies a perspective according to which it is structured. Though this perspective is not perceived, it plays a discernible structural role that can be traced through the organization of the image. If this is right, then we can individuate the perspective from which Johanna experiences a scene and Bernardo experiences the bottle merely by appealing to the structure of the image in each case.

Although I take this to be correct, it is also not of much further interest than that it bolsters the arguments of the previous section. Indeed, one might have doubts about how useful such a principle would be in any treatment of ordinary perceptual experience, in which the structure of the experience is inextricably linked to the subject's bodily nature. However, in the film case there is the additional possibility that we might appeal to the ways in which the perspectivally structured image is causally related to a spatiotemporal object, namely the camera, in order to individuate the location of the perspective in question. The camera is distinct from the perspective structuring the image it produces, just as the human body is distinct from the perspective structuring the experience of the subject. But, in each case, the perspective and the object in question are not merely coincident but systematically causally related, in a manner according to principles that I will now articulate.

Consider first a principle that I will call *anchoring*. Anchoring is nicely illustrated in Christopher Peacocke's discussion of how the orientations of a particular object, oneself as a body, can affect one's experience:

> Looking straight ahead at Buckingham Palace is one experience. It is another to look at the palace with one's face still toward it but with one's body turned toward a point on the right. In this second case the palace is experienced as being off to one side from the direction of straight ahead, even if the view remains exactly the same as in the first case. (Peacocke, 1992, p. 62)

In this example, the left–right axis is systematically causally related to the torso, such that changing its spatial properties (e.g., its orientation) affects one's perspectival experience. *Anchoring* is a term we can use to capture this kind of relation: a perspectival structure, or some part of a perspectival structure, is *anchored* to an object when variations in perspectivally structured content are systematically caused by variations in the anchoring object's spatial properties. In the scenario Peacocke describes, a part of an egocentric structure, its left–right axis, is anchored to the torso, causing systematic changes in the way in which objects are experienced.[13]

However, anchoring does not quite give us enough to capture the sense in which the perspective from which one experiences something is connected to a particular spatiotemporal object. For that we need the further idea that a perspective may exist at a particular location, in virtue of an object being at that location. To capture this, we can use the term *embedding*: a perspective is *embedded* within an object when it is located within an object to which its structure (or some part of its structure) is anchored. Embedding, as stated, requires anchoring. For a perspective to be embedded within an object it is not sufficient that it merely occupies the same location as that object. It needs to be causally connected to that object such that an anchoring relation obtains.

These principles provide a means by which we can individuate perspectives as distinct from but related to spatiotemporal objects. This is very straightforward in the film case. The perspective structuring a film can be individuated by its embedding within the camera (and not merely its colocation with it) as variations in its perspectivally structured content are systematically caused by variations in the camera's position and orientation. In this way, we can individuate the perspective from which Johanna experiences a filmed scene without appeal to Johanna representing her location, or indeed that of any subject within the narrative. The principles also straightforwardly apply to human perceptual experience, though, perhaps unsurprisingly, the overall situation is more complex. One of the main sources of complexity is in the fact that, in higher mammals at least, perceptual systems represent space surrounding the body according to multiple distinct egocentric frames of reference structured around the body's distinct individually mobile body parts.[14] If, for each of these egocentric structures, there is a corresponding perspective embedded within a distinct body part, then perceptual experience is complex, in so far as it is structured according to multiple distinct perspectives.

If this is correct, it would follow from PST that the subject would be located in multiple places within itself. To put the point more fully, recall the interpretative claim that we called *perspectival identity*: for a perceptually represented object a, a spatial relation R, a subject x at location l_x and a perspective p at location l_p, a perceptual experience represents aRx just because it represents aRp and l_p is represented as l_x. According to the preceding, a perspectivally structured experience might represent l_{p1-3}, which poses the question: Which of these is supposed to be represented as l_x?

One might think this puzzle could be easily resolved by the suggestion that perceptual processing in these body-part-specific spatial frameworks is ultimately translated into a single unified framework, such that a subject's experience is unified according to a single perspective. But there seems to be equally good motivation for this single perspective to be located within the head as within the torso. The head houses a great number of sensory organs that are particularly significant for spatial representation, namely the eyes, ears, and the vestibular labyrinth.[15] Yet, in the morphological structure of the body, the torso is the stable continent relative to which other parts are mere peninsulas and hence the most likely point of reference for the construction of a consistent egocentric representation.[16]

That there seem to be two equally viable options here presents something of a dilemma for any defender of PST, as it is not clear how the choice between these options would be resolved.[17] Yet, its defendant might want to grab the bull by the horns, so to speak, and run it to ground by claiming that the basic issue is no issue at all. For surely, the thought continues, as long as it follows that the subject's experience represents objects in relation to *some* location within the body, this is sufficient for locating the subject. But this only reveals a more fundamental issue. Now that we have on the table a robust conceptual distinction between the two entities, we can appreciate that the two locations in question have different extensity: l_p, qua perspective structuring the experience may be no more than a minimally extended point in space; l_x, qua bodily subject of experience is no less than a voluminous region. According to perspectival identity, it seems to follow from PST that the subject's location is not the location of the object that she is, it is a location within the object that she is.

Of course, this would not be an issue if we had the resources to make the step from representing something in relation to a location within a particular body part, to representing something in relation to ourselves as the fully extended bodies that we are. This would be to appeal to the notion of partial identity, that is, the sense in which a part is identical to any whole of which it is a part. By representing something in relation to a particular part of the body, one would represent it in relation to something partially identical with oneself. But PST is too bare a thesis to provide for even such a basic step as this. What would allow for such a step would be an account of the unity of the body, an account of how the parts of the subject's body are unified such that each is partially identical with the subject as a whole. The bare notion of perspectivally structured experience simply does not warrant such an addition. By contrast, the bare notion of bodily action does warrant such an addition. Thus it is an integral part of the account of spatial self-consciousness that I favor, as I will now argue.

6   Agentive Self-Location

Here is the central idea of an agentive account of spatial self-consciousness, as expressed by Brewer:

> perceptual contents are self-locating in virtue of their contribution to the subject's capacity for basic purposive action in the world. This mutually shaping psychological relation places the subject in the perceived world by bringing its objects into his environment as the focus of his perceptually controlled behavior (Brewer, 1992, p. 26)

From this, we may extract the agentive self-location thesis (AST).

AST: If an experience represents an object as the focus of its subject's possible action, then it represents its subject's location.[18]

On the face of things, AST could use some further motivation. If perspectival structure alone cannot serve to pick out the subject herself, why should representing the objects of perceptual experience as the focus of the subject's possible action be sufficient? The answer is that representing the subject's location as *both* the location from which she perceives *and* the location from which she would act, is necessary for representing an object of perceptual experience as the focus of the subject's possible action.

Accordingly, if a subject represents objects in this way it is a sufficient condition for her to represent her location. As Brewer puts it: "The interrelation between perception and action constitutes a kind of triangulation of the subject's location in the single world of each" (Brewer, 1992, p. 27).

In a great many cases, this single world of perception and action will be the actual world in which the subject is located. But it need not be. In some cases, the subject may represent an object as the focus of her possible action even if the object is not as it seems to be, or is nonexistent, merely virtual or imaginary. In each of these cases, it may be impossible to act on the object in the way it might seem to the subject that she can. Nevertheless, to the extent that her experience interfaces with her practical capacities, and in a manner that is equivalent to those cases in which the genuine article is present, the object is represented as the focus of possible action. Moreover, the intentions driving the actions in question directly concern that which is experienced. Whether the intention is to reach for or avoid the falling object, it is that object (whatever its nature) that would form the focus of the subject's action, were she to act upon what she perceives.[19]

It is significant here that the relevant class of action is bodily action, which I will take to consist of intentional actions that centrally involve movement of the body. Such actions are spatiotemporally constrained by the nature of the body itself as a unity of parts. Movement of any part of one's body will take as long as it does, and involve what physical displacements it does, precisely because that part is a part of the body as a whole. This relationship is made intelligible by conceiving of bodily structure in a way that highlights the constraints it imposes on bodily movement. For although there are various ways of conceiving of the bodily structure of creatures like us, the structure of interest here is that of a whole composed of interlocked parts, where interlocked parts constrain bodily movement due to the nature of their causal interaction.

A useful first attempt at giving such an account of bodily structure is José Luis Bermúdez's hinge analysis:

> The intuitive idea that I want to capture with this term is the idea of a body part that allows one to move a further body part. Examples of hinges are the neck, the jaw socket, the shoulders, the elbows, the wrists, the knuckles, the finger joints, the leg sockets, the knees, and the ankles. The distinction between moveable and immoveable body parts, together with the concept of a hinge, creates the following picture of how the human body is segmented. A relatively immoveable torso is linked by hinges to five moveable limbs (the head, two legs, and two arms), each of which is further segmented by means of further hinges. (Bermúdez, 1998, p. 155)

According to the hinge analysis, the body is segmented into major divisions by hinges: parts of the body whose role is to enable the movement of other parts. Notably, hinges are the only functionally salient parts (barring perhaps the torso) in the hinge analysis. The parts bounded by hinges correspond, roughly, to conventional body part names (with the exception of noses, ears and the like).

As useful as the hinge analysis may be for its original purpose, it has several shortcomings for an account of how bodily movement is constrained by the nature of the body itself.[20] A first shortcoming of the hinge analysis in this respect is that it fails to highlight the causal properties of other kinds of body parts than a hinge. For example, the rigidity of a body part, or even its length, might be causally efficacious in enabling a bodily movement. A second shortcoming is that the relevant causal interactions are limited to those between hinges and other parts. Barring reason to think otherwise, we ought to allow for causal interactions of various kinds: causal interactions between parts, and not only those due to the properties of hinges; as well as interactions between parts and the entire body, in virtue of the distinctive properties of each. A third shortcoming of the hinge analysis is that it fails to capture the crucial sense in which the unity of the body constrains actions performed with its parts. There is a sense in which parts of the body mutually affect one another to collectively constrain movement possibilities, and we would want an analysis of bodily structure to reflect this.

Using the hinge analysis as a foil, we can provide the following analysis of bodily structure. We can label the elements of a particular bodily movement as parts $\pi_1 - \pi_n$ and the whole that they comprise as ω. Call Π the relation of part–part causal interaction and Ω the relation of part–whole causal interaction. The structure of a body then consists of relations Π and Ω governing ω and $\pi_1 - \pi_n$.

Here is a little more detail to contrast with other possible analyses of bodily structure and to shed light on how the analysis deals with limit cases. One reason for the abstract labeling of parts $\pi_1 - \pi_n$ is to emphasize that these need not correspond to conventional body part names in English or other linguistic partonomies.[21] Rather they correspond to the causally efficacious elements of a particular bodily movement. In the limit case, the parts merely form a mereological sum ω_m, with no significant unity. Such a case is far from the normal case of bodily movement in which parts mutually affect one another in what Andy Clark (1997, chapter 8) calls "continuous reciprocal causation." Mike Wheeler usefully describes the core features as follows:

> This is causation that involves multiple simultaneous interactions and complex dynamic feedback loops, such that (i) the causal contribution of each systemic component partially determines, and is partially determined by, the causal contributions of large numbers of other systemic components, and, moreover, (ii) those contributions may change radically over time. (Wheeler, 2005, p. 260)

Considering the contrast from the limit case, we can say that a whole is unified to the extent that its parts are in continuous reciprocal causal interaction. The central case of a unified whole, w_u, corresponds to the interlocked structure of an animal body, in which parts can exert physical force in virtue of common boundaries. Tensegrity structures form a useful model of the ideal case in which an internally constrained system is formed by a set of continuous tension elements (e.g., muscles and connective tissue) balancing a set of discontinuous compression elements (e.g., bones).[22] But nothing conceptually precludes w_u consisting of partially discrete elements, such as hand-wielded tools and similar artifacts, or even fully discrete elements. Again, though, the extent to which such wholes are unified is determined by the extent to which they would be in continuous reciprocal causal interaction during the execution of a bodily action.

With the account of the unity of the body in action on the table, we can now discern its relevance for AST. And we can do so by returning to the final issue raised against PST at the end of the last section. That issue was that it does not seem sufficient for an experience to represent its subject's location by representing the location of a perspective within a part of the subject. Given that the subject and the perspective are distinct, the two may differ in extensity, and no account is offered as to how the object within which the perspective is embedded is related to the subject as a whole, PST seems to fall short of locating the subject per se. Now, on the face of things, AST might be confronted with its own version of this problem. Consider Schellenberg's expression of the idea that representing an object as the focus of possible action involves a kind of triangulation:

> One represents one's location in a dual mode: the point of origin of perception presents itself as the point of origin for bodily movement. One occupies one position from which one *both* perceives and would act were one to act. (Schellenberg, 2007, p. 621)

But say that a subject's visual experience represents an object from a perspective within her head. Her experience also represents the object as graspable, and the position from which she would act upon the object in grasping it is the current position of her hand, about a meter from her head. It is not clear, then, in what sense one does occupy a single position;

or better: it is not clear in what sense one represents oneself as occupying a single position.

However, the issue is easily resolved by properly appreciating the significance of the fact that the object is represented as the focus of the subject's possible action. To represent an object in this way is not to represent it in relation to a single position from which one perceives and acts. Rather it is to represent it in relation to a single, unified thing from which one perceives and with which one acts.[23] So, the basic account of spatial self-consciousness is this: Perceptual experience can be structured around a perspective, or multiple perspectives, embedded within one or more parts of the perceiver. If an experience represents an object as the focus of possible action, from a perspective that is embedded within a part of her, to the extent that the parts of her body form a unified whole, the experience represents her location, and will be sufficient for thoughts about her location.

7   Being Multiply or Singly Located

This penultimate section will bring out an important theme in the foregoing sections. Observing a distinction between perspectives and subjects reveals the possibility that perceptual experience is complex, in so far as it is structured according to multiple distinct perspectives. According to AST, if perspectivally structured perceptual experience is complex in this way, it is nevertheless unified in a certain respect: one represents oneself as singly located despite there being multiple locations within oneself from which one experiences the world. By contrast, according to PST, if perceptual experience is complex in this way, then it is not unified in that respect: one represents oneself as multiply located, in virtue of there being multiple locations within oneself from which one experiences the world. I take this to be a mark in favor of AST and against PST. What I will attempt to show is how this intuition aligns with a corresponding intuition that there is a contrast between the experience of a subject who experiences the world from multiple, spatially distant bodies and the experience of a subject who experiences the world from a single, spatially unified body. Assuming that there is such a contrast, my aim is to show that AST captures it for the very same reason it captures the intuition that, in the normal case, we represent ourselves as singly located; whereas PST does not capture either intuition, and for the very same reason in each case.

To demonstrate this, let me introduce a pair of imaginary scenarios which share the idea that a single subject might experience the world from multiple displaced objects simultaneously.[24] The first, described by Barry

Dainton (2000, pp. 66–87), involves an imagined subject, call him Barry, who experiences the world audiovisually from an artificial head and tactually from a body (the head of which has been anaesthetized), floating around in a distant sea. Tim Bayne (2010, pp. 262–266) raises a similar scenario that involves imagining a network mind, "Borgy," realized by three individually embodied brains in "wireless" cerebral communication.

Both of these scenarios involve the assumption that a single subject's experience can be structured around perspectives embedded in spatially distant bodies. And both PST and AST will provide similar answers to the question of where Barry and Borgy would represent themselves to be located, but for different reasons. From PST it would follow that Barry and Borgy would represent themselves as multiply located, because they experience the world from distinct perspectives with distinct locations. From AST it would also follow that Barry and Borgy would represent themselves as multiply located. But this would be because, in the cases so described, the multiple bodies of each subject do not causally influence one another such that they might be conceived as an integrated whole. Accordingly, if either Barry or Borgy were to represent objects from each of their distinct perspectives as the focus of possible action, their experience would represent those objects in relation to themselves as multiply located.

I should note that both of these scenarios are described by their authors as cases in which a single subject's *experience* may be unified, despite being structured around distinct bodies. Dainton claims that, in such a scenario, one's experience of the beautiful audiovisual scene at the mountaintop could be unified with a tugging sensation felt on the ankle of the underwater body (Dainton, 2000, pp. 69–70). That is, even though there are "no experienced spatial relations between your bodily experiences and your audio-visual experiences" it could be that "both sets of experiences are nonetheless co-conscious," that is, parts of one unified consciousness (Dainton, 2000, p. 71). Similarly, Bayne claims that despite his unusual constitution, Borgy's visual experience could still be unified. That is, he claims "it is plausible to suppose that [Borgy] could retain phenomenally unified consciousness despite the fact that neither his perceptual experiences nor his bodily sensations will be structured around a single physical object" (Bayne, 2010, p. 263). If you find this convincing, then your conception of unified perceptual experience is such that you can conceive of experiences being unified despite the fact that they are structured around distinct bodies. Nothing I have to say requires this, however. All that is required is the thought that Barry's and Borgy's experience contrasts with that of a subject who experiences the world from perspectives embedded in parts of a single, unified body.

Thus consider Barry United, a subject who experiences the world audio-visually from a head which is part of the same integrated whole as the hands from which he experiences the world tactually. Given that Barry United perceptually experiences the world in various modalities from a single body, it follows from AST that if his auditory, visual, or tactual experience represents an object as the focus of possible action, the experience will represent that object in relation to the single thing that he is. His experience would represent him as singly located in a way that Barry's experience, with his multiple, disunified bodies, would not. PST does not have the means to capture this very contrast, for all that PST can appeal to in an account of the self-locating content of Barry United's experience is its perspectival structure. As Barry United visually inspects a glass that he feels in his hand, he might experience the glass both from a visual perspective embedded within his head and from a tactual perspective embedded within his hand. Just as the perspectival structure of Barry's experience is structured around distinct bodies, the perspectival structure of Barry United's experience involves perspectives embedded in multiple parts of a single body. PST does not then give us any reason to think that Barry United's representation of his location, in virtue of his perceptual experience alone, would be significantly different from Barry's.

A corresponding modification to the Borgy scenario produces similar results. Borgy United is a subject who experiences the world visually from both the head and the chest of a body that forms an integrated whole. It follows from AST that his experience might nevertheless represent him as singly located in a way that Borgy, with his multiple disunified bodies, would not. Borgy United may visually experience the world from two places within himself, but if he represents what he sees as the focus of possible action, then he represents what he sees in relation to himself as a single thing. Once again, though, PST is unable to deliver the conclusion that Borgy United's experience would represent his location as singular in just the sense that Borgy's would not. When Borgy United looks at Buckingham Palace with his torso twisted away from it, it looks to be off to the side from one perspective and straight ahead from another. Just as the perspectival structure of Borgy's experience is structured around distinct bodies, the perspectival structure of Borgy United's experience involves perspectives embedded in the head and the torso of a single body. PST does not then give us any reason to think that Borgy United's representation of his location, in virtue of his perceptual experience alone, would be significantly different from Borgy's. It fails to provide an account of why an experience would represent a single location for a single subject who experiences the world from a single body.

8 Conclusion

Perceptual experience is perspectivally structured, in at least two respects. It has characteristic sensory limitations relative to a given location (limitation structure) and it presents objects as spatially related to a given location (egocentric structure). Perceptual experience is also self-locating, in the sense that an episode of perceptual experience may be sufficient for thoughts about one's location. But not all experience that is perspectivally structured has self-locating content. Moreover, we can individuate the location of a perspective independently of any subject who experiences the world from that perspective. Firmly distinguishing between perspectives and subjects in this way allows us to better to understand their connection in ordinary perceptual experience. Furthermore, it allows us to appreciate that the perspectival structure of perceptual experience is potentially complex, such that one might experience the world from multiple distinct perspectives embedded within one or more parts of oneself. On this basis, I have argued that any account of spatial self-consciousness based upon a simple inference from the perspectival structure of perceptual experience faces serious difficulties.

If this is correct, then we need to look beyond the perspectival structure of perceptual experience in order to account for its self-locating content. The agentive self-location thesis, as developed here, suggests that we look to the relationship between perceptual experience and bodily action, and to the unity of the body in mediating that relationship. This has the virtue of being compatible with the perspectival structure of perceptual experience, in however complex a form it may take. It also has the virtue of showing why we experience ourselves as singly located, despite the possibility that we experience the world from multiple perspectives, embedded within one or more parts of ourselves (or more fancifully, embedded within one or more bodies). In experiencing the world perspectivally, we can experience ourselves as singly located, because we experience the world as something we can potentially engage with as a dynamic unity.

Acknowledgments

Previous versions of this material have been significantly improved by feedback from fellow members of the Finding Perspective project (funded by the Volkswagen Foundation) at a series of events in Tübingen, and audiences at the Phenomenological Research Seminar and Philosophical Research

Colloquium at the University of Copenhagen. Thanks especially to Johan Gersel, Dan Zahavi, Thor Grunbaum, Hong Yu Wong, Thomas Sattig, and Matt Longo for useful discussion at these and other occasions. Frédérique de Vignemont, Alex Byrne, José Luis Bermúdez, and Christopher Peacocke also provided very constructive written comments on earlier drafts, which I hope to have adequately addressed and for which I am in any case very grateful. This work was funded by the Danish Council for Independent Research and the Volkswagen Foundation.

Notes

1. Agentive and intellectual accounts are distinguishable in so far as proponents of the former hold that it is possible to represent the objects one perceives as objects of one's actions without applying any concept of oneself. Though this commitment on the part of an agentive account is, strictly speaking, optional, this is clearly Brewer's (1992) view.

2. The presumed possibility of what Peacocke (2014) calls "degree 0 cases" illustrate some of the difficulties to be faced here. In such a case, there would be a subject capable of perception and action, and thus intentional action on perceived objects, that would not represent itself at all. For a proposal concerning the joint role that representations of actions, the body and its spatiotemporal properties must play in order that a subject may come to represent itself, see Peacocke (this volume). For a somewhat different treatment of the connection between agency and self-representation that instead appeals to a distinctive kind of experience involved in control of one's actions, see O'Brien (2007).

3. See Austen Clark (1996), Martin (1992), and Richardson (2010).

4. See Gibson, Kaplan, Reynolds, and Wheeler (1969).

5. Classic statements are found in Locke (1997, pp. 143–144) and Hume (1960, p. 56), but neither reached the extreme denial of visual experience of the third-dimension tout court associated with Berkeley (see, e.g., Berkeley, 2008, p. 21).

6. See, e.g., Gregory (2013, pp. 33–36) and Peacocke (1992, p. 62).

7. See, e.g., Evans (1982, p. 222), Brewer (1992, p. 17), Cassam (1997, pp. 44–55), Bermúdez (1998, pp. 103–129; 2002), Schellenberg (2007, pp. 619–621), and Peacocke (2001, pp. 215–216; 2008, pp. 101–103).

8. For a selection of cases in which the idea that an experience is perspectivally structured is often bound up with (i.e., not distinguished from) the idea that its content is self-locating, see, for example, Brewer (1992, p. 17), Cassam (1997, pp. 52–53), Zahavi (1999, pp. 92–93), Smith (2002, p. 145), Thompson (2005, p. 411), Schellenberg (2007, p. 619), Noë (2004, pp. 168–169), Gallagher and Zahavi (2008, pp. 141–142), and Bris-

coe (2009, pp. 424–426). I do not take it that all of these authors are committed to PST (for example, Brewer clearly is not), though some of their remarks might suggest it. For cases in which the relevant distinction is entertained, see Peacocke (2001, pp. 219–220; 2008, pp. 101–102; 2014, p. 31), Siegel (2006, p. 358), Gregory (2013, chap. 2), and Schwenkler (2014, pp. 138–140). The distinction is also required to highlight instances of what Peacocke (this volume) calls "the problem of avoiding redundancy" with respect to the transition from "*here*"-thoughts to thoughts genuinely involving the first-person.

9. Schwenkler (2014) responds that certain experiences with a dynamic egocentric structure can only be explained by assuming that their content includes the subject as a relatum. But if the arguments below are sound, then even if perspectival experience has a relational structure, it does not seem to be sufficient for self-locating content.

10. See, e.g., Schellenberg (2007, pp. 620–621).

11. Much of the discussion of these two cases is indebted to Williams (1976).

12. As Williams notes, it is deeply problematic to think that in doing so, Bernardo would be imagining that he himself is Giorgio (Williams, 1976, pp. 44–45). In any case, there is no reason why he would need to do so, for all that is required is that the imagined experience has a subject. Giorgio fulfills that role; there is no reason for Bernardo to do so. In Velleman's (1996) terms, Giorgio is the notional subject of the imagined experience, while Bernardo is the actual subject of the imagining.

13. Note that this is somewhat different to Peacocke's use of the term "anchoring" in his discussion of, e.g., relational spatial concepts being "anchored in subjects." See Peacocke (2014, p. 198).

14. See, e.g., Graziano, Yap, and Gross (1994), and Spence, Pavani, Maravita, and Holmes (2004).

15. Cf. Sherrington (1907, p. 480) on the primacy of the vestibular apparatus in a hierarchical ordering of "proprioceptors," in his original terminology. See also Wong (this volume).

16. Cf. Grush (2000, pp. 67–69) on coordinated egocentric spatial representations ultimately being stabilized with respect to the torso. My thanks to Matt Longo for the wonderful continent–peninsula analogy.

17. Empirical research on spatial representation suggests independent motivation for the head (e.g., Avillac, Denève, Olivier, Pouget, & Duhamel, 2005) and the torso (e.g., Grubb & Reed, 2002; Karnath, Schenkel, & Fischer, 1991). Moreover, systematic measures of intuitions suggest that our conception of ourselves as bodily subjects is vague with respect to bodily location at this level of granularity, picking out either the head or the torso merely as a matter of which is paid attention to first (Alsmith & Longo, 2014).

18. To claim that a subject represents an object of perceptual experience as the focus of her possible action is not to claim that her experience is constituted by her understanding of how what she experiences depends upon what she does (e.g., Noë, 2004). Rather, the implied relationship is somewhat the reverse: certain actions seem possible on the basis of what is perceived. For a nice discussion of the differences here, see Ward, Roberts, and Clark (2010).

19. Naturally, there would typically be a great many such foci. But for ease of discussion I will stick to the idealized case of a single object, rather than full-blown scenes with all the complications of convolved structures, and so on.

20. The original purpose of the hinge analysis was to provide a way of thinking about the relative position of bodily locations in giving an account of the spatial content of bodily experience. For further discussion, see Bermúdez (1998, pp. 154–161) and his contribution to this volume.

21. See, e.g., Brown (1976).

22. For a nice discussion of the kind of tensegrity structure that may be instantiated by the body and its parts, see Turvey and Fonseca (2014).

23. I should further clarify that I am assuming that the subject's experience involves a direct connection between perception and action. I do not mean to imply that the subject represents objects as the focus of her possible action, in virtue of also representing relations Π and Ω governing ω and $\pi_1 - \pi_n$. My thanks to Thomas Sattig for pressing me on this point.

24. Both of these cases owe a debt to the ingenious and thought provoking fictional autobiography of a disembodied brain (or a disembrained body?), recounted in Dennett (1981).

References

Alsmith, A., & Longo, M. (2014). Where exactly am I? Self-location judgements distribute between head and torso. *Consciousness and Cognition, 24*, 70–74. doi:10.1016/j.concog.2013.12.005.

Avillac, M., Denève, S., Olivier, E., Pouget, A., & Duhamel, J.-R. (2005). Reference frames for representing visual and tactile locations in parietal cortex. *Nature Neuroscience, 8*(7), 941–949. doi:10.1038/nn1480.

Bayne, T. (2010). *The unity of consciousness.* Oxford: Oxford University Press.

Berkeley, G. (2008). An essay towards a new theory of vision. In D. M. Clarke (Ed.), *Berkeley: Philosophical writings* (pp. 1–66). Cambridge: Cambridge University Press.

Bermúdez, J. L. (1998). Somatic proprioception and the bodily self. In J. L. Bermúdez (Ed.), *The paradox of self-consciousness* (pp. 131–162). Cambridge, MA: MIT Press.

Bermúdez, J. L. (2002). The sources of self-consciousness. *Proceedings of the Aristotelian Society (Hardback)*, *102*(1), 87–107. doi:10.1111/j.0066-7372.2003.00044.x.

Brewer, B. (1992). Self-location and agency. *Mind*, *101*(401), 17–34.

Briscoe, R. (2009). Egocentric spatial representation in action and perception. *Philosophy and Phenomenological Research*, *79*(2), 423–460. doi:10.1111/j.1933-1592 .2009.00284.x.

Brown, C. H. (1976). General principles of human anatomical partonomy and speculations on the growth of partonomic nomenclature. *American Ethnologist*, *3*(3), 400–424. doi:10.1525/ae.1976.3.3.02a00020.

Campbell, J. (1994). *Past, space, and self*. Cambridge, MA: MIT Press.

Cassam, Q. (1997). *Self and world*. Oxford: Oxford University Press.

Clark, A. (1996). Three varieties of visual field. *Philosophical Psychology*, *9*(4), 477–495. doi:10.1080/09515089608573196.

Clark, A. (1997). Being, computing, representing. In A. Clark (Ed.), *Being there: Putting brain, body, and world together again* (pp. 143–175). Cambridge, MA: MIT Press.

Dainton, B. (2000). *The stream of consciousness: Unity and continuity in conscious experience*. New York: Routledge.

Dennett, D. C. (1981). Where am I? In D. Hofstadter & D. C. Dennett (Eds.), *The mind's I: Fantasies and reflections on self and soul* (pp. 217–229). New York: Basic Books.

Evans, G. (1982). Self-identification. In G. Evans (Ed.), *The varieties of reference*. Oxford: Oxford University Press.

Gallagher, S., & Zahavi, D. (2008). *The phenomenological mind: An introduction to philosophy of mind and cognitive science*. New York: Routledge.

Gibson, J. J., Kaplan, G. A., Reynolds, H. N., & Wheeler, K. (1969). The change from visible to invisible. *Perception & Psychophysics*, *5*(2), 113–116. doi:10.3758/BF03210533.

Graziano, M., Yap, G., & Gross, C. (1994). Coding of visual space by premotor neurons. *Science*, *266*(5187), 1054–1057. doi:10.1126/science.7973661.

Gregory, D. (2013). *Showing, sensing, and seeming: Distinctively sensory representations and their contents*. Oxford: Oxford University Press.

Grubb, J. D., & Reed, C. L. (2002). Trunk orientation induces neglect-like lateral biases in covert attention. *Psychological Science*, *13*(6), 553–556. doi:10.1111/1467-9280.00497.

Grush, R. (2000). Self, world and space: The meaning and mechanisms of ego- and allocentric spatial representation. *Brain and Mind*, *1*(1), 59–92. doi:10.1023 /A:1010039705798.

Hume, D. (1960). *A treatise of human nature, Being an attempt to introduce the experimental method of reasoning into moral subjects* (reprint of the first edition in three volumes). Oxford: Oxford University Press.

Karnath, H. O., Schenkel, P., & Fischer, B. (1991). Trunk orientation as the determining factor of the "contralateral" deficit in the neglect syndrome and as the physical anchor of the internal representation of body orientation in space. *Brain, 114*(4), 1997–2014. doi:10.1093/brain/114.4.1997.

Locke, J. (1997). *An essay concerning human understanding.* London: Penguin.

Martin, M. G. F. (1992). Sight and touch. In T. Crane (Ed.), *The contents of experience: Essays on perception* (pp. 196–215). Cambridge: Cambridge University Press.

Martin, M. G. F. (2002). The transparency of experience. *Mind & Language, 17*(4), 376–425. doi:10.1111/1468-0017.00205.

Noë, A. (2004). *Action in perception.* Cambridge, MA: MIT Press.

O'Brien, L. (2007). *Self-knowing agents.* Oxford University Press.

Peacocke, C. (1992). Perceptual concepts. In C. Peacocke (Ed.), *A study of concepts* (pp. 61–98). Cambridge, MA: MIT Press.

Peacocke, C. (2001). First-person reference, representational independence, and self-knowledge. In A. Brook & R. DeVidi (Eds.), *Self-reference and self-awareness* (pp. 215–245). Philadelphia: John Benjamins.

Peacocke, C. (2008). *Truly understood.* Oxford: Oxford University Press.

Peacocke, C. (2014). *The mirror of the world: Subjects, consciousness, and self-consciousness.* New York: Oxford University Press.

Perry, J. (1986). Thought without representation. *Proceedings of the Aristotelian Society, Supplementary Volumes, 60*, 137–151.

Richardson, L. (2010). Seeing empty space. *European Journal of Philosophy, 18*(2), 227–243. doi:10.1111/j.1468-0378.2008.00341.x.

Schellenberg, S. (2007). Action and self-location in perception. *Mind, 116*(463), 603–632. doi:10.1093/mind/fzm603.

Schwenkler, J. (2014). Vision, self-location, and the phenomenology of the "point of view." *Noûs, 48*(1), 137–155. doi:10.1111/j.1468-0068.2012.00871.x.

Sherrington, C. (1907). On the proprio-ceptive system, especially in its reflex aspect. *Brain, 29*(4), 467–482. doi:10.1093/brain/29.4.467.

Shoemaker, S. S. (1968). Self-reference and self-awareness. *Journal of Philosophy, 65*(19), 555–567. doi:10.2307/2024121.

Siegel, S. (2006). Subject and object in the contents of visual experience. *Philosophical Review, 115*(3), 355–388.

Smith, A. D. (2002). *The problem of perception.* Cambridge, MA: Harvard University Press.

Spence, C., Pavani, F., Maravita, A., & Holmes, N. P. (2004). Multisensory contributions to the 3-D representation of visuotactile peripersonal space in humans: Evidence from the crossmodal congruency task. *Journal of Physiology, 98*(1–3), 171–189. doi: 10.1016/j.jphysparis.2004.03.008.

Thompson, E. (2005). Sensorimotor subjectivity and the enactive approach to experience. *Phenomenology and the Cognitive Sciences, 4*(4), 407–427. doi:10.1007/s11097-005-9003-x.

Turvey, M. T., & Fonseca, S. T. (2014). The medium of haptic perception: A tensegrity hypothesis. *Journal of Motor Behavior, 46*(3), 143–187. doi:10.1080/00222895.2013.798252.

Velleman, J. D. (1996). Self to self. *Philosophical Review, 105*(1), 39–76. doi:10.2307/2185763.

Ward, D., Roberts, T., & Clark, A. (2010). Knowing what we can do: Actions, intentions, and the construction of phenomenal experience. *Synthese, 181*(3), 375–394. doi:10.1007/s11229-010-9714-6.

Wheeler, M. (2005). *Reconstructing the cognitive world: The next step.* Cambridge, MA: MIT Press.

Williams, B. (1976). Imagination and the self. In B. Williams (Ed.), *Problems of the self* (pp. 26–45). Cambridge: Cambridge University Press.

Zahavi, D. (1999). *Self-awareness and alterity: A phenomenological investigation.* Evanston, IL: Northwestern University Press.

13   Philosophical Reflections on the First Person, the Body, and Agency

Christopher Peacocke

We can distinguish three degrees to which a subject's representation of itself may be involved in its conception of the way the world is (Peacocke, 2014). For some subjects, who merely represent events, objects, and processes taking place around what is in fact a perceptual point of origin, there may be no such self-representation in what it represents to be the case. These are subjects who represent the layout of world in a region around them, and some of what is going on there, but who do not represent themselves as being there (or anywhere else). That is what in my book *The Mirror of the World* I called Degree 0 of involvement of self-representation in a subject's conception of the world. At Degree 1, a subject has mental states with first-person content, but only of a nonconceptual kind. For those who admit the notion of nonconceptual intentional content at all, examples of mental states at Degree 1 would be hearing a noise to one's left, remembering climbing the stairs, being aware of raising one's hand. At Degree 2 of involvement of the first person, subjects enjoy mental states containing the first-person concept. This chapter addresses the question: What is required, as a constitutive matter, for a creature to be at Degree 1, to self-represent in a minimal nonconceptual way, as opposed to merely being at Degree 0?

There is a substantive question to address here independently of the framework and commitments in which I have just formulated it. Even if you think, for one reason or another, there are no possible examples of cases at Degree 0, there is still a substantive constitutive question of what it is for a creature to self-represent. The question remains of characterizing Degree 1 cases correctly, in a philosophical manner. Similarly, if you think that all intentional content is conceptual, there is still a substantive constitutive question of what it is for a creature to self-represent, even if the conceptual cases are the only ones you admit.

I think there are aspects of this substantive question about Degree 1 that I did not address in *The Mirror of the World*. In that book, when giving examples of organisms at Degree 0, at which subjects have representational states but do not self-represent, I considered only actions that do not involve bodily movement, do not involve control of location, and do not involve the position of limbs in relation to the rest of the body. I mentioned actions such as change of color or creation of an electric charge around the body of the creature. Those examples still seem fine, but the restricted range of cases I mentioned carried the apparent conversational implicature that if we were to include bodily movement and spatial control of the organism's limbs, we would already be above Degree 0, and have self-representation at Degree 1 or above. But that would not be true. There can be spatial, bodily action that is merely at Degree 0, as was rightly emphasized in Susanna Schellenberg's (2016) contribution to a symposium on *The Mirror of the World*. So the book did not offer, or even suggest, any answer to the question of the nature of the distinction between creatures at Degree 0 that do not self-represent and creatures at higher degrees that do self-represent.

That is the question I will be addressing here. I aim to offer a fuller positive account of Degree 1, and to trace out some of the many consequences of the account offered for the philosophy of mind, for possibilities in the theory of intentional content, for a correct account of the place of the first person in relation to interpersonal phenomena, and of epistemological phenomena involving the first person.

1 The Problem of Avoiding Redundancy

We can introduce the problem by considering a subject who uses an expression "I," but for whom a complete account of what is involved in this use is that this subject accepts, for instance

I am in front of a window

when and only when he accepts

Here [the location of his perceptual point of view] is in front of a window.

Similarly he accepts

There is a tree in that direction from me

when and only when he accepts

There is a tree in that direction from here.

That is, in general he accepts something of the form

I stand in relation R to things and events that are F

when and only when he accepts

Here stands in relation R to things and events that are F.

In this case, the seeming first-person acceptance is just a stylistic variant on the content of the second sentence of each of these pairs. If this is the full account of this person's use of an expression, that expression is not the genuine first person. This use of the expression "I" also does not give any new spatial content, a fortiori, not even by complex inference. It conservatively extends the subject's knowledge of propositions not involving "I." If we want to invoke the spirit of a Kantian point, we could say that this is a purely formal use of "I," it is a "merely logical subject."

The force of the consideration for present purposes is that exactly the same point applies at the level of nonconceptual content. Suppose there is a component c of nonconceptual content for which it is a full account of the subject's grasp of it that

c stands in relation R to things and events that are F

is equivalent to

Here stands in relation R to things and events that are F.

For the same reasons of redundancy, such a nonconceptual component c would not be the genuine nonconceptual first person, what I called i in *The Mirror of the World*.

Exactly parallel points apply to a subject for whom a full account of its use of "I" in

I am lying down

is that it is equivalent to

This body is lying down,

and similarly for whom

My left arm is extended

is equivalent to

This body's left arm is extended;

and more generally for whom it is a full account of their grasp that

I am F

is equivalent to

This body is F.

Again, the same points apply to a component c of nonconceptual content for which the above would be an exhaustive account of its role in a subject's psychological economy. Such a c would not be i.

Such notions as *this body* and *this hand* may be made available to a subject by proprioception of the subject's own body. There are also notions of the body and of limbs that are made available by the fact that the body or the hand in question is under the subject's control in action. A creature can represent something as *this hand*, even when not perceiving it proprioceptively, if the creature can reliably act with the hand in question. It can plan actions with that hand, thus represented. But thinking of a body, or limb, even in an action-based way, still does not by itself involve first-person content. Neither proprioception nor action-based modes of representation of the body and its parts bring a subject into the truth conditions of *this leg is bent*—into its content. The content *this leg is bent*, even based on proprioception, or capacities for action with the leg, or both, is not yet the content *my leg is bent*.

The combined effect of both of these points, about *here* and *this body*, means that it does not suffice for having states with first-person content that one has both an atlas of a world around a body that's *here*, and a history of that same body over time. The atlas and the history do not require more than a *here*, appropriate temporal updating, and perception of a body that's normally at that point of view, with memory of its movements over time.

So the question becomes pressing: What more is required to make a nonconceptual content c the first-person nonconceptual content i? This is equivalent to the question: What is it for an organism to be at Degree 1 of self-representation rather than Degree 0? It is also equivalent to the question: What minimally brings a subject into the (referential) content of a mental state?

A thinker brought up in the Western philosophical tradition may be inclined to smile at this question, and to answer it, almost as a matter of reflex, by saying, "Well, someone who is employing the genuine first person, and not merely something equivalent to *here* or to *this body*, will be able to make sense of the possibility that by some kind of brain transplant he might have had a different body; and similarly he might be representing himself in thought or imagination even when there is no perceptual *here* to get a grip, because the subject is not perceiving the world, but is still conscious." It is true that we can correctly entertain these possibilities and these kinds of thoughts and imaginings, and that using the first person is essential to doing so. But it is wholly implausible that the capacity to entertain these possibilities, thoughts, and imaginings has to be mentioned in a foundational, constitutive account of the nature of the grasp of the first person. Many creatures have mental states with a specifically first person content without the capacity for such sophisticated modal thought. Even when these capacities are present, its seems that their presence, and the genuine possibility of the modal contents entertained, rests on the nature of the first-person component itself. There must be features of the first-person component that make possible these distinctive capacities. Our task is to say what those features are.

2   A Proposal about the Nature of the First Person

It is uncontroversial that there are two different kinds of case in which a content

> This body is moving

can be true. The body in question may be passively moved, as when one is on an elevator, escalator, or on a moving walkway at an airport. In the other case, the subject whose body it is is moving the body, in a case of agency.

I suggest that there are two conditions, each of them necessary, and together jointly sufficient, for a nonconceptual component c of intentional content employed by a creature to be the genuine first person i:

(1) there is a range of action notions A for which the creature must be capable of being in mental states or of enjoying mental events with the content

> c is A-ing

where the state or event is produced by the initiation of an A-ing by the reference of c; and

(2) there is a range of notions F of bodily properties, spatial properties, and past tense properties F such that the creature is capable of being in mental states or enjoying mental events with the content c is F; where in these attributions,

> c is F

is accepted (in central basic cases) if and only if

> this body is F

is also accepted.

The range of notions F of bodily and spatial properties in condition (2) is to be understood as including the merely bodily and spatial properties involved in the creature's falling under one of the action notions A in condition 1, such as the merely bodily property one has when one raises one's arm.

The range of action notions A in condition (1) can include demonstrative notions of actions (*I am doing this*), as well as nondemonstrative notions such as *walking*, as in *I am walking*. Condition (1) links transitory events (initiations, actions) with a continuant, persisting entity, a subject. Certain kinds of binding must be in place for this to be possible.

Condition (1) alone would not be sufficient for a content c to be i. In the absence of condition (2),

c is A-ing

would have as its correctness condition merely that there is an event of A-ing, or that some particular event is an event of A-ing, an event that is in the circumstances an A-ing by the creature itself. That would not be a predication of a continuing entity. States with contents governed only by condition (1), and not by condition (2), could be produced simply by an action awareness, from the inside, of the relevant A-ing. A continuing entity would not be involved in the content itself; the earlier nonredundancy arguments would apply again. The earlier arguments about nonredundancy already show that condition (2) by itself would not be sufficient by itself for c to be i.

As I just implied, condition (1) can be fulfilled by the creature enjoying a distinctive action awareness, in phenomenal consciousness, of its own actions. But that is not the only way. Primitive first-person nonconceptual content is possible for a creature that is not conscious at all. Such a creature may still be an agent (there are probably many such in the universe), and there can be unconscious states with a content, *i am A-ing* that are produced in the creature by the events which cause the action. That content would still be distinct from a content, *i am being moved*, when for instance the creature is passively moved by a strong tide or current in its surrounding water.

If conditions (1) and (2) are severally necessary and jointly sufficient for content c to be the first person, it should not be surprising that the capacity to represent spatial relations, certain bodily properties, and even a bodily and spatial history too, are not sufficient for first-person representation. For none of these capacities involves the ability to represent something that has to have the capacity for agency.

All these considerations support the view that there is a much deeper role of agency in the first person than I indicated in previous writings. Henceforth I call the thesis that conditions (1) and (2) are jointly sufficient for a notion (and corresponding concept) to be that of the first person, *i*, "the agency-involving account."

The agency-involving account has implications for the correct characterization of the functional psychological organization of a creature that self-represents. In *The Mirror of the World*, I argued that the identity of a subject over time depends on the identity of an integrating apparatus. At the subpersonal level, the integrating apparatus operates to a produce a file that contains representations that underlie how the world seems to be to the subject whose integrating apparatus it is. The implication of the agency-involving thesis is that this file is properly labeled a "self-file" only if it includes representations of actions of the subject, where the inclusion of the representation is, in central cases, produced by the subject initiating an action of the type represented. A self-representing subject, a creature at Degree 1 rather than Degree 0, must not only be capable of action, but at least some range of its actions must be connected to representations of action, and to the file that is the output of the integrating apparatus, in the way just described. This requirement was not included or discussed in *The Mirror of the World*.

It is natural to wonder how this agency-involving account is related to the claim—endorsed in *The Mirror of the World*—that the first-person notion, like any other notion or indeed concept, is individuated by its fundamental reference rule. Does the argument above suggest that something more than the fundamental reference rule is involved in the individuation of the first-person notion? And if not, what is the need for all this argument, for can we not answer the question of what it is to be using the first-person notion by saying that it is the notion individuated by the fundamental reference rule that on any occasion of its occurrence in a mental state or mental event, it refers to the subject of that state or mental event?

We can indeed say that. The agency-involving account can rather be seen as an elaboration of what it is involved in the first-person notion's referring to a subject, rather than something else. The discussion above is meant as a contribution to the conditions that have to be fulfilled for a reference rule that mentions a subject as the notion's reference, rather than something else. Supplying further background on what it is for the notion a creature is employing to have one fundamental reference rule rather than another is entirely consistent with the fundamental reference rule's fully individuating the notion. This is a matter of what is involved in attributing the notion with its individuating fundamental reference rule to actual creatures.

In advocating the agency-involving account, I am rejecting a rival kind of experience-involving account. This rival view holds that what makes something the first-person notion *i* is that it is the *c* such that the subject represents it as being the case that

c has this experience

where "this experience" refers to the subject's current experience. There are at least two problems with this proposal. First, this cannot be a necessary condition for a notion to be the first person, because a subject can have representational states with a first-person content without being able to represent its experiences as such at all. The representational states can, for instance, concern the relations in which the subject, represented in the first-person way, stands to things and events around him, without the subject representing the experiences in which those things and events are presented. To be able to represent one's own experiences as such is a much more sophisticated matter than enjoying mental states and events with first-person content. Second, organisms that do not have phenomenally conscious mental states and events at all—perhaps organisms that have only the older, faster, dorsal route that leads to perceptual states—can still have states with first-person content.

These two objections do not apply to the agency-involving account. A subject can be an agent without being able to represent experiences as such. An organism can be an agent even if it has only the older dorsal route that ends in the production of nonconscious perceptual states.

The agency-involving account of the first person is formulated in terms of the capacity for attributing bodily actions. A creature may find itself in circumstances in which it cannot engage in bodily actions, perhaps because its efferent nerves have been blocked. It may still have the capacity for bodily action and action self-ascription when properly connected to the world. But could there be a creature capable only of mental action, action of a kind not fundamentally parasitic on the possibility of bodily action? Though I doubt that is possible, the question of its possibility would require at least a further paper. If there could be such a creature, I think an account of the first person in terms of agency would still be correct. The account would just need not to require that the agency be bodily agency. The possibility of such a case would mean that the reference to bodily agency in the above formulation of the agency-involving account would have to be removed. Many of the consequences of the agency-involving account, including those of the next section, would still apply. Those consequences noted later below that concern bodily action would need to be restricted to those subject using the first person who also enjoy embodiment.[1]

3   Instantiation-Dependence

Under the agency-involving account, a subject's ability to think about itself using the first person is made available by its being a subject, capable of action. A creature is able to represent itself in the first-person way only because it is suitably sensitive to the very events and states involving agency that make it a subject. This is not just a modal claim, but a constitutive claim. There is a way of representing, the first-person way, that in its nature requires what is so represented to be of a certain type (a subject), and requires sensitivity on the part of its possessor to what makes it of that type.

Just as there are phenomenal concepts of phenomenal states made available to a subject by the subject's being in those states, the first-person notion is made available by its user being a subject, capable of agency. Phenomenal concepts—concepts of an experience of red, pain, joy—have the characteristic that grasp of them requires the ability to apply them in response to a very instance of the property they pick out, an instance that is in the concept-user's own consciousness.

We can, in a similar spirit, introduce the idea of an *instantiation-dependent notion*. An instantiation-dependent notion is one whose fundamental reference rule requires its reference to be of a certain kind, and grasp of the notion, for constitutive reasons in the nature of the notion, is possible for a creature only if it is suitably sensitive to it itself being of that kind. In the present case, the kind is that of being a subject. If what I have said is correct, the first-person notion is instantiation-dependent. It is only because the subject is an agent, and its action ascriptions are suitably sensitive to the events that are its actions, that it can meet the conditions for using the first-person notion.

The ways of thinking expressed by a person's use of a personal proper name, such as "Napoleon," or a perceptual demonstrative *that person*, equally require their references to be subjects. But they do not require, purely in virtue of the nature of these ways of thinking, that the subject who is employing them be suitably sensitive, in his representations *Napoleon is thus and so*, or *that person is thus and so*, to the conditions that make the thinker himself a subject. Suppose Napoleon himself is thinking of himself in the third-personal way, as Napoleon (as such a person might well do). In that case, although Napoleon's representations of what Napoleon is doing are sensitive to what makes Napoleon, namely himself, a subject, that is not so purely in virtue of his use of the third-person notion *Napoleon*. The sensitivity depends also on his being Napoleon. By contrast, concerning the sensitivity required of any user of the first person to the states and events that make the user a subject: there is no such dependence on the subject being identical with something given in a third-personal way. The sensitivity to what makes the thinker himself a subject is required simply in virtue of the nature of the first-person notion itself.

These points also illustrate my favorite general thesis in philosophy, the metaphysics-first view, which holds that the metaphysics of a wide range of domains is prior, in the order of philosophical explanation, to a theory of meaning or theory of intentional contents about that domain. My general view is that a correct account of the nature of intentional contents and meanings concerning a given domain always involves the metaphysics of that domain. This involvement of the metaphysics can take two different forms. In metaphysics-first cases, there is genuine philosophical explanatory priority of the metaphysics of the domain. In no-priority cases, which would include certain social and legal properties, philosophical explanation of the intentional contents and philosophical explanation of the properties themselves would each involve the other. In the present case, the agency-involving account I have been offering is an example of a metaphysics-first thesis, here applied to the domain of subjects. The metaphysics of subjects, as agents, is explanatorily prior in philosophy to the nature of the first-person notion, and to the nature of the corresponding concept. An account of the nature of the first-person notion needs to refer to subjects as agents, and to the representational states that such agency makes available to subjects.

The case of the first person illustrates the metaphysics-first view in a particularly straightforward way. The basic argument for a general metaphysics-involving view proceeds in two steps. The first step is the principle that any notion or concept is individuated by the relation in which a subject must stand to something to be representing it under that notion or concept. The second step is that the relations in which a subject can stand to something are constrained by the correct metaphysics of that thing. If the agency-involving account of the first person is correct, the relations in which a thinker must stand to something to be representing it in the first-person way involve a sensitivity of its action ascriptions to the precursors of actions by that very thing. There is a level of action by a subject, the actions that are possible even at Degree 0, to which a subject's action ascriptions can be so sensitive. It is because there is a genuine possibility of a subject that perceives and acts, but does not yet self-represent, that the metaphysics-first view can be shown to be applicable in the domain of subjects and the first person.[2]

Perhaps the fact that the first-person notion and concept are instantiation-dependent can make understandable, and even partially justify, the idea of some writers that a special mode of acquaintance with its reference underlies the ability to employ the first person (see for example, Kripke, 2011). When acquaintance is construed as a causal notion, I have objected to that claim in *The Mirror of the World* (Peacocke, 2014, chap. 4, sec. 3). The hapless Cartesian subject who is deceived by the evil demon may have many beliefs about himself that are not caused by his being as those beliefs represent him to be. This hapless subject can still be using the first person to think about himself, even though he cannot use perceptual demonstratives to refer to things. If, however, we construe the kind of relation a subject can have to his own actions as a mode of acquaintance, such a mode of acquaintance with oneself is, on the present view, involved in the capacity for first-person representation. On the account I have been proposing, agency-based acquaintance does indeed have a special role to play in an account of first-person representation. The point may be a resource for elaborating the ideas of some of those wanting to give a special place to acquaintance and to being a subject in an account of the first person.

4   Consequences of the Agency-Involving Thesis

Consequence 1: Predicative Transfer and Its Ramifications
The agency-involving account implies a certain functional organization of a subject at Degree 1. Consider a subject at Degree 1 who represents it as being the case that

> this body is next to a ravine

where "this body" is a notion made available by proprioception, and refers to what is the subject's own body (not represented as such, of course, by the notion "this body"). Unlike the subject at Degree 0, the subject at Degree 1 will make a transition from representation of the displayed content as holding to representing it as being the case that

> i am next to a ravine.

This is a nontrivial transition, unlike the status it is accorded in the treatment considered at the outset of this article. It is nontrivial precisely because the first-person component of the second content has agency-involving and hence subject-involving connections that are not implicated in the first content itself. Here we have what we can call predicative transfer from predications involving *this body* to those involving the nonconceptual first person *i*. There will equally, for subject at Degree 1, be predicative transfer for representations concerning *here*, where that refers to subject's perceptual point of view. From

>   here is in the shade

the subject at Degree 1 will make the transition to

>   *i* am in the shade.

Such transitions, both at the nonconceptual and at the conceptual level, thus connect spatial representations about the body with the subject's desires, emotions, and intentions, when the subject also has the capacity to self-ascribe these mental states.

Consequence 1 opens up an explanation of the possibility of perceptual experiences with first-person content in which the subject does not perceive herself. From Consequence 1, it follows that when a subject at Degree 1 has a perception with the content

>   that object is coming toward here

such a subject will also represent, and may perceive, it as being the case that

>   that object is coming toward me.

But of course a subject can perceive something as coming toward here without perceiving any part of her body at all, either in proprioception, or by ordinary external perception of her limbs and body parts. In such a case, the subject can perceive that something is coming toward her, without perceiving her body in any way at all.

Consequence 2: The Metaphysics of First-Person Ownership

What makes a body mine is that it is, in normal circumstances and when all is functioning properly, the body whose movements I control. Some would elaborate this further by saying that it is the body controlled by my tryings.[3] Whether elaborated in terms of tryings or not, this statement about what makes a body mine is in itself entirely neutral on the metaphysics of ownership. The statement simply links ownership itself—not representation of ownership—with the first person, and with tryings if the statement is so elaborated. When however this statement is combined with the agency-involving account of the first person, we have a metaphysics-first account of ownership. For under the agency-involving account, what makes something the first-person notion can be explained in terms of a certain kind of sensitivity of the subject's first-person representations to the precursors of action, where action and the precursors of action are not explained in terms of the first-person notion. Actions and the precursors of action, and indeed in my view even the ownership of a body by a subject, can be present at Degree 0. They can all be elucidated without mention of the first-person notion, without the subject whose actions they are possessing the first-person notion at all.

Subjects who represent themselves, often reliably and knowledgeably, as agents of particular actions, and as owning body parts, succeed in doing so because of the systematic relation of their notions of themselves, of action, of ownership, to this metaphysically prior level of agency that does not need to involve the first person. Misrepresentations and illusions of ownership, as in the rubber hand illusions, are illusions that, for instance, the rubber hand is part of a body largely under one's own control.

Consequence 3: Individuation without Everyday Knowledge of What Individuates

We are faced with an interesting and potentially puzzling combination. What makes for the identity of a particular subject over time is identity of integrating apparatus (as I argued in *The Mirror of the World*), together, as I would now add, with an action-initiation apparatus. But of course the first person does not refer to this complex subpersonal apparatus. Nor does the ordinary user of the first person, whether their first person is nonconceptual or conceptual, need to have any conception or knowledge of this apparatus. Yet on the other hand, there must be something about the representing subject that makes it the case that in perception, registration, knowledge, memory, and the rest, the representing subject is latching onto a subject or person, rather than a mere body, or a mere point of view in space.[4]

I suggest that what makes it so is the constitutive link of the first person with representation of its own actions, as outlined in the agency-involving account of the first person. Only a subject with an integrating apparatus and action-initiation component can be the producer of an action. A point of view in space cannot be the producer. Insofar as it makes sense to say that a body is the producer of the action, that can mean only that the subject whose body it is, is the producer. The constitutive link of the first person with agency means that the first person must refer to something whose identity condition over time involves an integration apparatus and associated action-initiation apparatus.

I suggest also that it is the constitutive link of the first person with the representation of agency that is the ultimate source of our temptation, mentioned earlier, to cite the possibility of brain transplants when we initially object to attempts to identify *i* and *this body*. Ordinary thinkers do not need to have contemplated or to have taken a stance on such possibilities for their first-person notion to be distinct from notions like *this body*. Ordinary thinkers' use of the first person respects the constraints formulated in the agency-involving account. The agency-involving account is inextricably involved with the existence of a subpersonal action-initiation component. A subject's integration apparatus and action-initiation component are preserved if her brain is connected to a new body. The first-person intelligibility of a subject's own persistence without persistence of what *this body* refers to is something founded in the agency-involving nature of subjects, and in the agency-involving nature of the first person, rather than having some kind of primitive modal intelligibility on its own.

Consequence 4: The First Person without the Intersubjective, the Second Person, or the Social

The agency-involving account of the first person bears on the position of such diverse thinkers as G. H. Mead (1967) and Jean-Paul Sartre (1992) that there is no conception of self as object until a subject is involved in social relations of one kind or another. Mead is in my view convincing in his insistence that thought and perception concerning the body is not yet representation that involves the first person. "The self has the characteristic that it is an object to itself, and that characteristic distinguishes it from other objects and from the body" (Mead, 1967, p. 136). Mead's own positive view is that "it is impossible to conceive of a self arising outside of social experience" (1967, p. 140), and that "the language process is essential for the development of the self" (1967, p. 135). The agency-involving conception of the first person suggests that the positive claims of Mead are much too strong. The agency-involving account employs materials that do not make any mention of either social relations or language.

Sartre says that uses of the first person that seem to be independent of a subject's involvement in relations with other persons can all be understood as really reference to the body—"Body as illusory fulfillment of the I-concept," as he entitled one table in his book *The Transcendence of the Ego* (Sartre, 2004, p. 90). But as I argued above, uses of the first person in contents whose truth involves agency of the subject cannot be understood in purely bodily terms. There can be rich and extensive such attributions of agency without a subject participating in any social world at all.

The fact that there is no explicit mention of the social in the agency-involving account does not of course exclude the possibility that what it mentions does require, in less obvious ways, some relation to a social world. One claim for such less obvious involvement is that anyone capable of mental states with first-person content must be capable of being corresponding states with third-person content, states that attribute actions, for example. Gareth Evans's (1982) Generality Constraint, with its Strawsonian origins, and perhaps considerations of recombinability, might be cited in support of this claim. But those principles apply only to conceptualized content, not to nonconceptual content.[5] Though it is also a matter for a different paper, the nature of nonconceptual content, and the attributional, quasipredicative contents it involves, are answerable to explanatory roles that do not need to involve the generality and recombinability that are distinctive of conceptual content, meaning, and judgment.

I am thus inclined to conclude that a full account of the nature of what is involved in possessing the notion of the first person at Degree 1 undermines the thesis that interpersonal relations must be involved in first person representation. The Mead–Sartre arguments are but a small sample of the arguments that have actually been canvassed, and might plausibly be canvassed, for that thesis. All such arguments merit a detailed consideration that is not possible here. Nonetheless, I think that the agency-involving characterization of the nature of the first person tells against all of them.

This conclusion may make it seem that a good theory of the first person has nothing to contribute to a philosophical understanding of intersubjective relations and our conception of many minds. The very next consequence of the action-involving theory, Consequence 5, however, implies that that is not so.

Consequence 5: Links with Other Minds and Interpersonal Interactions
Despite Consequence 4 above, the agency-involving account of the first person connects it with resources that contribute to the explanation of our access to features of the minds of others; to the explanation of the character of our psychological ascriptions to others; and to the explanation of properties of an agent's interactions with other subjects, once a subject does have a conception of other minds.

There are at least two ways in which the agency-involving account bears on the possession of the conception of multiple subjects. One point of contact concerns the range of predications made of other subjects, and the resources that aid in rationally making such predications that are available even in advance of possession of a conception of many subjects. The other

point of contact concerns the conception of the nature of those other subjects themselves.

We can consider the first point of contact, on the range of predications
made rationally of other subjects. Events that are the subject's own actions
can be represented in ways that involve both action and perception, as in
the phenomena so extensively discussed by the mirror-neuron theorists
(for an overview, see Iacoboni, 2008). A subject can perceive what is in
fact the action of another subject, and know exactly how to perform such
an action himself, without inference at the personal level. Similarly, if the
subject himself acts in a certain way, he can perceive whether some action
on the part of another is of the same kind as he has just performed. When
events are so represented in this unified action–perception way by a subject
capable of first-person representation, that subject will be capable of seeing
events that are actions, but actions performed by others rather than himself, as actions, at least with a teleology. This subject may not yet possess
a conception of many subjects, but has already made a crucial step toward
it. If this subject wonders what unifies and explains these events over time,
occurring in a given body, the answer will be the presence of a subject, of
the same general kind as he is. In connecting grasp of the first person with
agency, the agency-involving account contributes to an explanation of the
significance of the resources available even in advance of possession of
the conception of many minds, resources for an explanation both of possible modes of acquisition of the conception of many minds, and of some
of the relations between levels once the conception is acquired. In fact,
in the case of humans, there is extensive evidence that even quite young
children expect events that are actions not merely to have a teleology—a
goal—but also to be produced by an agent (Carey, 2009, chap. 5). What the
present remarks imply is that when the subject does have the conception
of many minds, events that are perceived in the unified action–perception
way, available in advance of the conception of multiple subjects, can give
reasons for making action ascriptions to other minds.

The position I have just been outlining has a complex and interesting
relation to Vittorio Gallese's (2005) important conception of a shared manifold of intersubjectivity, provided by the content of unified action–perception representations of events. Gallese writes, "it is by means of this shared
manifold that we recognize other human beings as similar to us" (2005,
p. 115). I wholly agree; for Gallese's work can be seen as an elaboration of the
underlying representational states and formats that can sustain the points
of the previous paragraph. Gallese also says that the representational format
underlying unified action–perception representation of events meets the

condition that there be an "indifference of the representational format to the peculiar perspective spaces from which referents project their content; in other words, indifference to self-other distinctions" (2005, p. 107). It is true that representations underlying the unified action–perception way of representing an event can be applied both to one's own action and to those of others. We do, however, need to distinguish between the self/other distinction and the self/nonself distinction. To say that the shared intersubjective manifold contributes to our grasp and application of the self/other distinction is not to say that it contributes to our grasp and application of the self/nonself distinction. According to the agency-involving account of the first person, we do not need to invoke the shared manifold—the unified action–perception ways of representing events—in an account of first-person representation. On the agency-involving account as I have developed it, a subject can enjoy self-representation without other-representation. In fact, one can, to use Gallese's language, recognize other human beings as similar to oneself only if one already has some grasp of the first person. The agency-involving account specifies the nature of that prior grasp of the first person.

Let us consider a subject who employs the first person, even the conceptual first person, in thought. This subject may employ predicative concepts, true or false of particular events, such as *is a raising of a hand, is a reaching for a cup*, and these concepts may have the unified action–perception character we mentioned. These predicative concepts may, however, require for their satisfaction only that the events in question have a certain teleology, a goal-directed explanation, and not require that they be produced by a continuant agent, with a past and all the other structures normally involved in agency. For such concepts, we should not identify the contents *I'm A-ing* that the agency-involved account says are essential to the first person with the occurrence of such a merely teleologically specified event of *A*-ing in the body of the subject. There can be such an event without it's being an action of *A*-ing on the part of the subject. The phenomena of anarchic hand, illustrated by Dr. Strangelove's Nazi salutes, exemplifies this possibility (for discussion and further references, see Marcel, 2003). Real events of anarchic hand, such as undoing a series of buttons on the shirt the agent is wearing, contrary to the intentions—and to the immediately preceding actions of the subject in doing up the buttons—evidently have a teleology. The anarchic hand is a hand of the subject's body; but that does not make the undoing of the buttons one of the subject's actions. "*I'm* not undoing the buttons, it's not under my control, this wretched hand is doing it on its own," would be a true utterance by the unhappy subject suffering from anarchic hand. The upshot of this point is that the sense in which a subject enters the truth conditions of the action–predication *I'm A-ing* goes far beyond the occurrence of an event with the characteristic teleology of *A*-ings occurring with the participation of the agent's body.

In one of the later chapters of *The Mirror of the World*, I emphasized that capacities for certain kinds of self-consciousness can combine with other capacities to explain a certain kind of intellectual achievement on the part of the subject.[6] I suggest that a subject who has perspectival self-consciousness, and grasps the first person, already has the resources rationally to make other-ascriptions, even if he has not yet reached the point of marshaling those resources in that service. To oversimplify in ways that do not matter here, to be perspectivally self-conscious is to be capable of thinking of oneself, as such, as someone who is given in a way that is also third personal. Such a person may see a subject who is fact himself acting, and not realize it is himself. When he does gain the further information that the person given in a third-personal way is himself, he is in a position to see that he had a basis for ascribing a genuine action, of a subject, to someone presented in a third-personal way. Since someone presented in that third-personal way need not be him, this basis is a basis for genuine other-attributions of actions (and not merely events with a teleology). For a subject who is perspectivally self-conscious, and who also enjoys the unified action–perception ways of representing events, the move from self-attribution to other-attribution is no huge leap.

The other point of contact of the agency-involving account with the conception of many subjects concerns our thought about the nature of those subjects. This contact exists both at the constitutive level, and as an epistemological matter. According to the constitutive account that I offered in *Truly Understood* (Peacocke, 2008), to think of something as a subject is to think of that subject as something of fundamentally the same kind as oneself. To think of multiple subjects is to think of multiple entities of fundamentally the same kind as oneself. This gives the first person a constitutive place in the account of thought about other minds. Now if other subjects are conceived of the same general kind as me, and thinking of oneself involves conceiving of oneself as an agent, it follows that our thought about other subjects is thought about them as agents. This I would argue is indeed the basic form of perception of another as a subject, namely, as an agent. Our interaction with other subjects, in conversation, in contact attention, in joint activities and the formation of joint attitudes, is interaction with them as agents.

The constitutive role of the first person in thought about subjects in general can help to explain why the first person has a special role to play in the epistemology of attribution of mental states and events to other subjects. The first person has a distinctive epistemological role under the "like me" thesis of Andrew Meltzoff (2007), according to which a basic way of coming to know propositions about other subjects involves appreciating that they are like oneself. If to be a subject is to be of the same fundamental kind as me, then attributing mental states and events to others in accordance with an overarching principle that they are like me has a default reasonableness.

Consequence 6: Explanation and Unification of the Epistemology of Bodily and Mental Events Involving the First Person

The epistemological phenomena I have in mind pivot around what in earlier writing I called "the use of 'I' as agent" (Peacocke, 2007, p. 370). A use of "I" as agent is a use in a self-ascription that is made simply by the thinker taking her apparent action awareness, with its content *I'm A-ing now*, at face value. We need to explain why there is a use of the first person as agent in which, when so used, it is immune to error through misidentification in essentially Shoemaker's sense (1984b). (For the specialists, this is more strictly a case of immunity that is de facto and holds in normal and nearby possible circumstances.) Judgments in which there is a use of the first person as agent are also cases of knowledge. We also need to explain how it can be that there is such a diversity of cases of use of the first person that display this immunity to error through misidentification. The diverse uses include cases of self-ascription of bodily action; self-predications of bodily posture and states; self-predications based on spatial and temporal perception of the layout of one's environment, with a content concerning the subject's relation to events and objects therein; and self-ascriptions of such mental actions as judgments, decisions, inferences, and calculations.

On the agency-involving account of the first person as developed here, self-ascription of bodily agency is constitutively involved in possession of the first person. Such bodily self-ascriptions are knowledge when they are made on the basis of action awareness of the very bodily action self-ascribed. One way of explaining their status as knowledge is to cite the link between judging in accordance with the possession condition for a concept and knowledge of a content containing that concept. It is a plausible general principle, with a rationale in the theory of conceptual content, that coming to make a judgment in accordance with the possession condition for a concept in the content yields knowledge of that content (Peacocke, 1992). One could equally argue for this epistemological point from the fundamental reference rule for the first person, once it is recognized that the subject to which the first person refers must be an agent.

It is also a motivated part of the agency-involving account that the subject at Degree 1 or above who employs the first person also makes bodily ascriptions not necessarily involving action using that very first person notion. As we said, the basis for the latter ascriptions are such matters as bodily perception that can be present even for a subject at Degree 0. The subject experiencing proprioceptive states, and making bodily ascriptions by the means of predicative transfer outlined above, will be the same subject that makes the action ascriptions mentioned in the agency-involving account. So it is certainly no accident that, under that account, there are knowledgeable self-ascriptions both of actions and of bodily postures that are immune to error through misidentification. A similar point applies to the immunity to error through misidentification of spatial predications such as *I am on a bridge*, given the sufficiency, again by transfer of predicates, of *here*-perceptions for first-person predications.

If in general apparent action awareness with a content *I'm A-ing* in normal circumstances provides an entitlement to make a knowledgeable judgment that I'm *A*-ing, the point applies equally to the self-ascription of mental actions. When made on the basis of action awareness, self-ascriptions of judgments, decisions, inferences, calculations, suppositions, and other mental events are similarly immune to error through misidentification. The agency-involving account of the first person unifies our epistemological access to our own bodily and mental actions.

Acknowledgments

The first version of this material was written in Copenhagen the day before its presentation at the workshop in December 2015 on *The Body and the Self* organized by Adrian Alsmith and Frédérique de Vignemont. Frédérique's diplomatic, persistent, and effective prodding made me produce that first version. I learned from the general discussion, and in particular from the remarks of my commentator, José Luis Bermúdez, and from the observations of Patrick Haggard and Frédérique de Vignemont at the Copenhagen meeting. An expanded version was presented at the Harvard Workshop on Self-Knowledge in March 2016. At that meeting, I was helped by the comments of Matthew Boyle, Richard Moran, and Lucy O'Brien. At several meetings in London in the summer of 2016, I benefited from further comments from Patrick Haggard, Anthony Marcel, Michael Martin, and Hong Yu Wong. Issues very closely related to those addressed here are pursued in the Symposium on *The Mirror of the World*, see *Analysis*, volume 76, issue 3, published in 2016. The text above has been influenced by reflections on the contributions to that symposium made by Naomi Eilan, Karen Neander, and Susanna Schellenberg. I thank also the editors and an anonymous referee for helpful suggestions.

Notes

1. Two writers who have emphasized the importance of agency in first-person representation are Bill Brewer (1992) and Lucy O'Brien (2007, chap. 5). There are important insights in both these contributions. I may differ from Brewer in holding that there can be objective representation at Degree 0, and from O'Brien in holding that awareness is not required for first-person representation.

2. Here of course I am no longer giving answers to the opening question of this chapter that are neutral on whether examples at Degree 0 are possible. Prima facie, for someone who rejects the possibility of examples at Degree 0, the case of subjects and the first person will be a case in which the metaphysics-first view is not correct. The general characterization of such cases is that they are ones in which a subject's relation to elements of an ontology is not explanatorily prior to intentional contents and meanings concerning that ontology. This general characterization of the cases in which the metaphysics-first view does not hold is implicit in the very argument, outlined in the text, for the metaphysics-first view.

3. For further discussion, see Shoemaker's important paper "Embodiment and Behavior" (1984a).

4. "So we are grasped by what we cannot grasp" (Rilke)—or at least by what in everyday life we do not need to grasp.

5. Some of the arguments for recombinability and generality are clearly restricted to judgment and to the level of nonconceptual content. See *A Study of Concepts* (Peacocke, 1992, chap. 2).

6. See for instance the discussion of the way in which perspectival self-consciousness and reflective self-consciousness can combine to explain the operation of what Bernard Williams called "the absolute conception" (Peacocke, 2014, chap. 9, sec. 4).

References

Brewer, B. (1992). Self-location and agency. *Mind*, *101*(401), 17–34.

Carey, S. (2009). *The origin of concepts*. New York: Oxford University Press.

Evans, G. (1982). *The varieties of reference*. Oxford: Oxford University Press.

Gallese, V. (2005). "Being like me": Self-other identity, mirror neurons, and empathy. In S. Hurley & N. Chater (Eds.), *Perspectives on imitation: From neuroscience to social science* (Vol. 1, pp. 101–118). Cambridge, MA: MIT Press.

Iacoboni, M. (2008). *Mirroring people: The new science of how we connect with others.* New York: Farrar, Strauss, and Giroux.

Kripke, S. (2011). The first person. In *Philosophical troubles: Collected papers* (Vol. 1, pp. 292–321). New York: Oxford University Press.

Marcel, A. (2003). The sense of agency: Awareness and ownership of action. In J. Roessler & N. Eilan (Eds.), *Agency and self-awareness* (pp. 48–93). Oxford: Oxford University Press.

Mead, G. H. (1967). *Mind, self, and society: From the standpoint of a social behaviorist.* C. Morris (Ed.), Chicago: University of Chicago Press.

Meltzoff, A. (2007). The "like me" framework for recognizing and becoming an intentional agent. *Acta Psychologica, 124*(1), 26–43. doi:10.1016/j.actpsy.2006.09.005.

O'Brien, L. (2007). *Self-knowing agents.* Oxford: Oxford University Press.

Peacocke, C. (1992). *A study of concepts.* Cambridge, MA: MIT Press.

Peacocke, C. (2007). Mental action and self-awareness. In J. Cohen & B. McLaughlin (Eds.), *Contemporary debates in the philosophy of mind* (pp. 358–376). Malden, MA: Blackwell.

Peacocke, C. (2008). *Truly understood.* Oxford: Oxford University Press.

Peacocke, C. (2014). *The mirror of the world: Subjects, consciousness, and self-consciousness.* Oxford: Oxford University Press.

Sartre, J.-P. (1992). *Being and nothingness: A phenomenological essay on ontology* (H. Barnes, Trans.). New York: Washington Square Press.

Sartre, J.-P. (2004). *The transcendence of the ego: A sketch for a phenomenological description* (S. Richmond, Trans.). Abingdon: Routledge.

Schellenberg, S. (2016). *De se* content and *de hinc* content. *Analysis, 76*(3), 334–345. doi:10.1093/analys/anw019.

Shoemaker, S. (1984a). Embodiment and behavior. In S. Shoemaker (Ed.), *Identity, cause, and mind: Philosophical essays* (pp. 113–138). Cambridge: Cambridge University Press.

Shoemaker, S. (1984b). Self-reference and self-awareness. In S. Shoemaker (Ed.), *Identity, cause, and mind: Philosophical essays* (pp. 6–18). Cambridge: Cambridge University Press.

14   In and Out of Balance

Hong Yu Wong

With the sense of balance, the philosophy of perception reaches its outer boundaries. Either seen as a desert or tropical rainforest, desolate or resplendent yet treacherous, few have ventured there before. It is no philosopher's land. Aristotle did not include balance on his list of senses. Like another prominent exclusion from Aristotle's list, proprioception, balance seems to be everywhere and nowhere at once. Everywhere, because balance appears to be omnipresent and affects all aspects of behavior. Nowhere, because outside of episodes of dizziness and vertigo, balance, for the most part, does not seem to feature in lived experience. Like proprioception and other bodily senses, balance is a sense that one cannot turn off. One can close one's eyes, cover one's ears, hold one's nose, and shut one's mouth, but short of destroying one's vestibular labyrinths, the sense of balance is always operative.

Different reasons may have contributed to the neglect of balance. First, it is not a sense that we have voluntary control over. Second, it does not appear to provide a field or space where perceptual objects can be presented (Shoemaker, 1994). Third, one cannot turn it off. And, fourth, it seems to function largely outside consciousness. If we consider Grice's (1989) four criteria for individuating the senses—(1) proper sensibles, (2) proprietary phenomenology, (3) form of energy transduced, and (4) dedicated mechanisms—the vestibular system appears to already create problems. It has dedicated mechanisms, yet seems to be highly multisensory, and appears to either have no phenomenology at all or no proprietary phenomenology.

The vestibular system provides much philosophical food for thought. I will provide an overview of the vestibular system and argue that it relates self, body, and world.

1   Mechanism: Behind Balance

The vestibular system is engineered to answer two basic practical questions: (1) "Which way is up?" and (2) "Where am I heading?" How does the vestibular system do this? The vestibular labyrinths are situated in the inner ear and consist of two functional units: three semicircular canals, which sense changes in angular acceleration, and two otolithic organs, the utricle and the saccule, which sense changes in linear acceleration and gravity (see fig. 14.1).

The bilateral symmetry of the vestibular labyrinths allows the two labyrinths conjointly to measure angular acceleration about any axis and linear acceleration along any axis. Both the semicircular canals and otolithic organs detect accelerations through the inertia of their internal contents, which modulates the firing of afferent nerves. Angular accelerations generated by either active or passive rotatory motions, including the turning or tilting of the head, rotatory body movements, or turning movements during locomotion, are detected by the semicircular canals. Because the

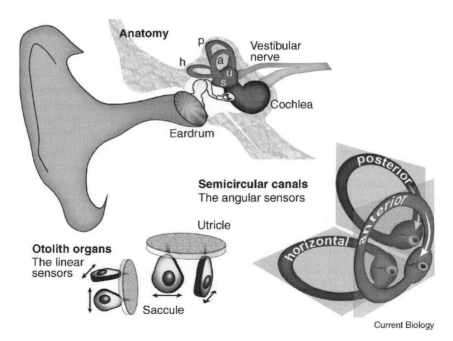

Figure 14.1
The vestibular organs (from Day & Fitzpatrick, 2005, reprinted with permission).

three semicircular canals in each labyrinth are located at right angles to each other, they can resolve rotation in any direction. Linear accelerations, which derive both from active and passive motions of the body and from gravity, are detected by the two otolithic organs, the utricle and the saccule. Because the utricle and saccule are located at right angles to each other, the overall pattern of receptor discharge encodes the direction of linear acceleration in three dimensions, while the firing rate encodes the magnitude of linear acceleration.[1]

2   Sense: Balance as a Sense

The peripheral and central mechanisms of the vestibular system allow us to mark four ways in which it differs from other more familiar senses.

Constancy: Unlike the other senses, vestibular afferents are continuously active even when we are motionless. Vestibular afferents continuously signal the gravitational force and do not adapt (Day & Fitzpatrick, 2005).

Silence: The constancy of the vestibular system may have consequences for the phenomenology of balance. Day and Fitzpatrick express the scientific consensus: "There is no overt, readily recognizable, localisable, conscious sensation from [the vestibular] organs. They provide a silent sense" (Day & Fitzpatrick, 2005, p. R583).

Absoluteness: Also unlike other senses the vestibular system allows for an absolute frame of reference for self-motion, in particular, absolute head motion in a head-centered frame of reference (Berthoz, 2000). (By self-motion, I mean motion of the subject regardless of whether it is active and passive, including whole body motion and head motion.) This is because the inertial frame of reference of the sensory cells is head-centered and does not depend on any external reference. This is unlike motion coding by other sensory modalities, which compares relative motion of the body and external objects or references. This is why one can experience visual vection (Mach, 1875), the illusion of self-motion due to the perception of background visual motion. The experience of visual vection is probably familiar from situations of sitting on a stationary train and seeing an adjacent train move. In contrast, self-motion coding by the vestibular system is absolute.

Multimodality: Finally, though the vestibular organs form a dedicated receptor system for gravity and self-motion, vestibular information and vestibular processing in the central nervous system is highly multisensory almost immediately (Angelaki & Cullen, 2008). Early on, vestibular signals are merged with visual, tactile, proprioceptive, and eye movement signals in the vestibular nuclei complex. All cortical areas involved in vestibular processing are multimodal, involving integration of vestibular, visual, tactile, and proprioceptive signals. The multisensory character of vestibular processing is mirrored in the neuroanatomy of the vestibular system. Unlike the other senses, there is neither a thalamic nucleus dedicated solely to vestibular processing nor a primary vestibular cortex (Grüsser, Guldin, Mirring, & Salah-Eldin, 1994; Lopez & Blanke, 2011). Rather, vestibular processing involves a highly distributed cortical network, with key areas in humans including the posterior insula and temporoparietal junction, the posterior parietal cortex, the somatosensory cortex, the anterior insula, and the premotor cortex.[2]

The multisensory character of vestibular processing can be seen as answering a functional demand. There is a need for vestibular information for a very wide range of functions, starting with reflexes for gaze stability and postural stability to motor control and the highest forms of perception and cognition. The multisensory character of vestibular processing is seen as another reason for the "silence" of the vestibular system (Angelaki & Cullen 2008, p. 126).

3 Pathologies: Out of Balance

The importance of the vestibular system is apparent when we reflect on pathologies of balance.[3] Pathologies provide us with a window on normal function. Typical vestibular disorders include benign positional vertigo (a displacement of the otoliths), labyrinthitis (infection), Ménière's disease (a hearing-related endolymphatic disorder), and loss of labyrinthine function (Baloh, Honrubia, & Kerber, 2010). What is life like when the sense of balance is compromised? Symptoms include dizziness, vertigo, disorientation, feeling imbalanced, blurry or double vision, and behavioral consequences, such as loss of balance, nausea, vomiting, and falls.

Dizziness and vertigo are key symptoms of vestibular disease. "Dizziness" is a notoriously evasive term. Baloh, Honrubia, and Kerber report that:

> The variety of symptoms that patients label as "dizziness" is large and includes visualized spinning of the environment, other types of movement of the environment (e.g., bouncing, rocking), "internal" movement sensations (i.e., movement sensation but no visualized movement of the environment), light-headedness, near-faint, unsteadiness standing or walking, disorientation or confusion, or even anxiety. (Baloh, Honrubia, & Kerber, 2010, p. 127)

And, they characterize vertigo as "an illusion of movement, usually that of rotation, although patients occasionally describe a sensation of linear displacement or tilt" (Baloh, Honrubia, & Kerber, 2010, p. 128). Vertigo is paroxysmal, occurring in episodes that begin abruptly.

The pathophysiology of vestibular symptoms is complex. The severity of the symptoms varies depending on the vestibular lesion, but is mostly due to either asymmetric operation of the bilateral vestibular receptors or the failure of vestibular-triggered reflexes. A key difference is between peripheral unilateral and bilateral vestibular lesions. After acute peripheral unilateral vestibular deafferentation, lower mammals initially cannot walk and develop postural and muscular irregularities. In humans, acute unilateral vestibular deafferentation is "dramatic and debilitating." Patients suffer "severe vertigo and nausea, are pale and perspiring, and usually vomit repeatedly." Patients are incapacitated, preferring to "lie quietly in a dark room but can walk if forced to (falling toward the side of the lesion)." In contrast, in bilateral vestibular deafferentation, patients "usually do not complain of vertigo, but they do report visual blurring or oscillopsia [= a condition where stationary objects are illusorily perceived as in motion] with head movements and instability when walking at night (due to loss of vestibulo-ocular and vestibulospinal reflex activity)" (Baloh, Honrubia, & Kerber, 2010, chap. 5).

In a physician's autobiographical account of his complete peripheral vestibular deafferentation and subsequent recovery, Crawford (1964) reported initially having problems standing with his eyes closed. Vertigo soon followed. "Every movement in bed gave rise to vertigo and nausea, even when I kept my eyes open. If I shut my eyes, the symptoms were intensified" (Crawford, 1964, p. 357). Crawford's vision was blurry and he suffered from oscillopsia; stationary things looked like they were moving and the world was in constant visual flux. He could not walk for a period.

What do these pathologies teach us about the function of balance? They show that the vestibular contribution to the stability of posture and the stability of gaze is vital. The maintenance of posture is dependent on a system of reflexes, such as the vestibulospinal and cervicospinal (neck-spinal) reflexes, which act synergistically to stabilize the body under different conditions of movement and posture (Jones, 2000). With vestibular deafferentation, the signals from vestibular nuclei to the spinal cord which are crucial to vestibulospinal reflexes are lost. Thus automatic postural corrections based on vestibular input are no longer present, leading to imbalance and falls.

Turning to gaze stability, it would not be expected a priori that balance is implicated in vision. But the reader will have noticed that one of the major symptoms cited above is blurry or double vision and oscillopsia, when stationary objects are illusorily perceived as in motion. This reflects the basic dependence of vision on gaze stability, which is in turn dependent on the vestibular-ocular reflex (VOR). Vestibular information is used to compensate for retinal slip. Stable images are better perceived on the retina than moving images. For example, when you are traveling in a fast moving vehicle, objects outside the vehicle can appear to be a blur. To ensure that this does not happen when the head moves, the eyes are stabilized by the VOR of eye muscles. The oculomotor system controlling eye movement uses information from the vestibular system to stabilize one's gaze so as to keep images still on the retina. The loss of the VOR affects basic visual functions such as reading and visual recognition when the agent is in motion, as we saw from Crawford's first-personal account of vestibular deafferentation above. These dysfunctions in vision and posture reflect the crucial contribution of the vestibular system in reflexes for gaze and postural stability.

4   Function: The Physiology of Balance

What are the main functions of the sense of balance? Our discussion of pathologies of balance makes it clear that balance is crucial for the stability of posture and gaze (Berthoz, 1991, 2000). The stability of gaze under head movements is dependent on the vestibulo-ocular reflex, which triggers eye movements in the direction opposite to head movements so as to stabilize the retinal image. Postural stability relies on vestibulospinal reflexes acting in synergy with cervicospinal reflexes to generate appropriate postural corrections for stability. These "stabilizing reactions" (Berthoz, 1991, p. 85) are essential to our basic capacities for perception and action.

Without stable gaze, because of retinal slip, vision would degenerate into a chaotic flux of sensations whenever vision is employed during any kind of movement. This would have a powerful negative impact on object perception, motion perception, and self-motion perception. Beyond this, thus degraded, vision could not contribute to the guidance of motion and the control of visuomotor actions. Without postural stability, bipedal locomotion would consist of lurching from one step to the next, eventually resulting in loss of balance and falling. Even crawling on all fours makes significant demands on postural stability, albeit less than bipedal locomotion. Postural stability is also the foundation for action. It is hard to reach and grab something if one is imbalanced oneself. Whether one is still or in motion, without a stable posture, it is difficult to plan and execute actions. Consequently, the vestibular system is part of the foundation for perception and action.

A third basic function of the vestibular system is the provision of gravity and, along with it, the gravitational (or "geocentric") frame of reference. Gibson observed that the ground is a fundamental surface of support for movement. The horizontal plane for movement defines the "ground" for the moving animal. The otolithic organs measure gravity, along with linear acceleration. In so doing, the otolithic organs provide for a horizontal plane for movement (Berthoz, 1991, p. 91). How do they do this? The otolithic organs provide the gravitational vertical that regulates posture, so that the spinal cord (cervical vertebral column) is kept parallel to gravitational force lines—even in absolute darkness (Vidal, Graf, & Berthoz, 1986). The importance of the otolithic organs in providing the gravitational vertical can be seen under microgravity conditions. Astronauts trying to keep their body perpendicular to the floor can perceive themselves as standing upright even though they are leaning as much as twenty degrees forward (Berthoz, 1991).

Postural stability allows for the head to provide an "inertial guidance platform" for the control of perception and action (Berthoz, 1991). The idea of an inertial guidance platform is an engineering concept of a control platform for a heavy mass. The key idea is that the control platform has sensors that will both stabilize the platform and control movements of the system (Berthoz, 1991, p. 97). This principle of guidance provides an elegant engineering solution to the problem of controlling a heavy mass in three-dimensional motion. With such a stable control platform, the head can provide a key reference point for frames of reference for the control of perception and action. The vestibular system provides an *absolute* head-centered frame of reference (Berthoz, 2000) that is key to the computation of various egocentric frames of reference for perception and action. It is absolute, because self-motion coding by the vestibular system is done with reference to head-centered inertial sensors and independent of any external reference. This head-centered egocentric frame of reference is dominant in the hierarchy of frames of reference and is used as a basic anchor for bodily self-motion (Berthoz, 1991, 2000; Paillard, 1991). Thus we see that balance is crucial for postural and perceptual stability and for providing a master frame of reference. I now turn to reflect on the philosophical significance of balance.

5   Phenomenology: In and Out of Balance

One of the most striking statements about the sense of balance is that it is silent.[4] By this, vestibular physiologists mean that conscious experience of balance does not figure—or at least not prominently—in lived experience. Two reasons are given for vestibular silence. The first is the constancy of vestibular signals. If consciousness reflected vestibular processing it would be overloaded with their "constant monologue" (Day & Fitzpatrick, 2005, p. R583). The second is the multisensory nature of vestibular processing.

Is balance silent though? Not entirely, as the vestibular physiologists note themselves. For one, the classical symptoms of vestibular disorders such as dizziness, vertigo, and imbalance are very strong experiences. But it is not only vestibular patients who have vestibular experiences. We have all experienced being out of balance in some way. Dizziness, vertigo, and other feelings of instability that precipitate motion sickness are all vivid examples of experiences of balance, because they are experiences of being *out* of balance.

Perhaps the claim about the silence of balance is best understood as a paucity of vestibular experiences in normal everyday experience. Allowing that we have some grip on the range of normal experiences, this once again raises the question of whether there is a phenomenology of balance. Here it is vital that we distinguish between the silence of a sense (in normal situations) as opposed to the sense lacking a proprietary phenomenology. To say that balance is normally silent is to claim that there is no phenomenology of balance—nothing it is like to be in balance—outside situations involving imbalance or vestibular disease. To say that balance lacks a proprietary phenomenology is not to deny that balance has a phenomenology, but to deny that there is a distinctive phenomenology of balance in the way each of vision, audition, touch, smell, and taste apparently have a proprietary phenomenology.

Is there something it is like to be in or out of balance? I have noted that there is something it is like to be out of balance. But it is not only when things go wrong that we have vestibular awareness. What is it like to be in balance? Even when we close our eyes there is still a sense of one's orientation, of where up is and where down is. And if someone spins you in your office chair with eyes shut, you can tell that you are spinning. When one bends down to tie one's shoelaces or pick up something from the floor, one has a distinct feeling of being a little upside down. And often one has a sense of movement when getting up after tying one's shoelaces. If one trips, one feels out of balance. If one balances on a narrow strip, walks on rocky terrain, or close to a cliff, one has vestibular awareness. Also, one experiences various sensations in cars, planes, and ships, and on bicycles, swings, and roller coasters. So we do have plenty of opportunities for vestibular experiences—they are perhaps just less regular than other sensory experiences or much more in the background. Thus there seems to be a phenomenology of the sense of balance in the normal case. This phenomenology is not prominent, but it is certainly not nothing. Balance is quiet, not silent.

Is this all there is to the phenomenology of balance? And does this make for a proprietary phenomenology of balance? I want to suggest that the phenomenology of balance is not proprietary to the sense. The phenomenology of the sense of balance, as I observed above, is what it is like to be in or out of balance. This is the phenomenology of one's heading and orientation, of how one is poised and one's motion. This sense of where "up" is, for example, is not exclusive to balance. It can be given by touch in normal terrestrial conditions when one's posture is upright and the ground resists one's feet. And it can be given by vision, as noted by Gibson (1979), who observed that optic flow in vision provides information about our own posture, balance, and movement. It is not just that in this case the object—one's orientation in the ambient environment and gravitation field—is the same. Rather, the phenomenology of balance does not differ between the senses of sight and balance. The phenomenology of balance qua balance isn't particularly different whether one's eyes are open or closed. In one case it is all dark, but one's feeling of balance doesn't seem to change. (There will of course be cases where there are differences due to a disagreement between sight and the vestibular system.) If these observations are on the right track, then the phenomenology of balance is marked in lived experience. It is marked in our experience of the world as having an "up" and a "down," in our having a multimodal sense of orientation and movement. Recognizing that balance doesn't have a proprietary phenomenology allows us to recognize how pervasive vestibular phenomenology is. Balance—when all is well—has no unique phenomenology, but it's there when we are walking, when we are up and about, when we are lying down.

6 Being Balanced: At One with Body in World

The philosophical significance of balance demands the articulation of a philosophical physiology of balance. There is only space here for a bare sketch. I outline the role of the vestibular system in agentive self-location (6.1), in anchoring the self to its body (6.2), and in orienting the subject to the world (6.3). I suggest that these three roles are complementary: the vestibular system can be seen as relating self, body, and world.

6.1 Agentive Self-Location

The question "Where am I?" can be answered unerringly with "Here." Let me contrast two models of "here": a referential as opposed to a functional one. On the referential model (e.g., Kaplan, 1989), the reference of "here" is given by a token-reflexive rule: "here" refers to the location of the speaker of the utterance or to the location of the thinker of a "here" thought. "Here" can refer to an arbitrarily large spatial region, as long as the utterance or thought is tokened in that region. In order to settle on the appropriate spatial region for the utterance context, pragmatic processes need to be brought in to narrow down the location referred to. For example, in an air-conditioned room in the summer, my utterance "It's cold here" refers to the room rather than any larger location where it is warm. On the functional model (Evans, 1982, pp. 151–170), a "here" thought gets a grip on a location because of the location's role in coordinating the subject's perception and action. "Here" refers to the nexus of perception and action and is part of a series of egocentric spatial terms with the subject at its point of origin, such as "up," "down," "left," "right," "in front," and "behind."

I don't think that the two models of "here" exclude each other. The functional model can be seen as providing a grasp of location that one can then refer to using a locution governed by the token-reflexive rule. The functional model can explain why the pragmatic processes settle on the region of space referred to. That region is the location that has the appropriate significance for the subject's perception and action.

How does a location from where the subject controls his perception and action enter into the picture? I want to suggest that the vestibular system can be seen as anchoring the subject to his location. Berthoz (1991, pp. 83–98, 2000, p. 32) and Paillard (1991, p. 472) have both suggested that the absolute head-centered geotropic frame of reference provided by the vestibular system dominates the hierarchy of reference frames used for perception and action and thereby links together the diverse frames of reference used in the control of perception and action (e.g., centered on different body parts, such as the hand, the trunk, the retina, etc., or centered on objects in the world). I propose that the vestibular anchoring of frames of reference, along with contributions from vision, touch, and the location's role in controlling the subject's perception and action is what typically determines the referent of "here." If so, the vestibular system would be playing a crucial role in anchoring agentive self-location.

Once we see the vestibular system as anchoring agentive self-location, a tantalizing connection to the psychology of "essential indexicality" (Perry, 1979; Campbell, 1993) opens up. The relevant aspect of essential indexicality I am interested in concerns a contrast in behavioral significance between situations, for example, when there is a fire *here* as opposed to *there* or when the shark is heading *here* as opposed to *there*. Happenings *here* have "immediate implications for action" (Campbell, 1993). I want to suggest that in setting up a master frame of reference, the vestibular system is simultaneously anchoring self-location and providing for a condition of possibility for sensorimotor action. We can see this by revisiting the case of vertigo.

What does vertigo take away from agents? In bouts of vertigo, the sensations of whirling and imbalance are exacerbated by movement. If patients are up and about, head movements may result in them falling. Patients very quickly learn to stay motionless during vertigo attacks. Thus, vertigo incapacitates the agent.

In providing for a sense of balance, the vestibular system is providing a sense of which way is up and a sense of self-motion. In vestibular disease, confusion about self-motion and orientation result in vertigo and difficulties in moving, which paralyze the agent. All the agent can do is keep still. Core behavioral capacities for movement are disabled. Immediate possibilities for action appear to be abolished. In this way vestibular malfunction brings the agent to a standstill. This demonstrates the foundational role of vestibular functioning for action: it provides a condition of possibility for action. My contention is that the vestibular system is anchoring the self to its location in a way that opens up a structure of possibilities of action.

6.2 Being-in-My-Body

A potential role for the vestibular system in embodiment has been recognized since vestibular interventions were shown to alter body perception and bodily experience in neurological patients. Vestibular interventions have been shown to alleviate neglect (Vallar, Guariglia, & Rusconi, 1997; Rossetti & Rode, 2002), anosognosia for hemiplegia (Cappa, Sterzi, Vallar, & Bisiach, 1987; Ronchi et al., 2013), hemianesthesia (Bottini et al., 1995, 2005), and somatoparaphrenia (Bisiach, Rusconi, & Vallar, 1991; Rode et al., 1992; Schiff & Pulver, 1999).

The vestibular modulation of somatoparaphrenia is of especial interest. Somatoparahrenic patients report that a limb feels alien and deny that the limb in question is theirs, often ascribing it to a relative or even the experimenter (Vallar & Ronchi, 2009; Garbarini, Pia, Fossataro, and Berti, this volume). One patient denied her left arm was hers, attributing it to her mother instead. After caloric vestibular stimulation, there was a temporary remission of the somatoparaphrenia when the patient reclaimed ownership of her arm (Bisiach et al., 1991). (Caloric vestibular stimulation involves introducing either cold or warm water in the ear, thus differentially activating vestibular afferents by causing convection of the endolymphatic fluid in the semicircular canals.) Somatoparaphrenia is a disorder of body ownership. The finding that vestibular interventions alleviate somatoparaphrenia suggests that there is a vestibular contribution to body ownership. This cannot be attributed to vestibular stimulation alleviating somatosensory deficits, which are typically present in somatoparaphrenics. Rode and colleagues (1992) found that vestibular stimulation improved somatoparaphrenia, neglect, and anosognosia for hemiplegia, but did not alleviate somatosensory (hemianesthesia) and visual deficits (hemianopia).[5] So the effect of vestibular stimulation seems to be specific to body ownership. This suggests that there is a vestibular role in body ownership.

This suggestion has been corroborated in a number of ways in pathologies of body ownership (as we will see below) and in direct modulations of body ownership in experiments on healthy subjects. In the standard paradigm for studying body ownership, the rubber hand illusion (Botvinick & Cohen, 1998), a subject has a rubber hand in view while their own hand is hidden. When the rubber hand and the subject's hidden hand are synchronously stroked, most subjects report that they feel ownership over the rubber hand. Lopez and colleagues (2010) found that galvanic vestibular stimulation—electrical stimulation of the vestibular receptors applied through a pair of electrodes placed behind the ears—increased the sense of ownership that subjects felt over the rubber hand. The vestibular modulation of hand ownership is further evidence of vestibular mechanisms underlying ordinary embodiment. But so far we have only examined cases involving individual body parts.

A proper study of embodiment must consider ownership of the body as a whole and not only of body parts. Blanke (2012) has identified three key aspects of bodily self-consciousness: (1) body ownership (the experience of owning one's body), (2) self-location (the experience of where one is in space), and (3) the first-person perspective (the experience of the perspective from which I perceive the world). It might be expected that there is a vestibular role in embodiment since vestibular signals concern the orientation and disposition of the body as a whole. Is there evidence of this?

Evidence of vestibular involvement comes from disorders of embodiment of the body as a whole. This is clear in neurological patients who experience various "autoscopic phenomena," such as out-of-body experiences and heautoscopic experiences (see fig. 14.2 for illustrations of their phenomenology).[6] Patients who have out-of-body experiences exhibit a three-way dissociation from their biological body, illustrating Blanke's three aspects of bodily self-consciousness. These patients typically experience ownership over an illusory body in external space (defective body ownership), experience themselves to be located above their biological body (defective self-location), and experience themselves as having an altered first-person perspective where they are looking back down on their biological body (defective first-person perspective) (Pfeiffer, Serino, & Blanke, 2014, p. 4). In heautoscopic patients, they experience seeing a second body of theirs in external space, which they have a sense of ownership over, and they sometimes report feeling located in both bodies or switching between the two.

In patients suffering from out-of-body experiences and heautoscopic experiences, there are failures of multisensory integration, in particular, the integration of body-related information (vestibular, proprioceptive, and tactile cues) and mismatches between vestibular and visual information. The vestibular element comes out if we contrast the pathophysiology of patients suffering from out-of-body experiences and heautoscopic experiences as opposed to those suffering from autoscopic hallucinations. Patients suffering from autoscopic hallucinations visually experience a hallucination of their own body in external space, but they neither feel a sense of ownership over the illusory body nor locate themselves in the illusory body. This is in contrast to the patients suffering from out-of-body experiences and heautoscopic experiences, who both have illusory body ownership and erroneous self-location. Critically, out-of-body experiences and heautoscopy were associated with vestibular disturbances, whereas autoscopic hallucinations did not have such a component. Furthermore, patients who suffer from autoscopic hallucinations had little or no vestibular impairment, whereas patients suffering from out-of-body experiences and heautoscopy had impaired vestibular and proprioceptive processing. The latter group of patients typically have damage to vestibular-related areas, such as the temporoparietal junction and posterior insula, suggesting a key role for vestibular processing in embodiment.

The importance of the vestibular system in embodiment is also reflected in how it affects the perceived shape of one's own body. This can be seen in a number of different scenarios. In microgravity conditions, one of the most common illusions experienced is the inversion illusion (Lackner, 1992). One experiences telescoping downward through one's body, toward one's feet, and then being inverted. Note that this involves a change in the basic shape of one's body and not only a change in posture, as one

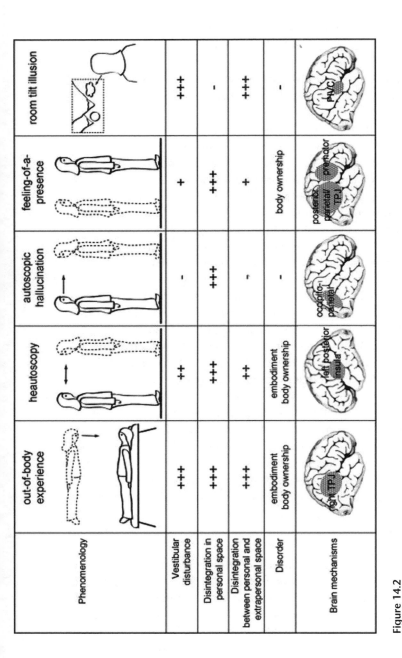

Figure 14.2

This figure from Lopez et al. (2008) illustrates the phenomenology and physiopathology of various autoscopic phenomena and the room tilt illusion. The position of the subject's biological body is represented by dashed lines. The position of the experienced illusory body is represented by dashed lines. The origin and direction of the first-person visuospatial perspective of the subject is indicated by an arrow pointing away from where the subject feels him or herself to be located. Note that Lopez et al. (2008) use the term "embodiment" to refer to ownership of the body as a whole and "body ownership" to refer to ownership of individual body parts. The figure has been revised to reflect new lesion analyses showing the left posterior insula as the primary site of damage in the case of heautoscopy (Heydrich & Blanke, 2013). Figure revised by Gregor Hochstetter and reprinted with permission.

experiences telescoping downward (and telescoping upward when returning to normal gravitational conditions). Another vestibular modulation
of body shape is that of the induction of phantom limbs. Caloric vestibular
stimulation has been used to induce temporary phantom limbs in amputees and paraplegics who had previously not experienced phantom limbs
(André et al., 2001; Braun et al. 2001; Chapelain, Beis, & André, 2001).
Finally, Lopez and colleagues (2012) examined the impact of the vestibular
system on hand shape and size in an experiment with healthy subjects. To
determine hand shape and size, Lopez and colleagues used Longo's method
for extracting the internal representation of hand shape through proprioceptive localization of landmarks on the hand. Subjects perceived their hands as
being larger under caloric vestibular stimulation, as compared to a control
condition.

We may conclude that the vestibular system has a powerful impact on
ownership of one's body and on the perceived shape of one's own body. So
the vestibular system is vital to being-in-my-body.

6.3 Being-in-the-World

I will now argue that there is a key vestibular role in being embedded in the
world. The vestibular system is a bodily sense, but not exclusively so—for
it provides information about the orientation, movement, and disposition
of the body in its ambient environment and gravitational field. So balance
plays a role in giving one a sense of the world.

We can already see that balance is providing a sense of the world from
our earlier discussion on vertigo. When one suffers from vestibular disorders
and consequently from vertigo, one is severely spatially disoriented. One
loses a sense of up and down and how the world is. In microgravity, there
is a loss of orientation as well. Besides the inversion illusion I discussed in
the previous section, subjects often experience the room tilt illusion, where
the space that they are situated in is experienced as upside down (Lackner,
1992). The room tilt illusion is so compelling that in parabolic flights where
microgravity experiments are conducted in cycles of free fall and normal
flight, when the free fall period ends and subjects are to resume their positions, subjects often resume the incorrect positions.

Spatial disorientation is not the only problem arising from vestibular
alterations. Subjects may not only lack the appropriate spatial relatedness
to the world, but also lack the appropriate affective and cognitive relatedness to the world. This is clearest when we consider how balance deficits
result in a loss of reality in depersonalization and derealization disorders.
In depersonalization and derealization disorders, patients feel detached

and alienated from their thoughts, actions, and bodies; often this is accompanied by derealization, where patients experience the external world as appearing hazy, strange, or unreal (Baker et al., 2003; Sierra, 2009; Billon, this volume). Sang and colleagues (2006) found that vestibular patients experienced symptoms of depersonalization and derealization more often and with greater severity than healthy controls. Alongside more classical symptoms of vestibular disease, such as dizziness and vertigo, patients also reported experiencing derealization symptoms such as "surroundings seeming strange and unreal," "feeling as though in a dream," "feeling as if walking on shifting ground," "feeling not being in control of self," "feeling detached or separated from surroundings," and "feeling 'spacey' or 'spaced out'" (items from the standard depersonalization/derealization inventory, see Cox & Swinson, 2002). Furthermore, healthy controls reported symptoms of depersonalization and derealization when they underwent caloric vestibular stimulation, while vestibular patients reported experiencing symptoms of a sort that they were familiar with from vestibular disease. Sang and colleagues suggest that experiences of derealization result from a mismatch of vestibular with other sensory signals, creating an "incoherent frame of spatial reference which makes the patient feel he or she is detached or separated from the world" (Sang et al., 2006, p. 760).

6.4 Challenges

Could the contributions of the vestibular system be merely modulatory? To begin, if we see the vestibular system as providing a master frame of reference that coordinates a subject's perception and action, then there is no question about the critical contribution of balance on this front. Here the constitutive role of balance in the perception–action nexus and in anchoring self-location is manifest. It is critical for spatial orientation in the world and for the immediate implications for action that characterize perceptual orientation. The loss of one's orientation toward the world under microgravity conditions, as can be seen by combinations of the inversion illusion and the room tilt illusion (Lackner, 1992), is telling. The incapacitation that comes with vertigo is another clear indication of the significance of the vestibular system.

When it comes to embodiment, things become trickier. This is in part because we do not yet have a clear idea of the underlying neural mechanisms responsible for body representations, including those for body shape and size, and more complex ones for body ownership. Although we have strong clinical and behavioral evidence that the vestibular cortex is involved in embodiment, we do not have a clear understanding of what the vestibular cortex does beyond its basic functions related to maintaining perceptual and postural stability and detecting gravity. A promising hypothesis is that the vestibular cortex is involved in processing self-related information and is a multisensory network coding for body ownership and embodiment (Lopez, Halje, & Blanke, 2008; Ferrè, Lopez, & Haggard, 2014; Lopez, 2016). But until we have some account of how vestibular processing is yielding this information, we have to remain agnostic. One way in which vestibular processing could be crucial is if the vestibular system provides a master frame of reference which dominates and coordinates spatial, bodily, and affective processing. Current science does not give us enough materials to mount a full sketch of an explanatory account; but it will be seen that my account has already gone beyond a correlational one and that the vestibular system has a role that goes beyond being a mere enabling condition.

Another question that could be raised concerns the predictions of my account for vestibular deafferentation. If the vestibular system plays such a critical role in anchoring the self to its body in the world, we would expect that patients who are vestibularly deafferented would fare poorly. Interestingly, the patients who have a bilateral loss of vestibular function show relatively little disability. These patients do not in general suffer from vertigo—because there are no conflicting vestibular signals to cause disorientation—and never get motion sick (Baloh, Honrubia, & Kerber, 2010). However, they do suffer from problems with vision and instability when walking, especially at night or on uneven ground (due to the loss of the reflexes for postural and perceptual stability). The recovery of function in vestibular deafferentation is due to the ability of patients to use various compensatory strategies for maintaining balance, such as using distal visual cues along with tactile and proprioceptive cues (Crawford, 1964; Baloh, Honrubia, & Kerber, 2010). The relative well-being of vestibularly deafferented patients need not count against my account. If there is no longer an intact vestibular system, then there is an absence of the master frame of reference provided by the vestibular system that dominates and coordinates perception and action. However, other frames of reference can take over. Nothing in my account requires that this cannot be the case. Also, from the fact that vestibularly deafferented subjects have certain capacities, it does not follow that in healthy subjects these same capacities are not underpinned by the vestibular system.[7]

7 Synthesis: Being-in-My-Body-in-the-World

I have argued that balance plays a vital role in self-location, in embodiment, and in being embedded in the world. The role of balance in each of these domains complements the others. These roles of balance can be naturally brought together to reflect the vestibular system as balancing self, body, and world. Balance, through providing a master frame of reference that coordinates perception and action, is critical to agentive self-location. It grounds the perception–action nexus and makes for its behavioral significance. Thus, balance is critical to being *here*. As we have seen, the vestibular system has a strong impact on ownership of one's body, both from clinical and experimental evidence. Thus, balance is significant for being-in-my-body. Finally, we saw that balance is key for the subject's appropriate orientation to the world, both spatially and affectively. Thus, balance is vital to being-in-the-world.

We can synthesize the roles of balance in self-location, embodiment, and embeddedness in the world. We have seen that vestibular problems result in problems with embodiment. Thus, to be out of balance is to be out of touch with one's body. We have seen that vestibular problems result in problems with being embedded in the world, both spatially and affectively. Thus, to be out of balance is to be out of touch with the world. We may conclude that to be out of balance is to be out of touch with both one's body and the world. Conversely, to be in balance is then to be at one with one's body in the world.

8 Conclusion: Balance

Based on empirical and philosophical considerations, I have argued that the vestibular system is critical for self-location, for anchoring the self to its own body, and for situating this embodied self in the world. So the sense of balance maintains our equilibrium in two senses: physical stability and attunement between self, body, and world. Thus balance is an aspect of the anchor of existence: I am here in my body in the world. In a Heideggerian turn of phrase, balance is *being-in-my-body-in-the-world*.

Acknowledgments

Patrick Haggard incited my interest in the vestibular system. I am indebted to the editors, Bigna Lenggenhager, Christophe Lopez, and Krisztina Orbán for their feedback on this paper. Finally, I wish to thank audiences in Tübingen, London, and Bochum for discussion, especially Chiara Brozzo, Elisa Ferrè, Gregor Hochstetter, Matthew Longo, Michael Martin, Jean Moritz Müller, and Casey O'Callaghan. I gratefully acknowledge funding from the Volkswagen Foundation for the project *Finding Perspective* (Az.: 89435).

Notes

1. For fuller reviews, see Day and Fitzpatrick (2005); Angelaki and Cullen (2008); Baloh, Honrubia, and Kerber (2010, chap. 1); Goldberg, Walker, and Hudspeth, (2013); Lenggenhager and Lopez (2015); and Lopez (2016).

2. See, for review, Lopez and Blanke (2011). The posterior insula and temporoparietal junction are considered the human homologue of the parieto-insular vestibular cortex (PIVC) identified by Grüsser and colleagues (1990) in monkeys. The PIVC is the only vestibular area that is connected to all other vestibular regions identified so far.

3. All quotations in this section are to Baloh, Honrubia, and Kerber (2010, chap. 5), unless otherwise stated.

4. In this chapter I am using the terms "sense of balance" and the "vestibular system" interchangeably. It is important to distinguish between this narrower use of "balance" to denote the vestibular system and a broader notion of the sense of balance. The latter is what provides a multimodal percept of balance that may draw on multiple perceptual systems, such as the vestibular system (proper), vision, audition, touch, proprioception, etc. My discussion in section 5 concerns the narrower notion of balance.

5. Considering other cases where the reverse is found—an improvement of hemianesthesia but not somatoparaphrenia (Bottini et al., 1995; Moro, Zampini, & Aglioti, 2004)—Vallar and Ronchi suggest that there is a "double dissociation between somatoparaphrenia and sensory impairments" (Vallar & Ronchi, 2009, p. 547).

6. See Lopez et al. (2008); Blanke, Arzy, and Landis (2008); Pfeiffer et al. (2014); and Lopez (2016.)

7. I have argued for an analogous claim with respect to peripheral proprioceptive deafferentation elsewhere (Wong, 2017, forthcoming).

References

André, J. M., Martinet, N., Paysant, J., Beis, J. M., & Chapelain, L. L. (2001). Temporary phantom limbs evoked by vestibular caloric stimulation in amputees. *Neuropsychiatry, Neuropsychology, and Behavioral Neurology, 14*(3), 190–196.

Angelaki, D. E., & Cullen, K. E. (2008). Vestibular system: The many facets of a multimodal sense. *Annual Review of Neuroscience, 31,* 125–150. doi:10.1146/annurev.neuro.31.060407.125555.

Baker, D., Hunter, E., Lawrence, E., Medford, N., Patel, M., Senior, C., et al. (2003). Depersonalisation disorder: Clinical features of 204 cases. *British Journal of Psychiatry, 182*(5), 428–433. doi:10.1192/bjp.182.5.428.

Baloh, R. W., Honrubia, V., & Kerber, K. A. (2010). *Baloh and Honrubia's Clinical neurophysiology of the vestibular system* (4th ed.). Oxford: Oxford University Press.

Berthoz, A. (1991). Reference frames for the perception and control of movement. In J. Paillard (Ed.), *Brain and space*. Oxford: Oxford University Press.

Berthoz, A. (2000). *The brain's sense of movement*. Cambridge, MA: Harvard University Press.

Bisiach, E., Rusconi, M. L., & Vallar, G. (1991). Remission of somatoparaphrenic delusion through vestibular stimulation. *Neuropsychologia, 29*(10), 1029–1031. doi:10.1016/0028-3932(91)90066-H.

Blanke, O. (2012). Multisensory brain mechanisms of bodily self-consciousness. *Nature Reviews: Neuroscience, 13*(8), 556–571. doi:10.1038/nrn3292.

Blanke, O., Arzy, S., & Landis, T. (2008). Illusory perceptions of the human body and self. In G. Goldenberg & B. Miller (Eds.), *Handbook of clinical neurology* (Vol. 88, pp. 429–458): *Neuropsychology and behavioral neurology*. Amsterdam: Elsevier. doi:10.1016/S0072-9752(07)88022-5.

Bottini, G., Paulesu, E., Sterzi, R., Warburton, E., Wise, R. J., Vallar, G., et al. (1995). Modulation of conscious experience by peripheral sensory stimuli. *Nature, 376*(6543), 778–781. doi:10.1038/376778a0.

Bottini, G., Paulesu, E., Gandola, M., Loffredo, S., Scarpa, P., Sterzi, R., et al. (2005). Left caloric vestibular stimulation ameliorates right hemianesthesia. *Neurology, 65*(8), 1278–1283. doi:10.1212/01.wnl.0000182398.14088.e8.

Botvinick, M., & Cohen, J. (1998). Rubber hands "feel" touch that eyes see. *Nature, 391*(6669), 756. doi:10.1038/35784.

Braun, M., Chapelain, L. L., Beis, J. M., Opincariu, J., & André, J. M. (2001). Feet dorsal imaginary flexion in paraplegic patients: fMRI of motor areas before and through vestibular stimulation. *NeuroImage, 13*(6), S1135. doi:10.1016/S1053-8119(01)92459-0.

Campbell, J. (1993). The role of physical objects in spatial thinking. In N. Eilan, R. McCarthy, & B. Brewer (Eds.), *Spatial representation* (pp. 65–95). Oxford: Oxford University Press.

Cappa, S., Sterzi, R., Vallar, G., & Bisiach, E. (1987). Remission of hemineglect and anosognosia during vestibular stimulation. *Neuropsychologia, 25*(5), 775–782. doi:10.1016/0028-3932(87)90115-1.

Chapelain, L. L., Beis, J. M., & André, J. M. (2001). Vestibular caloric stimulation evokes phantom limb illusions in patients with paraplegia. *Spinal Cord, 39*(2), 85–87.

Cox, B. J., & Swinson, R. P. (2002). Instrument to assess depersonalization-derealization in panic disorder. *Depression and Anxiety, 15*(4), 172–175. doi:10.1002/da.10051.

Crawford, J. (1964). Living without a balancing mechanism. *British Journal of Ophthalmology*, *48*(7), 357–360. doi:10.1136/bjo.48.7.357.

Day, B. L., & Fitzpatrick, R. C. (2005). The vestibular system. *Current Biology*, *15*(15), R583–R586. doi:10.1016/j.cub.2005.07.053.

Evans, G. (1982). *The varieties of reference*. Oxford: Clarendon Press.

Ferrè, E. R., Lopez, C., & Haggard, P. (2014). Anchoring the self to the body: Vestibular contribution to the sense of self. *Psychological Science*, *25*(11), 2106–2108. doi:10.1177/0956797614547917.

Gibson, J. J. (1979). *The ecological approach to visual perception*. Boston: Houghton-Mifflin.

Goldberg, M. E., Walker, M. F., & Hudspeth, A. J. (2013). The vestibular system. In E. R. Kandel, J. H. Schwartz, T. M. Jessell, S. A. Siegelbaum, & A. J. Hudspeth (Eds.), *Principles of neural science* (5th ed.). New York: McGraw-Hill Medical.

Grice, H. P. (1989). Some remarks about the senses. In H. P. Grice (Ed.), *Studies in the way of words* (pp. 248–268). Cambridge, MA: Harvard University Press.

Grüsser, O. J., Pause, M., & Schreiter, U. (1990). Localization and responses of neurones in the parieto-insular vestibular cortex of awake monkeys (Macaca fascicularis). *Journal of Physiology*, *430*(1), 537–557. doi:10.1113/jphysiol.1990.sp018306.

Grüsser, O. J., Guldin, W. O., Mirring, S., & Salah-Eldin, A. (1994). Comparative physiological and anatomical studies of the primate vestibular cortex. In B. Albowitz, K. Albus, U. Kuhnt, H. C. Nothdurf, & P. Wahle (Eds.), *Structural and functional organization of the neocortex* (pp. 358–371). Berlin: Springer.

Heydrich, L., & Blanke, O. (2013). Distinct illusory own-body perceptions caused by damage to posterior insula and extrastriate cortex. *Brain*, *136*(6), 790–803. doi:10.1093/brain/aws364.

Jones, G. M. (2000). Posture. In E. R. Kandel, J. H. Schwartz, & T. M. Jessell (Eds.), *Principles of neural science* (4th ed.). New York: McGraw-Hill.

Kaplan, D. (1989). Demonstratives. In J. Almog, H. Wettstein, & J. Perry (Eds.), *Themes from Kaplan* (pp. 481–563). New York: Oxford University Press.

Lackner, J. R. (1992). Spatial orientation in weightless environments. *Perception*, *21*(6), 803–812.

Lenggenhager, B., and Lopez, C. (2015). Vestibular contributions to the sense of body, self, and others. *Open MIND* 23(T). doi:10.15502/9783958570023.

Lopez, C. (2016). The vestibular system: Balancing more than just the body. *Current Opinion in Neurology*, *29*(1). 74–83. doi:10.1097/WCO.0000000000000286.

Lopez, C., & Blanke, O. (2011). The thalamocortical vestibular system in animals and humans. *Brain Research. Brain Research Reviews, 67*(1), 119–146. doi:10.1016/j .brainresrev.2010.12.002.

Lopez, C., Halje, P., & Blanke, O. (2008). Body ownership and embodiment: Vestibular and multisensory mechanisms. *Neurophysiologie Clinique. Clinical Neurophysiology, 38*(3), 149–161. doi:10.1016/j.neucli.2007.12.006.

Lopez, C., Lenggenhager, B., & Blanker, O. (2010). How vestibular stimulation interacts with illusory hand ownership. *Consciousness and Cognition, 19*(1), 33–47. doi:10.1016/j.concog.2009.12.003.

Lopez, C., Schreyer, H. M., Preuss, N., & Mast, F. W. (2012). Vestibular stimulation modifies the body schema. *Neuropsychologia, 50*(8), 1830–1837. doi:10.1016/j.neuro psychologia.2012.04.008.

Mach, E. (1875). *Grundlinien der Lehre von der Bewegungsempfindung.* Leipzig: Engelmann.

Moro, V., Zampini, M., & Aglioti, S. M. (2004). Changes in spatial position of hands modify tactile extinction but not disownership of contralesional hand in two right brain-damaged patients. *Neurocase, 10*(6), 437–443. doi:10.1080/13554790490894020.

Paillard, J. (Ed.). (1991). *Brain and space.* Oxford: Oxford University Press.

Perry, J. (1979). The problem of the essential indexical. *Noûs, 13*(1), 3–21. doi:10.2307 /2214792.

Pfeiffer, C., Serino, A., & Blanke, O. (2014). The vestibular system: A spatial reference for bodily self-consciousness. *Frontiers in Integrative Neuroscience, 8*(31). doi:10.3389/ fnint.2014.00031.

Rode, G., Charles, N., Perenin, M. T., Vighetto, A., Trillet, M., & Aimond, G. (1992). Partial remission in a case of hemiplegia and somatoparaphrenia through vestibular stimulation in a case of unilateral neglect. *Cortex, 28*(2), 203–208. doi:10.1016/ S0010-9452(13)80048-2.

Ronchi, R., Rode, G., Cotton, F., Farnè, A., Rossetti, Y., & Jacquin-Courtois, S. (2013). Remission of anosognosia for right hemiplegia and neglect after caloric vestibular stimulation. *Restorative Neurology and Neuroscience, 31*(1), 19–24. doi:10.3233/ RNN-120236.

Rossetti, Y., & Rode, G. (2002). Reducing spatial neglect by visual and other sensory manipulations: Non-cognitive (physiological) routes to the rehabilitation of a cognitive disorder. In H.-O. Karnath, A. D. Milner, & G. Vallar (Eds.), *The cognitive and neural bases of spatial neglect* (pp. 375–396). Oxford: Oxford University Press.

Sang, F. Y. P., Jáuregui-Renaud, K., Green, D. A., Bronstein, A. M., & Gresty, M. A. (2006). Depersonalisation/derealisation symptoms in vestibular disease. *Journal of Neurology, Neurosurgery, and Psychiatry, 77*(6), 760–766. doi:10.1136/jnnp.2005.075473.

Schiff, N. D., & Pulver, M. (1999). Does vestibular stimulation activate thalamo-cortical mechanisms that reintegrate impaired cortical regions? *Proceedings of the Royal Society of London. Series B, Biological Sciences, 266*(1417), 421–423. doi:10.1098/rspb.1999.0654.

Shoemaker, S. (1994). Self-knowledge and "inner sense": Lecture I: The object perception model. *Philosophy and Phenomenological Research, 54*(2), 249–269. doi:10.2307/2108488.

Sierra, M. (2009). *Depersonalization: A new look at a neglected syndrome.* Cambridge: Cambridge University Press.

Vallar, G., & Ronchi, R. (2009). Somatoparaphrenia: A body delusion. A review of the neuropsychological literature. *Experimental Brain Research, 192*(3), 533–551. doi: 10.1007/s00221-008-1562-y.

Vallar, G., Guariglia, C., & Rusconi, M. L. (1997). Modulation of the neglect syndrome by sensory stimulation. In P. Thier & H.-O. Karnath (Eds.), *Parietal lobe contributions to orientation in 3D space* (pp. 555–578). Heidelberg: Springer-Verlag.

Vidal, P. P., Graf, W., & Berthoz, A. (1986). The orientation of the cervical vertebral column in unrestrained awake animals. *Experimental Brain Research, 61*(3), 549–559. doi:10.1007/BF00237580.

Wong, H. Y. (2017). Embodied agency. *Philosophy and Phenomenological Research.* doi:10.1111/phpr.12392.

Wong, H. Y. (forthcoming). On proprioception in action: Multimodality versus deafferentation. *Mind & Language.*

15 The Material Me: Unifying the Exteroceptive and Interoceptive Sides of the Bodily Self

Manos Tsakiris

1 Introduction

As the leading social psychologist, Roy Baumeister famously wrote: "Everywhere in the world, self starts with body" (1991, p. 2). By grounding the self in the body, psychology could at last overcome Cartesianism and make the *bodily self* the starting point for a science of the self. This approach has been exemplified recently by two influential research paradigms. First, research on the sense of agency over one's actions and the sense of ownership of one's body has shown how these fundamental experiences of the self rely on specific processes of sensorimotor interactions and multisensory integration, respectively (Tsakiris, Longo, & Haggard, 2010). Second, the evidence for a mirror system in humans has shown how events observed on others' bodies are mirrored onto one's own sensorimotor system, thus opening a window into other minds (Gallese & Sinigaglia, 2011). To date, these paradigms have been instrumental in explaining the nature of the bodily self and certain aspects of social cognition. Across both paradigms, however, the focus has been on the perception of one's own and others' bodies from the *outside*, in terms of observable sensory and motor events. Consequently, awareness of the self and of others has been assumed to rely largely on the processing of exteroceptive signals, at the expense of another side of embodiment—the unobservable (yet felt) interoceptive body.

A distinction can be drawn between perceptual information channels (which encompass both exteroception and proprioception) and visceral information channels. Multisensory conveying information about the body as perceived from the outside, such as through vision or touch, represents only one channel of information available for self-awareness. Interoception, defined here as the sense of the physiological condition of the body, is a ubiquitous information channel used to represent one's body from within (Craig, 2009). At the physiological level, autonomic interoceptive processing ensures the stability of the organism, in other words its homeo-stasis. Beyond physiology, hitherto psychological research on interoception has focused mainly on classic debates regarding the role of interoception on emotion, as well as on a number of related cognitive abilities such as attention and decision making. More radically, the interoceptive body has been linked to phenomenal consciousness (Craig, 2009; Damasio, 1999). The aim of the present chapter is twofold: first to briefly describe these two important models of the self, relying on the exteroceptive and the interoceptive sides of embodiment respectively, and second to put forward a unifying model of the bodily self that integrates the exteroceptive and interoceptive sides of the body, using existing empirical data to support it and generating new empirically testable hypotheses.

2   An Exteroceptive Model of the Bodily Self: The Case of Body Ownership

The basic question of how the brain produces the experience of this body as *mine*, known as body ownership, has been addressed mainly in the context of multisensory integration. For example, in the rubber hand illusion (RHI) (Botvinick & Cohen, 1998), watching a rubber hand being stroked synchronously with one's own unseen hand causes the rubber hand to be experienced as part of one's body (for a review see Tsakiris, 2010).

Over the last twenty years, the RHI paradigm has been established as one of the most important experimental paradigms that allows the con-trolled manipulation of the experience of body ownership. While the underlying mechanisms, behavioral, physiological, and phenomenologi-cal consequences of the illusion have been described in detail elsewhere (Tsakiris, 2010; Blanke, 2012), it is important to highlight here certain key features that are particularly relevant for understanding the relation between the exteroceptive and interoceptive models of the self. First, while not sufficient by itself, synchronous multisensory (i.e., visuotactile in most cases) stimulation is the main cause that drives the RHI and the resulting change in body ownership. Multisensory processing aims at the integra-tion of sensory signals and the resolution of potential conflicts to generate a coherent representation of the world and the body on the basis of the available sensory evidence. Therefore, the RHI reflects a three-way weighted interaction between vision, touch, and proprioception: vision of tactile stimulation on the rubber hand captures the tactile sensation on the par-ticipant's own hand, and this visual capture results in a mislocalization of the felt location of one's own hand toward the spatial location of the visual percept.[1] Second, at the phenomenological level, the RHI has been success-fully used as a model instance of embodiment. Longo, Schüür, Kammers, Tsakiris, and Haggard (2008) characterized the subjective experience of body ownership during the RHI, revealing that this consists of dissociable components, such as ownership of the limb, its location, and the sense of control over it. Third, the change in body ownership as a result of the RHI can in turn change one's body image. For example, participants who expe-rienced the RHI perceived their hand and the rubber hand as significantly more similar (Longo et al., 2009), than participants who did not experi-ence the illusion, suggesting that ownership leads to changes in perceived similarity. Taken together these findings from this classic bodily illusion highlight the intriguing interactions between different sensory modalities that underpin changes in the phenomenology of which one is my body, as well as in one's body image (i.e., what my body looks like).

Beyond these changes, the RHI literature has indicated that the experi-ence of owning the rubber hand results in significant alterations in the way one's own real hand is processed at the introspective (Longo et al., 2008) and physiological level (Moseley et al., 2008). Introspectively, participants feel as if their own hand had disappeared (Longo et al., 2008), suggesting that the changes caused by RHI do not consist of an addition or exten-sion of one's body, but instead they produce incorporation and replace-ment of one's own hand. Intriguingly, the same phenomenon seems to be present at the physiological level. Moseley and colleagues (2008) provided evidence that the experience of ownership during RHI is also accompanied by significant changes in the homeostatic regulation of the real hand, beyond changes in the subjective experience of one's body. In particular, skin temperature of the real hand decreased when participants experienced the RHI (but see Kammers, Rose, & Haggard, 2011; Rohde, Wold, Karnath, & Ernst, 2013; Sadibolova & Longo, 2014). Additionally, the magnitude of the decrease in skin temperature on the participant's own hand was posi-tively correlated with the vividness of the illusion. Importantly, this effect occurred only as a result of the experience of ownership, and not simply as a consequence of synchronous stimulation. Thus, a change in conscious experience of body ownership has direct consequences for the homeostatic regulation of real body parts that occur once participants experience the RHI. Even more strikingly, histamine reactivity increases in the "rejected" arm during the rubber hand illusion (Barnsley et al., 2012), implying that the interoceptive system begins to disown the real hand in favor of the prosthetic and recalling Damasio's definition of "the self" as "what[ever] the immune system identifies as belonging to the body" (Damasio, 2003,

p. 227). Further support for the effects that changes in body ownership have on interoception comes from functional neuroimaging studies that showed a correlation between the strength of the rubber hand illusion and the amplitude of blood oxygenation level dependent (BOLD) responses triggered by physical threats toward the rubber hand in key areas related to interoception such as the insula and the anterior cingulate cortex (ACC) (Ehrsson, Wiech, Weiskopf, Dolan, & Passingham, 2007). Similarly, Guterstam and colleagues (2015) not only found activation in insular cortex and ACC when threats were applied to an owned stranger's body during a full body illusion, but also reported that the stronger the full body illusion the weaker the threat-evoked BOLD responses in insular cortex and ACC when threats where directed toward the real body in view. These findings corroborate the link between the responsiveness of the central interoceptive system and the (exteroceptive) rubber hand illusion, and represent an ecologically relevant approach to probe the homeostatic stability of the organism. Therefore, cognitive processes that update or disrupt the awareness of our physical self may in turn alter the physiological regulation of the self. The changes caused in the physiological regulation of the self as a result of the experience of body ownership over and above multisensory integration suggests that processes other than multisensory integration may be involved in generating, maintaining, or disrupting the awareness of the bodily self.

Beyond ownership of a limb, the same principles of exteroceptive multisensory integration have been used to probe questions of full body ownership and self-identification. Ehrsson (2007) used synchronous or asynchronous visuotactile stimulation to elicit out-of-body experiences: synchronous but not asynchronous visuotactile stimulation induced a shift in the first-person perspective such that participants experienced being located at some distance behind the visual image of their own body as if they were looking at someone else. Lenggenhager, Tadi, Metzinger, and Blanke (2007) induced a full body illusion (see also Petkova & Ehrsson, 2008) by having participants viewing a virtual body presented at a distance of two meters ahead of them through the use a 3D video head-mounted display. As with the RHI, after synchronous stimulation, participants felt as if the virtual body was their body. To further investigate the extent to which current multisensory input may influence the sense of self-identity, I extended the paradigm of multisensory integration to self-face recognition (Tsakiris, 2008). Participants were stroked on their face while they were looking at a morphed face being touched in synchrony or asynchrony. Before and after the visuotactile stimulation participants performed a self-recognition task. The results showed that synchronized multisensory signals had a significant effect on self-face recognition. Synchronous tactile stimulation while watching another person's face being similarly touched produced a bias in recognizing one's own face, in the direction of the other person included in the representation of one's own face. (See also Sforza, Bufalari, Haggard, & Aglioti, 2010; Tajadura-Jiménez, Longo, Coleman, & Tsakiris, 2012; Tajadura-Jiménez & Tsakiris, 2014.) This effect suggests that our mental representation of our self, such as self-face representation, is not solely derived from mnemonic representations, but instead, as with body ownership, these representations are susceptible to current multisensory evidence.

Following the aforementioned literature, it seems that multisensory integration can update cognitive representations of one's body, such as the sense of ownership of body parts (Longo et al., 2008) or whole body (Ehrsson, 2007; Lenggenhager et al., 2007; Petkova & Ehrsson, 2008), the physical appearance of one's body (Longo et al., 2009), and the representation of one's identity in relation to other people (Tsakiris, 2008). Taken together, these results speak in favor of an exteroceptive model of the self, within which self-awareness is highly malleable, and subject to the influence of exteroception (i.e., the perception of the body from the *outside*). However, exteroceptive input represents only one set of channels of information available for self-awareness, as we are also interoceptively aware of our body.

3   Interoceptive Processing and Interoceptive Awareness

Interoception, as a sensory system, is the *sense of the physiological condition of the body* (Craig, 2009) originating from within its visceral organs (e.g., heart, lungs, stomach, bladder, etc.), that signal their state (e.g., heartbeat, hunger, dyspnea, distension of the bladder, stomach, rectum, or esophagus, etc.). While vestibular and proprioceptive signals also seem to originate from within, interoception plays a unique role in allowing the brain to ensure the efficient physiological function of the organism (i.e., homeostasis). Interoception is therefore critical for ensuring the homeostatic stability and survival of the organism in a changing environment, in a way that other systems are not. Interoceptive signals arise within four systems—the cardiovascular, respiratory, gastrointestinal, and urogenital. Of those, the cardiovascular has emerged as the main focus of study of the interaction between the visceral body and the brain (Critchley & Harrison, 2013), because of the informationally rich and bidirectional connections between these two most important organs of the body—the heart and the brain. Another historical reason that explains the focus of neurophysiology and psychology on the heart–brain interactions is linked to the known role that the balance between the sympathetic and parasympathetic systems plays in emotion processing.

Of particular interest for understanding the heart–brain interactions are a set of well-studied autonomic functions. Heart rate variability (HRV) indexes the variation in the beat to beat interval and reflects the balance between sympathetic and parasympathetic influences that seek to respectively increase and decrease heart rate (HR). A critical node in the heart–brain system is the vagus nerve, a primary component of the parasympathetic branch that has both afferent and efferent pathways, enabling efficient coregulation of the heart and the brain, promoting flexible responsiveness to environmental changes. Vagal tone (VT) is an index of the functional state of the parasympathetic system, as the vagus nerve decreases HR by inhibiting the firing rate of the sinoatrial node. High VT reflects greater parasympathetic control of the heart. In general cardiac signals are relayed by the vagus nerve to subcortical and cortical areas, including the insula, which is the central interoceptive hub (Craig, 2009), in order to convey information about the physiological state of the body. Overall, these variables are instrumental in enabling and shaping the heart–brain dialogue below the level of awareness.

Undeniably, while we may not be aware of our HRV or VT, we can become aware of interoceptive states, such as our accelerating heart rate or empty stomach. As with awareness of other sensory modalities, awareness of interoceptive states confers significant biological advantages. However, in contrast to the vast empirical data on visual or somatosensory awareness, our understanding of interoceptive awareness is limited by the difficulties in causally manipulating interoceptive states (e.g., controlling inputs to the system), as well as by the available measurement methods. Research into interoceptive awareness has focused mainly on awareness of heartbeats because these are distinct events that can be easily measured, unlike other interoceptive changes. Heartbeat detection procedures typically require individuals to perceive and count the number of heartbeats occurring during short intervals, or to detect the a/synchronicity between individual heartbeats and external stimuli. Both methods produce measures of interoceptive accuracy (IAcc), which correlate with each other and with measures in other interoceptive modalities (see for review Garfinkel et al., 2015). There are significant interindividual differences in performance, allowing us to distinguish between people with high and low IAcc. IAcc is thought to reflect a trait-like sensitivity to one's visceral signals that has important consequences for health, feelings, and cognition. Similar methods have been applied in other interoceptive systems, to measure for example respiratory or gastric sensitivity. A fundamental question concerns the interrelation of awareness across different interoceptive systems. Some studies report significant correlations between cardiac and respiratory sensitivity (Whitehead, 1980), and cardiac and gastric sensitivity (Herbert, Muth, Pollatos, & Herbert, 2012), while others do not (Harver, Katkin, & Bloch, 1993). Interestingly, the available neuroimaging findings suggest potential commonalities, as they implicate the insula across interoceptive modalities (for review see Craig, 2009). Therefore, on the basis of the current but limited data, the assumption that cardiac awareness represents an indicator of "general" interoceptive awareness seems plausible, but future studies should attempt to conclusively clarify this issue.

Individual differences in cardiac IAcc have been linked to mental health with very high IAcc predisposing to anxiety, while in patients with alexithymia, symptom severity is inversely related to IAcc. Low IAcc characterizes sufferers from depersonalization disorder, those with personality disorders, psychosomatic complaints, and patients with eating disorders (for review see Herbert & Pollatos, 2012). In healthy adults, research into interoceptive awareness has been almost exclusively concerned with emotion. IAcc is crucial for the intensity of emotional experience and emotion regulation (Wiens, 2005). Individuals with high IAcc report higher arousal than people with low IAcc, despite comparable physiological arousal, are more able to self-regulate their behavior (Herbert & Pollatos, 2012), and tend to follow their intuitions more in decision-making tasks (Dunn et al., 2010). Taken together, the classical view on interoceptive awareness, deriving mainly from the study of emotion and psychopathology, suggests that it is important for emotional awareness and mental well-being.

However, beyond these domains, cognitive neuroscience has indirectly revealed the ubiquitous role interoception may play for cognitive processing and self-awareness. Countless functional neuroimaging studies have reported activations in the insula, the central interoceptive hub in the brain, across a wide range of tasks. Craig (2009) suggested that the common denominator of insula activity is the central role of this area in integrating bodily and environmental information to optimize homeostatic efficiency, and in representing the "material me" in the brain. Beyond homeostasis, a set of intriguing findings that relate to self-awareness have captured our attention (for review see Craig, 2009; Tsakiris, 2010). Right anterior insula activity correlates with performance in IAcc (Critchley et al., 2004; but see also Khalsa, Rudrauf, Feinstein, & Tranel, 2009). Ronchi et al. (2015) reported a single-case study showing that heartbeat awareness decreased after insular resection. In terms of the neural mechanisms that underpin body ownership, functional neuroimaging studies on the RHI and lesion studies implicate a network of areas (for review see Tsakiris, 2010), comprised of premotor (Ehrsson et al., 2004), temporoparietal (Tsakiris, Costantini, & Haggard, 2008), and occipital areas (Limanowski & Blankenburg, 2015), as well as the insula (Tsakiris et al., 2007). Intriguingly, the hypothesis that the right posterior insula is linked to the experience of body ownership is also supported by available evidence on somatoparaphrenia—a neuropsychological syndrome where loss of experienced ownership over one's own limb is the key feature. A lesion mapping study that focused specifically on patients with somatoparaphrenic symptoms Baier and Karnath revealed that the right posterior insula is indeed the critical structure involved in phenomena of "disturbed sensation of limb ownership" (Baier & Karnath, 2008, p. 487).

These findings suggest that the exteroceptive and the interoceptive sides of the bodily self are represented across the insular cortex, from the posterior to anterior subregions respectively (Simmons et al., 2013). Beyond the representation of the body, the insular cortex is also linked to affective processing of self and others, and a wide range of social cognition processes such as empathy (Bernhardt & Singer, 2012). Taken together, these findings suggest that interoception may play a role for self-awareness that goes beyond its known role for emotion and phenomenal consciousness. Notwithstanding the importance of the neuroimaging results showing where in the brain the interoceptive and exteroceptive sides of the self are integrated, they do not answer a fundamental *psychological* question: Are the interoceptive and exteroceptive representations simply added or do they interact, and what is the functional importance of the balancing act between the two, *for* the self in its natural embodiment *and* perhaps in the self's social world?

4   Interactions between Exteroceptive Processing and Interoceptive Awareness

Awareness of the interoceptive body has rarely been considered in direct relation to *the* awareness of the sensorimotor body. Even though we are aware of this *one* body as *ours*, psychology has not as yet understood how the bodily signals *from within* are integrated with signals *from the outside* to give rise to this unified experience.

The first study that tested the potential link between exteroceptive and interoceptive awareness of the body measured and quantified IAcc and compared this measure with the change in body ownership caused by multisensory stimulation, using the RHI as a paradigmatic case of the exteroceptive self. My colleagues and I (Tsakiris et al., 2011) observed a negative correlation between IAcc and RHI, such that people with lower IAcc showed a stronger RHI measured behaviorally and homeostatically (i.e., drop in skin temperature), suggesting that in the absence of accurate interoceptive representations, one's model of self is predominantly exteroceptive. While Moseley et al. (2008) had shown how a change in the body ownership during RHI affects homeostatic regulation, my colleagues and I (Tsakiris et al., 2011) showed for the first time that both the experience of body ownership and the same subsequent changes in homeostatic regulation depend partly on levels of IAcc. Following that initial finding, the same negative correlation was observed in children aged eight to seventeen years (Schauder, Mash, Bryant, & Cascio, 2015). Similarly, using the enfacement illusion (Sforza et al., 2010), Tajadura-Jiménez and colleagues (2012), and Tajadura-Jiménez and Tsakiris (2014) found that people with low interoceptive awareness showed larger behavioral changes in a self-recognition paradigm, indicative of a stronger sense of identification with the other's face. Interestingly, a similar but inverse relationship holds between interoception and attitudes toward one's body. For example, we showed (Ainley & Tsakiris, 2014) that levels of IAcc are inversely correlated with self-objectification, which is the tendency to experience one's body principally as an object (Fredrickson & Roberts, 1997). Others have found an inverse relationship with body-image satisfaction (Emanuelsen, Drew, & Köteles, 2015). These observations suggest that interoceptive influences extend from the basic levels of multisensory integration to the conscious (affective) *attitudes* that we hold about our body, highlighting the role that interoception may play across different hierarchical levels of body representations. These findings suggest an *antagonism* between interoceptive and exteroceptive cues in bodily self-awareness. Moreover, this was a seminal finding that could not have been predicted by existing accounts of interoceptive awareness or by models of the exteroceptive self, suggestive of the limitations of our current theories of the bodily self.

Since then, recent studies have tried to modify the conditions of multimodal stimulation by including cardiac feedback to examine in greater detail the potential role of interoceptive signals in creating a sense of body ownership. Suzuki, Garfinkel, Critchley, and Seth (2013) using a novel "virtual hand" paradigm, dispensed altogether with a prosthetic hand, by filming the subject's own hand and replaying this film to them in real time, in the location where the rubber hand would usually be placed. They showed that, if the participant's filmed hand was made to flush slightly, in synchrony with the subject's heartbeat, then the rubber hand illusion was induced (Suzuki et al., 2013). Contrary to my own results (Tsakiris et al., 2011), in this paradigm it was the people with high interoceptive awareness who experience the greater proprioceptive drift. The important difference between these two experimental manipulations is that in the classic rubber hand illusion the interoceptive cues of the individuals with good heartbeat perception serve to anchor those participants in their own bodies and enable them to resist the illusion. However, in Suzuki and colleagues' (2013) novel method, the salient interoceptive cues are now located on the true, filmed hand, predisposing people with high interceptive awareness to recognize it as their real body part. It has similarly been shown that causing an avatar to flash in synchrony with the participant's own heartbeat (to enhance self-identification with the avatar's body) facilitates performance on a task that requires participants to judge the perspective of the avatar (Aspell et al, 2013). It has also recently been demonstrated that respiratory cues can be used to induce changes in some aspects of body-representations, using methods similar to the cardiovisual stimulation. People who saw a virtual body flashing synchronously with their breathing reported a change sense of self-location toward the virtual body, similar to the one observed in classic visuotactile versions of the full body illusion than when the flashing was asynchronous (and also when compared with an inanimate control object), although no changes in self-identification were observed in either condition (Adler, Herbelin, Similowski, & Blanke, 2014).

On the basis of these findings, we could argue that, if the exteroceptive model of the self highlights the *malleability* of body awareness given the striking effects that multisensory integration has on body ownership, the interoceptive model of the self should primarily serve the *stability* of the body and its mental representation in response to external changes, thus reflecting thus the biologically necessary balance between adaptability and stability.

5   The Free Energy Self: Predictive Coding as a Unifying Theory of Self

The idea that there is more than one side to the self is as old as psychology but theories that integrate the interoceptive and exteroceptive sides of self have been lacking (Legrand & Ruby, 2009). Some theories have focused mostly on the idea of coherence (Zahavi, 2005), thus neglecting the fact that certain aspects of the self may be antagonistic or competitive. Others (Metzinger, 2003), inspired by Hume, have focused on antagonism to argue against the unity of the self. We here provide a different approach by focusing on the dynamic relations between bodily modalities, so that processes of both *integration* and *competition* can be accounted for, contributing to the *unity* and *stability* of the bodily self, respectively.

5.1 The Brain as an Inference Machine

Psychological science has struggled to propose a unifying theory that accommodates the different sides of our self in a biologically plausible way. Predictive coding (PC) has emerged as a prominent unifying theory of cortical function to explain brain processes underlying perception, action, and more recently interoception (Friston, 2010; Seth, 2013). According to the theory, incoming sensory data is compared with internal models, that is, with the brain's probabilistic "prediction" or best guess about the environmental causes that affect the organism's nervous system. If predictions and data are not compatible, then "prediction errors" arise. However, organisms must maintain their bodies within a narrow range of desirable states, and therefore prediction errors *must be minimized*. A central tenet of PC models is the free energy principle that states that biological agents resist a natural tendency toward disorder in a constantly changing environment (Friston, 2005). Mathematically speaking, the brain (as the organ within an agent that evaluates information about the external and internal milieu and resists disorder) must have a low level of *entropy*, entropy being the surprise averaged over all events encountered (Friston, 2005). To do this the brain only needs to minimize surprise associated with the current event by making predictions about what sensorial consequences will be evoked by events in the environment. Predictions are updated and optimized continuously over time in order that a low level of entropy is maintained across the brain. In the long-term, this means that the brain as a whole minimizes the average of surprise in all sensory systems, learning how best to model and predict incoming sensory input. Additionally, it means that short-term phasic surprises ("prediction errors"), which are processed locally at each node of each sensory system, are avoided by actions that minimize surprise. This can be achieved by updating and optimizing predictions, or by acting to increase the sampling of environmental data (Friston, 2010).

The brain is therefore processing dynamically shifting generative models of what is causing incoming sensory events, based on probabilistic predictions about how likely something is to have happened and what the likely causes are. In essence this means that a surprising sensory event causes short-term phasic prediction errors, which are avoided by actions with minimal predicted surprise, and by changes in the representations (i.e., the probability distribution) of what was likely to have caused the sensory input.

Predictive coding argues for complimentary hierarchical top-down and bottom-up processes, which are distinguished by the nature of the information that they process. Bottom-up information flowing through the hierarchy reflects the impact of a sensory event, that is, prediction errors. Top-down information flowing through the hierarchy is in the form of predictions about the sensory consequences of events. At the top of the hierarchies are multisensory areas that will process abstract, supramodal representations of sensory input. Within each level of the hierarchy, there is a considerable exchange of information between representational (which process probabilistic representations or predictions about upcoming sensory input) and error units, which code prediction errors when there is a divergence between expected and actual sensory events (Clark, 2013; Friston, 2005). In summary, predictive coding suggests that probabilistic representations act as a top-down influence on expectations explaining away bottom-up prediction errors. The inferred cause of a sensory event will be the posterior probability distribution when error has been minimized.

5.2   The Exteroceptive Self from the Predictive Coding Perspective

We recently extended this framework to self-awareness to account for the malleability of the exteroceptive self (Apps & Tsakiris, 2014), and argued that one's body is processed in a probabilistic manner as the most likely to be "mine" (see Limanowski & Blankenburg, 2015 and Samad, Chung & Shams, 2015 for empirical support). Such probabilistic representations are created through the integration of top-down "predictions" about the body and of bottom-up "prediction errors" from unimodal sensory systems that are then explained away. The mental representation of the physical properties of one's self are therefore also probabilistic. That is, one's own body is the one which has the highest probability of being "mine" as other objects are probabilistically less likely to evoke the same sensory inputs. This information can be considered as highly abstract with respect to the low-level properties of the stimuli and can only be represented as "self" when different streams of multisensory information are integrated. That is, the self-face will only be recognized as "self" when a visual stimulus has been processed hierarchically for its low-level visual properties, its configural features and then its identity. The self-face will therefore be represented as an abstract, supramodal representation of visual input, for example, this is a face that I have seen before, that I am familiar with, and that is associated with congruent corollary discharge, vestibular, somatosensory, and interoceptive information when seen on a reflective surface.

In predictive coding accounts, abstract information is encoded in terms of posterior beliefs at high levels of a hierarchical model; that is, probability distributions of abstract supramodal events (Clark, 2013). In hierarchical models, beliefs at intermediate levels of the hierarchy are referred to as empirical priors because they are constrained and (plastically) optimized by both top-down and bottom-up influences—in other words, they are prior beliefs that are sensitive to empirical sensory evidence. High-level empirical priors are essentially the same as low-level empirical priors but generally represent abstract multimodal beliefs about states of the world that change slowly over time. Such beliefs are learned through associations being formed between congruent, low-level sensory events from different systems, that over time result in one event having a high probability of predicting another sensory event (Ballard, Hayhoe, Pook, & Rao, 1997). However, to produce these parallel (multimodal) predictions, there must be a high-level representation (of self) that elaborates descending predictions to multiple unimodal systems. This has implications for the processes that underpin body awareness such as body ownership and self-recognition, as it highlights how sensory events in one system can become associated with events in another and therefore how abstract representations of one's body may be formed. To illustrate, visually observed touch on the skin that is temporally congruent with touch detected by the somatosensory system will become associated with each other, resulting in a prediction of a somatosensory event when contact to the skin is about to occur. In contrast, touch between two other noncorporeal objects will never evoke a somatosensory event, and thus the prior probability of a somatosensory event following touch on such objects is very low. So one's own body is probabilistically likely to become and be the object that touch is predicted to be experienced upon. The visual properties of different body parts will also be perceptually learned such that when any object approaches the body, a somatosensory event will be predicted. Thus, perceptual learning within the free energy and predictive coding frameworks leads to generative models where aspects of one's body are processed as probabilistically the most likely object (or collection of objects) that when touched, moved, threatened, or acted upon in any way, evokes events in the other sensory systems that detect the state of the body. In short, the notion that there is a "self" is the most parsimonious and accurate explanation for sensory inputs. In mathematical terms, this parsimonious accuracy is exactly the quantity that is optimized when minimizing free energy or prediction error.

How can the free energy account explain changes in body awareness that are driven by multisensory inputs, such as the ones used in the bodily illusions reviewed above? The free energy principle highlights how surprising events in one sensory system can be explained away by more parsimonious information in another by the convergence of information at multimodal nodes in the cortex. In each of these illusions there is considerable bottom-up sensory surprise evoked in one system. The somatosensory experience of touch on one's hand that is temporally congruent with the vision of touch on the rubber hand is surprising, as prior to stimulation participants cannot see the touch on their own hand and would not predict that touch on the rubber hand would evoke a sensation of touch. Similarly, there is surprise in the somatosensory system during the enfacement illusion and surprise in the auditory system during the rubber voice illusion (Zheng et al., 2011). This surprise will be explained away by top-down effects from multisensory areas. In turn, perceptual learning processes will update representations of one's appearance or voice, such that the probabilistic representation of one's body and voice is different after synchronous multisensory stimulation. These illusions highlight how representations of one's body are malleable and can be updated when expectations about multisensory events are violated. We argue that such effects can be accounted for by top-down explaining away of the bottom-up surprise evoked by an unexpected event.

The same principles can explain the processes involved in the recognition of one's self in the mirror. At the ontogenetic level, self-recognition in the mirror poses two challenges. First comes the challenge of matching the sensorimotor experience of the body with the sensorimotor behavior of the reflected image. The second challenge relates to how a mental representation of facial and bodily appearance is acquired in the first place. Given that the infant cannot have a priori knowledge of their appearance, the infant encountering a mirror for the first time must succeed in matching their sensorimotor experience with the observed sensorimotor behavior of the object seen inside the mirror. This matching between felt and observed sensorimotor signals will lead to the formation of a mental representation of visual appearance (i.e., "that is my body reflected in the mirror; therefore that is what I look like"). This process of self-identification allows successful performance in the classic "rouge" task of mirror self-recognition, in which infants are exposed to their mirror reflection and their response to a spot of rouge covertly applied to their nose is registered (e.g., they might respond by touching their own nose (see Brooks-Gunn & Lewis, 1984). When looking in a mirror there are several surprising features that need to be explained away. First is the spatially surprising nature of reflective surfaces, as the agent perceives the visual (sensory) consequences of bodily movements in an allocentric frame of reference. Second is the temporally surprising nature of the event as there is an object (i.e., a body) that moves in a temporally congruent manner to the corollary discharge of the agent. In this setting, corollary discharge is no more, or less, than any other descending prediction other than that it produces movement by containing some proprioceptive and kinesthetic components. Third, is the surprise that the body seen in the mirror has a specific visual form. How can these surprises be explained away? The surprises evoked during mirror exposure will be explained away in multisensory areas that integrate visual information with corollary discharge, updating the probability that actions will result in movement of that body in the mirror. This will explain away the visual surprise. In turn, perceptual learning will lead to the visual features of one's body being processed as a highly likely input when one looks in a reflective surface. Thus, the viewing of an agent's own actions in a mirror (including arm movements, facial expressions, etc.), will lead to optimized high-level empirical priors about one's body, which will in turn modulate expectations in the visual system about the expected visual consequences of one's own actions. The agent will also therefore begin to recognize her face as "mine" because it is typically the face that is processed when looking in a mirror, and *that* face rarely violates expectations instantiated by the agent's actions. One's body is therefore represented as the most probable to be "mine" when seen in a mirror due to it being the most likely visual input when viewing a reflective surface.

Within a predictive coding framework, top-down predictive information processed in multisensory association cortices, plays an important role in altering the perception of sensory input. Prior beliefs will therefore modulate how self-stimuli are recognized. In addition, predictive coding argues that surprise in one system can be minimized by the top-down effects of multisensory nodes (Lee & Mumford, 2003). This suggests that surprise in any system could be explained away by probabilistic representations that are derived from information in any other system, if this is the optimal manner in which free energy can be minimized. The free energy account discussed here is therefore distinct from others in highlighting how information from any system can be used to explain away information in any other system (Mitchell, 1993). This distinguishes the present theoretical perspective from previous accounts of self-recognition, which have argued that self-processing is tied to processing in one "self" network (Northoff et al., 2006), or arises as a result of congruencies between sensory input and motor efference alone (Legrand & Ruby, 2009). The suggestion here is that self-recognition is more complex, with information from each and every sensory system potentially able to modulate self-recognition. This is particularly important, given the evidence to suggest that the continuity of the self may be underpinned by many different types of information, the integration of which leads to a coherent sense of one's body (Blanke, 2012; Tsakiris, 2010). This treatment of illusions—in the context of self recognition—is entirely consistent with current understanding that illusory phenomena are a result of Bayes optimal inference. In other words, almost universally, illusions can be explained as an unusual set of sensory circumstances being interpreted under prior beliefs about their causes in a Bayes optimal fashion. In the examples reviewed above, these prior beliefs reflect the fact that most of our sensations are caused by ourselves.

5.3   Interoceptive Predictions and Interoceptive Awareness

However, as one's body is not simply perceived exteroceptively—it is also felt interoceptively—a unifying model of the self must account for their integration. Consider the experience of body ownership during the RHI. The exteroceptive evidence suggests that what I am looking at (i.e., the rubber hand) is *my* hand. However if this is my hand, then there are interoceptive prediction errors that need to be explained away between how my *true* hand feels (i.e., the interoceptive prediction) and the fact that I cannot feel the rubber hand interoceptively. An important contribution of this and other free energy models (see Allen & Friston, 2016; Seth, 2013) is the proposal that the self is hierarchically distributed and underpinned by many different types of information. Signals and predictions from any modality may thus be brought to bear to resolve a conflict between cues in another, including higher-level, abstract, and amodal assumptions (predictions). Therefore, exteroceptive and interoceptive streams must be integrated for a body to be represented as "self." What determines the weighting of the different streams?

Both predictions and the incoming sensory data vary in the *precision* (i.e., reliability) of the information that they convey (e.g., how noisy they are). Precision is defined as the inverse variance of the distribution associated with each variable (Friston, 2009). In any modality and context, and at each level of the hierarchy, the brain therefore not only makes a "first order" hypothesis about what most probably accounts for the incoming sensory data but has also, equally crucially, to make a "second order" estimate of the variance (the precision, i.e., reliability) of the prediction errors that are set up by the incoming data versus the precision of the prior (Brown, Friston, & Bestmann, 2011; Hohwy, 2012). Sensory signals (and consequent prediction errors) that are compatible with only a narrow range of potential predictions have "high precision" and thus carry information that is reliable. By contrast, sensory signals with "low precision" are compatible with a wide range of potential predictions such that the resulting imprecise prediction errors they set up are likely to be treated as unreliable information and consequently suppressed by a precise prediction. If their interoceptive signals are precise, this would explain why individuals with high IAcc experience a weaker body ownership during the RHI by contrast with individuals with low IAcc. Precision is crucial when selecting information among various modalities because the brain preferentially weights signals that are the most precise in the given context. We therefore propose that individual differences in IAcc can be explained in terms of variations in the "precision" with which interoceptive signals from within the body are represented (Friston, 2010). The central assumption of the model is that good heartbeat perceivers (i.e., with high IAcc) are those individuals who have precise interoceptive prediction errors, relative to less precise interoceptive priors for the heartbeat (Fotopoulou, 2013; Seth, 2013). As a result, for high IAcc the brain weights interoceptive prediction errors as more reliable compared to those with low IAcc.

To experience body ownership during the RHI, participants must form a percept that the prosthetic hand is their own, by minimizing prediction errors across all available sensory modalities. Importantly in this context, information from any sensory modality can be used to explain away prediction error in any other (Apps & Tsakiris, 2014). It is precision that dictates which part of the conflicting evidence is presumed to be reliable. The illusion appears to invoke a high-level prior that seen touch and felt touch usually co-occur and thus enhances the precision of these cues (Apps & Tsakiris, 2014). Attention to vision during the illusion also deliberately enhances the precision of the visual input. The final (illusory) percept is thus determined by the high precision of the visual and somatosensory prediction errors, which the brain explains away by predicting that the rubber hand must actually be one's own. However, neither vision nor touch, is self-specific and it is potentially surprising that their integration is sufficient to cause the illusion (Legrand & Ruby, 2009). Interoceptive cues provide uniquely self-specifying sensory input to the rubber hand illusion, and the experience of embodiment in general. Their importance is evidenced by the effects of threats to the prosthetic hand, (Ehrsson et al., 2007); by histamine reactivity in the "rejected" hand (Barnsley et al., 2012); and by cooling of the participant's true hand during the illusion (Moseley et al., 2008). People with good interoceptive accuracy resist the illusion. We suggest that for these people the fake hand does not have the internal feelings attached to one's own hand because their daily interoceptive experience is characterized by the continuous updating of interoceptive priors as they are sensitive to changes in interoceptive states, as a function of highly precise interoceptive prediction errors. These serve to anchor a sense of ownership of their true hand. By contrast, people with lower interoceptive accuracy are not sensitive to interoceptive changes, experiencing little moment to moment updating of interoceptive priors and they can hence be persuaded that a fake hand is their own. This account can also explain why in the case of interoceptive rubber hand illusion (Suzuki et al., 2013; see also Aspell et al., 2013 for a similar full body illusion) it is the people with *higher* interoceptive accuracy who now experience the greater illusion, illustrating the crucial effect of context. The interoceptive cues in this version of the experiment indicate that the hand is one's own because its visual appearance is congruent with the individual's continually experienced updating of interoceptive priors. People for whom interoceptive prediction errors are precise (i.e., good heartbeat perceivers) are therefore now more, rather than less, likely to claim ownership of the virtual hand, as this experiment has demonstrated (Suzuki et al., 2013).

The model described above provides a plausible explanation of how exteroceptive evidence can be used to minimize prediction errors during the construction of our body awareness but also how exteroceptive with interoceptive information are integrated in this process. In order to minimize prediction error, the organism must learn over time to assign the best possible set of weights and thus to optimize the relative precisions of predictions and prediction errors across all modalities. This process has large explanatory value when considering the interaction between *interoceptive stability* and the *malleability of the exteroceptive self*, as it explains individual differences in interoceptive or exteroceptive precision and their effects for the awareness of the bodily self.

6 Beyond the Apparent Antagonism: Self and Unity

We used the sense of body ownership and the process of mirror self-recognition as a paradigmatic case of the interaction between the exteroceptive and interoceptive sides of embodiment. Even though we are aware of this *one* body as *ours*, psychology and neuroscience have not yet understood how the bodily signals from within are integrated with signals from the outside to give rise to the unity of the bodily self. We here proposed that in a way analogous to the homeostatic function that interoception serves at the physiological level, awareness of the interoceptive body is fundamental

to the unity and stability of the bodily self, as the other side of the exteroceptive body. Unity of the self depends on interoception for the experience
of a coherent, nonhollow body that anchors the self; while stability of the
self depends on interoception to provide a distinctive, self-specific experience in response to external changes.

Ours and others' recent findings on the link between levels of IAcc
and exteroceptively-based representations of the body together with the
development of a unifying theoretical framework described above provide
the motivation for new hypotheses that should be empirically tested in
future research. This requires first and foremost substantial methodological
advances. Despite recent developments (Garfinkel et al., 2015; Kleckner,
Wormwood, Simmons, Barrett, & Quigley, 2015), there is consensus that
interoception research must develop a wider and more grounded measurement model and a fuller characterization of the links between different
interoceptive systems, if it is to achieve its appropriate place within psychology. In addition, psychological research on interoceptive awareness
often relies on correlations that can be partly explained by the fact that
unlike exteroception, it is particularly difficult to have experimental control over the inputs to the interoceptive system, or to interfere causally with
it, or both. Therefore, the testing of new empirical hypotheses should be
preceded by methodological solutions that will address hierarchical relations in interoceptive processing, horizontal relations across interoceptive
modalities, and causal relations between interoception and awareness,
instead of mere correlations between them. It will then become possible to
test empirically the role that precision and individual differences in precision of predictions and predictions errors play in shaping the individual
characteristics of body awareness to determine the relative weight of exteroceptive and interoceptive contributions. Lastly, a hitherto unmet challenge
relates to the ontogenetic development of interoceptive awareness. Even
though the question of how self-awareness emerges in early infancy (Lewis,
2011; Rochat, 2003, or changes through development (e.g., adolescence, see
Sebastian, Burnett, & Blakemore, 2008), has been a central focus of developmental psychology, the question of when and how interoceptive awareness
emerges resulting in marked individual differences remains unexplored. In
particular, why the precision accorded to interoceptive signals might differ
between individuals has not yet been fully elucidated. Crucially however,
precision is refined by learning (Feldman & Friston, 2010; Apps & Tsakiris,
2014). In order to minimize free energy (and thus PEs), the brain must
continually optimize the relative precisions of PEs and priors, over time
and across all sensory modalities and contexts, for the particular individual

(Friston, 2009; Fotopoulou, 2013). The model put forward here implies that in people with higher IAcc this optimization involves the prioritizing of interoceptive sensations such that they can be called into awareness, with attention. Potentially higher IAcc may, at least in part, result from learned attention to internal bodily changes (interoceptive PEs), relative to other sensory modalities, presumably due to various neurophysiological and psychosocial parameters in development and during the life span. Understanding the roots of such processes in development is one of the key future research challenges in this area.

The novel conceptualization of interoceptive awareness presented here has far-reaching consequences for our understanding of bodily self-awareness, as well as the ontogenetic development of the self, and for the self's social relatedness. The theory that interoception plays an important role in cognitive and emotional processes is well established. The model we put forward here goes beyond this view to advance a ground breaking, high-risk hypothesis about the psychological role of interoception, namely that interoception serves the unity and stability of the self. This role is inspired by the homeostatic principles that keep the organism within certain ranges of physiological function in adaptive response to external changes. At the same time, we are aware of the long-lasting dichotomies (inside/out; self/ other) that have fractionalized the psychological study of the self. We therefore go beyond existing psychological models of the self to integrate two influential traditions that until now have been kept separate: the awareness of the self from the outside and from within. Rather than focusing on their apparent differences, our model considers their antagonism from a predictive coding perspective that can explain their integration for the unity of the self, and how their relationship is reflected in the balance between stability and adaptation.

Acknowledgments

This work was supported by the European Research Council Starting Investigator Grant (ERC-2010-StG-262853) to M.T. and by a Neuropsychoanalysis Foundation Fellowship.

Notes

1. Proprioceptive drift has been used as a behavioral measure of the sense of body ownership in RHI since the first description of the illusion (Botvinick & Cohen, 1998), while later studies refined its use (Tsakiris & Haggard, 2005; Costantini &

Haggard, 2007; Longo et al., 2009). However, it has recently come under criticism as to whether it truly reflects changes in body ownership. While it is true that changes in proprioception can occur without changes in body ownership (Holmes, Snijders & Spence, 2006; Rohde, Luca & Enst, 2011), it seems that changes in body ownership are accompanied by changes in proprioception (Longo et al., 2009). More recently, Abdulkarim and Ehrsson (2016) investigated the link between the strength of subjective experience of the RHI and proprioceptive drift, and found a correlation between the two, but also presented evidence that the proprioceptive drift is not causing the subjective illusion. However, it could still be the case that the subjective experience of the illusion causes the drift.

References

Abdulkarim, Z., & Ehrsson, H. H. (2016). No causal link between changes in hand position sense and feeling of limb ownership in the rubber hand illusion. *Attention, Perception & Psychophysics, 78*(2), 707–720. doi:10.3758/s13414-015-1016-0.

Adler, D., Herbelin, B., Similowski, T., & Blanke, O. (2014). Breathing and sense of self: Visuo-respiratory conflicts alter body self-consciousness. *Respiratory Physiology & Neurobiology, 203*, 68–74. doi:10.1016/j.resp.2014.08.003.

Ainley, V., & Tsakiris, M. (2013). Body conscious? Interoceptive awareness, measured by heartbeat perception, is negatively correlated with self-objectification. *PLoS One, 8*(2), e55568. https://doi.org/10.1371/journal.pone.0055568.

Allen, M., & Friston, K. J. (2016). From cognitivism to autopoiesis: Towards a computational framework for the embodied mind. *Synthese*, 1–24. doi:10.1007/s11229-016-1288-5.

Apps, M. A. J., & Tsakiris, M. (2014). The free-energy self: A predictive coding account of self-recognition. *Neuroscience and Biobehavioral Reviews, 41*, 85–97. doi:10.1016/j.neubiorev.2013.01.029.

Aspell, J. E., Heydrich, L., Marillier, G., Lavanchy, T., Herbelin, B., & Blanke, O. (2013). Turning body and self inside out: Visualized heartbeats alter bodily self-consciousness and tactile perception. *Psychological Science, 24*(12), 2445–2453. doi:10.1177/0956797613498395.

Baier, B., & Karnath, H. O. (2008). Tight link between our sense of limb ownership and self-awareness of actions. *Stroke, 39*(2), 486–488. doi:10.1161/STROKEAHA.107.495606.

Ballard, D. H., Hayhoe, M. M., Pook, P. K., & Rao, R. P. N. (1997). Deictic codes for the embodiment of cognition. *Behavioral and Brain Sciences, 20*(4), 723–767.

Barnsley, N., McCauley, J. H., Mohan, R., Dey, A., Thomas, P., & Mosley, G. (2012). The rubber hand illusion increases histamine reactivity in the real arm. *Current Biology, 21*(23), R945–R946. doi:10.1016/j.cub.2011.10.039.

Baumeister, R. F. (1991). The nature and structure of the self: An overview. In R. Baumeister (Ed.), *The self in social psychology* (pp. 1–21). Philadelphia: Psychology Press.

Bernhardt, B. C., & Singer, T. (2012). The neural basis of empathy. *Annual Review of Neuroscience, 35*, 1–23. doi:10.1146/annurev-neuro-062111-150536.

Blanke, O. (2012). Multisensory brain mechanisms of bodily self-consciousness. *Nature Reviews: Neuroscience, 13*(8), 556–571. doi:10.1038/nrn3292.

Botvinick, M., & Cohen, J. (1998). Rubber hands "feel" touch that eyes see. *Nature, 391*(6669), 756. doi:10.1038/35784.

Brooks-Gunn, J., & Lewis, M. (1984). The development of early visual self-recognition. *Developmental Review, 4*(3), 215–239. doi:10.1016/S0273-2297(84)80006-4.

Brown, H., Friston, K., & Bestmann, S. (2011). Active inference, attention, and motor preparation. *Frontiers in Psychology, 2*, 218. doi:10.3389/fpsyg.2011.00218.

Clark, A. (2013). Whatever next? Predictive brains, situated agents, and the future of cognitive science. *Behavioral and Brain Sciences, 36*(3), 181–204. doi:10.1017/S0140525X12000477.

Costantini, M., & Haggard, P. (2007). The rubber hand illusion: Sensitivity and reference frame for body ownership. *Consciousness and Cognition, 16*(2), 229–240. doi:10.1016/j.concog.2007.01.001.

Craig, A. D. (2009). How do you feel—now? The anterior insula and human awareness. *Nature Reviews: Neuroscience, 10*(1), 59–70. doi:10.1038/nrn2555.

Critchley, H. D., Wiens, S., Rotshtein, P., Ohman, A., & Dolan, R. J. (2004). Neural systems supporting interoceptive awareness. *Nature Neuroscience, 7*(2), 189–195. doi:10.1038/nn1176.

Critchley, H. D., & Harrison, N. (2013). Visceral influences on brain and behavior. *Neuron, 77*(4), 624–638. doi:10.1016/j.neuron.2013.02.008.

Damasio, A. (1999). *The feeling of what happens: Body and emotion in the making of consciousness.* New York: Harcourt Brace.

Damasio, A. R. (2003). Mental self: The person within. *Nature, 423*(6937), 227. doi:10.1038/423227a.

Dunn, B. D., Galton, H. C., Morgan, R., Evans, D., Oliver, C., Meyer, M., et al. (2010). Listening to your heart: How interoception shapes emotion experience and intuitive decision making. *Psychological Science, 21*(12), 1835–1844. doi:10.1177/0956797610389191.

Ehrsson, H. H. (2007). The experimental induction of out-of-body experiences. *Science, 317*(5841), 1048. doi:10.1126/science.1142175.

Ehrsson, H. H., Spence, C., & Passingham, R. E. (2004). That's my hand! Activity in premotor cortex reflects feeling of ownership of a limb. *Science, 305,* 875–877.

Ehrsson, H. H., Wiech, K., Weiskopf, N., Dolan, R. J., & Passingham, R. E. (2007). Threatening a rubber hand that you feel is yours elicits a cortical anxiety response. *Proceedings of the National Academy of Sciences of the United States of America, 104*(23), 9828–9833. doi:10.1073/pnas.0610011104.

Emanuelsen, L., Drew, R., & Köteles, F. (2015). Interoceptive sensitivity, body image dissatisfaction, and body awareness in healthy individuals. *Scandinavian Journal of Psychology, 56*(2), 167–174. https://doi.org/10.1111/sjop.12183.

Feldman, H., & Friston, K. (2010). Attention, uncertainty, and free-energy. *Frontiers in Human Neuroscience, 4,* 215. doi:10.3389/fnhum.2010.00215.

Fredrickson, B. L., & Roberts, T. A. (1997). Objectification theory. *Psychology of Women Quarterly, 21,* 173–206. doi:10.1111/j.1471-6402.1997.tb00108.x.

Friston, K. (2005). A theory of cortical responses. *Philosophical Transactions of the Royal Society of London, 360*(1456), 815–836. doi:10.1098/rstb.2005.1622.

Friston, K. (2009). The free-energy principle: A rough guide to the brain? *Trends in Cognitive Sciences, 13*(7), 293–301. doi:10.1016/j.tics.2009.04.005.

Friston, K. (2010). The free-energy principle: A unified brain theory? *Nature Reviews: Neuroscience, 11*(2), 127–138. doi:10.1038/nrn2787.

Fotopoulou, A. (2013). Beyond the reward principle: Consciousness as precision seeking. *Neuro-psychoanalysis, 15*(1), 33–38.

Gallese, V., & Sinigaglia, C. (2011). What is so special about embodied simulation? *Trends in Cognitive Sciences, 15*(11), 512–519. doi:10.1016/j.tics.2011.09.003.

Garfinkel, S. N., Seth, A. K., Barrett, A. B., Suzuki, K., & Critchley, H. D. (2015). Knowing your own heart: Distinguishing interoceptive accuracy from interoceptive awareness. *Biological Psychology, 104,* 65–74. doi:10.1016/j.biopsycho.2014.11.004.

Guterstam, A., Björnsdotter, M., Gentile, G., & Ehrsson, H. H. (2015). Posterior cingulate cortex integrates the senses of self-location and body ownership. *Current Biology, 25*(11), 1416–1425. doi:10.1016/j.cub.2015.03.059.

Harver, A., Katkin, E. S., & Bloch, E. (1993). Signal-detection outcomes on heartbeat and respiratory resistance detection tasks in male and female subjects. *Psychophysiology, 30*(3), 223–230. doi:10.1111/j.1469-8986.1993.tb03347.x.

Herbert, B. M., & Pollatos, O. (2012). The body in the mind: On the relationship between interoception and embodiment. *Topics in Cognitive Science, 4*(4), 692–704. doi:10.1111/j.1756-8765.2012.01189.x.

Herbert, B. M., Muth, E. R., Pollatos, O., & Herbert, C. (2012). Interoception across modalities: On the relationship between cardiac awareness and the sensitivity for gastric functions. *PLoS One*, *7*(5), e36646. doi:10.1371/journal.pone.0036646.

Hohwy, J. (2012). Attention and conscious perception in the hypothesis testing brain. *Frontiers in Psychology*, *3*, 96. doi:10.3389/fpsyg.2012.00096.

Holmes, N. P., Snijders, H. J., & Spence, C. (2006). Reaching with alien limbs: Visual exposure to prosthetic hands in a mirror biases proprioception without accompanying illusions of ownership. *Perception & Psychophysics*, *68*(4), 685–701. doi:10.3758/BF03208768.

Kammers, M. P., Rose, K., & Haggard, P. (2011). Feeling numb: Temperature, but not thermal pain, modulates feeling of body ownership. *Neuropsychologia*, *49*(5), 1316–1321. doi:10.1016/j.neuropsychologia.2011.02.039.

Khalsa, S. S., Rudrauf, D., Feinstein, J. S., & Tranel, D. (2009). The pathways of interoceptive awareness. *Nature Neuroscience*, *12*, 1494–1496. doi:10.1038/nn.2411.

Kleckner, I. R., Wormwood, J. B., Simmons, W. K., Barrett, L. F., & Quigley, K. S. (2015). Methodological recommendations for a heartbeat detection-based measure of interoceptive sensitivity. *Psychophysiology*, *52*(11), 1432–1440. doi:10.1111/psyp.12503.

Lee, T. S., & Mumford, D. (2003). Hierarchical Bayesian inference in the visual cortex. *Journal of the Optical Society of America*, *20*(7), 1434–1448. doi:10.1364/JOSAA.20.001434.

Legrand, D., & Ruby, P. (2009). What is self-specific? Theoretical investigation and critical review of neuroimaging results. *Psychological Review*, *116*(1), 252–282. doi:10.1037/a0014172.

Lenggenhager, B., Tadi, T., Metzinger, T., & Blanke, O. (2007). Video ergo sum: Manipulating bodily self-consciousness. *Science*, *317*(5841), 1096–1099. doi:10.1126/science.1143439.

Lewis, M. (2011). The origins and uses of self-awareness or the mental representation of me. *Consciousness and Cognition*, *20*(1), 120–129.

Limanowski, J., & Blankenburg, F. (2015). Network activity underlying the illusory self-attribution of a dummy arm. *Human Brain Mapping*, *36*(6), 2284–2304. doi:10.1002/hbm.22770.

Longo, M. R., Schüür, F., Kammers, M. P., Tsakiris, M., & Haggard, P. (2008). What is embodiment? A psychometric approach. *Cognition*, *107*(3), 978–998. doi:10.1016/j.cognition.2007.12.004.

Longo, M. R., Schüür, F., Kammers, M. P., Tsakiris, M., & Haggard, P. (2009). Self-awareness and the body image. *Acta Psychologica*, *132*(2), 166–172. doi:10.1016/j.actpsy.2009.02.003.

Metzinger, T. (2003). *Being no one: The self-model theory of subjectivity*. Cambridge, MA: MIT Press.

Mitchell, R. W. (1993). Mental models of mirror-self-recognition: Two theories. *New Ideas in Psychology, 11*(3), 295–325. doi:10.1016/0732-118X(93)90002-U.

Moseley, G. L., Olthof, N., Venema, A., Don, S., Wijers, M., Gallace, A., et al. (2008). Psychologically induced cooling of a specific body part caused by the illusory ownership of an artificial counterpart. *Proceedings of the National Academy of Sciences of the United States of America, 105*(35), 13169–13173. doi:10.1073/pnas.0803768105.

Northoff, G., Heinzel, A., de Greck, M., Bennpohl, F., Dobrowolny, H., & Panksepp, J. (2006). Self-referential processing in our brain—a meta-analysis of imaging studies on the self. *NeuroImage, 31*(1), 440–457. doi:10.1016/j.neuroimage.2005.12.002.

Petkova, V. I., & Ehrsson, H. H. (2008). If I were you: Perceptual illusion of body swapping. *PLoS One, 3*(12), e3832. doi:10.1371/journal.pone.0003832.

Rochat, P. (2003). Five levels of self-awareness as they unfold early in life. *Consciousness and Cognition, 12*(4), 717–731.

Rohde, M., Di Luca, M., & Ernst, M. O. (2011). The rubber hand illusion: Feeling of ownership and proprioceptive drift do not go hand in hand. *PLoS One, 6*(6), e21659. https://doi.org/10.1371/journal.pone.0021659.

Rohde, M., Wold, A., Karnath, H.-O., & Ernst, M. O. (2013). The human touch: Skin temperature during the rubber hand illusion in manual and automated stroking procedures. *PLoS One, 8*(11), e80688. doi:10.1371/journal.pone.0080688.

Ronchi, R., Bello-Ruiz, J., Lukowska, M., Herbelin, B., Cabrilo, I., Schaller, K., et al. (2015). Right insular damage decreases heartbeat awareness and alters cardio-visual effects on bodily self-consciousness. *Neuropsychologia, 70*, 11–20. doi:10.1016/j.neuro psychologia.2015.02.010.

Sadibolova, R., & Longo, M. R. (2014). Seeing the body produces limb-specific modulation of skin temperature. *Biology Letters, 10*(4), 20140157. doi:10.1098/rsbl .2014.0157.

Samad, M., Chung, A. J., & Shams, L. (2015). Perception of body ownership is driven by Bayesian sensory inference. *PLoS One, 10*(2), e0117178. doi:10.1371/journal.pone .0117178.

Schauder, K. B., Mash, L. E., Bryant, L. K., & Cascio, C. J. (2015). Interoceptive ability and body awareness in autism spectrum disorder. *Journal of Experimental Child Psychology, 131*, 193–200. doi:10.1016/j.jecp.2014.11.002.

Sebastian, C., Burnett, S., & Blakemore, S.-J. (2008). Development of the self-concept during adolescence. *Trends in Cognitive Sciences, 12*(11), 441–446. doi:10.1016/j.tics .2008.07.008.

Seth, A. K. (2013). Interoceptive inference, emotion, and the embodied self. *Trends in Cognitive Sciences*, *17*(11), 565–573. doi:10.1016/j.tics.2013.09.007.

Sforza, A., Bufalari, I., Haggard, P., & Aglioti, S. M. (2010). My face in yours: Visuo-tactile facial stimulation influences sense of identity. *Social Neuroscience*, *5*(2), 148–162. doi:10.1080/17470910903205503.

Simmons, W. K., Avery, J., Barcalow, J., Bodurka, J., Drevets, W. C., & Bellgowan, P. (2013). Keeping the body in mind: Insula functional organization and functional connectivity integrate interoceptive, exteroceptive, and emotional awareness. *Human Brain Mapping*, *34*(11), 2944–2958. doi:10.1002/hbm.22113.

Suzuki, K., Garfinkel, S. N., Critchley, H. D., & Seth, A. K. (2013). Multisensory integration across exteroceptive and interoceptive domains modulates self-experience in the rubber-hand illusion. *Neuropsychologia*, *51*(13), 2909–2917. doi:10.1016/j.neuropsychologia.2013.08.014.

Tajadura-Jiménez, A., Longo, M. R., Coleman, R., & Tsakiris, M. (2012). The person in the mirror: Using the enfacement illusion to investigate the experiential structure of self-identification. *Consciousness and Cognition*, *21*(4), 1725–1738. doi:10.1016/j.concog.2012.10.004.

Tajadura-Jiménez, A., & Tsakiris, M. (2014). Balancing the "inner" and the "outer" self: Interoceptive sensitivity modulates self-other boundaries. *Journal of Experimental Psychology. General*, *143*(2), 736–744. doi:10.1037/a0033171.

Tsakiris, M. (2008). Looking for myself: Current multisensory input alters self-face recognition. *PLoS One*, *3*(12), e4040. doi:10.1371/journal.pone.0004040.

Tsakiris, M. (2010). *My* body in the brain: A neurocognitive model of body-ownership. *Neuropsychologia*, *48*(3), 703–712. doi:10.1016/j.neuropsychologia.2009.09.034.

Tsakiris, M., Costantini, M., & Haggard, P. (2008). The role of the right temporoparietal junction in maintaining a coherent sense of one's body. *Neuropsychologia*, *46*, 3014–3018.

Tsakiris, M., Hesse, M. D., Boy, C., Haggard, P., & Fink, G. R. (2007). Neural signatures of body ownership: A sensory network for bodily self-consciousness. *Cerebral Cortex*, *17*(10), 2235–2244. doi:10.1093/cercor/bhl131.

Tsakiris, M., Longo, M. R., & Haggard, P. (2010). Having a body versus moving your body: Neural signatures of agency and body-ownership. *Neuropsychologia*, *48*(9), 2740–2749. doi:10.1016/j.neuropsychologia.2010.05.021.

Tsakiris, M., Tajadura-Jiménez, A., & Costantini, M. (2011). Just a heartbeat away from one's body: Interoceptive sensitivity predicts malleability of body-representations. *Proceedings of the Royal Society: Biological Sciences*, *278*(1717), 2470–2476. doi:10.1098/rspb.2010.2547.

Whitehead, W. E., & Drescher, V. M. (1980). Perception of gastric contractions and self-control of gastric motility. *Psychophysiology, 17*(6), 552–558. doi:10.1111/j.1469 -8986.1980.tb02296.x.

Wiens, S. (2005). Interoception in emotional experience. *Current Opinion in Neurology, 18*(4), 442–447.

Zahavi, D. (2005). *Subjectivity and selfhood: Investigating the first-person perspective.* Cambridge, MA: MIT Press.

Zheng, Z. Z., MacDonald, E. N., Munhall, K. G., & Johnsrude, I. S. (2011). Perceiving a stranger's voice as being one's own: A "rubber voice" illusion? *PLoS One, 6*(4), e18655. doi:10.1371/journal.pone.0018655.

16 Why Should Any Body Have a Self?

Jakob Hohwy and John Michael

1 Introduction

We use a general computational framework for brain function to develop a
theory of the self. The theory is that the self is an inferred model of endogenous, deeply hidden causes of behavior. The general framework for brain
function on which we base this theory is that the brain is fundamentally an
organ for prediction error minimization.

There are three related parts to this project. In the first part (sections
2 and 3), we explain how prediction error minimization must lead to the
inference of a network of deeply hidden endogenous causes. The key concept here is that prediction error minimization in the long term approximates hierarchical Bayesian inference, where the hierarchy is critical to
understand the place of the self and the body in the world.

In the second part (sections 4 and 5), we discuss why such a set of hidden
endogenous causes should qualify as a self. We show how a comprehensive
prediction error minimization account can accommodate key characteristics of the self. It turns out that, though the modeled endogenous causes
are just some among other inferred causes of sensory input, the model is
special in being—in a special sense—a model of itself.

The third part (sections 6 and 7), identifies a threat from such self-modeling: How can a self-model be accurate if it represents itself? We propose that
we learn to be who we are through a positive feedback loop: from infancy
onward, humans apply agent-models to understand what other agents are
up to in their environment, and actively align themselves with those models. Accurate self-models arise and are sustained as a natural consequence of
humans' skill in modeling and interacting with each other.

The concluding section situates this inferentialist yet realist theory of
the self with respect to narrative conceptions of the self.

2   Bayesian Inference and Prediction Error Minimization

On the picture of the human brain that we shall work with, organisms like us construct internal models of the world in order to interact meaningfully in our environment. The inputs that our senses receive are caused by objects and states of affairs in the world, including other people and endogenous states of our own bodies. Sensory input is all the brain has to go by in constructing its model of the world (Helmholtz, 1867). A series of sensory inputs is a sample of some size, for example, samples for an estimate of the location of a flash of light. Such a sample will be subject to noise, and we can assume it will be normally distributed (i.e., a Gaussian distribution). This is what the brain has to work with in its attempt to learn the true cause (the location of the flash of light). Assume for simplicity that samples come in one at a time. The brain needs to learn something from each sample, so that it can arrive at an estimate of the true, underlying cause. The first sample comes in and suggests location a, so the brain represents the location as location a. The next sample comes in and suggests location b. Now the brain could stick to location a, but would then have learned nothing from the second sample; this strategy is tantamount to assuming falsely that a first sample is veridical and the rest misleading. The brain could switch to location b, but would then have thrown out all information carried by the first sample; this strategy is an example of overfitting. Instead, a location between the two samples should be picked: a location, m, that results from weighting the existing evidence against the new evidence.

This is an exceedingly simple example, but it is instructive. Notice that the estimate of location m is a *model* fitted to the samples, and that the brain never receives direct confirmation of this inferred location. In other words, if the sensory input is noisy, then the brain must be entertaining internal models that are in some sense removed from the states of affairs— the hidden causes—that are being modeled.

Bayes' rule specifies the optimal location of m, namely in terms of the probability of location a, also known as the prior—what is already believed— and the probability of the new sample given location a, also known as the likelihood. Bayesian *inference* is the process of updating the prior in the light of the new evidence to arrive at a new estimate—the posterior. In inference, the prior works as a *prediction* ("the next input will be a"), and the likelihood encodes the *prediction error*, which would be zero if the next sample were indeed a. In our example, the new prediction error is b, so the prediction error is $(a - b)$. Crucially, the amount learned from this prediction error should depend on how robust the prior and likelihoods are. If it is not sample one and two, but sample 1001 and 1002, then even a large prediction error should not change the posterior very much; similarly, if the prediction error itself is very noisy then it should not be allowed to update the posterior very much. Bayes' rule takes care of this weighting. It turns out that for a normal distribution, this estimate turns out to be the mean, hence "m."

Consider now what happens to the long-term average of prediction error as Bayesian inference converges on the mean. There will still be prediction error for every new, noisy sample. Most samples will be within a couple of standard deviations, and there will be some outliers, but overall, by sticking to m, error will be minimized. In contrast, any other, non-Bayesian, estimate will tend to create greater error in the long run (e.g., if the true mean is 0, and the samples -1 and 1, then a non-Bayesian estimate of -3 will generate a prediction error of 6 rather than 2; for this approach to Bayes in terms of relative precisions, and subsequent application to hierarchical learning, see Mathys et al., 2012, 2014).

If Bayesian inference is prediction error minimization, then (assuming normal distributions) any system that minimizes prediction error in the long run will be approximating Bayesian inference. This is crucial to appreciate how the brain solves the problem of building a model of the world on the basis of sensory input.

It is not plausible to say that the brain knows and applies Bayes' rule—neurons don't know probability theory. But it is plausible to say that neuronal populations harbor expectations about what the sensory input should be, the strength of which is based on past learning. These expectations are compared against the actual input to extract the prediction error, and the activity of the neuronal population is adjusted in the light of the size and variance of the ensuing prediction error.

In other words, it is plausible that the brain can minimize prediction error, even if it does not explicitly apply Bayes' rule. Moreover, if the brain simply aims to keep prediction error as low as possible (taking into account irreducible noise and assuming normal distributions) on average and over the long run, then it will be guaranteed to approximate Bayesian inference (Friston, 2003). This is the fundamental idea of predictive processing: a system—like the brain—that minimizes prediction error on the long-term average will approximate Bayesian inference.

The challenges to prediction error minimization become much more prevalent in a world as complex as ours, where there is not just a single source of visual input but multiple interacting causes. In such an environment, the system must constantly assess hypotheses and compare them against each other to arrive at the best overall model. For example, the light, represented with the mean location *m*, may periodically disappear and thus create a situation where the absence of a predicted input causes a prediction error (cf. den Ouden, Friston, Daw, McIntosh, & Stephan, 2009). The system may then try to introduce a further hidden cause into its model, also normally distributed, that represents an occluder (e.g., someone waving their hand in front of the light). Then the system may be able to get prediction error minimization back on track, when the causal interaction of the occluder and the light is correctly modeled.

A prediction error minimization system in the real world, exposed to its manifold of causes, would build up a vast repertoire of beliefs about all sorts of hidden causes and their interactions. This would be hierarchically ordered in a spatiotemporal sense, such that small receptive fields and regularities operating at fast timescales would be at the bottom (e.g., the intensity and location of the light), and larger fields and longer-term causal regularities higher up (e.g., the movement of a hand periodically occluding the light). The hierarchy would also include expectations not just about means but also of the variances (or *precisions*) of the prediction errors it may encounter, in order for it to steer an informed route between underfitting and overfitting.

The claim now is that *we* are like this (Hohwy, 2013; Clark, 2013, 2016). We manage to represent the world by being prediction error minimizers—neural mechanisms that realize Bayesian inference in the long run. Equivalently, we minimize uncertainty about our model of the world—accumulate evidence for it—by minimizing error. On some versions of the prediction error minimization framework, this is *all* we ever do (Friston, 2010; Hohwy, 2013, 2015).

If all we ever do is minimize prediction error, what could it mean to have a *self*? It seems prediction error minimization is just a matter of inferring causes in the world, so expecting there to be a self could appear as unreasonable as expecting the mean location of a series of visual samples, arrived at through Bayesian inference, to have a self. However, by working with the notion of a prediction error minimizing system we will show how it can in fact accommodate many of our preconceptions about the self.

Interestingly, there are now a number of studies attempting to connect different aspects of body and self with the predictive processing framework. Our approach here builds upon an early approach developed in Hohwy (2007; 2013, chap. 12). It also resonates with and draws upon several other recent approaches, including Limanowski and Blankenburg (2013), who connect the framework to minimal phenomenal selfhood; Apps and Tsakiris (2014), who explain bodily self-awareness in terms of the framework;

Seth, Suzuki, and Critchley (2011), who focus on interoceptive predictive coding and self; Moutoussis, Fearon, El-Deredy, Dolan, and Friston (2014), who focus on predictive processes in the relation of self and other; Friston and Frith (2015), who focus on social understanding in terms of coupled oscillations of selves; Fotopoulou (2012) and Carhart-Harris and Friston (2010), who connect the framework to psychodynamical notions of self; and finally, an important precursor to the Bayesian approach is Thomas Metzinger's (2004, 2009) work on self-models (see Limanowski & Blankenburg 2013 for discussion).

In the simple example of a flash of light, we considered the possibility of causal interaction with other causes, such as an occluder making the light disappear periodically. Interactions create nonlinearity in the sensory input that cannot be explained away well on the basis of a model of a simple, normal distribution. Instead, it becomes necessary to postulate multiple causes that, when convolved, are able to fit the sensory input. Of course, a good explanation for why a light periodically disappears could be that the perceiver is blinking their eyes, which technically speaking occludes the light source. If the perceiver models this, then they are modeling part of what happens to be their *own body* in order to minimize prediction error. This can be generalized and extended to any part of the body or the trajectory of the body as a whole (e.g., Why are the flashes of light moving at an accelerating pace? You have begun a sprint; Why is the chair creaking? You have put on weight). In this simple sense, modeling the body is the automatic upshot of prediction error minimization, which allows perception of the world. A full body model will be finessed over time, as we accumulate evidence, learn about precisions, and learn how to actively test hypotheses through our own behavior (for discussion, see Hohwy, 2013, chaps. 1–4; Seth, 2015).

By taking the perspective of long-term prediction error minimization, it is thus quite easy to see how internal models of agents will end up including representations of the agent's own body and its trajectories and interactions with other causes in the world. Agents will represent their own bodies simply because prediction error minimization of necessity leads to representing the worldly causes of the agent's sensory input, and the agent's body is in fact itself one of these causes.

3   The Self in the Body

Perception is perfused with the interaction of the body with the environment, mandating internal representation of the body. The body is nothing special, it is just one among many causes interacting with each other in the environment, and in the course of this impacting on the senses. Representation of the body is nothing special either; it is just one among many causes that get represented in the internal model used for prediction error minimization.

As we noticed, internal models need to be hierarchical to be efficient at minimizing prediction error in the long run. For example, in the short timescale, you might be well-served to use an umbrella whenever it rains, but it also helps to model how the seasons influence the probability of rainfall so you know better when to bring your umbrella. The long-term representation of seasons is higher in the hierarchy in the sense that it helps control the predictions of rainfall, and of course, perception of actual rainfall is evidence that filters upward and helps to shape the long-term representations of seasons. Seasons are in this sense more deeply hidden causes than rainfall itself, they (or the tilt of the Earth's rotational axis in its orbital plane) are causes that operate behind, but are perceivable in, the more directly observable causes, such as rainfall.

As it is for rain and seasons, so also for the body and its more deeply hidden causes. For example, an agent who blinks at a normal rate will blink more when exposed to an unexpected, startling auditory stimulus. In this case, fear is an internal mental state that causally interacts with the body and thereby modulates the evolution of sensory input. Eye blinks can also be brought about by a puff of air to the eye. Here we have an ambiguous situation where two different hypotheses could explain the same visual input: something scary or a mere puff of air. Contextual information such as additional auditory input or the presence of an air puffer can help disambiguate and arrive at the best hypothesis. Similar examples can be run for other cases of body-involving prediction error. If you begin experiencing repeatedly removing yourself from parties and social get-togethers before everyone else, then there is, assuming you are normally keen to socialize, prediction error concerning the trajectory of your body. This can be explained away by hypothesizing that you are beginning to develop introversion as a character trait, or, as alternative hypotheses to test over time, social phobia, depression, or, again, as something non-self-related such as the deterioration of your social scene.

Over time, the overall internal model will be populated with states and parameters for not just the less hidden bodily causes of sensory input but also the more deeply hidden internal causes of the agent, which interact with each other (e.g., fear plus hunger gives one trajectory of sensory input, fear plus pain gives another) and in turn with worldly influences (e.g., fear and presence of tigers vs. fear and no presence of tigers).

The model of causes hidden within the body captures an integrated net of character traits, biases, reaction patterns, affections, standing beliefs, desires, intentions, base-level internal states, and so on. This representation comes about through prediction error minimization just as naturally as representations of deep hidden causes in the wider environment, such as seasons. Without representation of these deep causes we would be much worse off in our ability to minimize moment to moment prediction error over the long run. Causes within the body can be thought of as *endogenous* (i.e., as changes initiated within the organism in a sense we will specify more below), and causes in the environment as *exogenous* (i.e., as changes initiated outside of the organism).

Our proposal is to conceive of this internal model of endogenous causes as a representation of *the self*. The suggestion then, is that agents model the self as a hierarchy of hidden, endogenous causes, and further, that the self is identical to these causes. As we shall explain later on, this modeling in turn becomes an endogenous cause serving to stabilize the hierarchy of causes constituting the self, so the self-model is part of the self. Our proposal is motivated by the basic idea that who we are is determined by the regularities in our constitution that determine what we feel, think, and decide, and how we act. This proposal sits well with earlier notions of self-models, in particular Thomas Metzinger's approach: "A self-model, an inner image of the organism as a whole [is] built into the world-model, and this is how the consciously experienced first-person perspective develop[s]" (2009, p. 64; see also 2004).

This proposal presents the self as more than a mere bundle of causes. The self-model is a hierarchical construct whose levels are linked by message-passing as top-down predictions are generated and bottom-up prediction errors minimized. For example, the agent's desire for ice cream manifests every day but its magnitude is modulated by longer-term regularities associated with the desire to lose weight, which manifest predominantly at the beginning of the calendar year. All the parts of the self-model are thus tied together and interact causally with each other. This captures the idea that one's self is comprised of both long-term characteristics and the expression of these in shorter-term behaviors, and, vice versa, that our long-term characteristics must depend on relatively stable patterns in our shorter-term behaviors.

Over time, noise and uncertainty are filtered out of the self-model, just as they are in the modeling of the broader environment in which the self is causally enmeshed. This means that more coincidental events do not make it as parts of the self-model. For example, if one summer day the ice-cream loving agent by happenstance refrains from eating ice cream, this doesn't mean the parameters of the self-model should be revised. If such coincidental events are included, then the self-model risks being overfitted to coincidentally varying behavior, which is not so clearly self-related. However, if this kind of variability reduction happens too much, then the model becomes uninformative (underfitted) and fails to capture actual patterns of behavior. This balancing act between overfitting and underfitting corresponds to what happens in any kind of Bayesian modeling, as described above.

A balanced self-model of endogenous causes may be paraphrased in simple terms as a *theory* or *narrative* that appeals to regularities or plotlines at different, interlocked timescales. Such a theory or narrative can be seen as an answer to the question: Which kind of agent am I? For a simplistic agent, this might be "I am an ice-cream loving person who worries about my weight, and this manifests in the way I go through life, where I am often eating ice cream though I manage to refrain in the couple of months after my New Year's resolution." For realistic agents, the narrative will be much longer and more complicated. Crucially—and in contrast to narrative accounts of the self (as we will explain in more detail in section 8)—this account does not imply that agents generally make such narratives fully explicit, nor that the narratives in questions take a linguistic form, nor that they are coherent in the sense of forming a coherent plot or story (cf. Dennett, 1991a, 1991b; Velleman, 2006). Rather, it is a narrative account, in the first instance, in the sense that the subsumption of events under higher-level regularities (i.e., hierarchical Bayes) structures and constrains our interpretation of those events. As we shall see later in sections 6 and 7, the self-model is also narrative in the sense that it actively shapes itself over time to align with those higher-level regularities.

Above, we briefly noted that *action* is a useful tool for disambiguation of models of the body. The reliance on action is unsurprising on a prediction error minimization scheme since action is an efficient tool for reducing uncertainty in causal inference. Action, or intervention in the world, allows us to go beyond mere associative evidence (e.g., A is statistically associated with B) and on to learning causal relations (e.g., A causes B) (Pearl, 2000; Woodward, 2003). Accordingly, action is also crucial for forming the self-model—in shaping the narrative. For example, if you suspect that your fear of heights is subsiding then you may seek out tall buildings to accumulate evidence for this hypothesis. James Russell neatly ties action in with forming a conception, or model, of the self in causal terms:

> The freer we are to alter our perceptual inputs, the more we learn of the *refractory* nature of the world and, correlatively, the richer the conception we gain of ourselves as determiners of our immediate mental life. This refractoriness, therefore, sets limits on what our agency can achieve in determining our experiences, thereby engendering a conception in us of something as setting these limits, as causing them to be set. (Russell, 1995, p. 134)

Through action, the self-model stands out more sharply and with less uncertainty. Of course, we have also argued that it is action itself that leads to the need for a self-model in the first place. The agent's causal interaction with the world causes changes to sensory input of a kind that is best explained away by positing a body and a self. We thus represent the self because we in general are active creatures, and we act so that we can represent the self. This circularity is a springboard for discussing some of the deeper aspects of the prediction error minimization approach to the self (sections 4 and 5), as well as the developmental dynamics in the shaping of the self (sections 6 and 7).

4 Body, Self, and Existence

The self-model is hierarchical, which means that it encompasses causal regularities governing events at many timescales. At the low levels of this hierarchy are regularities that represent the body and its movement, which happens at relatively fast timescales (e.g., one to two seconds for reaching, a few hours for moving around town to do the shopping). At intermediate levels are regularities that represent medium-term endogenous causes (e.g., days for reading up for an exam, months for a new learning objective). At higher levels are stable regularities such as character traits (e.g., being fastidious).

What we label the "self" is constituted by more deeply hidden causes than what is represented in the body-model specifically. Given the hierarchical ordering of the overall model, this does not imply that body and self are separate entities. They are tied up in one causal nexus, just as daily rainfall and seasons are tied up together. We can certainly talk about the movement of the body on its own, and we can talk about dynamics of the self on its own, but it is very hard to understand or predict the movements of the body or the dynamics of the self without connecting them to each other in just the way hierarchical Bayes suggests. For example, knowing character traits enables predictions of bodily movement, and character traits that never manifest in bodily movement will quickly begin to look spurious.

By treating body and self as just more hierarchical modeling of the causes in the world we thus get an appealing picture of body and self as separate and yet related. This makes good sense of core intuitions about body and self. When we speculate about the self it is hard to avoid involving thoughts about the body, and conversely, it is difficult to divorce thoughts about one's own body from thoughts about one's self. Yet our conceptions of body and self allow that they can be referred to separately (e.g., "my body may be old but I still feel young inside").

There is nothing special about this hierarchically mediated relation between body and self. The self-model represents them together, just as the model of the world represents snowfall and seasons together. One analogy here would be biological cells. Body and self are as connected as subcellular components are to the detailed activity at the cell membrane. There is no great mystery in either case; the main difference would be that in the case of the body and self, there are causes at more levels of hierarchical depth than in the cell (even though cells are rather complex biological entities; see Friston, 2013 for a prediction error minimization account of basic organic entities).

In his delightful thought experiment "Where Am I?" Daniel Dennett (1981) imagines that his endogenous causes, harbored in the brain, are dislodged from the body but connected to it wirelessly. Dennett notes the profound uncertainty he feels in trying to locate himself either where his brain is or where his body is. We would feel the same kind of uncertainty if a similar thought experiment were made for the cell: Is the cell where the membrane is or where the subcellular components are? We feel something has been left out of the story if either is ignored. The Bayesian explanation is simple: the causal hierarchy ties body and self (or membrane and subcellular components) together such that the processes in one only makes sense in the context of the other. The thought experiment works because on the one hand the mathematical detail is left unchanged such that the causal hierarchy is intact (Dennett's body still is the lower level of the causal hierarchy and the endogenous causes in his brain at the higher levels). On the other hand the self-model is challenged because we have learned over time that the self and the body are co-located. In this sense, this type of philosophical reflection about the self is very similar to self-related illusions like the rubber hand illusion or full body illusion (Botvinick & Cohen, 1998; Lenggenhager, Tadi, Metzinger, & Blanke, 2007; see also the theoretical background for this work on self-models, developed by Metzinger, 2004, 2009, which also challenge the core belief of spatial collocation associated with the self-model).

We next offer a consideration about the self-model, which helps tie it to a very traditional notion of the self, namely that having or being a self is in some inchoate sense tied to *existence* or *being*—to the fact or thought *that I am*. At the low level of the overall self-model we have parameters representing the body. These parameters are modulated in part by higher-level causes, the set of which we identified with the self. We said that at the higher levels of the hierarchy we have stable regularities concerning, for example, character traits. At the very highest levels, details are stripped out and only more general beliefs are found. This leads, in the end, to just the belief that *I exist*. In the most ambitious versions of prediction error minimization schemes, which are based on free energy minimization, the belief that I exist is equivalent to the belief that I act to maintain myself in certain states (Friston & Stephan, 2007; for further discussion, see Limanowski & Blankenburg, 2013). The reasoning is that I cease to exist if I cannot maintain myself in a limited number of states, that is, if my body begins to disperse across many states. I must act to prevent dispersion: inaction leaves me open to the unfettered impact of the second law of thermodynamics. So if I exist I must be acting, and if I act I must exist. Put differently, the highest-level belief is that I am a cause in the world, or an agent. This belief permeates all the levels below in the sense that they would all generate large prediction errors in the long run if agency ceased. Conversely, that highest-level belief in being an agent is itself based on just the kind of Bayesian inference exemplified above: the best prediction error minimization is obtained by modeling the self and its body as partial causes of changes in sensory input. Here we see how the circularity mentioned earlier (I act to model myself and model myself because I act) is grounded in the free energy principle (for this kind of approach, see Friston & Stephan, 2007; Friston, 2011).

This speculative link to the free energy minimization account enables substantial characteristics of our conception of self to emerge from hierarchical Bayesian processing. Being a self is in a fundamental sense tied to existence and to agency, rather than merely to having a certain narrative, certain character traits, certain desires, or a certain bodily configuration.

The hierarchical Bayesian perspective can be illustrated through David Hume's famous failure to identify the self through introspection:

> For my part, when I enter most intimately into what I call *myself*, I always stumble on some particular perception or other, of heat or cold, light or shade, love or hatred, pain or pleasure. I never catch *myself* at any time without a perception, and never can observe any thing but the perception. (Hume, 2000, B1, p. 4, §6)

When he stumbles upon his perceptions he is reporting on low-level causes, and failing to report that the trajectory of sensory experience is governed by more deeply hidden causes, which are not directly perceivable in the same sense and yet are represented. Hume might as well have complained that he never perceives seasons but only snowfall, blooming flowers, ripening fruit, and falling leaves. He is looking in the right place but focusing on the wrong timescale. As a result, Hume succumbs to what might be termed the *short-timescale fallacy*, failing to pick up the real patterns that unfold at longer timescales and which underlie more rapidly fluctuating perceptual states. In particular, he fails to appreciate the more deeply hidden causes that pertain to his own interaction with the world and which are informed by the highest-level belief that he exists and is an agent in the world.

5   The Model That Models Itself

The self is just one set of causes among other causes of sensory input. By minimizing prediction error, the self can be modeled just as other causes can be modeled. If the cause is a leafy tree in the environment, then the internal model represents that leafy tree. Seen from an outside, third-person perspective, there is clear separation of the causal relata—of the model and what is modeled. The model is harbored in the brain and the tree is outside the brain. The less the prediction error, the more the mutual information between them.

The situation is less straightforward with the self-model and the self. Seen from the outside, third-person perspective, it is not immediately clear what the causal relata are. In some sense, the self-model must be representing itself rather than things external to itself. But this notion of self-representation is somewhat mystifying. Metzinger discusses this, explaining a weak version of the self in terms of "a self-organizing and self-sustaining physical system that can represent itself on the level of global availability" (2009, p. 208). Metzinger denies the existence of a self in a stronger sense, based on the idea that the self-model is a mere process, a "biological data format" (2009, p. 288; see also Metzinger, 2011). We agree with much of this but below we offer a seemingly more metaphysically robust account of self-representation in terms of inferred hidden causes.

Consider first that inference of the deeply hidden causes constituting the self is mediated through the impact of these causes on less deeply hidden nonself causes in the body and the environment—these are the states that the agent can control through action. Blinking or moving a cup are examples of this. For inference of other hidden causes such as seasons, migrations, and economic downturns, the causal flow can be pictured as relatively straight, going through deeply hidden to less deeply hidden causes, and then together impacting on the sensory organs of the organism in question and shaping its internal model. In the case of the self, this flow simply bends back on itself such that the deeply hidden causes stem from the organism itself. This is part of what is modeled: the self-model represents the circular character of the causal flow.

The notion of self-involving circular causation does not wholly demystify self-modeling. This is because it is clear that *action* must be central to understanding what is going on: without action there would be no need to posit endogenous causes to explain changes in prediction error. It will therefore help to clarify what action is, according to the prediction error minimization approach.

Above we noted that a system that minimizes prediction error on average and in the long run will approximate Bayesian inference. Prediction error can be minimized by changing the model to fit the data, as happens in perception. But prediction error can obviously also be minimized by acting in the world. For example, you move the source of sound to the location you expect it to be at. Since average long-run prediction error minimization will approximate Bayesian inference, it follows that considered in the long term, action is inference just as much as perception is; it is *active inference* (Friston, Daunizeau, & Kiebel, 2009). Inference is the job of the model, so active inference too stems from the model. It follows that the part of the model that is involved in active inference is the self: this part of the model (the active states and their more deeply hidden causes) are the very endogenous causes that can be inferred in perceptual inference, which therefore become part of the self-model that in turn, in a dynamic downstream manner, shape active inference.

Self-modeling can now be demystified further. The self is modeled in perceptual inference, as the system learns what its own self is. What is learned are hierarchical patterns of active inference: the deeply hidden expectations that the system relies upon in active inference (for example, a pattern may be that you consistently move classical music sound sources closer to yourself, but other types of music further away, revealing something about your deeper desires). The self-model's learned patterns of active inference in turn inform the next volley of active inference (e.g., relocating to Vienna to make classical music encounters more likely). If this process manages to keep prediction error low on average and over the long run, then uncertainty about the model is gradually reduced. The model thus comes to know itself—represent itself—through action (as anticipated in the quote by Russell above).

It is worth taking a moment to let the strangeness of this idea sink in. It may seem that there must be ways of reducing prediction error about the self other than revising the self-model. In particular, it seems that I could simply move to a new environment that does not elicit behavior from me which generates the prediction error. For example, if I notice that I have been attending lots of Schoenberg concerts even though I don't believe myself to be a fan of atonal music, do I really need to revise my self-model in order to do away with the discrepancy? Can't I just move to a place where there is no possibility of going to Schoenberg concerts? In fact, however, this would be a form of active inference, and its successful execution (i.e., choosing a place where there is no Schoenberg to tempt me) would require me to be sensitive to just the right hidden cause in myself (when offered the opportunity to listen to Schoenberg, I tend to take it). In other words, it turns out that this move, too, would constitute a form of Bayesian inference about my self.

Self-modeling as a process of coming to learn one's own model through action implies that there are two related stages in the flow of activity in the brain of a prediction error minimizing agent from sensory states, impacted by the worldly causes, through the internal states and on to the active states that enslave bodily movement, which in turn affect changes in the world's hidden causes. The key is that active states are the downstream effects of what we have called deeply hidden endogenous states, and these endogenous states are the downstream effects of sensory states. Self-modeling is thereby a process that can be described in causal terms, as first finessing a model of the self, and then engaging that model in action, leading to further finessing of the model, and more action. This approach applies the notion of a Markov blanket, which is essential to the free energy principle (cf. Friston, 2013), to the case of the self.

For this dynamic inferential process to make sense, it cannot be that any inference about the patterns of active inference is as good as any other; the self-model would be cluttered with all sorts of more or less plausible beliefs, and prediction error would not be minimized. But since some actions are more likely than others to minimize prediction error, the system is constrained insofar as it needs to learn which patterns of active inference are associated with long-term prediction error minimization. That information is available to the model, since prediction error is the one quantity the brain can compute. This means that patterns of active inference can be ranked according to their ability to minimize error.

A ranking of patterns of active inference will facilitate decision making, on the assumption that agents believe they will occupy low prediction error states in the long run (i.e., that they will exist). This in turn implies that the highly ranked patterns will reflect how probable it is that the agent harbors these patterns, that is, that those patterns go into constituting the self. In other words, the better the pattern of active inference is at minimizing error, the more likely it is that it belongs to the agent. This is because the agent has learned one overarching belief, as we mentioned above, namely that it exists as an agent—as an active prediction error minimizer in the long run. The mere belief in existence therefore makes it probable that the agent harbors patterns of active inference that are good at minimizing error in the long run. Self-related prediction error minimization will infer to those well-performing patterns over poor performing patterns, and they will then become part of what we here call the self. This means the self-modeling approximates Bayesian inference about the self, through action, because it minimizes error in the long run, fundamentally with respect to the hypothesis that the agent exists.

Of course, a self-model will only minimize prediction error in the long run if it can maintain a fairly high degree of *accuracy*. Given the circular causality associated with self-modeling, it may seem that the process can float free of any constraints. To address this concern, we will (in the next two sections) explain in some detail how to think about accuracy for such a self-modeling system. The core idea is that self-models and selves are fitted together as a natural consequence of humans' skill in modeling and interacting with each other. More concretely, infants and young children apply agent-models to others during the course of development, and use these agent-models to guide imitation and other forms of cultural learning. From the perspective of the prediction error minimization framework, this appears as a form of active inference: infants and young children shape their selves progressively to match the agent models that they have been using to interpret others. Thus, the predictive processing framework is able not just to underpin key notions of body and self but also to provide us with a novel way of thinking about recent findings from developmental psychology pertaining to cultural learning and the development of self-understanding.

6   Agent-Modeling, and Cultural Learning as Active Inference

There is a wealth of research in developmental psychology suggesting that infants differentiate between agents, on the one hand, and nonagents on the other. In particular, they are sensitive to core features of agents, such as faces and gaze direction (Senju & Csibra, 2008; Farroni et al., 2002), as well as contingent motion (Gergely & Watson, 1999; Carey, 2009).

Over the course of the first year of life, this sensitivity to such features comes increasingly to inform and be informed by representations of agents' goals (Woodward, 1998), of their strategies for attaining those goals (Gergely & Csibra, 2003), and of basic mental states such as attention (Reddy, 2003), emotions (Stern, 1998), and intentions (Behne, Carpenter, Call, & Tomasello, 2005). Indeed, there is an ever-increasing body of evidence suggesting that infants are able to represent and reason about other agents' beliefs by the second year of life (Surian, Caldi, & Sperber, 2007; for reviews, see Christensen & Michael, 2015; Michael & Christensen, 2016; Apperly, 2011, chap. 3; Baillargeon, Scott, & He, 2010), and perhaps as early as the middle of the first year (Kovacs et al., 2010; Southgate & Vernetti, 2014).

What this evidence indicates is that infants and young children not only identify agents as a subset of the objects around them, but that they are predicting the behavior of those agents by applying an increasingly hierarchical model of what agents are like: Agents have particular desires and preferences, which they act upon in ways that are informed and constrained by doxastic representations which in turn are acquired through perception and through inferences.

We will now explain how the application of an agent-model, in particular in infancy and early childhood, supports imitation and other forms of *cultural learning*. For present purposes, we will adopt Tomasello, Kruger and Ratner's (1993) conception of cultural learning as a form of learning that depends upon learners and teachers understanding each other as beings who "have intentional and mental lives like their own" (Tomasello, 1999, p. 7).

One important type of cultural learning is imitative learning. Following Tomasello (1999; cf. also Tomasello, Carpenter, Call, Behne, & Moll, 2005) we will regard imitation (which is sensitive to an observed agent's goals and strategies), but not emulation (where the learner focuses on the environmental effect of an observed action) as a type of cultural learning. In other words, imitation relies upon a deeper model of the observed agent's mental states in their relation to her movements and to the environmental affordances and constraints. When engaged in imitative learning, the learner understands the agent as rationally selecting an appropriate sequence of actions to realize a goal. From about eighteen months, infants tend to imitate incomplete but intended actions rather than replicating the exact behavior they have seen, for example, when an agent tries but fails to close a drawer (Meltzoff, 1995). This demonstrates that they are modeling other agents' intentions and using those intentions to structure and guide their own learning. Similarly, Gergely and colleagues (2002) have found evidence that, by around fourteen months, infants are able to selectively imitate features of an action that are relevant to the goal of the action, and to ignore extraneous or idiosyncratic features. In other words, they interpret observed agents' behavior in terms of goals and rational strategies to attain those goals, and their imitative learning is guided by this interpretation.

These findings indicate that, in order to understand what the adults in their environment are up to, children apply agent-models that are structured by coherent relations among mental states, environmental constraints and affordances, and bodily movements. In addition, however, it also reveals that children have a tendency to align themselves actively with what those adults are up to—at least with what those adults appear to be up to when viewed through the lens of the agent-models which children apply to them.

This is perhaps most obviously the case for imitation, since it involves children manifestly acting to align themselves with a model. But it is also just as true, though perhaps more subtly, for other forms of cultural learning. In social-referencing situations, for example, which occur by around nine months (Baldwin & Moses, 1994) and perhaps earlier at five or six months (Vaillant-Molina & Bahrick, 2012), infants are sensitive to the objects of caregivers' emotional expressions and adopt those attitudes toward the same objects. That is, infants treat as dangerous or disgusting objects toward which the caregiver has expressed fear or disgust. Here we see how the emotional evaluation of the object is influenced by a sophisticated understanding of the adult's visual attention in order to track not only the type of emotional state but also its intentional object, and to adopt an emotion of the same type toward the same intentional object.

Furthermore, there has been a great deal of research documenting how children's understanding of adults' attentional states and intentions is crucial for language acquisition. For example, if an adult announces her intention to "find the toma" and then searches in a number of locations, scowling upon seeing some objects and smiling upon seeing one object, children will learn the new word "toma" for the object the adult smiles at (Tomasello & Barton, 1994). In fact, Southgate and colleagues (2010) found that seventeen-month-olds learned to apply a novel word ("sefu") to a toy that an adult falsely believed was hidden in a box if the adult pointed at that box and pronounced the word (after being out of the room while the toy was moved from the box to a different location) (for a review of several similar studies, see Tomasello, 1999, pp. 114–116). Moreover, as Tomasello (1999) has emphasized, language acquisition gets going around twelve months, at which time children engage in triadic interactions with an adult and an object, and exhibit pointing behavior to inform others of events they do not know about or to share an attitude about mutually attended events others already know about (Liszkowski, Carpenter, & Tomasello, 2007). As with the case of imitation, then, we see that language learning also requires children to apply agent-models to others, and to actively align themselves with those agent-models.

These central forms of cultural learning also provide the foundation for additional, more nuanced and elaborate forms of cultural learning further downstream. Language, for example, enables a multitude of further effects upon cognitive development—"from simply exposing children to factual information to transforming the way they understand and cognitively represent the world by providing them with multiple, sometimes conflicting, perspectives on phenomena" (Tomasello, 1999, p. 163). In acquiring a natural language, children learn to partition the world into objects and events in a way specific to their culture, to categorize the objects and events so partitioned, and to take different perspectives upon them. Thus, one object can be described as "the dog," "Fido," "the dog over there," "the golden retriever," and so on, and one event can be described as "The dog bit the man," "The man was bitten by the dog," and "Fido bit Daddy." Which of these descriptions is appropriate depends upon the speaker's communicative goals and upon her evaluation of the listener's interests, knowledge, and so forth. The ability to switch among these perspectives and to deploy them flexibly is entrenched through early experiences of disagreeing with others who take different perspectives and in reformulating utterances that have not been understood. Language also enables children to internalize rules, to memorize information and procedures, to talk about their own reasoning processes and other experiences, and to redescribe previously implicit procedural knowledge in explicit symbolic terms, thus enabling greater flexibility and systematicity.

Moreover, sensitivity to others' mental states is also of crucial importance in understanding all manner of norms that structure human sociality, since these derive their binding force not from physical facts but from agreement in people's attitudes about the statuses of entities, the entitlements and obligations they entail, and so on (cf. Searle, 1995; Gilbert, 1990). And there is evidence that children as young as two are sensitive to conventional ways of doing things or using objects, and treat these conventions as normatively binding (Rakoczy, Warneken, & Tomasello, 2008; Schmidt, Rakoczy, & Tomasello, 2010).

Finally, language is also important in shaping children's emerging understanding of themselves as unique individuals with their own preferences, as well as their own distinctive perspectives on and evaluations of events. In particular, as Fivush and Nelson (2006) have emphasized, talking about events together with adults helps children to become more fluent in linking their own emotions and other mental states with external events (e.g., "I was sad because my balloon flew away"). Moreover, shared remembering of past events, and of their own attitudes toward those events, helps children to develop a more reflective understanding of themselves as agents with distinctive perspectives on the world, some of whose thoughts and feelings can change over time, whereas some other mental states are much more lasting, such as some preferences, some beliefs, and many memories (Nelson, 2003).

The upshot of these various forms of cultural learning is that infants and young children progressively refine their agent-models through interaction with others, and also, through active inference, increasingly conform to those models themselves.

7 Active Inference and the Reciprocal Shaping of Self-Models

We have seen in the previous section that cultural learning can be conceptualized as a form of active inference by which children progressively converge upon the agent-models which they initially apply to interpret *other* agents. One effect of this is that children become increasingly similar to the adults in their culture. More precisely, they become increasingly similar to the adults around them *as those adults appear to them on the basis of the interpretations they generate by applying agent-models*. This effect ensures that the application of agent-models during development increases the predictive power of those agent-models. For children's use of agent-models will have shaped their own development such that they themselves approximate the intentional agents that they take others to be. And, if so, they will themselves be more easily intelligible for other interpreters who are also applying agent-models.

The flip side of this is that *adults* also apply agent-models toward young children, and that this also plays a key role in structuring children's cognitive development, that is, by setting up expectations for them to fulfill, and by acquainting them with culture-specific objects, practices, narratives, social roles, and so forth. For example, gender-specific interpretations of infant behavior (such as boys' cries more often being interpreted as expressions of anger as opposed to sadness) create expectations that children then conform to (Mameli, 2001). Insofar as adults' interpretation of young children as potentially rational intentional agents facilitates children's enculturation, it also increases the predictive power of agent-models, and thus becomes, as Mameli (2001) puts it, a "self-fulfilling prophecy."

And of course this structuring effect[1] of agent-models continues into adulthood. Consider, for example, how we sanction others for departing from rational or social norms. Thus, as McGeer puts it, folk psychology is "a *regulative* practice, moulding the way individuals act, think and operate so that they become well-behaved folk-psychological agents: agents that can be well-predicted and explained using both the concepts and the rationalizing narrative structures of folk psychology" (McGeer, 2007, p. 139). Similarly, Alfano (2013) has recently argued that similar ideas can play an important role in shaping people's ethical behavior: labeling somebody as generous, for example, may lead her to think of herself as generous, or to believe that others think of her this way, or both, and motivate her to want to live up to this expectation and to maintain this image. As he puts it: "Trait attributions of the right sort function as self-fulfilling prophecies" (Alfano, 2013, p. 83).

Alfano's analysis also underscores the point that our interpretations of our own behavior and biographies have an influence on our own actions and choices, and are thus also sometimes self-fulfilling prophesies. Some research with split-brain patients serves as a dramatic illustration of this. One woman, whose right hemisphere received the instruction that she should get up and leave the room, and who was then presented with a request to her left hemisphere to explain what she was doing (Gazzaniga, 1995, p. 1393), confabulated that she had gotten up in order to get a soda—and, crucially, she then really did go and get a soda. Thus, to borrow Zawidzki's gloss on this example: "whether or not our public self-interpretations are justified or true, we actively work to confirm them" (Zawidzki, 2013, p. 231).

The mechanism proposed here is circular, but not viciously so. It does not require that young children have the intentional states ascribed by interpreters applying agent-models, nor that agent-models have a high degree of predictive power when applied to very young children. It requires merely that young children have imprecise predictions to this effect about other agents and about themselves. If they do so, and if this provides them with role models to learn from and thereby to become more similar to, then they will develop in such a way that they subsequently become intelligible to others who also apply agent-models—including themselves. Moreover, becoming more like the agents in their culture they are modeling also adds to children's interpretive resources, which, in turn, enable more learning and thereby more similarity, and so forth. In this sense, agent-modeling and cultural learning constitute a positive feedback loop.

8 Is the Bayesian Self a Narrative Self?

As we have seen, the prediction error minimization framework presents an elegant and novel way of understanding how agents come to model the self, namely as a hierarchy of hidden endogenous causes, and of how human agents—through active inference in development and in social interaction throughout the life span—reciprocally align their selves with their agent-models. The upshot is increasing controllability and decreasing prediction error (for a fully developed view of alignment within the free energy principle, see Friston & Frith, 2015, who essentially treat interaction as coupled oscillation that entails alignment). In this final section, we will flesh out this conception a little more by considering similarities it bears to narrative accounts of the self—but also some interesting differences.

The key feature of narrative accounts is that the self is conceptualized as an abstraction emerging from autobiographical narratives. As Dennett, for example, has expressed this view:

> A self . . . is an abstraction defined by the myriad of attributions and interpretations (including self-attributions and self-interpretations) that have composed the biography of the living body whose centre of narrative gravity it is. As such it plays a singularly important role in the ongoing cognitive economy of that living body, because, of all the things in the environment an active body must make mental models of, none is more crucial than the model the agent has of itself. (Dennett, 1991a, p. 427)

And:

> And where is the thing your self-representation is about? It is wherever you are. And what is this thing? It's nothing more than, and nothing less than, your centre of narrative gravity. (Dennett, 1991a, p. 429)

This approach is attractive insofar as it offers a way of conceptualizing the self as real and robust (like centers of gravity) without postulating mysterious immaterial entities. In fact, insofar as descriptions of the self and its traits can be used to identify behavioral and interactive patterns that facilitate predictions and to specify norms and ideals to conform to, it can also be a tool for structuring and controlling actions over time. Building on this point, Velleman (2006) articulates a narrative theory which emphasizes that the descriptions that constitute the self feed back into the decision making and planning of the agent, and thus have real causal powers, akin to self-fulfilling prophesies (see also Mackenzie, 2007; for discussion, see Menary, 2008).

Despite the prima facie attraction of the basic idea of the self as a narrative center of gravity, the metaphor of the narrative also raises several important questions and challenges. First of all, the concept of a narrative implies linguistic representation, and perhaps also explicit recounting. This implies that prelinguistic children and nonlinguistic creatures do not have selves. And if they do have some more primitive form of self, it is difficult to see how a narrative self would arise from or otherwise relate to this more primitive form of self (Menary, 2008). Second, as some (e.g., Strawson, 2004) have objected, the concept of a narrative appears to imply coherence, whereas in fact life (and one's autobiographical memories) may seem more like a desultory collection of fragments than a coherently crafted narrative. Third, narrative accounts make it difficult to make sense of the possibility of error. While narratives about fictional characters are unconstrained by objective facts, it is possible to be mistaken in thinking that one is, for example, kind or well-loved.

Like narrativist accounts, the account we have been articulating resolutely avoids postulating an immaterial entity as the bearer of psychological properties or of experiences. And, also like narrativist accounts, it stops short of eliminating altogether the self. Instead, it avoids Hume's short-timescale fallacy by understanding the self as an abstraction that is useful in recognizing deeply hidden, longer-term patterns among endogenous psychological properties, experiences, and sensory inputs.

In contrast to narrative accounts, however, this account does not imply that the form of representation in question is linguistic. Instead, it is a hierarchical Bayesian model that passes messages among its levels to reduce prediction error in the long term. One important consequence of this modification is that the account does not rely on narrative *coherence* (see Strawson's objection above). This is because the self-model is not a representation of events or sequences of events in the life of the agent. Instead, it captures the hidden patterns of endogenous causes of those events. Different models can however have different depths. For example, a very shallow self-model will have trouble subsuming regular events under longer-term regularities; conversely, an overly deep model will tend to explain irregular happenstance as manifestations of longer-term regularities. This speaks to differing degrees of narrative coherence and the long-term task of arriving at a model of appropriate depth: a shallow model will have a fragmented narrative and a deep model will be more structured. Individual differences in the depth of the self-model are to be expected, given the dynamic nature of active self-alignment.

However, no matter how deep or shallow the self-model, in order for it to contribute to the reduction of prediction error, a different kind of coherence is always required. Specifically, the hierarchically superordinate layers of the model can only have predictive power if the parameters that they include are really somehow connected to each other and to the parameters of hierarchically subordinate layers. For example, the postulation of clusters of psychological properties like preferences, beliefs, and personality traits must make it possible to generate predictions about behavior, and the error in predictions about behavior help shape the clusters of psychological properties. In other words, there must be a coherent link between these psychological properties, the behavior, other causes in the world, and back on to sensory input. The notion of coherence is here given a precise meaning, namely in terms of how a system that minimizes prediction error will approximate Bayesian inference ensuring that all levels are maximally predictive of each other (given expected levels of noise in the self-model).

Finally, the account is better positioned than narrative accounts to explain how we can be wrong in our self-representations. The self is not merely the fictitious subject of a narrative. Instead, it is the set of endogenous causes being referred to by self-models, which are constrained by their embeddedness in a positive feedback loop constituted by worldly causes, bodily states, sensory states, internal states at various levels of causal depth, and active states.

While this constitutes a departure from the way in which narrativist theorists such as Dennett have explicitly characterized the self, it is a departure that in fact builds upon core insights of narrative theorists. In particular, the developmental feedback loop we have described can be understood as the product of applying Dennett's intentional stance theory to the development of self-understanding and the self: young children's use of the intentional stance enables them to learn from and thereby to become more similar to the adults in their culture. As a result, they themselves become increasingly intelligible to other people taking the intentional stance. Thus, the intentional stance and cultural learning constitute a feedback loop that (partially) explains the reliability of the intentional stance. Michael (2015) has even argued that this developmental perspective on the intentional stance—contra Dennett—provides grist to the mill for a *causal* realist interpretation of the reference of intentional terms and of the self, insofar the causal interaction between intentional interpretations of behavior and cognitive development provides an anchor that links intentional terms to the endogenous hidden causes constituting the self.

This realist interpretation of intentional states and of self also means that—contra narrativism—correctness does enter into the picture with respect to the self. In particular, the agent can accumulate more or less evidence for a self-model over different time spans. Of course, it is often not a straightforward matter to evaluate the probability of an attribution of a psychological property, such as whether I am generous or hot-tempered. But the attribution is constrained by all the evidence that I have accumulated about myself, and can be contested by others who have access to an overlapping set of evidence about me. Thus, attributions of properties to the self can be more or less consistent with evidence, and they are open to revision according to how well they predict the evidence.

In summary, the predictive processing approach to brain function has a central role for both body and self, as inferred entities in the world that are represented in the agent's internal model of the world. The inference is based on filtering out patterns of causation that are best explained away by the model inferring that it is itself a cause of changes to its sensory input. Various aspects of this inferential account speak to the conception of the self as something more than mere inference but indeed something connected to existence and agency. These abstract ideas are not only consistent with recent research on self-conceptions in infants and young children, they allow us to see social interaction and cultural learning as key elements in the dynamic process of shaping one's self through action and interaction. Overall, we arrive at an idea of the embodied self, which harkens back to but also significantly revises well-known narrative accounts of the self.

Note

1. Mameli (2001) coined the term "mindshaping" to denote this structuring effect of adults' intentional interpretations of children; Zawidzki (2013, chap. 2) generalizes it to include cases, such as imitative learning, where an agent actively converges upon some external model—for instance, models of other agents, generated by taking the intentional stance toward them.

References

Alfano, M. (2013). *Character as moral fiction.* Cambridge: Cambridge University Press.

Apperly, I. (2011). *Mindreaders: The cognitive basis of "theory of mind."* New York: Psychology Press.

Apps, M. A. J., & Tsakiris, M. (2014). The free-energy self: A predictive coding account of self-recognition. *Neuroscience and Biobehavioral Reviews, 41,* 85–97. doi:10.1016/j .neubiorev.2013.01.029.

Baillargeon, R., Scott, R. M., & He, Z. (2010). False-belief understanding in infants. *Trends in Cognitive Sciences, 14*(3), 110–118. doi:10.1016/j.tics.2009.12.006.

Baldwin, D. A., & Moses, L. J. (1994). Early understanding of referential intent and attentional focus: Evidence from language and emotion. In C. Lewis & P. Mitchell (Eds.), *Children's early understanding of mind: Origins and development* (pp. 133–156). Hillsdale, NJ: Lawrence Erlbaum.

Behne, T., Carpenter, M., Call, J., & Tomasello, M. (2005). Unwilling versus unable: Infants' understanding of intentional action. *Developmental Psychology, 41*(2), 328– 337. doi:10.1037/0012-1649.41.2.328.

Botvinick, M., & Cohen, J. (1998). Rubber hands "feel" touch that eyes see. *Nature, 391*(6669), 756. doi:10.1038/35784.

Carey, S. (2009). *The origin of concepts.* New York: Oxford University Press.

Carhart-Harris, R. L., & Friston, K. J. (2010). The default-mode, ego-functions and free-energy: A neurobiological account of Freudian ideas. *Brain, 133*(4), 1265–1283. doi:10.1093/brain/awq010.

Christensen, W., & Michael, J. (2015). From two systems to a multi-systems architecture for mindreading. *New Ideas in Psychology.* doi:10.1016/j.newideapsych.2015 .01.003.

Clark, A. (2013). Whatever next? Predictive brains, situated agents, and the future of cognitive science. *Behavioral and Brain Sciences, 36*(3), 181–204. doi:10.1017/ S0140525X12000477.

Clark, A. (2016). *Surfing uncertainty.* New York: Oxford University Press.

Csibra, G., Gergely, G., Biró, S., Koós, O., & Brockbank, M. (1999). Goal attribution without agency cues: The perception of "pure reason" in infancy. *Cognition, 72*(3), 237–267. doi:10.1016/S0010-0277(99)00039-6.

Dennett, D. (1981). Where am I? In *Brainstorms: Philosophical essays on mind and psychology* (pp. 310–323). Cambridge, MA: MIT Press.

Dennett, D. (1991a). *Consciousness explained.* London: Allen Lane.

Dennett, D. (1991b). Real patterns. *Journal of Philosophy, 88*(1), 27–51. doi:10.2307/ 2027085.

den Ouden, H. E. M., Friston, K. J., Daw, N. D., McIntosh, A. R., & Stephan, K. E. (2009). A dual role for prediction error in associative learning. *Cerebral Cortex, 19*(5), 1175–1185. doi:10.1093/cercor/bhn161.

Farroni, T., Csibra, G., Simion, F., & Johnson, M. H. (2002). Eye contact detection in humans from birth. *Proceedings of the National Academy of Sciences of the United States of America*, *99*(14), 9602–9605.

Fivush, R., & Nelson, K. (2006). Parent–child reminiscing locates the self in the past. *British Journal of Developmental Psychology*, *24*(1), 235–251. doi:10.1348/0261510 05X57747.

Fotopoulou, A. (2012). Towards psychodynamic neuroscience. In A. Fotopoulou, D. Pfaff, & M. A. Conway (Eds.), *From the couch to the lab: Trends in psychodynamic neuroscience* (pp. 25–47). New York: Oxford University Press.

Friston, K. (2003). Learning and inference in the brain. *Neural Networks*, *16*(9), 1325–1352. doi:10.1016/j.neunet.2003.06.005.

Friston, K. (2010). The free-energy principle: A unified brain theory? *Nature Reviews: Neuroscience*, *11*(2), 127–138. doi:10.1038/nrn2787.

Friston, K. (2011). Embodied inference: Or "I think therefore I am, if I am what I think." In W. Tschacher & C. Bergomi (Eds.), *The implications of embodiment* (pp. 89–125). Exeter, UK: Imprint Academic.

Friston, K. (2013). Life as we know it. *Journal of the Royal Society, Interface*, *10*(86). doi:10.1098/rsif.2013.0475.

Friston, K., Daunizeau, J., & Kiebel, S. J. (2009). Reinforcement learning or active inference? *PLoS One*, *4*(7), e6421. doi:10.1371/journal.pone.0006421.

Friston, K., & Frith, C. (2015). A duet for one. *Consciousness and Cognition*, *36*, 390–405. doi:10.1016/j.concog.2014.12.003.

Friston, K., & Stephan, K. (2007). Free energy and the brain. *Synthese*, *159*(3), 417–458. doi:10.1007/s11229-007-9237-y.

Gazzaniga, M. (1995). Consciousness and the cerebral hemispheres. In M. Gazzaniga (Ed.), *The cognitive neurosciences* (pp. 1391–1400). Cambridge, MA: MIT Press.

Gergely, G., Bekkering, H., & Kiraly, I. (2002). Developmental psychology: Rational imitation in preverbal infants. *Nature*, *415*(6873), 755. doi:10.1038/415755a.

Gergely, G., & Csibra, G. (2003). Teleological reasoning in infancy: The naïve theory of rational action. *Trends in Cognitive Sciences*, *7*(7), 287–292. doi:10.1016/ S1364-6613(03)00128-1.

Gergely, G., & Watson, J. S. (1999). Early socio-emotional development: Contingency perception and the social-biofeedback model. *Early Social Cognition: Understanding Others in the First Months of Life*, *60*, 101–136.

Gilbert, M. (1990). Walking together: A paradigmatic social phenomenon. *Midwest Studies in Philosophy*, *15*(1), 1–14. doi:10.1111/j.1475-4975.1990.tb00202.x.

Helmholtz, H. v. (1867). *Handbuch der physiologishen Optik*. Leipzig: Leopold Voss.

Hohwy, J. (2007). The sense of self in the phenomenology of agency and perception. *Psyche, 13*(1). http://journalpsyche.org/files/0xab11.pdf.

Hohwy, J. (2013). *The predictive mind*. Oxford: Oxford University Press.

Hohwy, J. (2015). The neural organ explains the mind. In T. Metzinger & J. M. Windt (Eds.), *Open MIND* (pp. 1–23). Frankfurt am Main: MIND Group.

Hume, D. (2000). *A treatise of human nature*. Oxford: Clarendon Press.

Kovács, Á. M., Téglás, E., & Endress, A. D. (2010). The social sense: Susceptibility to others' beliefs in human infants and adults. *Science, 330*(6012), 1830–1834.

Lenggenhager, B., Tadi, T., Metzinger, T., & Blanke, O. (2007). Video ergo sum: Manipulating bodily self-consciousness. *Science, 317*(5841), 1096–1099. doi:10.1126/science.1143439.

Limanowski, J., & Blankenburg, F. (2013). Minimal self-models and the free energy principle. *Frontiers in Human Neuroscience, 7*, 547. doi:10.3389/fnhum.2013.00547.

Liszkowski, U., Carpenter, M., & Tomasello, M. (2007). Pointing out new news, old news and absent referents at 12 months of age. *Developmental Science, 10*(2), F1–F7. doi:10.1111/j.1467-7687.2006.00552.x.

Mackenzie, C. (2007). Bare personhood? Velleman on selfhood. *Philosophical Explorations, 10*(3), 263–281. doi:10.1080/13869790701535287.

Mameli, M. (2001). Mindreading, mindshaping, and evolution. *Biology & Philosophy, 16*(5), 595–626. doi:10.1023/A:1012203830990.

Mathys, C., Daunizeau, J., Iglesias, S., Diaconescu, A. O., Weber, L. A. E., Friston, K. J., et al. (2012). Computational modeling of perceptual inference: A hierarchical Bayesian approach that allows for individual and contextual differences in weighting of input. *International Journal of Psychophysiology, 85*(3), 317–318. doi:10.1016/j.ijpsycho.2012.06.077.

Mathys, C. D., Lomakina, E. I., Daunizeau, J., Iglesias, S., Brodersen, K. H., Friston, K. J., et al. (2014). Uncertainty in perception and the Hierarchical Gaussian Filter. *Frontiers in Human Neuroscience, 8*, 825. doi:10.3389/fnhum.2014.00825.

McGeer, V. (2007). The regulative dimension of folk psychology. In D. D. Hutto & M. Ratcliffe (Eds.), *Folk psychology re-assessed* (pp. 137–156). Dordrecht, Netherlands: Springer.

Menary, R. (2008). Embodied narratives. *Journal of Consciousness Studies, 15*(6), 63–84.

Metzinger, T. (2004). *Being no one: The self-model theory of subjectivity*. Cambridge, MA: MIT Press.

Metzinger, T. (2009). *The ego tunnel*. New York: Basic Books.

Metzinger, T. (2011). The no-self alternative. In S. Gallagher (Ed.), *The Oxford handbook of the self*. Oxford: Oxford University Press. doi:10.1093/oxfordhb/9780199548019.003.0012.

Meltzoff, A. N. (1995). Understanding the intentions of others: Re-enactment of intended acts by 18-month-old children. *Developmental Psychology, 31*(5), 838–850. doi:10.1037/0012-1649.31.5.838.

Michael, J. (2015). The intentional stance and cultural learning: A developmental feedback loop. In C. Muñoz-Suárez & F. De Brigard (Eds.), *Content and consciousness revisited: With replies by Daniel Dennett* (pp. 163–183). New York: Springer; 10.1007/978-3-319-17374-0_9.

Michael, J., & Christensen, W. (2016). Flexible goal attribution in early mindreading. *Psychological Review, 123*(2), 219–227.

Moutoussis, M., Fearon, P., El-Deredy, W., Dolan, R. J., & Friston, K. J. (2014). Bayesian inferences about the self (and others): A review. *Consciousness and Cognition, 25*, 67–76. doi:10.1016/j.concog.2014.01.009.

Nelson, K. (2003). Narrative and self, myth and memory: Emergence of the cultural self. In R. Fivush & C. A. Haden (Eds.), *Autobiographical memory and the construction of a narrative self: Developmental and cultural perspectives*. Hove: Psychology Press.

Pearl, J. (2000). *Causality*. Cambridge: Cambridge University Press.

Rakoczy, H., Warneken, F., & Tomasello, M. (2008). The sources of normativity: Children's understanding of the normative structure of games. *Developmental Psychology, 44*(3), 875–881. doi:10.1037/0012-1649.44.3.875.

Reddy, V. (2003). On being the object of attention: Implications for self–other consciousness. *Trends in Cognitive Sciences, 7*(9), 397–402. doi:10.1016/S1364-6613(03)00191-8.

Russell, J. (1995). At two with nature: Agency and the development of self-world dualism. In J. L. Bermúdez, A. J. Marcel, & N. Eilan (Eds.), *The body and the self* (pp. 127–151). Cambridge, MA: MIT Press.

Schmidt, M., Rakoczy, H., & Tomasello, M. (2010). Young children attribute normativity to novel actions without pedagogy or normative language. *Developmental Science, 14*(3), 530–539. doi:10.1111/j.1467-7687.2010.01000.x.

Searle, J. (1995). *The construction of social reality*. New York: Free Press.

Senju, A., & Csibra, G. (2008). Gaze-following in human infants depends on communicative Signals. *Developmental Science, 18*(9), 668–671. doi:10.1016/j.cub.2008.03.059.

Seth, A. K., Suzuki, K., & Critchley, H. D. (2011). An interoceptive predictive coding model of conscious presence. *Frontiers in Psychology, 2*, 395. doi:10.3389/fpsyg .2011.00395.

Seth, A. K. (2015). The cybernetic Bayesian brain. In T. K. Metzinger & J. M. Windt (Eds.), *Open MIND*. Frankfurt am Main: MIND Group.

Southgate, V., Chevallier, C., & Csibra, G. (2010). Seventeen-month-olds appeal to false beliefs to interpret others' referential communication. *Developmental Science, 13*(6), 907–912. doi:10.1111/j.1467-7687.2009.00946.x.

Southgate, V., & Vernetti, A. (2014). Belief-based action prediction in preverbal infants. *Cognition, 130*(1), 1–10.

Stern, D. (1998). *The interpersonal world of the infant: A view from psychoanalysis and developmental psychology*. London: Karnac.

Strawson, G. (2004). Against narrativity. *Ratio, 17*(4), 428–452. doi:10.1111/j.1467-9329 .2004.00264.x.

Surian, L., Caldi, S., & Sperber, D. (2007). Attribution of beliefs by 13-month-old infants. *Psychological Science, 18*(7), 580–586.

Tomasello, M. (1999). *The cultural origins of human cognition*. Cambridge, MA: Harvard University Press.

Tomasello, M., & Barton, M. E. (1994). Learning words in nonostensive contexts. *Developmental Psychology, 30*(5), 639–650. doi:10.1037/0012-1649.30.5.639.

Tomasello, M., Carpenter, M., Call, J., Behne, T., & Moll, H. (2005). Understanding and sharing intentions: The origins of cultural cognition. *Behavioral and Brain Sciences, 28*(5), 675–691. doi:10.1017/S0140525X05000129.

Tomasello, M., Kruger, A., & Ratner, H. (1993). Cultural learning. *Behavioral and Brain Sciences, 16*(3), 495–511. doi:10.1017/S0140525X0003123X.

Vaillant-Molina, M., & Bahrick, L. E. (2012). The role of intersensory redundancy in the emergence of social referencing in 51/2-month-old infants. *Developmental Psychology, 48*(1), 1–9. doi:10.1037/a0025263.

Velleman, J. D. (2006). *Self to self: Selected essays*. New York: Cambridge University Press.

Woodward, A. L. (1998). Infants selectively encode the goal object of an actor's reach. *Cognition, 69*(1), 1–34. doi:10.1016/S0010-0277(98)00058-4.

Woodward, J. (2003). *Making things happen*. New York: Oxford University Press.

Zawidzki, T. (2013). *Mindshaping: A new framework for understanding human social cognition*. Cambridge, MA: MIT Press.

Contributors

Adrian J. T. Alsmith   Center for Subjectivity Research, University of Copenhagen, Denmark

Brianna Beck   Institute of Cognitive Neuroscience, University College London, UK

José Luis Bermúdez   Department of Philosophy, Texas A&M University, USA

Anna Berti   Department of Psychology, University of Turin, Italy

Alexandre Billon   Department of Philosophy, Université Lille 3, France

Andrew J. Bremner   Department of Psychology, Goldsmiths, University of London, UK

Lucilla Cardinali   The Brain and Mind Institute, Western University, Canada

Tony Cheng   Department of Philosophy, University College London, UK

Frédérique de Vignemont   Institut Jean Nicod, CNRS-ENS-EHESS, Institut d'Études Cognitives, PSL, France

Francesca Fardo   Interacting Minds Center, Aarhus University, Denmark

Alessandro Farnè   IMPACT, INSERM, France

Carlotta Fossataro   Psychology Department, University of Turin, Italy

Shaun Gallagher   Department of Philosophy, University of Memphis, USA

Francesca Garbarini   Department of Psychology, University of Turin, Italy

Patrick Haggard   Institute of Cognitive Neuroscience, University College London, UK

Jakob Hohwy   Department of Philosophy, Monash University, Australia

Matthew R. Longo   Department of Psychological Sciences, Birkbeck College, University of London, UK

Tamar R. Makin   Institute of Cognitive Neuroscience, University College London, UK

Marie Martel   Laboratoire Dynamique du Langage, CNRS, France

Melvin Mezue   Oxford Centre for Functional MRI of the Brain, University of Oxford, UK

John Michael   Department of Philosophy, University of Warwick, UK

Christopher Peacocke   Department of Philosophy, Columbia University, USA

Lorenzo Pia   Department of Psychology, University of Turin, Italy

Louise Richardson   Department of Philosophy, University of York, UK

Alice C. Roy   Laboratoire Dynamique du Langage, CNRS, France

Manos Tsakiris   Department of Psychology, Royal Holloway, University of London, UK

Hong Yu Wong   Werner Reichardt Centre for Integrative Neuroscience, University of Tübingen, Germany

Index

Action, 290, 293. *See also* Motor control; Agency
computational model of, xii, 62–67
defensive movements, 209, 223–225, 228–232
development of, 3, 5, 8–9, 11–13
instrumental movements, 223–224
knowledge of, 150–151, 301, 307–308
representation of, xi–xii, 3, 7–9, 12, 78–80, 97, 220, 223–225, 264, 274–275, 277–278, 282n2, 293–295, 301, 304–306
and self-location, 263–264, 274–281, 282n1, 319–323, 328
with tool and prosthesis, 51–59, 277
Affective
affective processing, 56–57, 327–328, 342–343
affective response, 56, 207, 230, 327–328
and depersonalization, 199–200, 206–208, 325
and sense of bodily ownership, 190, 193, 209, 226–227, 232
Agency
agentive feelings, 10–11, 122–124, 146, 155–157, 205, 210, 219, 282n2, 294, 329–330 (*see also* Sense of agency)
anarchic hand sign, 218–219, 305–306

delusion of control, 219, 301
and sense of bodily ownership, 122–124, 146, 155–157, 180–182, 190, 192, 193, 196, 203–205, 210, 217–223, 227, 231, 301
Amputation, 33–43, 56–57, 219, 222, 325. *See also* Phantom limb
Amygdala lesion, 230
Anosognosia
for hemianesthesia, 169
for hemiplegia, 219–220, 321–322
Asomotagnosia. *See* Somatoparaphrenia
Audition, 4, 10, 12, 15, 17, 109, 225, 375
rubber voice illusion, 348
Autoscopic experience, 322–324

Bimanual coupling effect, 167, 169
Blindness, 13, 15, 24, 38, 61, 125, 201
Bodily ownership. *See* Sense of bodily ownership
Bodily self, xiii, 5, 18, 218, 222, 328, 335–339, 342–345, 352–354
implicit representation, 5, 131, 243, 245, 258, 260n12, 269
as the "material me," 341
stability of, 345, 353–354
unity of, 344–345, 352–354
visual representation of, 242, 266–268, 273–274